WESTERN MEDICAL GUIDE
for
ENERGY HEALING PRACTITIONERS

DISCLAIMER: This book is intended only for educational purposes and not for diagnosis and treatment purpose. The information in this book is not intended to replace the diagnosis and treatment of a physician. Neither the publisher nor the author can be held responsible for any consequences arising from misuse of information in this book.

Copyright © 2013 – Syed A. Afzal

All rights reserved.

All rights reserved. No part of this book may be reproduced or transmitted in any form or by any means electronic or mechanical including photocopying or recording or by any information storage and retrieval system without permission in writing from the publisher.

International Standard Book Number : 978-0-9917015-3-7

Book title   : Western medical guide for Energy Healing Practitioners

Written by   : Syed A. Afzal

Graphic design   : Boopathi MK (Colour Krafts)

Second Edition printed in 2013,

First Edition Printed in 2007

DEDICATION

This work is dedicated to my beloved parents and to
my beloved and respected Teacher,
Grandmaster Choa Kok Sui.

FOREWORD

TThis book *'Western Medical Guide for Energy Healing Practitioners'* describes the Anatomy, Physiology, Pathology and Psychiatric disorders of the human body in a simple manner.

Hence it could be easily understood by any person without a medical background. This can be used as ready reckoner for quick reference.

Signed
Dr.C.S. Vijay Shankar
Cardio Thoracic Surgeon,
Senior Consultant, Apollo Hospital, Chennai

INTRODUCTION

"If you cannot be a king, be a healer" – An ancient Sinhalese saying.

How this book came about

While practicing Pranic healing with my colleagues who did not have a medical background, back in 1996 before internet was widely used, I felt that these Pranic Healers and other Energy Healing Practitioners had great healing skills but did not have enough understanding about the human body. Some had books on Anatomy, Physiology or Pathology (diseases), which were very detailed and complex for a layperson to understand.

Many Healers were not sure which books to buy to understand Psychiatric Disorders and Laboratory Values. When patients showed their lab reports to their Healers, assuming they understood it, many healers were not sure what to do or how to interpret the results. These patients expected their Healers to know and interpret their basic lab values and vital signs. All of these topics are available in different books, but are complicated to understand for a Healer without a medical background.

The purpose of this book

This book is intended to provide Energy Healing Practitioners information on various topics such as Anatomy, Physiology, Pathology, Lab values and their interpretations, Psychiatric disorders , commonly used medical terminology and Cancers and Tumors in a single book. We realize that Energy Healers need forms for assessment, treatment and follow-up, if they have a professional healing clinic or want to have a professional practice, therefore, we have added these form

We added a chapter 'Aromatherapy and its Colored Energy' since we felt this chapter is essential because it gives a basic understanding about the properties of various healing oils and how they can be used during practice depending on the Color Energy they contain.

We have done our best to keep the language simple and readable. We hope this book will truly be giving you more confidence in your abilities and add a professional touch to your healing practice.

Syed A.Afzal

ACKNOWLEDGEMENTS

To Divine Providence, for the Divine Blessings to complete this work.

To my Teacher, Master Choa Kok Sui for His priceless teachings and blessings.

To my parents, my wife, and my children for their constant support and love.

I express my immense gratitude to Boopathi MK (Colour Krafts) for his graphic design work, his creativity, organization skills and enormous contribution towards the completion of this book.

Thank you to my friend Murali Krishnan for his major contribution towards the book.

Thank you to Dr. Suhasini for her contribution, support and having overseen this book. A very special thanks to her for playing a major role in completion and publishing this book.

My sincere thanks to Smriti Tyagi and Arti for their work on psychiatric disorders.

A special thank you to Dr. Saira for editing the chapter on psychiatric disorders.

Thanks to Iniyan, Preeth Cherian, Mr. Sudhakar Reddy, all my friends, colleagues and associates for their help, support and encouragement.

TABLE OF CONTENTS

GASTROINTESTINAL SYSTEM 4

RESPIRATORY SYSTEM 27

CARDIOVASCULAR SYSTEM 45

NERVOUS SYSTEM 72

URINARY SYSTEM. 93

REPRODUCTIVE SYSTEM 103

MUSCULOSKELETAL SYSTEM 123

SKIN. 152

ENDOCRINE SYSTEM 162

EYE AND EAR 178

BLOOD 194

CANCERS AND TUMORS 204

VITAL SIGNS, COMMON LAB VALUES AND INTERPRETATIONS 222

PSYCHIATRIC DISORDERS 231

AROMATHERAPY AND COLORED ENERGY. 246

GENERAL HEALTH FORMS 266

COMMONLY USED MEDICAL TERMINOLOGY 277

INDEX 283

Chapter 1

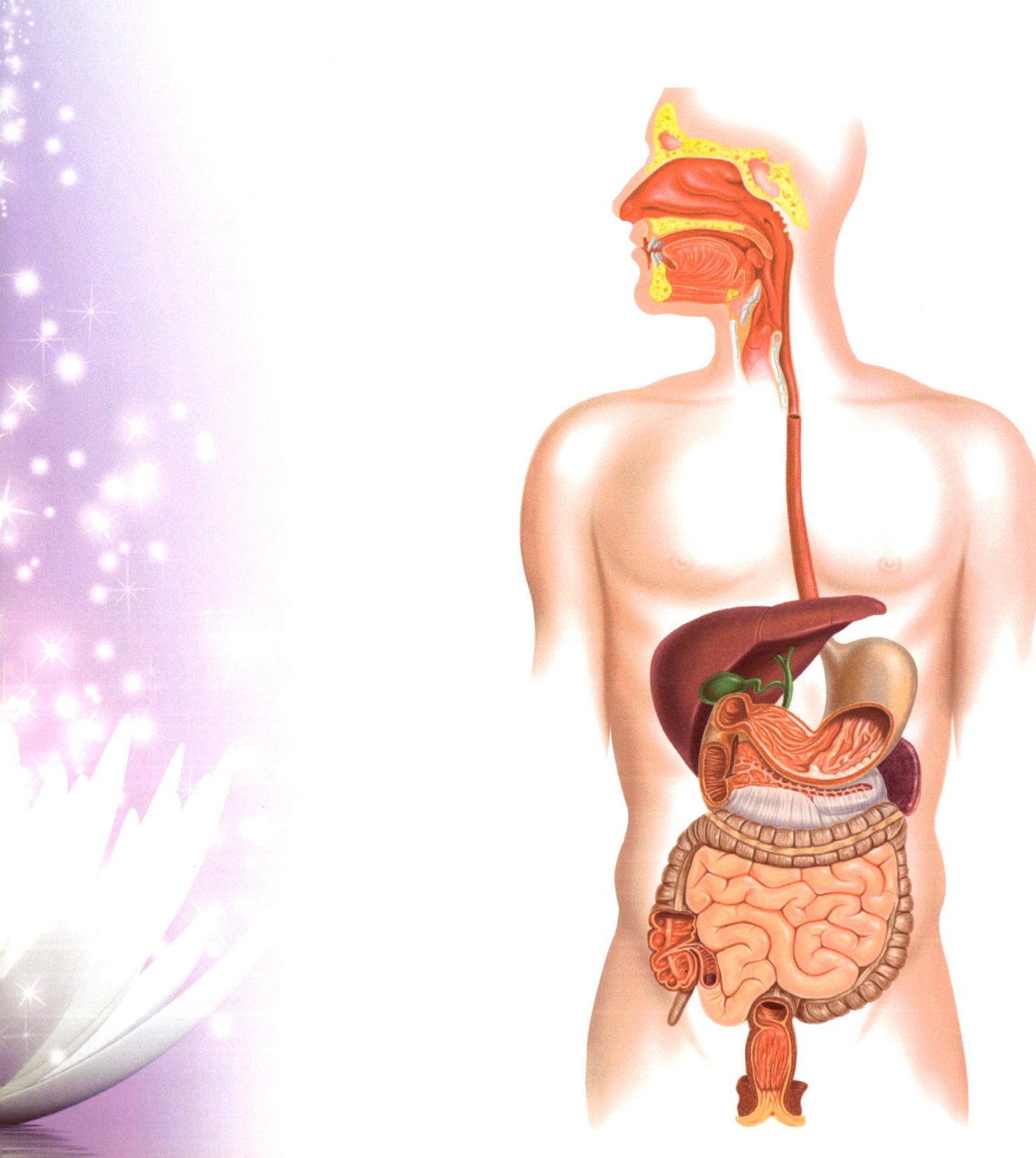

Gastrointestinal system

TABLE OF CONTENTS

- GASTROINTESTINAL TRACT 4
- ANATOMY 5
- MOUTH 5
- TEETH 6
- DISORDERS OF THE TEETH 8
  - Stages of tooth decay 8
- SALIVARY GLANDS 9
- PHARYNX AND ESOPHAGUS 10
- STOMACH 11
- SMALL INTESTINE 12
- LARGE INTESTINE 12
- LIVER AND GALLBLADDER 13
- PANCREAS 14
- PHYSIOLOGY 14
- DISORDERS OF GASTROINTESTINAL TRACT SYSTEM 15
  - Acid regurgitation (Heart burn) 15
  - Abdominal Pain 16
  - Appendicitis 17
  - Constipation 18
  - Diarrhea 18
  - Diverticulosis 18
  - Dysentery 20
  - Gastric Ulcer, Duodenal Ulcer (Peptic Ulcer) 20
  - Hiatal Hernia 21
  - Gastritis 22
  - Rectal prolapse 22
  - Ulcerative colitis 23
- LIVER & GALL BLADDER 23
  - Physiology 23
- DISORDERS OF LIVER & GALL BLADDER 24
  - Alcoholic liver disease 24
  - Ascites 24
  - Cirrhosis of liver 24
  - Gallstones 25
  - Hepatitis 26
  - Jaundice 26

GASTROINTESTINAL TRACT

The digestive system, medically referred to as the gastrointestinal tract, is primarily concerned with the intake, digestion and absorption of the nutrients from the food we eat. The food is broken down into microscopic particles or molecules, and separated by successive digestive organs into nutrients and waste matter. Nutrients enter the blood stream through the channels in the intestinal wall and are then distributed to nourish every cell within the body. The undigestible waste materials are disposed in the form of fecal matter.

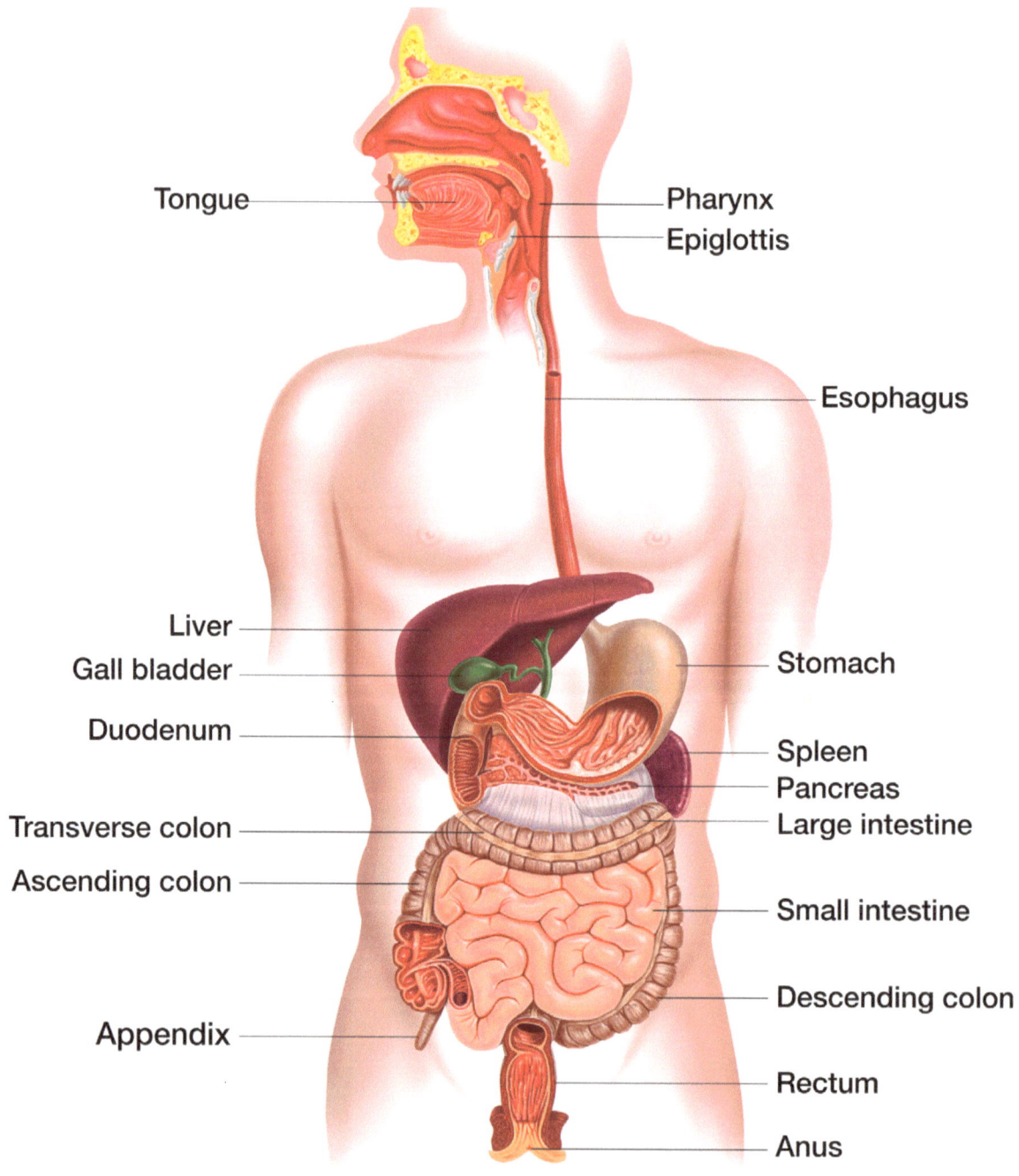

Figure 1-1 Gastrointestinal system

The functions of the GI tract include the following:
- Mechanical decomposition of the complex food materials into smaller digestible substances.
- Storage and processing of the food into absorbable substances.
- Propulsion of the food materials by muscular action called peristalsis.
- Secretion of digestive juices called enzymes, which enhance the food processing and different lubricants that allow for the smooth passage of food particles.
- Absorption of digested food materials.
- Elimination of the unwanted materials.

The GI tract consists of the following components:

1. Mouth – oral or buccal cavity
2. Pharynx
3. Esophagus - food pipe
4. Stomach
5. Small intestine
   - duodenum
   - Jejunum
   - Ileum
6. Large intestine
   - Cecum
   - Ascending colon
   - Transverse colon
   - Descending colon
   - Sigmoid colon
7. Rectum and Anus
8. Three pairs of salivary glands, liver, and pancreas which secrete digestive juices

ANATOMY

Digestion begins in the mouth. Food is broken down by the teeth, and mixed with saliva, which moistens it for easy swallowing.

MOUTH

The mouth (i.e. the buccal cavity) consists of inner and outer parts separated by the teeth. In a proper oral cavity, the outer part is narrower compared to the larger inner part. The lips are fleshy folds surrounding the oral orifice. They are externally lined by skin and internally with the mucosa. The maxilla that forms the upper jaw is immovable while the mandible or the lower jaw is movable. Skeletal muscles and considerable amount of fat called the buccal fat pad, and the salivary glands cover the maxilla.

TEETH

Teeth are the hard conical structures set in the alveoli of the upper and lower jaws. A tooth is composed of dentin encased in cementum on the anatomic root and enamel on its anatomic crown. It consists of a root buried in the alveolus, a neck surrounded by the gum, and an exposed portion called the crown. In the center is the pulp cavity filled with a connective tissue reticulum containing a jelly-like substance called dental pulp, and blood vessels and nerves entering through a canal at the apex of the root called the root canal.

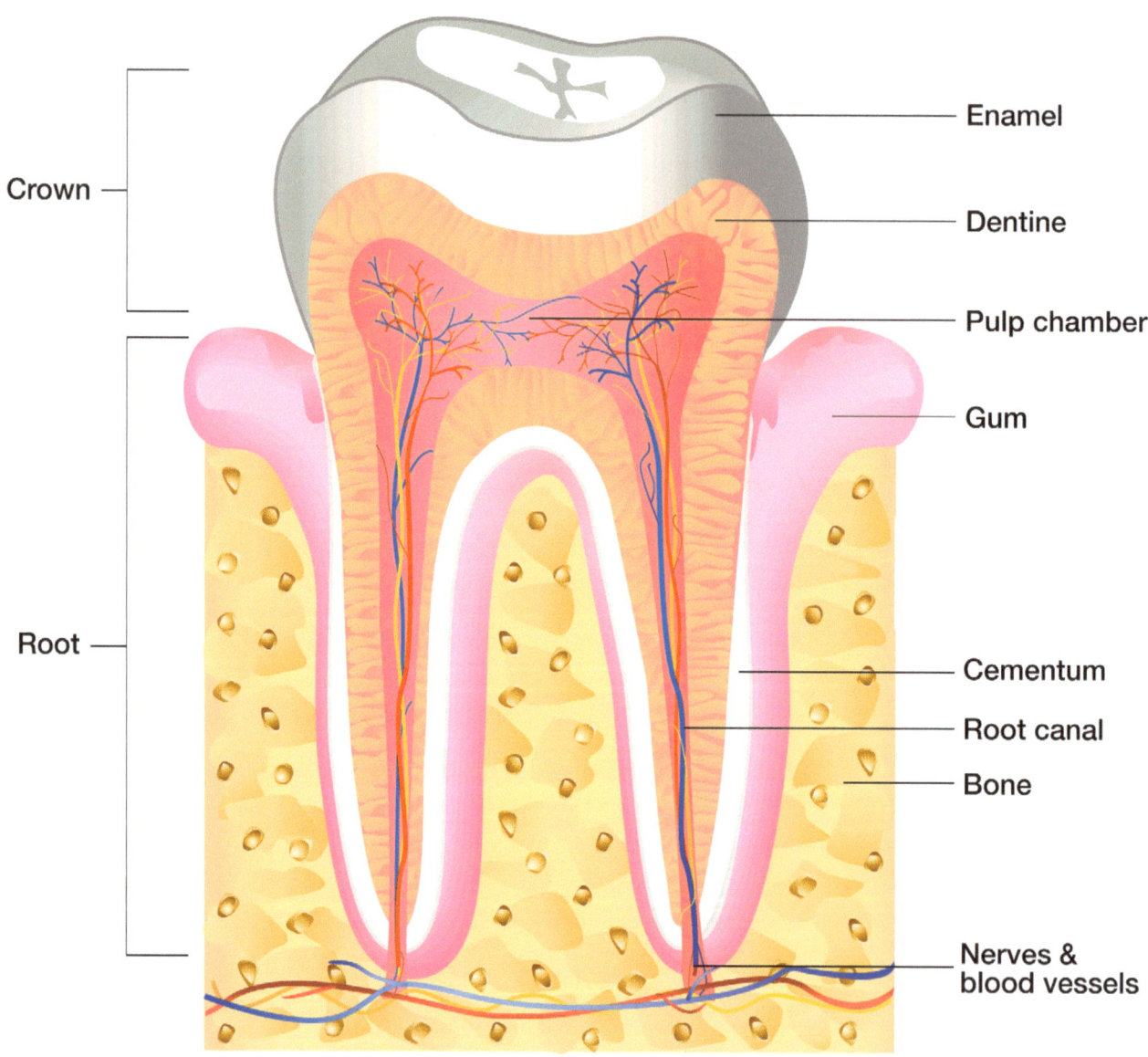

Figure 1-2 Tooth anatomy

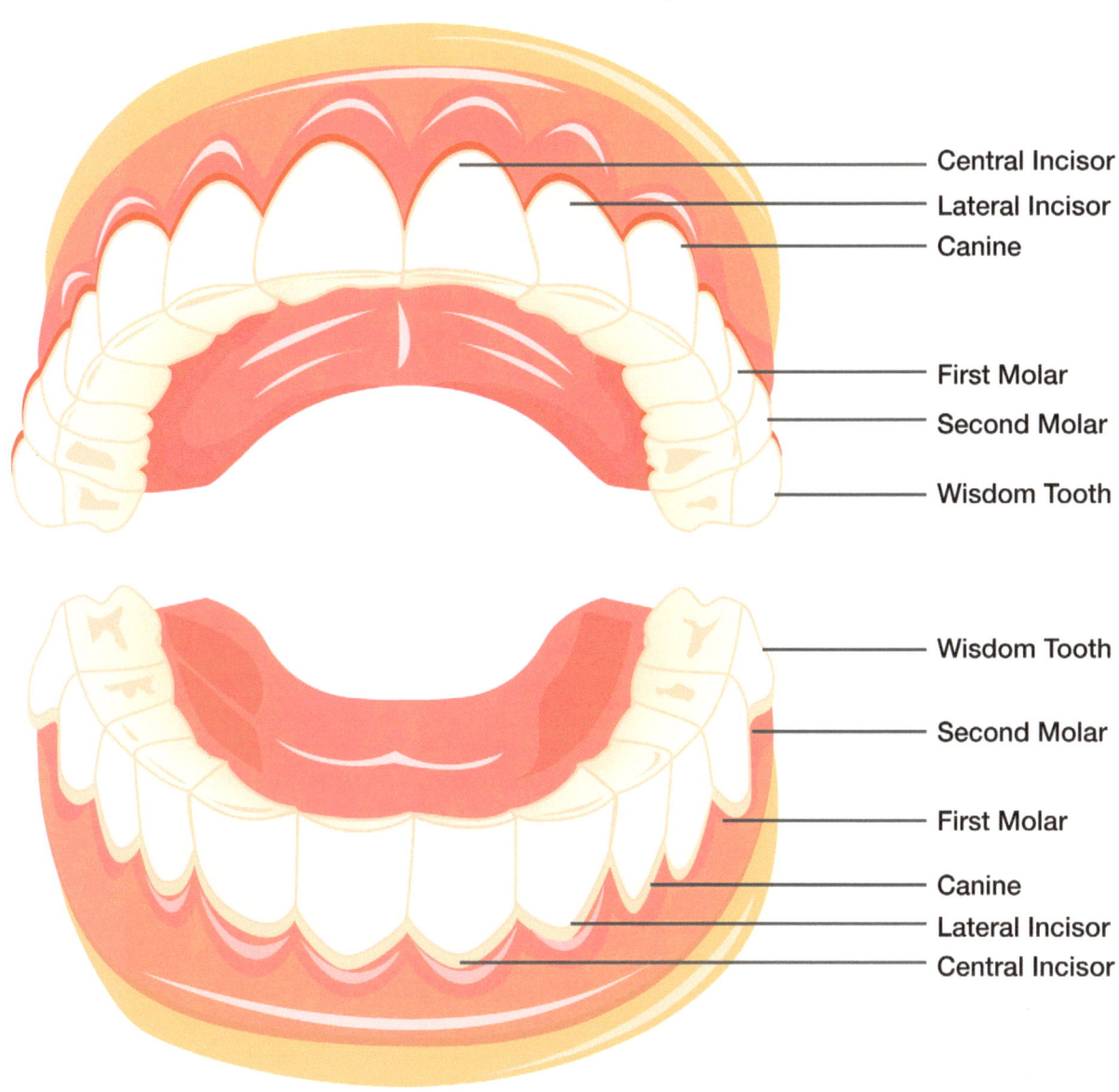

Figure 1-3 Dental arches

The 20 deciduous teeth or primary teeth appear at the 6th, 9th and the 24th month of life; these fall out eventually and are replaced by the 32 permanent teeth appearing between the 5th and 7th year and the 17th to the 23rd year. In general, there are four kinds of teeth: incisor, canine, premolar, and molar. Each jaw has 16 teeth and are arranged symmetrically on the two sides. Each half of the jaw has 8 teeth; 2 incisors, 1 canine, 2 premolars and 3 molars.

DISORDERS OF THE TEETH

STAGES OF TOOTH DECAY

There are different stages of the tooth decay. Plaque formation occurs in the first stage, the loss of calcium and presence of white spots on the enamel due to initiation of acid dissolution and weakening of the enamel. In the second stage, the decay grows in the enamel of the tooth if the demineralization process extends beyond the natural remineralization level. The enamel begins to break down in this stage.In the third stage, the decay stretches to the dentin if left untreated, this lead to the formation of a cavity. This results in decay of the pulp which is the living part of the tooth. Since the pulp is infected and invaded by the bacteria at this stage, the blood vessels and the nerves become severely damaged. In the fourth stage there is decay in the pulp.

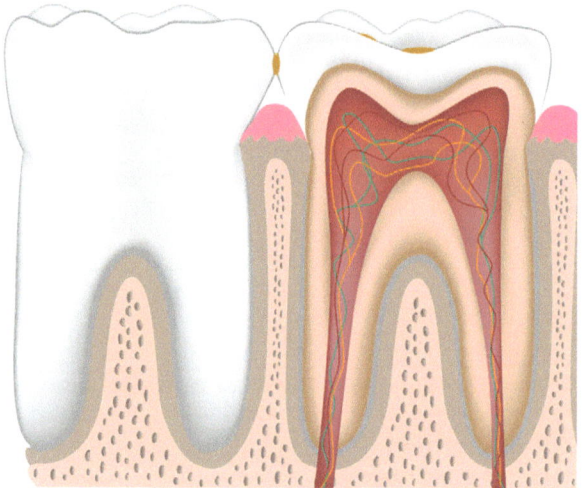
1. Healthy tooth with plaque

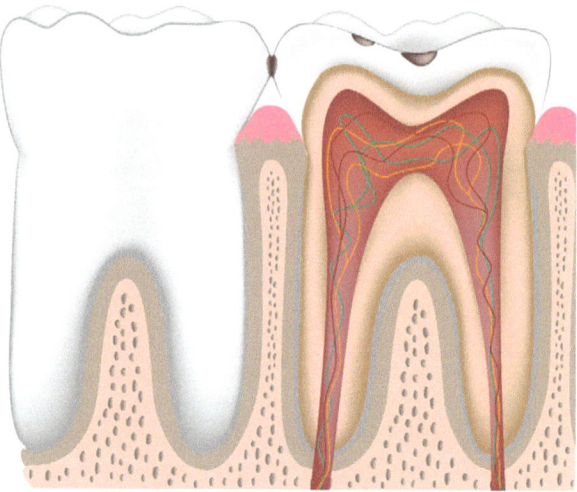
2. Decay in enamel

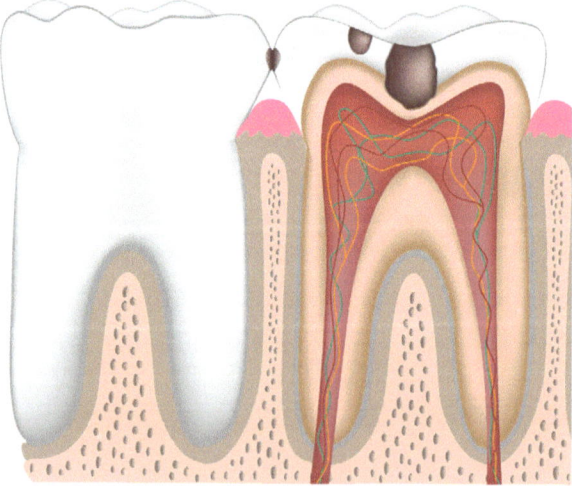
3. Decay in dentine

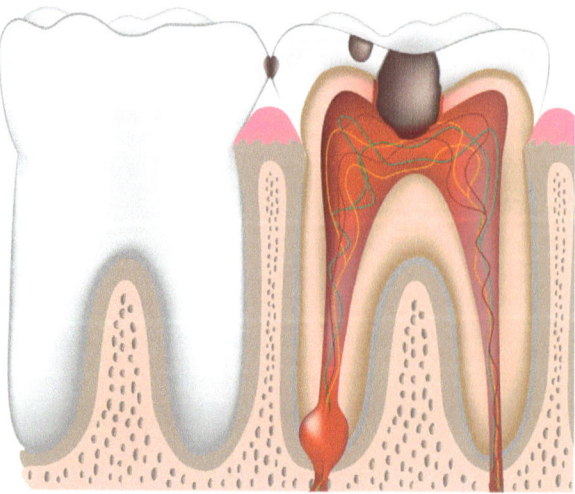
4. Decay in pulp

Figure 1-4 Stages of decay in the tooth

SALIVARY GLANDS

The salivary glands secrete the saliva into the oral cavity. There are three pairs of salivary glands in the oral cavity; parotid, sub-mandibular, and sub-lingual glands. The parotid glands are the largest of salivary glands, located at the angle of the mandible below the ear. There is a pair of sub-mandibular glands about the size of a walnut sitting below the angle of the jaw and a pair of sub-lingual glands lying below the tongue. In addition to the major glands, minor salivary glands exist in the tongue, the region of the tonsils, the soft palate, the lips, and the cheeks. The palate or the roof of the mouth is divided into the hard palate in the front and the soft palate located behind the tongue. The soft palate is movable while the hard palate is fixed. The tongue is a highly muscular organ used for chewing, tasting and speech. The moist lining called mucosa contains a lot of taste buds and is the chief organ for sensation of taste.

- We make around one and a half liters of saliva a day which means we produce enough saliva to fill two swimming pools in our life time
- We can only taste something when our saliva can dissolve it

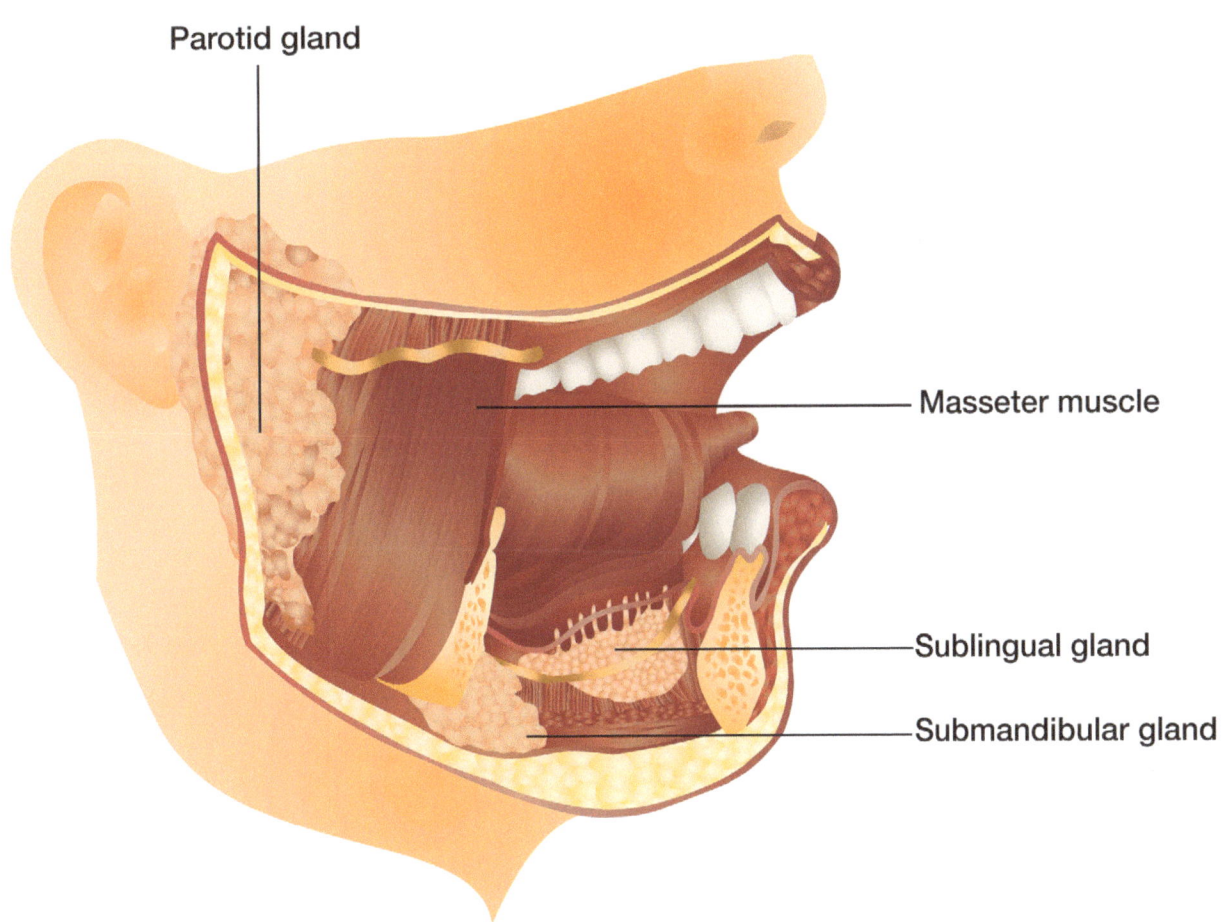

Figure 1-5 Salivary glands

Gastrointestinal System

PHARYNX AND ESOPHAGUS

Food passes through the mouth down to the pharynx. The pharynx is about 12 cm long and is the common passageway for food and air. A muscular flap called the epiglottis guards the opening of the windpipe and prevents food from entering into the lungs while swallowing. The food from the pharynx then moves down to a muscular tube called the esophagus. The esophagus is about 25 cm long and connects stomach at the lower end.

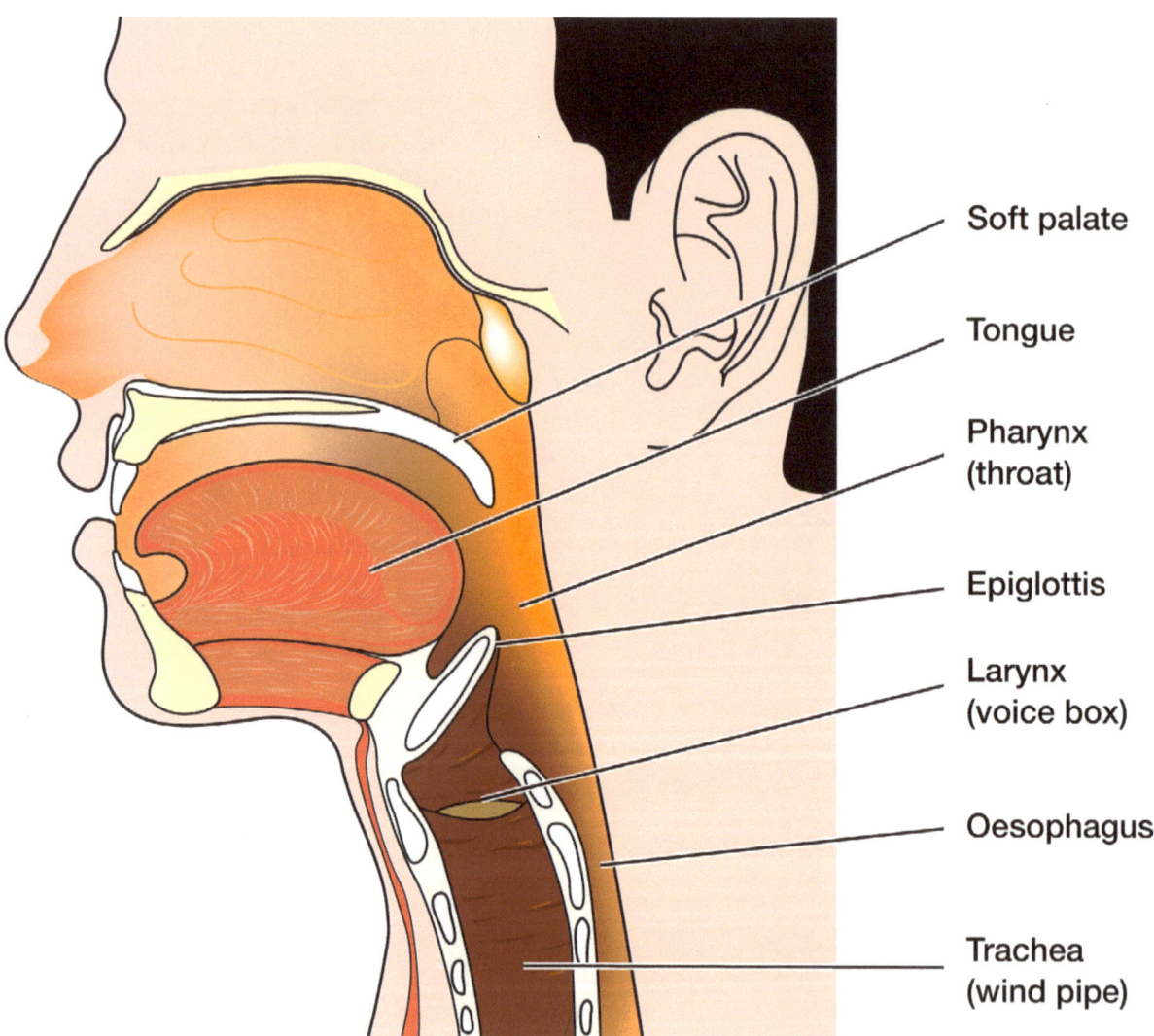

Figure 1-6 Pharynx and Esophagus

STOMACH

The stomach is a hollow muscular organ located in the left side of the abdomen below the diaphragm. The stomach size varies based on the contents. The esophagus or the food pipe opens into the upper side of the stomach guarded by a weak muscular valve called cardiac sphincter or lower esophageal sphincter. It prevents regurgitation or the backward flow of the food into the esophagus. The exit from the stomach is guarded by a strong muscular valve called pyloric sphincter. Pyloric sphincter opens into the duodenum, which is the first part of the small intestine. The stomach is a J-shaped muscular organ with a smooth outer layer and an inner layer thrown in many foldings called the rugae. The inner layer is further covered by mucosal lining, which protects the stomach from hydrochloric acid and digestive juices secreted for digestion.

- The esophagus is approximately 20 cm long
- The stomach of an adult has a capacity to hold approximately 1.5 liters of material
- The average man consumes about 50 tonnes of food during his lifetime

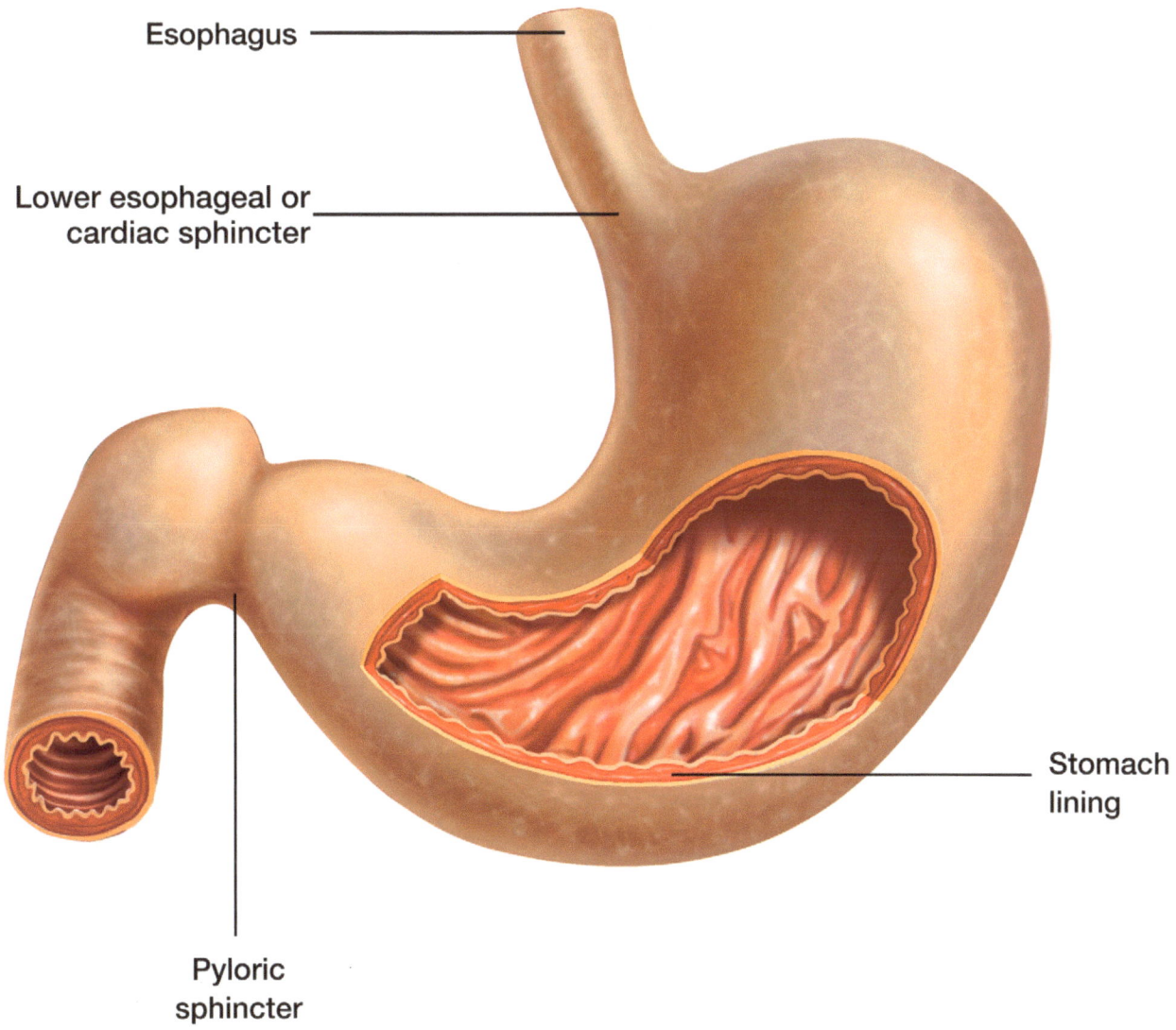

Figure 1-7 Stomach

Gastrointestinal System 11

SMALL INTESTINE

The stomach empties into the small intestine, which digests the food chemically so that the body can absorb it into the bloodstream. The small intestine is further subdivided into three parts. The first part of the small intestine, the duodenum is 25 cm in length and is the shortest and widest part. It is entirely above the umbilicus and adjacent to the stomach. The duodenum consists of superior, descending, horizontal and ascending parts and connects to the jejunum at the lower end. The jejunum is the coiling midsection of the small intestine measuring about 2.2 meters in length. The jejunum lies mostly in the umbilical region but may extend to the surrounding areas. The ileum, the final section of small intestine is about 4 meters long. It is the continuation of the jejunum and it is mainly in the pelvic region. After coiling it ascends to open into the large intestine between the cecum and colon. The inner wall of the small intestine is covered with microscopic finger-like projections called the villi. The villi are the parts transferring the nutrients into the blood stream.

- The small intestine is the length of 3 grown men and is two fingers wide making it the largest internal organ
- In small intestine the food is mixed with enzymes, bile and pancreatic juice and over 90% of digestion and absorption takes place here

LARGE INTESTINE

The large intestine receives undigested remainder of the food and water from the small intestine. The large intestine is made up of three parts; the cecum, the colon and the rectum.

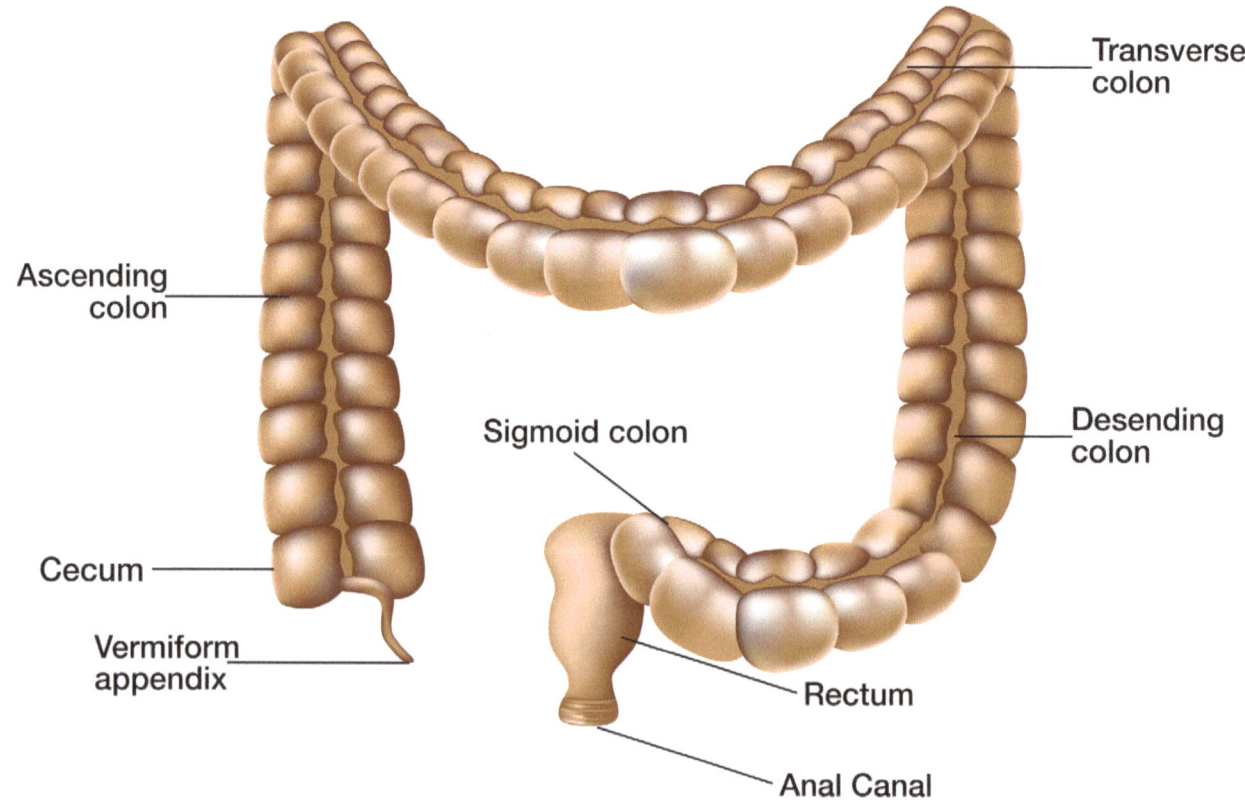

Figure 1-8 Large intestine

Gastrointestinal System

The cecum is a small sac-like section of large intestine at the end of which the appendix hangs. The colon extends from the cecum up the right side of the abdomen, across the upper abdomen, and then down the left side of the abdomen. The colon is further divided into ascending, transverse, descending, and sigmoid colons based on the location. The last part of the colon is connected to the rectum, which then terminates at the anus.

The cecum and the colon are about 5 feet long each, while the rectum is only 5 inches long. Water is removed as waste products move along the length of the large intestine. By the time the final products of digestion reach the rectum, they are in the form of solid waste called feces. The rectum stores the feces until the body is ready to eliminate it out through the anus as a bowel movement.

LIVER AND GALLBLADDER

The liver is located beneath the ribcage of the right upper part of the abdomen, the gallbladder is located just below the liver, and the pancreas beneath the stomach are the three major glands

- Consuming alcohol, coffee and tea containing caffeine, drugs, fried and processed foods can affect liver. Foods that contain Anti- oxidants are beneficial to the liver

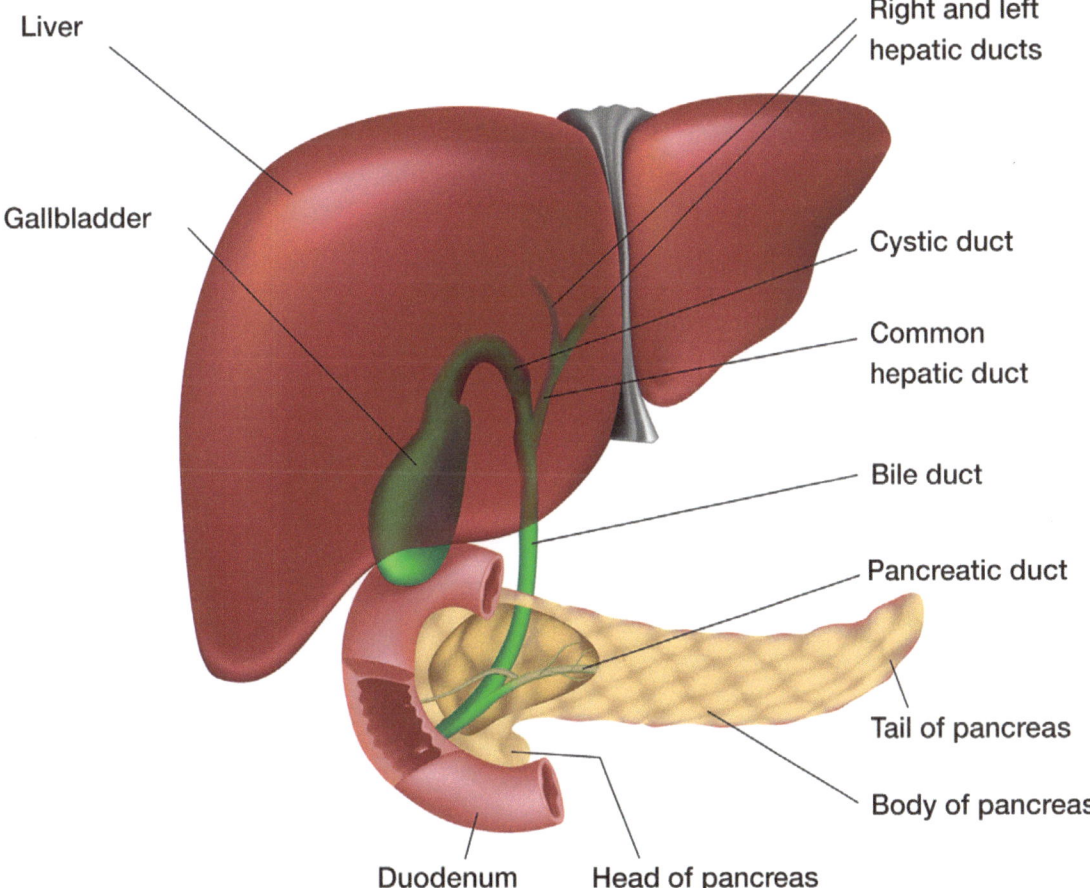

Figure 1-9 Liver, gall bladder & pancreas

which produce enzymes and substances that travel via special ducts directly to the small intestine to aid in digestion. The liver is the largest gland of the body. It is reddish brown and lies immediately beneath the diaphragm on the upper right side of the abdomen. It is a wedge shaped organ that has a remarkable blood supply. A normal liver is firm and non-greasy. It gradually increases in size and becomes soft, greasy, and yellow as fat starts to accumulate in the liver cells. The liver consists of a large right lobe and a small left lobe. The liver cells are called the hepatocytes, which secrete the bile. The gall bladder is a pear-shaped, hollow organ closely attached to the backside of the liver. The gallbladder acts as a reservoir for the bile. The bile from the gallbladder is emptied into the duodenum through the bile duct.

PANCREAS

The pancreas is a leaf-shaped organ, grayish pink in color located below the stomach at the left side of the upper abdomen. The secretions of the pancreas are released through the pancreatic duct. The pancreatic duct joins the bile duct and empties the secretions from the pancreas into the duodenum.

PHYSIOLOGY

In fact, the digestion process starts at the smell or sight of food. When we see, smell, taste, or even imagine a tasty food our salivary glands begin to produce saliva. This is brought about by a brain reflex that is triggered when we sense a desirable food. This sensory stimulation causes the brain to send impulses through the nerves that control the salivary glands, instructing them to prepare for a meal.

As soon as the food enters the body through the mouth, the mechanical process of breaking down the food starts by chewing. The teeth are the specially designed tools to transform chunks of food into easy to swallow substances .As we chew, saliva softens and moistens food and its enzymes help with breaking down the starches into simpler sugars.

The food passes through the mouth into the pharynx by the act of swallowing which is a voluntary coordinated muscle movement. The epiglottis reflexively closes the windpipe while food is being swallowed, to effectively prevent food from entering the lungs.

Food is then forced down the esophagus towards the stomach by the waves of muscular contractions called peristalsis. Peristalsis is an involuntary muscular action controlled by the nervous system. During normal digestion we are not aware of the movements of the esophagus, the stomach, and most of the intestine.

The stomach temporarily stores food and the peristalsis of the stomach churns food back and forth, mixing it with mucus and gastric juices. These juices contain enzymes and hydrochloric acid, forming the acidic environment required for digestion in the stomach. Only a small amount of absorption takes place in the stomach; however, water, glucose and alcohol are directly absorbed from the stomach. This is why one may experience an enhanced alcohol effect while drinking with an empty stomach. The food leaving the stomach is processed into a thick liquid called chyme. The outlet of the stomach is guarded by the pyloric sphincter, which keeps the chyme in the stomach until it reaches the right consistency to pass into the small intestine.

Most digestion including the digestion of all fats and proteins along with most of the absorption process takes place in the small intestine. The pancreas and the liver connect with the small intestine and send secretions into it to aid digestion. These include the pancreatic juice, which contains enzymes helping the digestion of carbohydrates, proteins, and fat. The bile breaks down the fats and aids in its absorption. Though bile is produced in the liver, it is stored in the gallbladder, and sent into the small intestine through the bile duct.

Gastric juice produced in the stomach is highly acidic which the stomach delivers to the duodenum. The secretions of the pancreas consists of sodium bicarbonate, that neutralizes the acidity of the chyme. If this process fails, the person gets stomach ulcer since the highly acidic gastric juice can eat up the mucous membrane covering the wall of the duodenum. This is the most common site of an ulcer.

The pancreatic secretion also consists of amylase which decomposes the carbohydrates into sugars. Another pancreatic enzyme called lipase, along with the bile, breaks down the fats into fatty acids and glycerol. The trypsin transforms proteins into amino acids. Once broken down, the soluble food products are dissolved and absorbed directly into the bloodstream through the walls of the small intestine, along with vitamins and minerals. This process is called absorption.

By the time the food reaches the large intestine, the digestion process is almost complete. The main function of the large intestine is to remove water from the undigested matter and form the matter into feces to be eliminated from the body. The contents of the small intestine enter the cecum through another sphincter muscle, which prevents their return to the small intestine. The cecum passes these contents to the colon. Fluids and salts are absorbed in the ascending colon, more water is removed from waste materials in the transverse colon, and the descending colon holds the resulting waste. Bacteria in the colon aid in digestion of the remaining food products. The final waste product, the feces, is then stored in the rectum until it exits the body through the anus.

Besides its role in digestion, the liver acts as a detoxifier. It absorbs all poisons and toxic substances such as nicotine, and various drugs and gets swollen. It allows the blood without poisonous substances to circulate to the heart. The liver has a significant regenerative capacity. It can rebuild itself to normal size, even if 80 percent of its size is cut away. It produces between 600 and 1200 ml of bile a day, which is stored in the gall bladder and released when necessary. The bile helps in digestion of fat and also serves as a means for excretion of several waste products from the blood.

The bile consists of two pigments; Bilirubin and Biliverdin. Occasionally, these pigments may get into the blood stream in excess quantity and produce jaundice-yellow staining of skin and eyes.

DISORDERS OF GASTROINTESTINAL TRACT SYSTEM

ACID REGURGITATION (HEARTBURN)

A condition in which the contents of the stomach including the stomach juices, flow back into the esophagus, cause inflammation and irritation of the lining of the esophagus. These conditions may arise due to over eating or lax musculature at the lower end of the esophagus (cardiac sphincter) where it connects to the stomach allowing the stomach acid to flow back. Most people describe heartburn as a feeling of burning chest pain, localized behind the breastbone moving up toward the neck and throat. Some even experience the bitter or sour taste of the acid in the back of the throat. The burning and pressure symptoms of heartburn can last as long as 2 hours and are often worsened by eating.

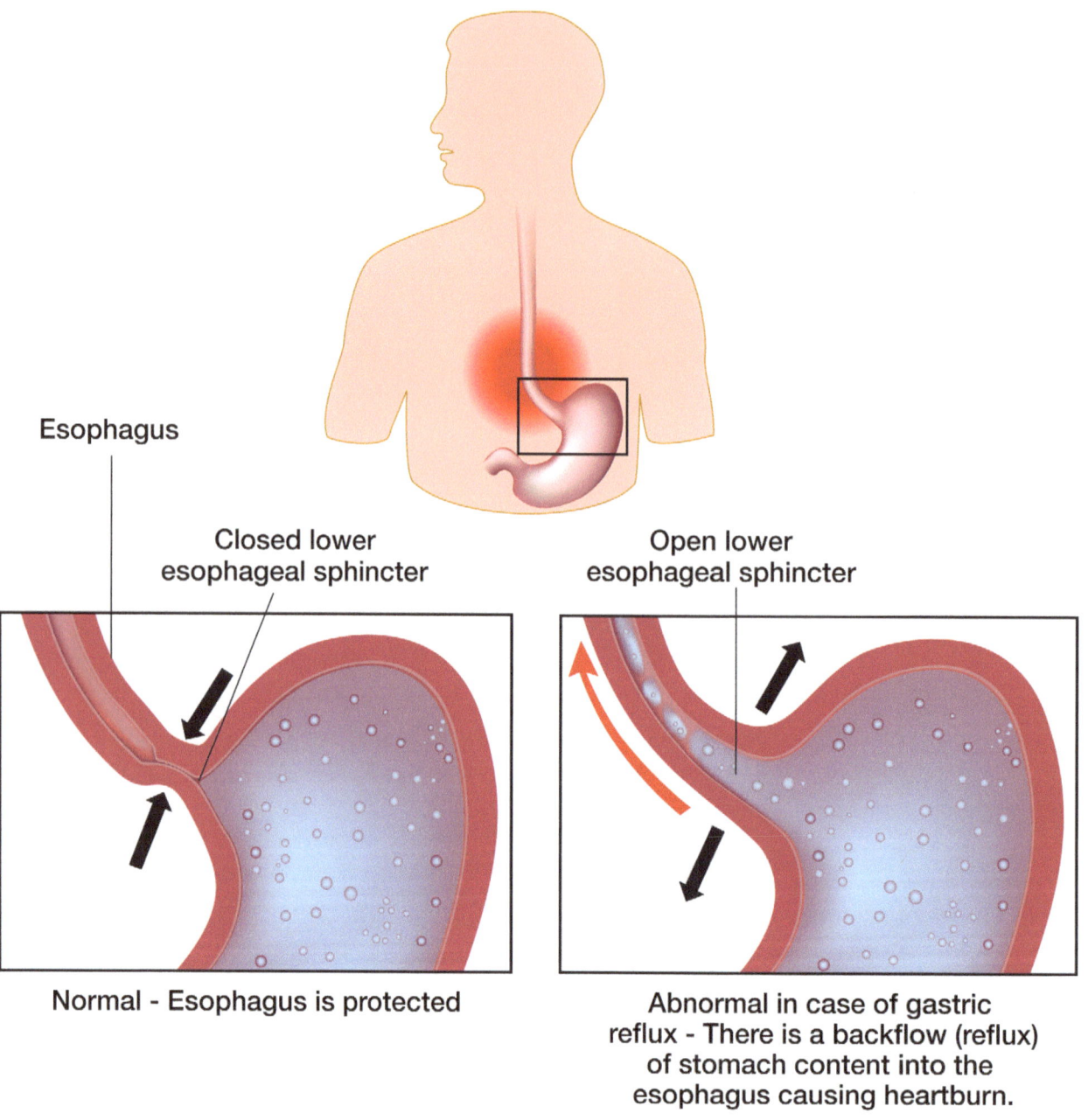

Figure 1-10 Gastric reflux causing heartburn

ABDOMINAL PAIN

Sometimes, it is difficult to find out the cause of a stomach ache. The pain may be due to trivial reasons such as a hot spicy acidic meal while in some cases it can occur as a result of a serious illness such as an ulcer. The possible causes of stomach pain are listed below:

- Gastric ulcer – A lesion in the inner wall of the abdomen caused by superficial loss of tissue due to erosion by acid and associated with inflammation.
- Peritonitis – Inflammation of the peritoneum.

- Mechanical obstruction in the tract, a stone which may be intestinal, biliary or renal.
- Disturbances in blood supply or injury to abdominal wall muscles.
- Associated with other conditions such as diabetes, uremia, lead poisoning etc. Pain may radiate from kidney to the stomach in kidney disorders, e.g., stones in the kidneys.
- The lower abdominal pain in women can be due to problems in the female genital system. The causes may include menstrual problems, discharge or abnormal bleeding from the vagina, the cervical or adnexal masses etc.

APPENDICITIS

Appendicitis is a condition of inflammation of the vermiform appendix. This is caused by the blockage of the open end of the appendix due to a hard mass of fecal material getting trapped inside the appendix and resulting swelling inside the wall. This can lead to an infection flaring up into an abscess resulting in further complications.

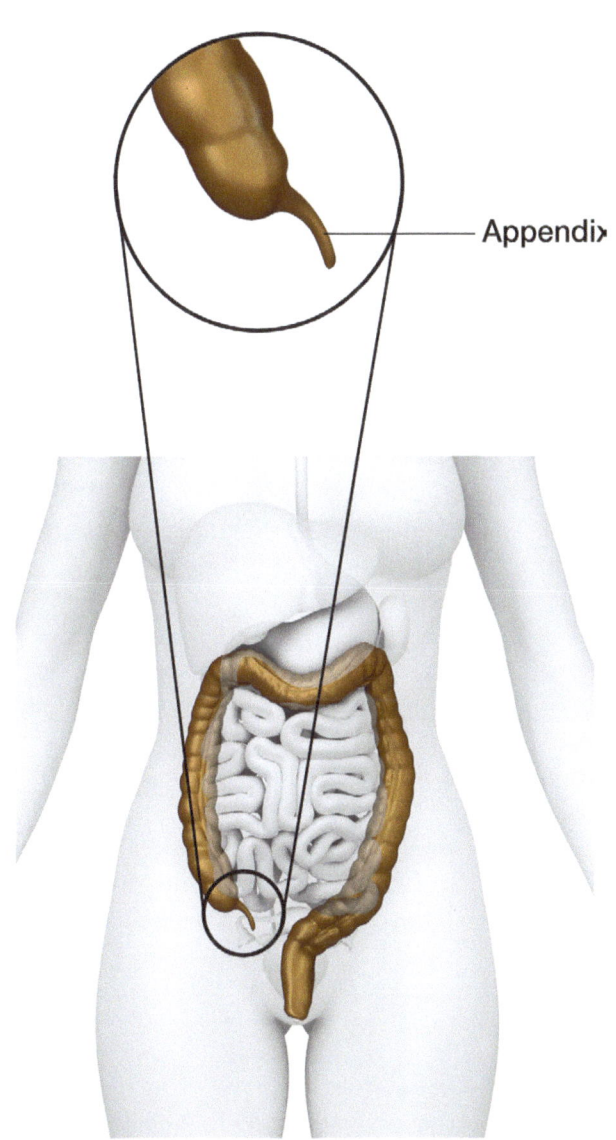

Figure 1-11 Vermiform Appendix

The pain starts intermittently and is usually felt near the navel or sometimes only in the right lower abdomen. It may hurt while walking or during urinating. It is also tender to pressure and there will be a moderate rise in temperature. The patient usually feels nauseous under these conditions and may vomit. In severe cases, an abscess in the appendix may burst open leaking its content in to the abdominal cavity. This is an emergency and an immediate surgery is needed to save the patient.

CONSTIPATION

Constipation is a condition in which bowel movements are infrequent or incomplete and large quantities of dry and hard feces are accumulated in the descending colon. There is a slow movement of feces through the large intestine, and the excess of water absorbed from the stools make them hard. Irregular bowel habits that have developed by inhibition of normal defecation reflexes can cause constipation. That is why infants are seldom constipated, but as they learn to control defecation, natural defecation reflex is inhibited which may lead to constipation. Decreased amount of fiber in diet, stress, tumors in GI tract and the adhesions that constrict the intestine can trigger constipation obstructing the movement of intestinal contents.

The common complaints of constipation include the feeling of abdominal fullness or bloating, gaseousness, an experience of rectal pressure or discomfort, abdominal distension, and the feeling of incomplete elimination of the fecal matter.

DIARRHEA

Diarrhea is an abnormally frequent discharge of semi-solid or fluid fecal matter from the bowel. Diarrhea results from rapid movement of fecal matter through the large intestine. Viral or bacterial infections in the intestinal tract or infections present in the large intestine irritate the mucosa increasing the rate of secretion of fluid that is made available to wash away the infective agent. These, coupled with strong propulsive movements of the intestines propel the fluid forward leading to diarrhea. Diarrhea also occurs in ulcerative colitis, a condition in which extensive areas of the walls of the large intestine become inflamed and ulcerated due to which colon's secretions are significantly enhanced. Diarrhea sometimes occurs as a result of nervous tension causing strong propulsive movement and an increase in the secretion of mucus in the distal colon.

DIVERTICULOSIS

Diverticulosis is a common digestive disease of the large intestine where there is outpocketing or bulging sacs of the intestine through the weak muscle layers of the walls of the colon or the intestine. Each pouch is called a diverticulum and multiple pouches are called diverticula. This condition of having diverticula is called diverticulosis. Inflammation of the diverticula is called diverticulitis.

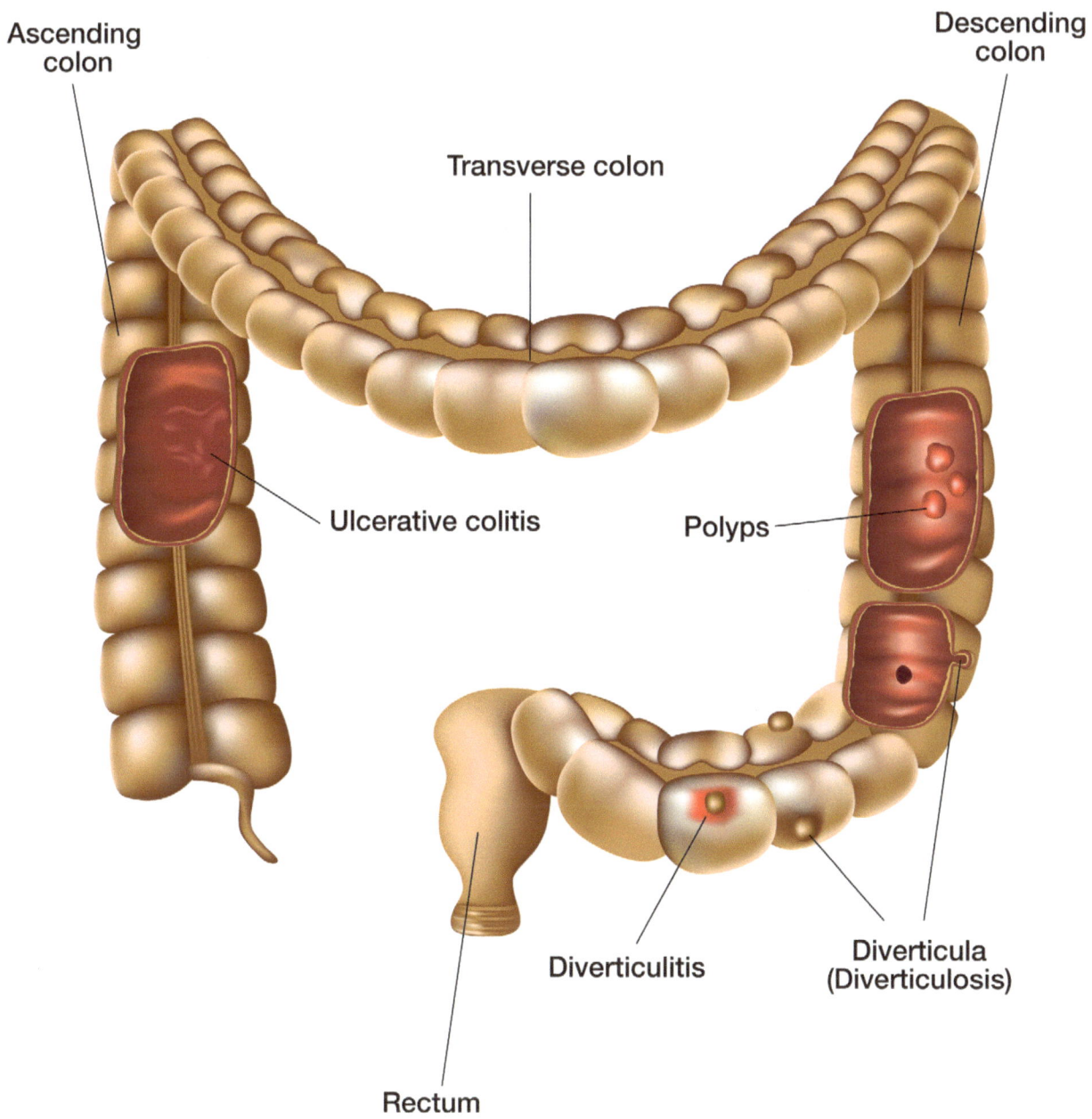

Figure 1-12 Colon diseases

Diverticula usually occurs in the lower portion of the intestine, though it may also take place in the gastrointestinal tract above the stomach, as in the esophagus. They tend to appear after the age of 40 years. The exact cause is still unknown. Eating a low- fiber diet including processed food is an associated cause. This may result in constipation and formation of hard stools which increases the pressure in the colon during passing stools. The increased pressure in the colon can lead to the formation of these pouches. Consequent infection or inflammation may occur when small pieces of fecel matter (stools) get trapped in these pouches. Some patients may experience severe abdominal pain, fever, nausea and changes in their bowel habits. Additionally, bleeding can happen in some cases.

Gastrointestinal System

DYSENTERY

Dysentery is an infection of the bowel leading to severe diarrhea consisting of watery stools, often streaked with blood, pus or mucus. There may be gripping pain in the abdomen and also a rise in the body temperature. Diarrhea may be experienced as many as twenty times a day for children with dysentery.

GASTRIC ULCER, DUODENAL ULCER (PEPTIC ULCER)

An ulcer is a focal area of the stomach or the duodenum destroyed by the digestive juices and the stomach acid. The most common symptom of an ulcer is a burning pain in the abdomen located between the navel and the bottom of the breastbone. The pain often is felt between meals and sometimes awakens people from sleep. The pain can last from minutes to hours and is often relieved by eating or taking antacids. Other symptoms of an ulcer include nausea, vomiting and loss of appetite and weight.

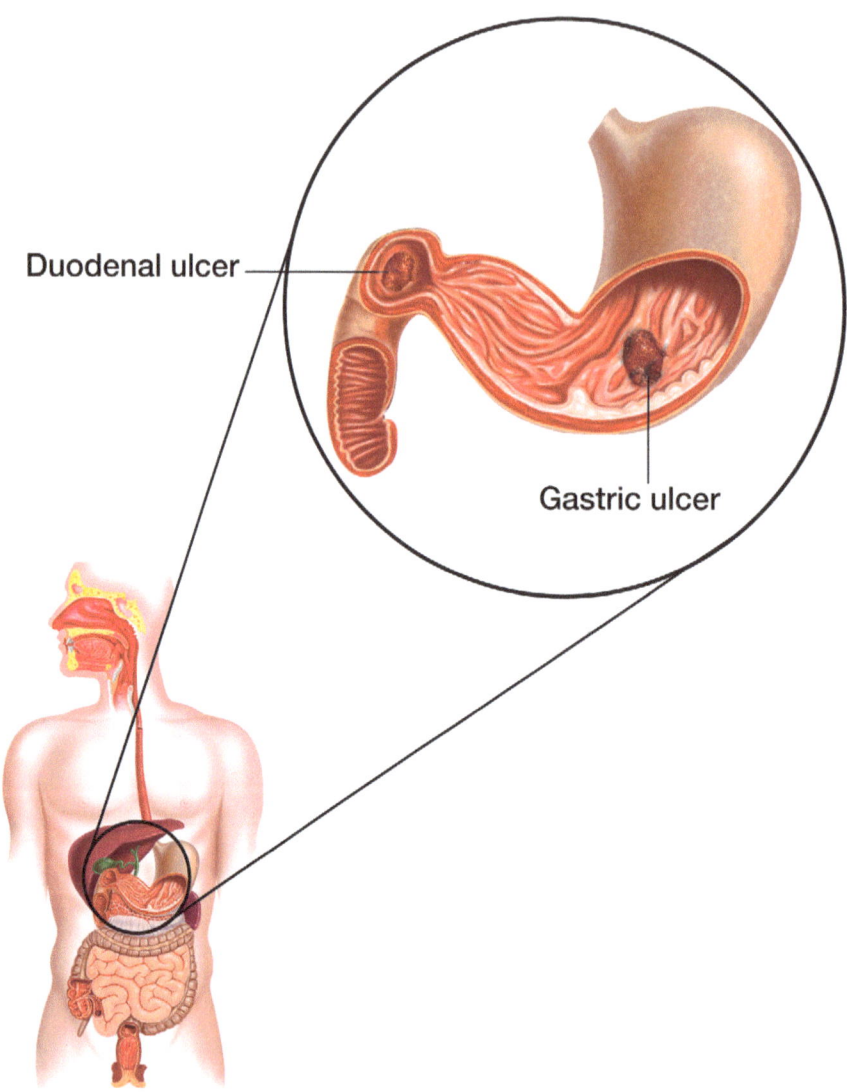

Figure 1-13 Stomach Ulcer

Complications brought about by an ulcer include bleeding resulting in tarry black stools; perforation of intestinal wall with spillage of food and bacteria into the abdominal cavity causing intense pain; obstructions caused by scarring at the ulcer site and blocking the passage of the food along the ulcer site.

Gastric ulcer is caused by the destruction of the small area of lining of the mucosa of the stomach by gastric juices.If it is located in the duodenum it is called duodenal ulcer. The main symptom is a cramp like pain in the upper abdominal area with localized tenderness. In gastric ulcer, the pain is usually experienced left of the midline, and in duodenal ulcer the pain is felt towards the right side, or in the middle of the upper abdomen radiating upwards.

Experiencing the pain half an hour to one hour after a meal is suggestive of a gastric ulcer while pain two or three hours before meal may indicate a duodenal ulcer. Alcohol, tobacco, irregular meals, anxiety, stress and overwork may all provoke the symptoms. Some types of drugs may precipitate an ulcer in susceptible people. Erosion of the blood vessels may cause sudden bleeding and blood vomiting, with either a bright red or a brownish color, like coffee grounds. Peritonitis is another complication where the deepest ulcers may perforate through the stomach wall and release the contents into the abdominal cavity causing a sudden severe pain. Chronic gastric ulcers may become cancerous.

HIATAL HERNIA

The hiatus hernia or hiatal hernia is an anatomical abnormality of the upper digestive system in which the upper part of the stomach protrudes or herniates into the thorax or the chest.

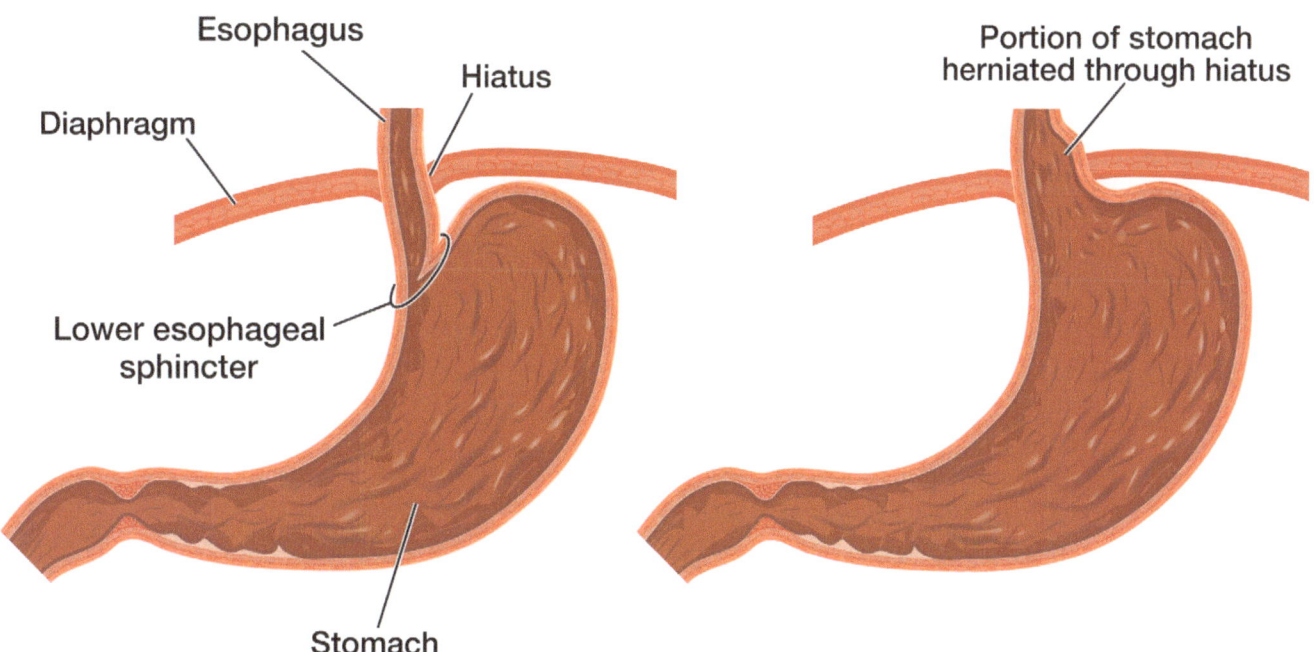

Figure 1-14 Hiatal hernia

Gastrointestinal System

The hiatus or the opening of the diaphragm through which the esophagus passes from the chest into the abdomen is reasonably tight and firmly grips the esophagus just above the stomach. In some cases, the hiatus becomes larger than normal allowing the esophagus to slip out of its normal position causing the upper part of the stomach to be herniated through the opening.

Different types of hiatus hernia:

In the sliding hiatus hernia, the herniated part of the stomach moves or slides back and forth, into the thorax or the chest. This is the most common type of hiatus hernia which does not usually reveal any symptoms; however, symptoms such as heartburn and acid regurgitation may be observed.

In the second type of hiatus hernia, known as the fixed hiatus hernia, the upper part of the stomach is caught up in the chest. There may be symptoms such as chronic acid reflux into the esophagus for this type of hiatus hernia.

GASTRITIS

Gastritis is the inflammation of the inner lining of the stomach, accompanied by abdominal pain, nausea and vomiting. Fever and diarrhea may also be experienced as a result of an accompanying infection.

RECTAL PROLAPSE

Prolapse means the displacement of an organ from its normal position. Rectal prolapse occurs when a part of the rectum is forced downwards and protrudes from the anus. In some cases, the whole rectal wall may be prolapsed protruding uncomfortably through the anus and look like a moist and swollen tissue which is red or pink in color. It may occur due to straining for a long time to empty the bowels. This condition may be associated with internal piles in adults.

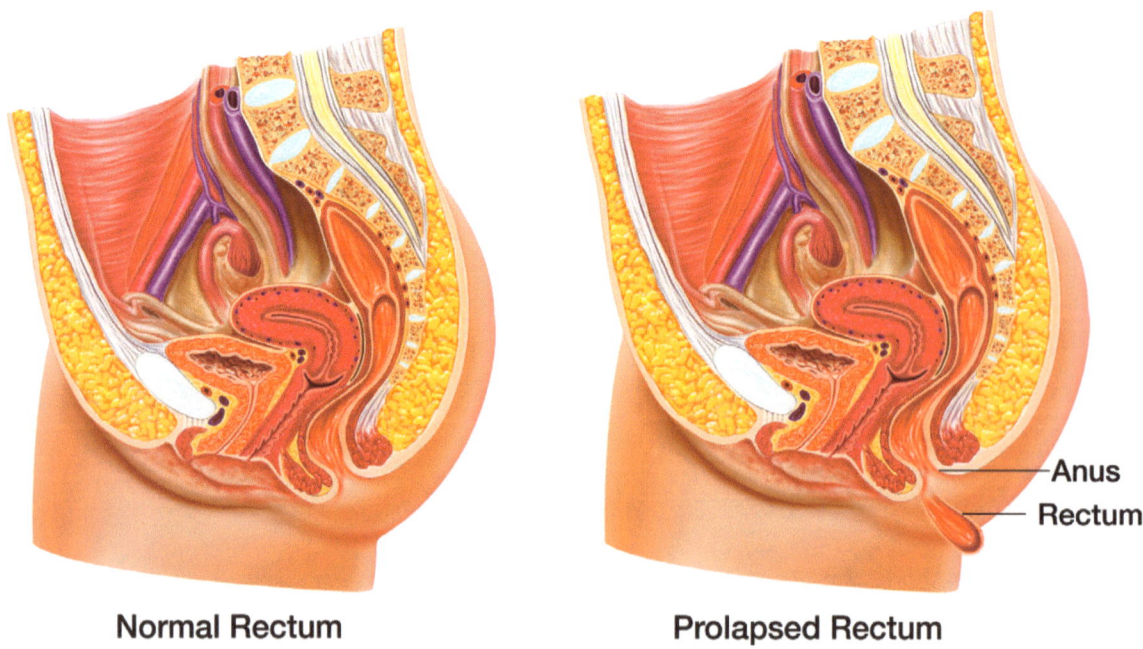

Normal Rectum   Prolapsed Rectum

Figure 1-15 Rectal prolapse

ULCERATIVE COLITIS

A chronic inflammation of the large bowel(colon) causing ulceration, the cause of which is unknown. Common symptoms include mild cramps in the lower part of the abdomen, fever, loss of appetite and loss of weight, frequent attacks of diarrhea with blood in the stools. Sometimes the diarrhea consists of water, blood and pus only. In severe cases diarrhea may occur 10 to 20 times a day. Complications such as hemorrhage occur and it may spread to involve the whole colon. The risk of cancer of the bowel is high in children with colitis.

LIVER & GALL BLADDER

The liver and the gall bladder are the major organs associated with the G.I. tract. Their proper performance is vital since they carry out a remarkable part of the metabolic activities. The liver is the largest gland of the body. It is reddish brown in color and lies immediately beneath the diaphragm on the upper right side of the abdomen. As pointed out previously, a normal liver is firm and non-greasy. As a result of fat accumulation in the liver cells, the liver gradually increases in size and becomes soft, greasy, and yellow. It has a significant blood supply and is wedge shaped. It consists of a large right lobe and a small left lobe. The cells in the liver which are called hepatocytes secrete the bile. The gall bladder is a pear-shaped, hollow organ closely attached to the back side of the liver. The gall gladder acts as the reservoir for the bile.

- The medical words used to describe the liver are 'hepato' or 'hepatic'
- The liver performs more than 500 different functions!

PHYSIOLOGY

The liver acts as a detoxifier. It absorbs all poisons and toxic substances such as nicotine, and various drugs and consequently swells. As a result, the blood without the poisonous substances is circulated to the heart. The liver has a great regenerative capacity and can rebuild itself to normal size, even if 80 percent of its body is cut away. It produces between 600 and 1200 ml/day of greenish-yellow digestive juice called bile which is stored in the gall bladder. The bile is released at meal time and passes through a duct to the duodenum to act on the food. The bile helps with the digestion of fat and also serves as a means for excretion of several important waste products from the blood. The bile consists of two pigments; bilirubin and biliverdin. These pigments may occasionally get into the blood stream in excess quantities and produce jaundice-yellow staining of skin and eye. Jaundice is a symptom, not a disease, which announces that there is something wrong with the liver.

- The liver acts as detoxifier and removes toxins and poisons including, cigarette smoke, alcohol and drugs from the blood
- The liver filters more than one litre of blood each minute
- If the liver is not functioning properly the skin and eyes may have a yellowish colour. There may also be loss of appetite, nausea and fatigue, frequent headaches, chronic constipation and intolerance to greasy food

DISORDERS OF LIVER & GALL BLADDER

ALCOHOLIC LIVER DISEASE

Alcohol induced liver injury results from chronic alcohol ingestion. Alcohol has a detrimental effect on the liver. Following are the conditions that result due to chronic alcohol ingestion.

1. Alcoholic fatty liver – Due to fat deposition in the liver and enlargement of liver, it becomes painful.
2. Alcoholic hepatitis – Chronic inflammation of the liver leading to jaundice and liver damage.
3. Alcoholic cirrhosis of liver – Irreversible damage to the liver parenchyma resulting in impairment of liver of liver functions, especially fat digestion.

ASCITES

In certain liver conditions, the blood flow through the blood vessels of the liver gets impeded. When there is excess pressure in the hepatic veins (veins of the liver carrying blood to the heart), excessive amounts of fluids leak through the outer surface of the liver directly into the abdominal cavity. As a result of further pressure increase, the "sweating" from the surface of the liver may increase enough to cause a large amount of fluid to accumulate in the abdominal cavity. This condition is known as ascites.

CIRRHOSIS OF LIVER

Cirrhosis of the liver is a condition where fat infiltrates into the liver and is replaced by fibrous tissue followed by scarring and conversion of the normal liver tissue into abnormal hard nodules. It may eventually constrict the blood vessels thereby impeding the flow of blood through the liver. This condition will consequently increase the blood pressure in the abdomen. This can lead to multiple issues such as collection of fluid in the abdomen, enlargement of the spleen, kidney problems and swelling of the ankles. The liver becomes shrunken, hard, sickly and yellowish in color. Cirrhosis of the liver is often associated with alcoholism, malnutrition, uncontrolled negative lower emotions, or a complication of infection of the liver. If the disease can be stopped in a timely manner, the undamaged liver can regenerate itself back to its normal state.

Cirrhosis is more common in men and its symptoms include feeling ill, atrophy (shrinking) of the testicles, anemia, and a pale slightly 'dirty' complexion.

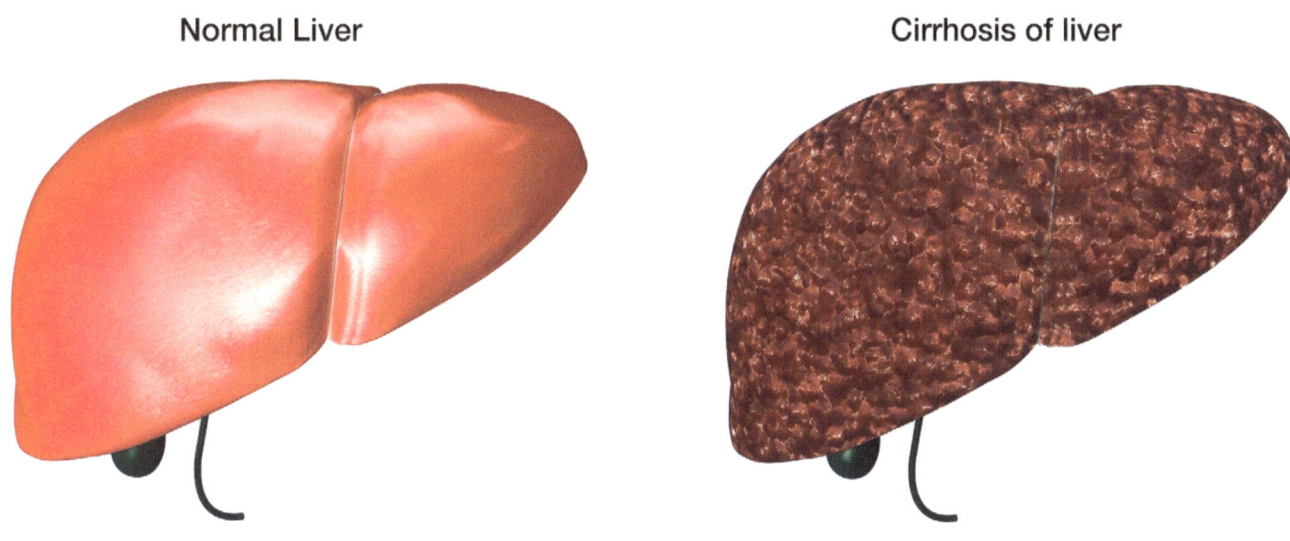

Figure 1-16 Cirrhosis of liver

In men, the breasts may swell since the diseased liver cannot inactivate the female hormones that are present to a small degree. Other symptoms include the loss of sex drive, appetite and weight.

GALLSTONES

Gallstones are hard stone-like precipitates which form in the gallbladder and get lodged in the bile duct. They are formed as a result of the chronic inflammation of the gall bladder or due to elevated levels of cholesterol in the bile (a product of the liver, employed in digestion and stored in the gall bladder). It may also occur due to excessive fat in the diet or due to decreased secretion of bile.

- Gallstones are formed when there is excess cholesterol in the bile, or due to excessive fat in the diet or due to decreased secretion of bile

The cholesterol which is digested by the bile secreted from liver gets precipitated in chronic diseases of the gall bladder resulting in the formation of gallstones.

The stones present in the gall bladder rarely lead any major problem; however, if they appear in the bile duct, various symptoms arise including nausea, vomiting, fever, intermittent pain in upper, middle and right abdomen near the right lower ribs.

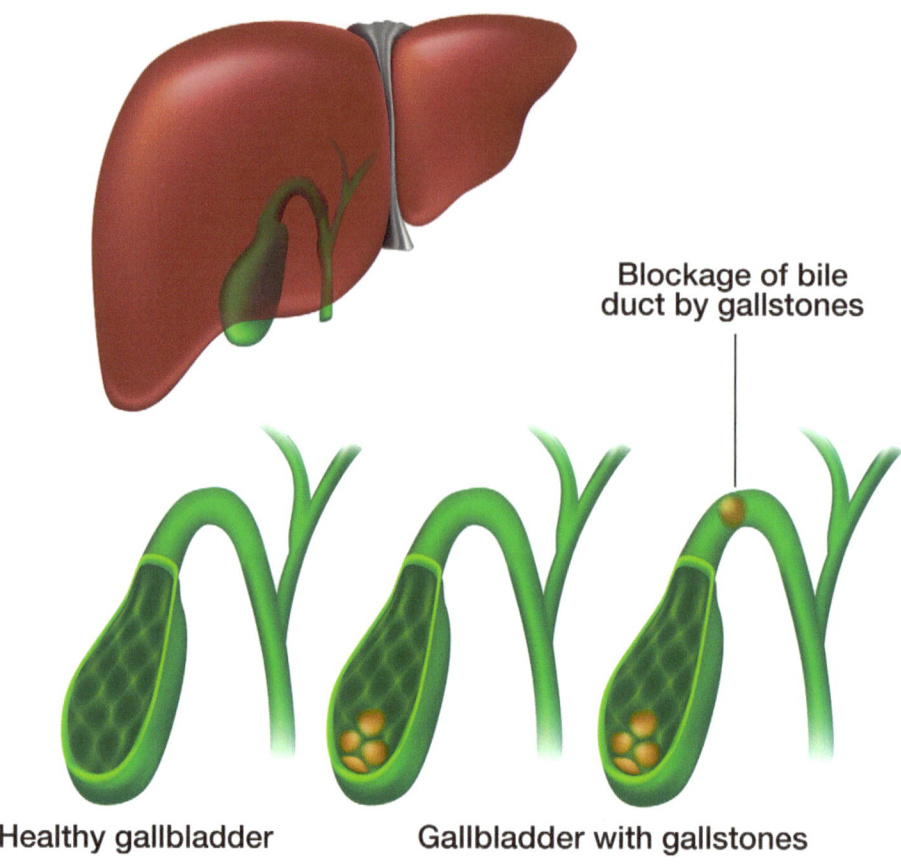

Figure 1-17 Gallstones

HEPATITIS

Hepatitis is an inflammation of the liver cells caused by viral infection. The patient usually experiences headache, nausea, vomiting, general malaise and diarrhea initially. Generally, about two weeks after the onset of the infection, the patient becomes jaundiced, the skin and eyes turn yellow and the urine darkens. The liver grows large and tender. The duration of the illness varies, and even after the jaundice disappears the patient will continue to feel malaise for a few days.

JAUNDICE

Jaundice is characterized by excessive yellow pigment-bilirubin. This pigment is produced when the red blood cells are broken by the spleen and are further removed by the liver and discharged as bile into the intestines to help digestion. When this pigment is produced in excessive amounts due to some sort of disease, it accumulates in the body tissues. The yellowish color may be visible in the skin and white of the eyes. The urine gets a dark brown color. Therefore, jaundice includes a set of symptoms indicating a type of liver malfunction. It may be caused by infections, which damage the liver or any other disorder which obstruct the flow of the bile into the intestine through the bile duct. Jaundice is seen in three to five day old babies because the baby's body has more bilirubin than it can get rid of. During pregnancy the bilirubin was removed through the placenta but after birth the baby's body need to get rid of bilirubin on its own. This condition causes a mild jaundice.

Chapter 2

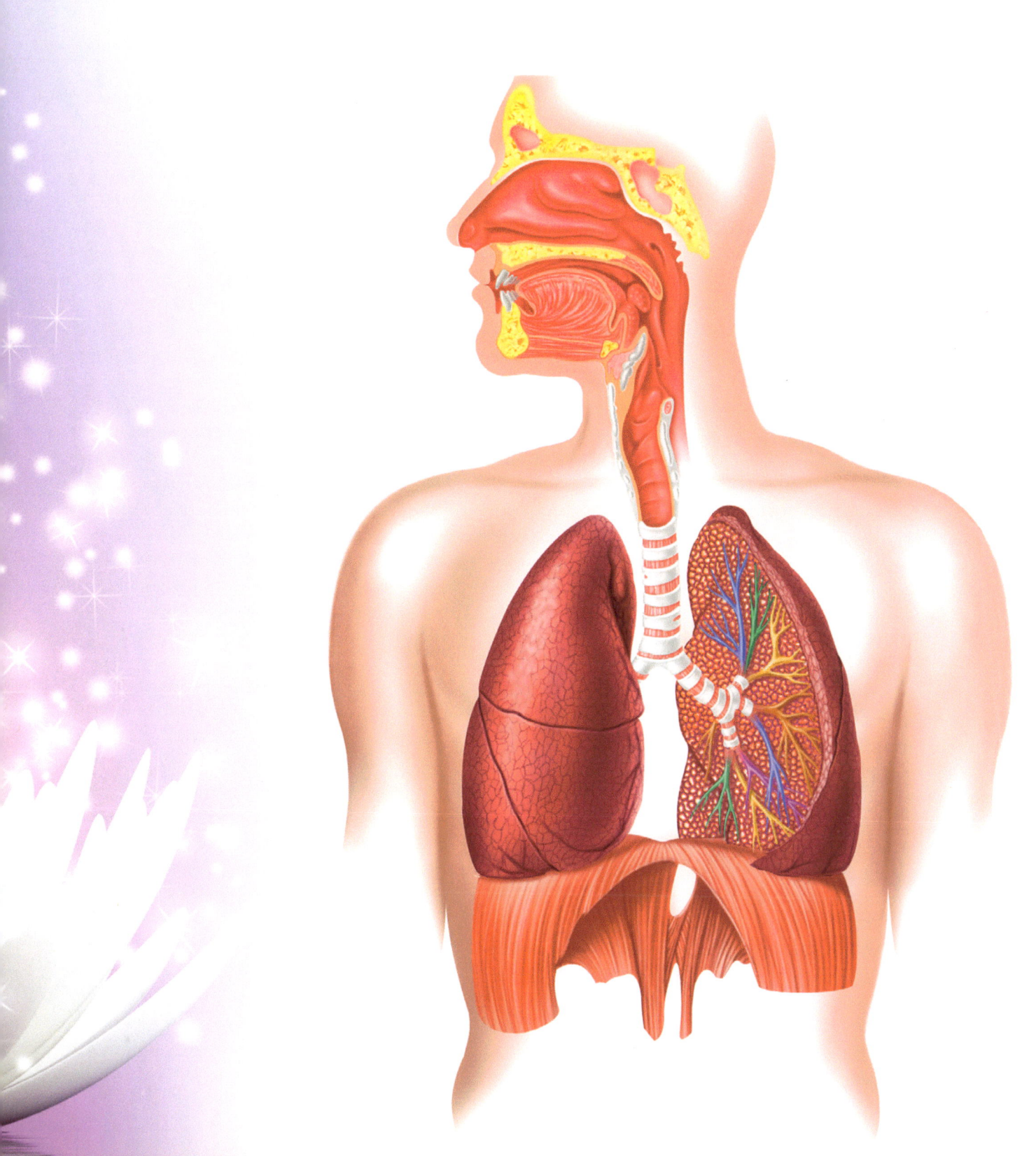

Respiratory system

TABLE OF CONTENTS

- ANATOMY 29
- NOSE 30
- SINUSES 30
- PHARYNX 31
- LARYNX 31
- TRACHEA 32
- BRONCHI 33
- BRONCHIOLES 33
- ALVEOLI 33
- PLEURA 33
- PHYSIOLOGY 34
  - Pulmonary ventilation 34
  - Diffusion or exchange of oxygen and carbon dioxide between the alveoli and blood 35
  - Transport of oxygen and carbon dioxide in the blood and body fluids to and from the cells 35
- DISORDERS OF NOSE AND NASAL PASSAGES 37
  - Sinusitis 37
- DISORDERS OF PHARYNX 38
  - Adenoiditis 38
  - Pharyngitis 38
  - Tonsillitis 38
  - Epistaxis 39
  - Laryngitis 39
- DISORDERS OF LUNGS 39
  - Asthma 39
  - Bronchiectasis 40
  - Bronchiolitis 40
  - Bronchitis 40
  - Emphysema 41
  - Pleurisy 42
  - Pneumothorax 42
  - Pneumonia 43
  - Tuberculosis 44

RESPIRATORY SYSTEM

ANATOMY

The term respiration is often understood as the mechanical process of breathing which is repetitive exchange of air between the lungs and the external environment. This exchange of air at the lungs is also known as external respiration. The tissues of our body require oxygen for their normal functioning and metabolic reactions. The obvious goal of respiration is to provide oxygen to the tissues and to remove carbon dioxide. Internal respiration is the exchange of gases not at the lungs but at the cells within all the organs of the body. In this process, oxygen passes out of the bloodstream into the tissue cells. At the same time, carbon dioxide passes from the tissue cells into the bloodstream and is carried by the blood back to the lungs to be exhaled.

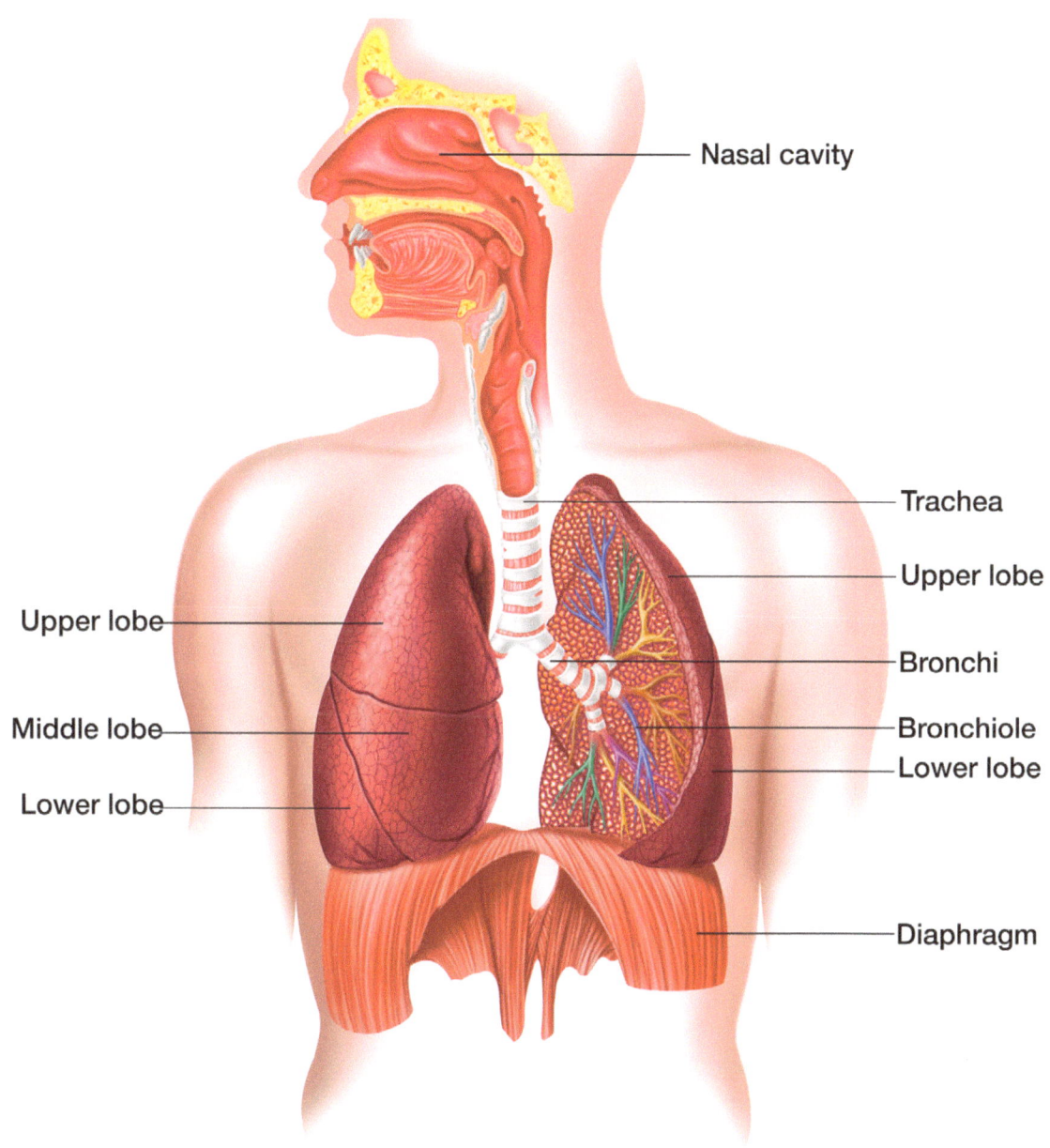

Figure 2-1 Respiratory system

The respiratory tract is comprised of the nose and the nasal passages, the trachea, pharynx, and the lungs. Associated with the nasal passages are a series of bony sacs, the para nasal sinuses. The respiratory system is divided into the following two parts:

1. The upper respiratory tract, which is comprised of nostrils, nasopharynx, and oropharynx.

2. The lower respiratory tract, which is comprised of the larynx, trachea, bronchi and the rest of the respiratory tree (bronchioles and air sacs or alveoli).

NOSE

The upper respiratory tract starts at the nose. The nose has a bony partition called the nasal septum. The inner wall of the nose is lined by the mucous membrane. The nasal cavity opens to the exterior through the nares or the nostrils. The walls of the nasal cavity have bony infoldings that are referred to as turbinates.

- The length of our thumb and our nose is the same
- We breathe 23,000 times a day on an average
- We inhale over 10,500 liters of air every day

SINUSES

Air sinuses are the air-filled expansions in the bones of the skull. There are sinuses present around the nose that open into the nasal passage and are called paranasal sinuses; these sinuses are called the maxillary sinuses; located above the cheeks, frontal sinuses; located in the frontal bone over the eyes, ethmoid sinuses; located in the wall between the nose and eyes, sphenoid sinuses; which are located at the back of the nasal cavity.

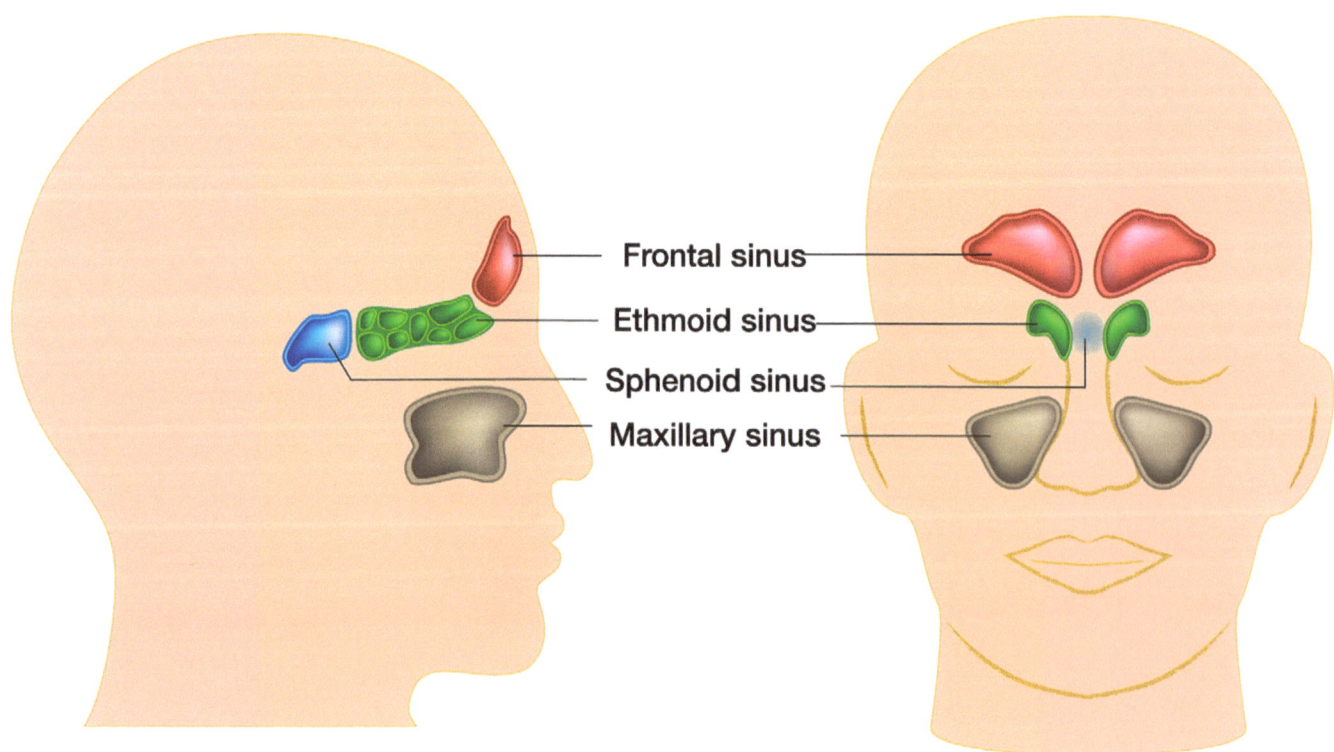

Figure 2-2 Sinuses

Their major function is to warm, humidify and filter the particles in the inhaled air. The cold air is warmed in the nose and upper respiratory tract before reaching the larynx. This process prevents the larynx from becoming dry and keeps the airways pliable and patent thus allowing a smooth and fresh passage for the act of ventilation (namely inspiration and expiration).

PHARYNX

The air travels from the nasal passages to the pharynx commonly known as the throat. The throat has two components; the nasal part which is called the nasopharynx, and the oral part that communicates with the mouth is called the oropharynx. The nasopharynx has small lymphatic tissues called adenoids and the oropharynx contains lymphatic nodes called tonsils. These tonsils can be observed when the individual's mouth is open. Refer fig 1-6, page 10 and fig 2-10, page 38.

LARYNX

The oropharynx is connected to another chamber called the larynx. This is also known as the voice box. The larynx is guarded by the epiglottis which closes when the individual swallows food or water. The voice box is constructed mainly of cartilage, which is a flexible connective tissue. The vocal cords are two pairs of membranes that are stretched across the inside of the larynx. As the air is expired, the vocal cords vibrate. We can control the vibrations of the vocal cords to make sounds.

- The voice box is called larynx and the windpipe is called trachea

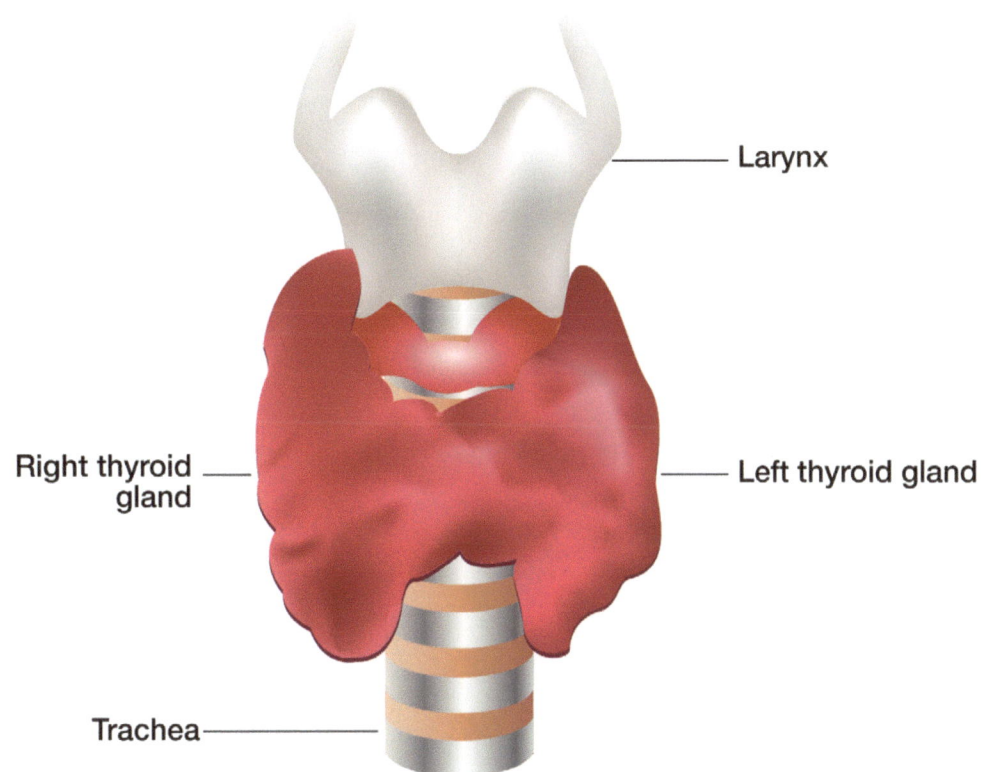

Figure 2-3 Larynx

Respiratory System

TRACHEA

The trachea or the windpipe begins below the larynx and runs down in front of the neck into the chest and is divided into right and left main bronchi. It is formed of cartilages and fibromuscular membrane lined internally by mucosa. The trachea is 10 to 11 cm long. There are about 20 C-shaped hyaline cartilaginous rings on the trachea each of which are deficient in the back. The trachea bifurcates into two branches which enter the lung. The point of bifurcation is called the carina. This point when stimulated, results in coughing, preventing any aspiration in the normal healthy individual.

- The trachea also filters the air we breathe

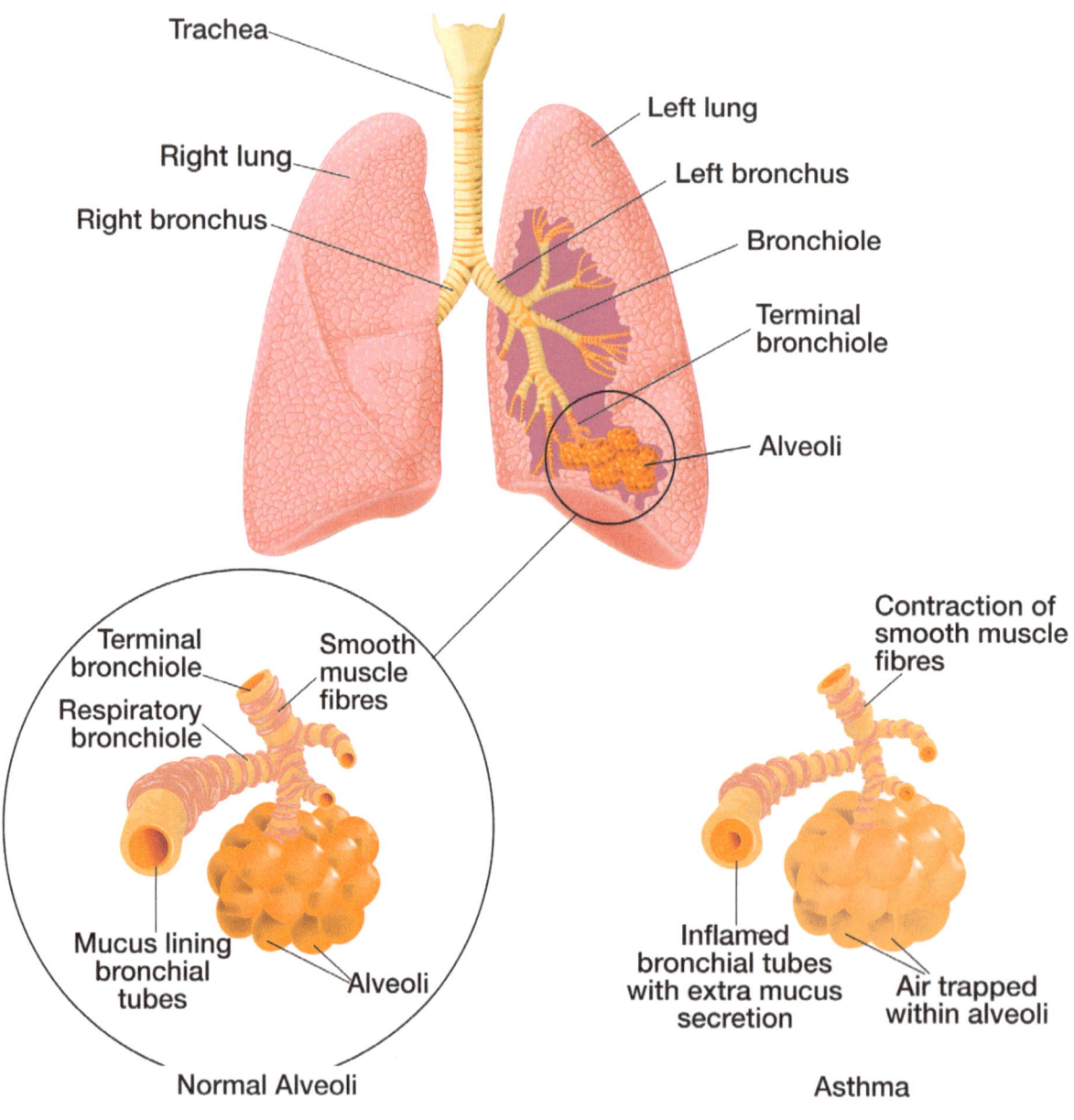

Figure 2-4 Lung anatomy

Respiratory System

BRONCHI

The branches of the trachea that act as a passageway into the air spaces of the lung are called the bronchi or bronchial tube. This part of the respiratory tract is lined with ciliated epithelial cells. The bronchus is also lined with a mucous membrane and fine hairs called cilia to help filter out external objects.

BRONCHIOLES

The bronchial tubes further divide to form smaller branches called bronchioles. Their walls become thinner and have less and less cartilage. Eventually, they become a tiny group of tubes called the terminal bronchioles.

ALVEOLI

The terminal bronchiole ends in a tiny air chamber. Each chamber contains many cup-shaped cavities or air sacs known as alveoli. The walls of the alveoli are one cell thick and they form the respiratory surface where the gas exchange takes place. They are thin, moist, and are surrounded by several capillaries. The exchange of oxygen and carbon dioxide between blood and air occurs through these walls. The lungs contain about 300 million alveoli. Their total surface area would be about 70 square meters. That is 40 times the surface area of the skin.

- There are about 300 million alveoli in each lung
- The lungs have a surface area of approximately the same size as a tennis court

PLEURA

The lungs are covered by a double-layered membrane called pleura. The inner layer that is adherent to the lung is called the visceral pleura and the outer layer which is loose and attached to the thoracic cavity is called the parietal pleura. The pleura is lubricated by a thin film of fluid present between the two layers that allows the lungs to expand and contract smoothly while breathing and prevents friction during movement.

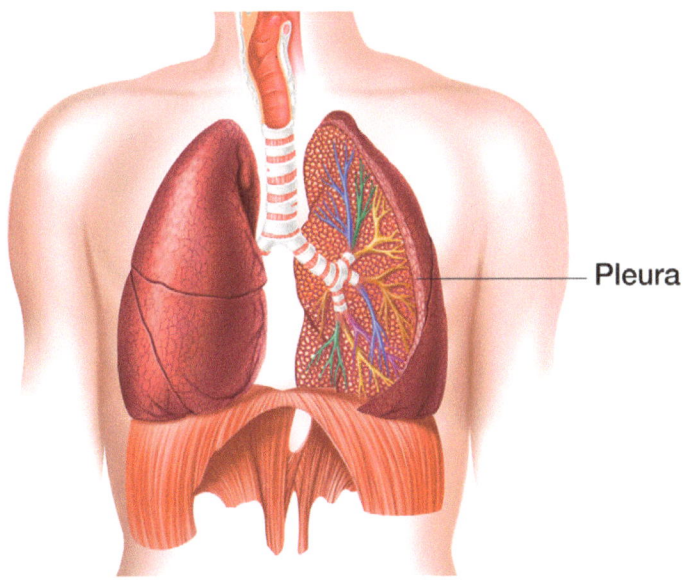

Figure 2-5 Pleura

Respiratory System

PHYSIOLOGY

Gaseous exchange is the primary role of the respiratory system. To achieve this, respiration can be divided into three major functional events:

1. Pulmonary ventilation.
2. Diffusion or exchange of oxygen and carbon dioxide between the alveoli and blood.
3. Transport of oxygen and carbon dioxide in the blood and body fluids to and from the cells.

1. PULMONARY VENTILATION

Pulmonary ventilation is the entry of air to the lungs. The air enters through the nose and passes through the nasopharynx, oropharynx, larynx, trachea, bronchi, secondary bronchi, terminal bronchioles and finally into the alveoli where the gas exchange takes place. This is brought about by the expansion of lungs. This process is called inhalation or inspiration.

- We breathe 12 to 15 times a minute
- The sneeze speed is more than 100 mph. We cannot keep our eyes open and sneeze at the same time

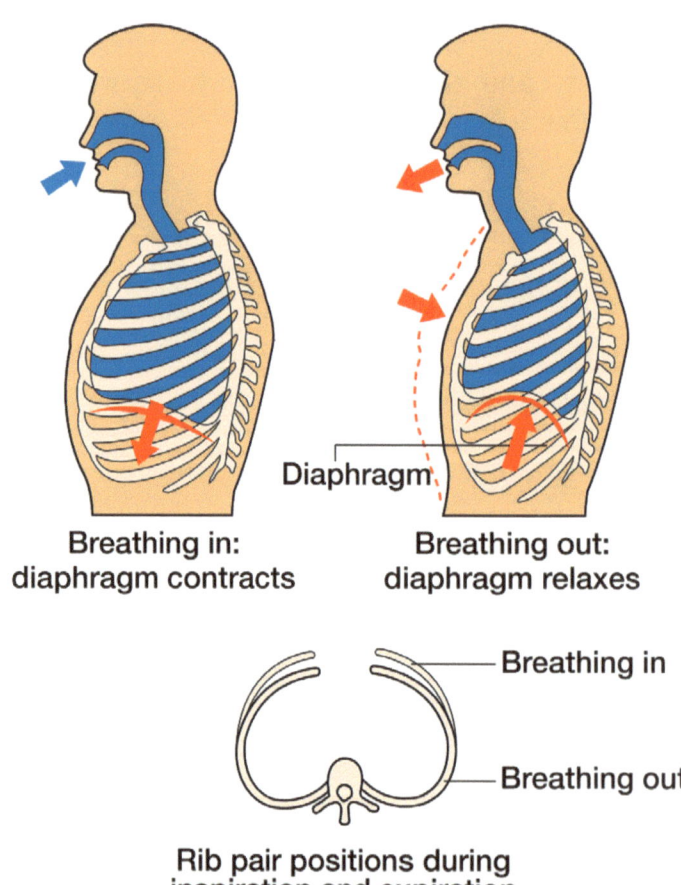

Figure 2-6 Respiration

During inhalation, the diaphragm moves downward increasing the vertical dimension of thoracic cavity. This lowers the air pressure in lungs and causes the air to move into lungs through the above mentioned route. After the exchange of gases, the air is expelled out of the lungs by a process called expiration or exhalation. During exhalation, relaxation of the external intercostal muscles returns the diaphragm to its original resting position. This restores the thoracic cavity to its pre-inspiratory volume. The increased pressure in the lungs aided with the elastic recoil of the lungs pushes the air outside the lungs where it is exhaled.

2. DIFFUSION OR EXCHANGE OF OXYGEN AND CARBON DIOXIDE BETWEEN THE ALVEOLI AND BLOOD

The exchange of gases oxygen (O_2) and carbon dioxide (CO_2) between the alveoli and the blood occurs by a simple diffusion process. Oxygen diffuses from the alveoli into the blood while carbon dioxide from the blood into the alveoli. Diffusion takes place based on a concentration gradient. Therefore, the concentration (or pressure) of O_2 in the alveoli must be kept at a higher level than in the blood while the concentration (or pressure) of CO_2 in the alveoli must be kept at a lower level than in the blood. We do this, of course, by breathing continuously into and out of the lungs.

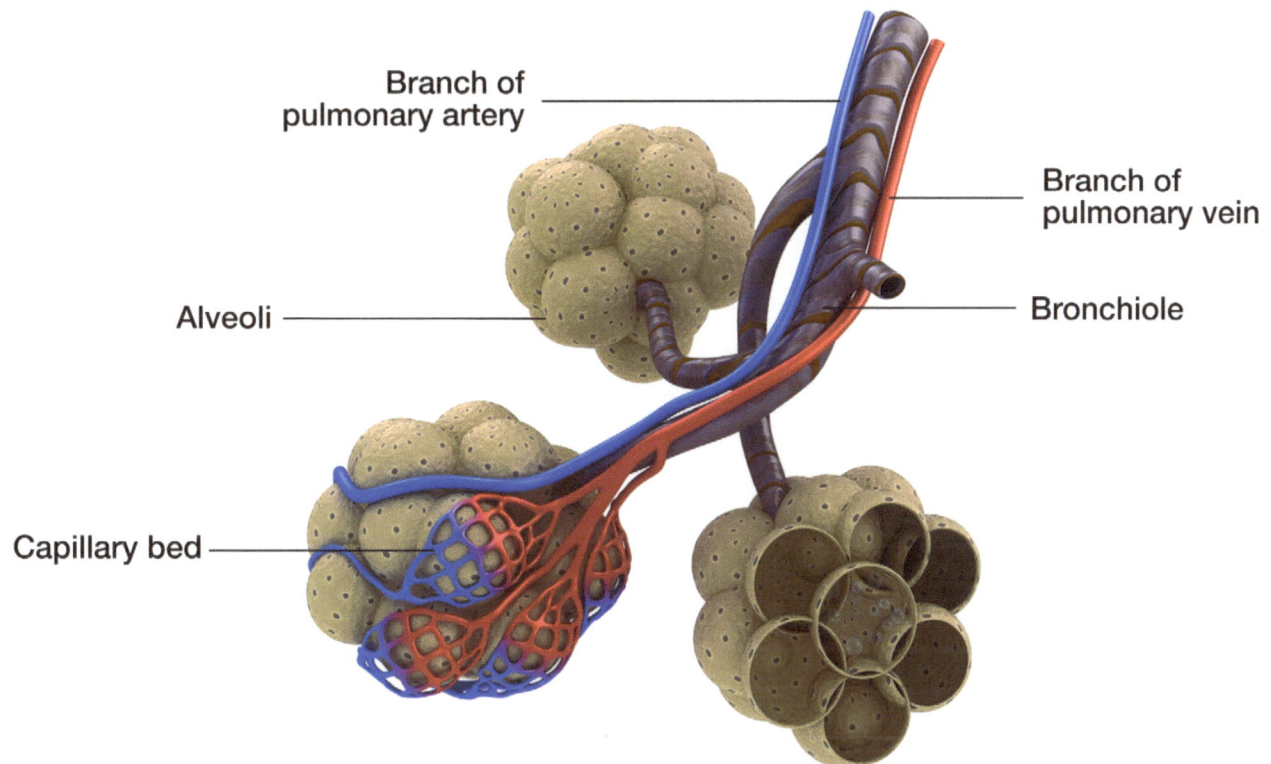

Figure 2-7 Gaseous exchange in alveoli

3. TRANSPORT OF OXYGEN AND CARBON DIOXIDE IN THE BLOOD AND BODY FLUIDS TO AND FROM THE CELLS

Gases are transported in association with molecules in the blood or dissolved in the plasma. Over 98% of oxygen carried in the blood is bound to the hemoglobin of the red blood cells, producing oxyhemoglobin. In areas of low oxygen concentrations, oxyhemoglobin is unstable and gives up its oxygen molecules. More oxygen is released as the blood concentration of carbon dioxide increases, as the blood becomes more acidic, or as blood temperature increases. A deficiency of oxygen reaching the tissues is called hypoxia and has a variety of causes.

Respiratory System

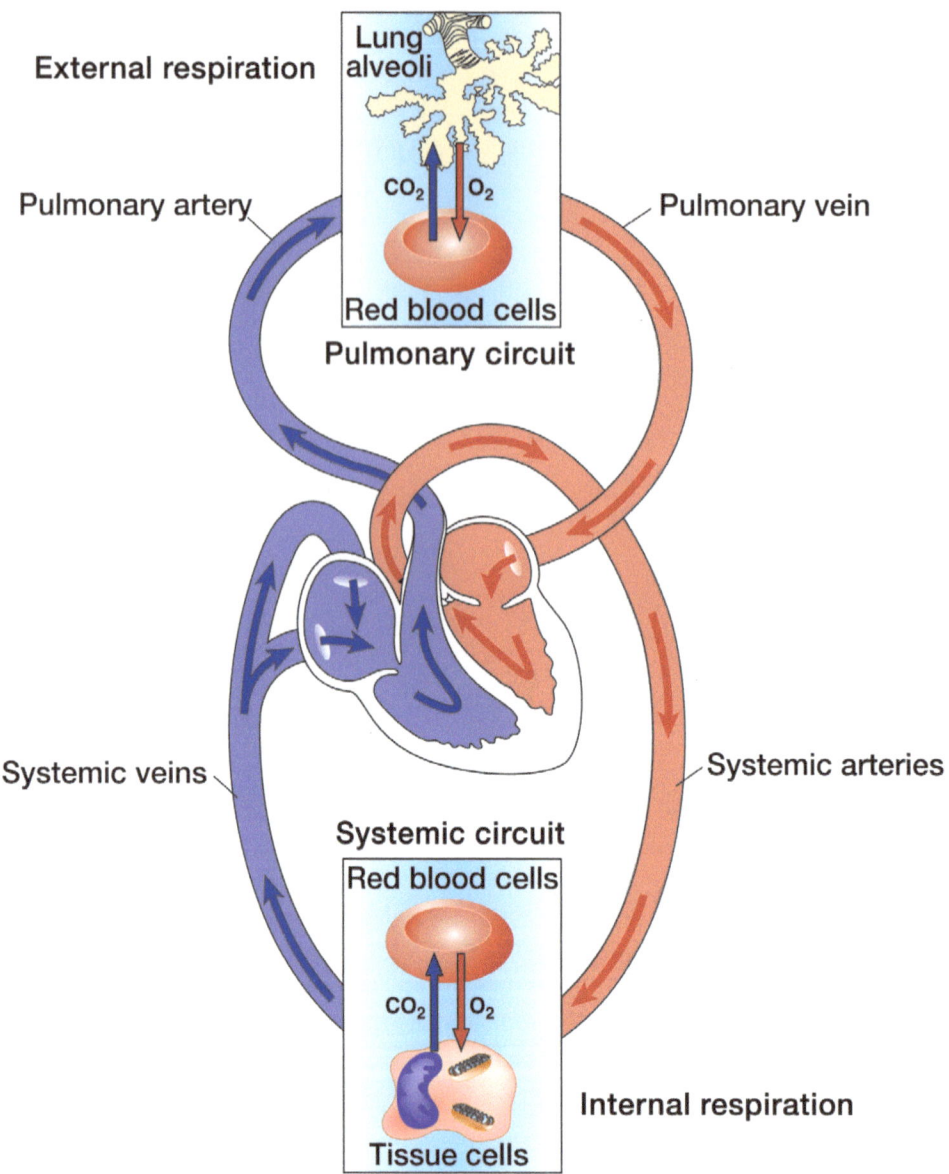

Figure 2-8 Transport of oxygen and carbon dioxide in the blood and body fluids to and from the cells

Carbon dioxide is transported dissolved in blood plasma, as carbaminohemoglobin, or as bicarbonate ions. Most carbon dioxide is transported in the form of bicarbonate. When carbon dioxide reacts with water in the plasma, carbonic acid is formed in a slow rate; however, much of the carbon dioxide enters the red blood cells, where the enzyme carbonic anhydrase accelerates this reaction. The resulting carbonic acid dissociates immediately, releasing bicarbonate and hydrogen ions. Carbaminohemoglobin also releases its carbon dioxide which diffuses out of the blood into the alveolar air. Therefore, the oxygen drawn into the blood from lungs is delivered to the cells and tissues while the carbon dioxide taken into the blood from the cells and tissues is released into the lungs and exhaled.

DISORDERS OF NOSE AND NASAL PASSAGES

SINUSITIS

It is a condition of inflammation of the paranasal sinuses caused by microorganisms or allergic reactions. Swelling of the membranes that line the openings of the sinuses into the nasal cavities blocks drainage of secretions from the sinuses. This results in fever, headache, dizziness and tenderness when pressure is applied on the affected sinus. Sinusitis may be acute or chronic and treatments may be directed towards opening the exits of the sinuses to promote the drainage and relieve the pressure.

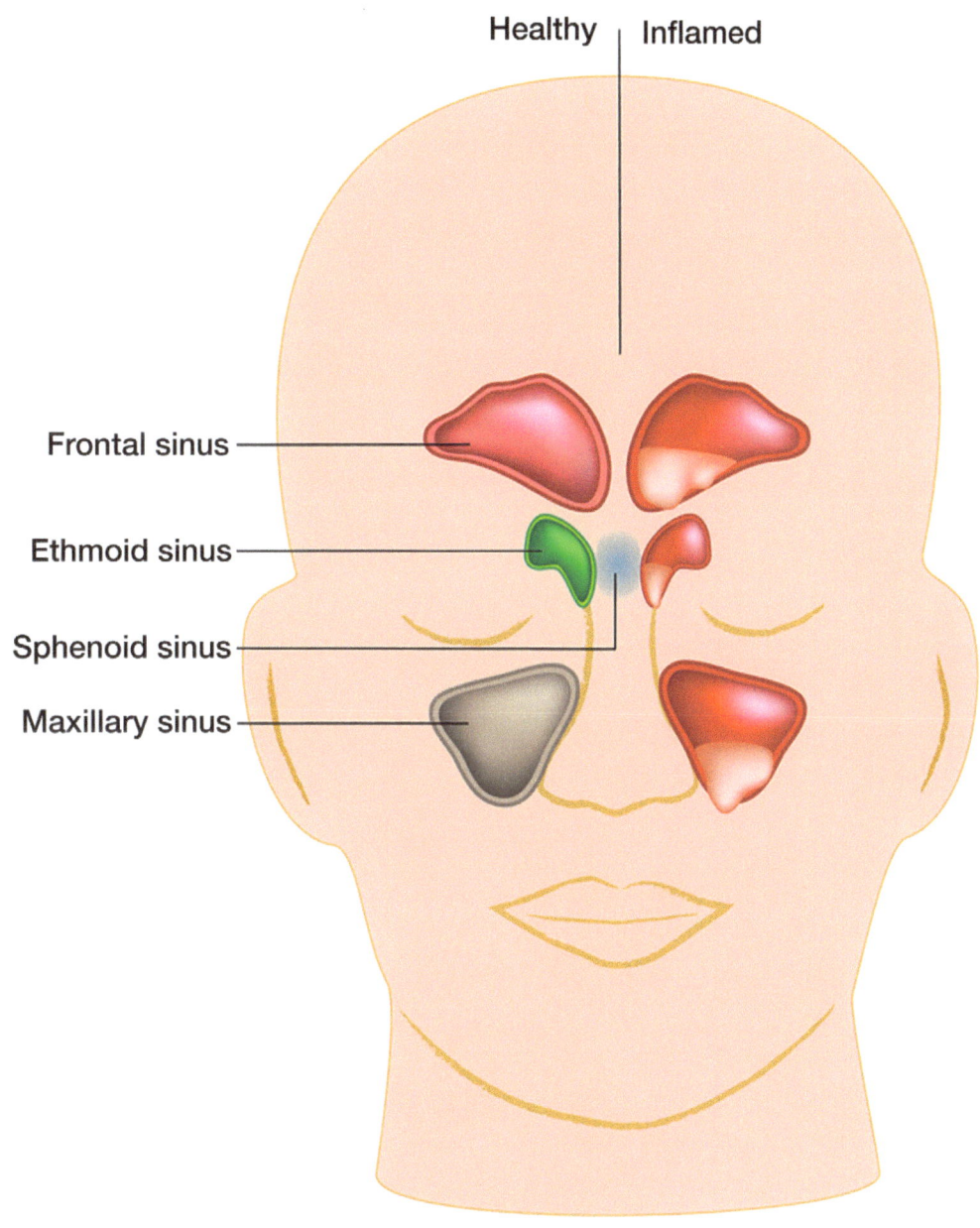

Figure 2-9 Sinusitis

DISORDERS OF PHARYNX

ADENOIDITIS

The adenoids are lymphoid tissues present in the nasopharynx. They get inflamed when microorganisms enter via the upper respiratory tract to the throat. Enlarged adenoids may obstruct the flow of air from the nose to the throat forcing the individual to breathe through the mouth. This could cause the lack of normal moistening, warming and cleansing functions.

PHARYNGITIS

Pharyngitis is the infection of pharyngeal wall. The symptoms and signs include sore throat, raised temperature, headache, dry cough, and redness of the pharyngeal wall. It presents as a postnasal drip with a thin watery nasal discharge.

TONSILLITIS

Tonsils are lymphoid tissue, which are located in the oropharynx. Inflammation of the tonsils is called tonsillitis, which is most common in children. Symptoms are rise in temperature, sore throat, inflamed posterior pharyngeal wall often covered with a white fleck of pus, and swollen glands in the neck. The tongue is coated white with malodorous breath. Tonsillitis infected by streptococcal organism and left untreated may lead to rheumatic heart disease.

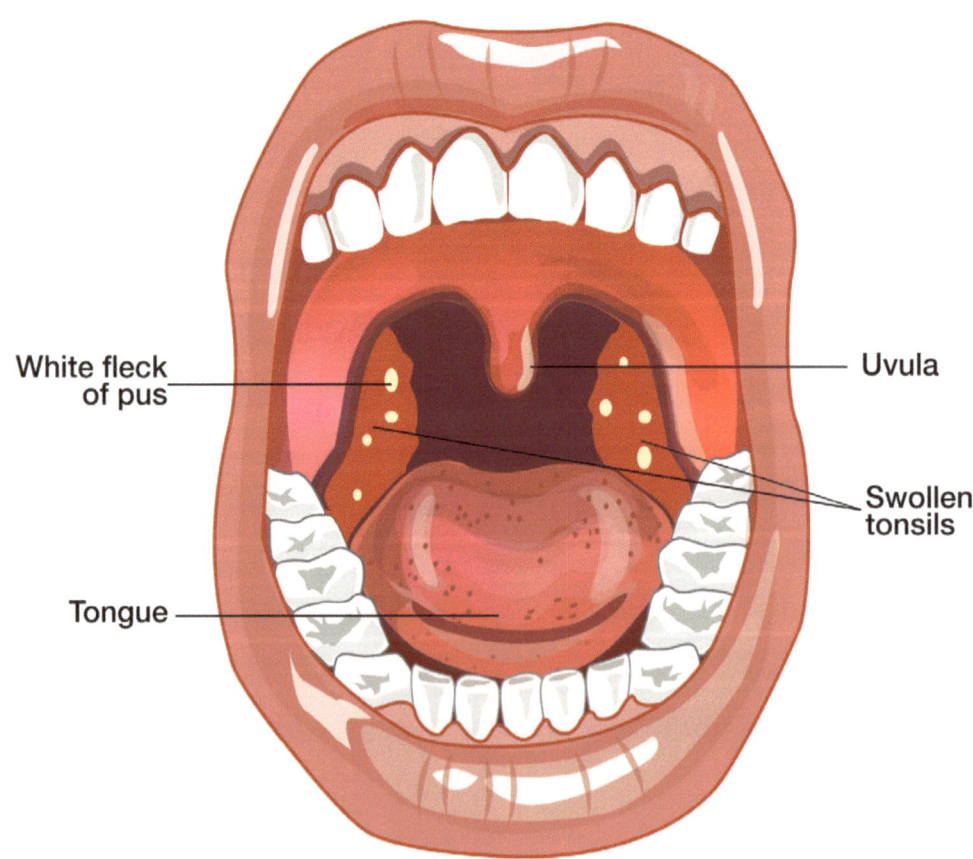

Figure 2-10 Tonsillitis

EPISTAXIS

Epistaxis refers to hemorrhage or bleeding from the nose. Epistaxis can be caused due to various reasons such as trauma, allergic response, fractures of the skull, intracranial bleeds, infections, severe environmental conditions of mental and physical stress, and systemic disorders such as leukemia, low platelet levels and hemophilia. The bleeding should be stopped as early as possible, as there is the risk of aspiration (sucking) of blood into the lungs and obstruction of the airway by the clotted blood in the nasal passageway.

- A nose bleed is also called epistaxis

LARYNGITIS

Laryngitis is the inflammation of the larynx. It produces hoarseness or sometimes loss of voice. It may be associated with sore throat, with pain, discomfort or hoarseness of voice on speaking, accompanied with a squeaky voice and hoarse cough.

DISORDERS OF LUNGS

ASTHMA

Asthma is a disease characterized by contraction or narrowing of the bronchioles resulting in airway obstruction and extreme difficulty in breathing. Asthma is caused due to hypersensitivity of the bronchioles to allergens such as pollen grains, dust particles, fur, dander, feather, etc. or other factors such as anxiety, cold and exercise. The symptoms include paroxysmal (sudden) dyspnea, wheezing, and cough. Sudden acute asthma attacks result in shortness of breath and wheezing and the individual tries to breathe fresh air from windows or open spaces. This condition is referred to as status asthmaticus.

- In the year 2009, about 8% of the US population had asthma.

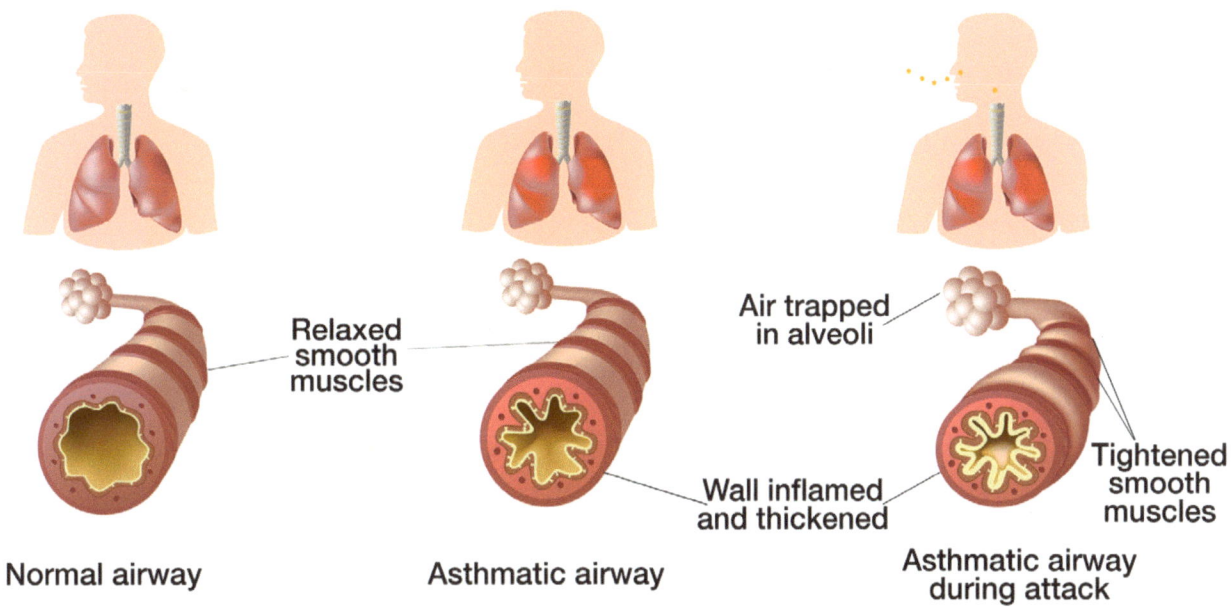

Figure 2-11 Pathology of Asthma

BRONCHIECTASIS

Bronchiectasis is a disease condition where a dilation or widening of lower bronchial airways occurs following a contraction in the upper bronchial airways. This condition may be congenital (present at birth), but occurs more commonly after a lung disease or infection. The area of lung tissue is reduced and the bronchi become weakened and widened as a result. Any infection like pneumonia, tuberculosis, bronchitis in which the amount of air that reaches the lungs is reduced is likely to cause bronchiectasis. Bronchiectasis commonly leads to chronic obstruction of a bronchus.

BRONCHIOLITIS

Bronchiolitis is the inflammation of the bronchioles. This illness affects infants and the lungs become filled with mucus and pus cells causing the baby to be seriously ill. It commonly occurs in winter. The illness starts with a cough or cold; then as the infection spreads down to the small air tubes deep in the lungs, symptoms such as shortness of breath with rapid breathing, sometimes accompanied by a wheeze developing in a few hours. The condition is associated with lower ribs and upper abdomen getting sucked in with each breath taken and the baby might look pale.

BRONCHITIS

Bronchitis is the inflammation of the larger air passages (bronchi) leading to the lung. There are two categories of bronchitis - acute and chronic bronchitis.

ACUTE BRONCHITIS

Acute bronchitis is accompanied by wheezy breathing, persistent cough, general fatigue, loss of appetite and fever. Phlegm produced during this condition is yellowish or greenish in color.

CHRONIC BRONCHITIS

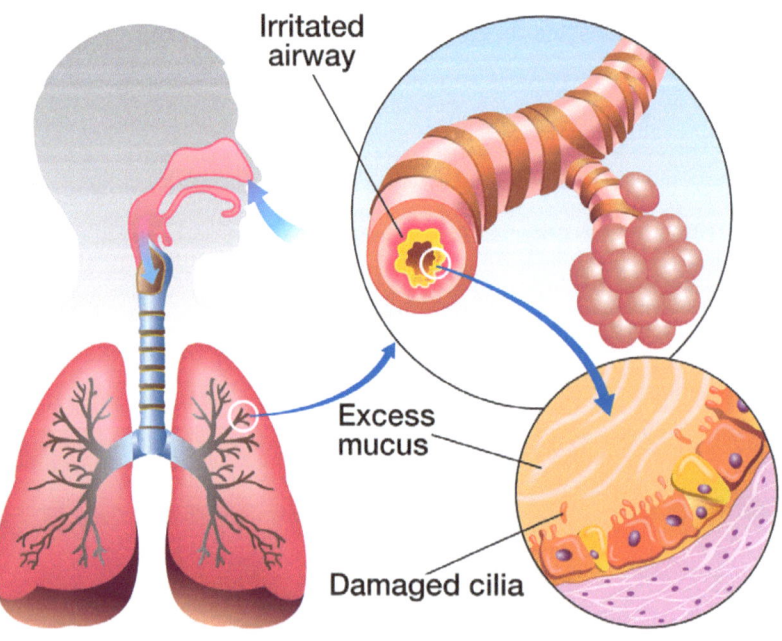

Figure 2-12 Chronic bronchitis

Chronic bronchitis is the condition of the bronchial tree characterized by cough, hypersecretion of mucus, and expectoration of sputum over a long period of time, associated with frequent bronchial infection. It is usually caused due to inhalation over a prolonged period of air contaminated by dust or by noxious gases of combustion. The cough and daily sputum production should be present at least for three months in two successive years for the condition to be called as chronic bronchitis. There is difficulty in breathing with chronic cough. The patient usually expectorates white and frothy sputum. A general feeling of illness, malaise, fatigue and ill-defined chest pain are experienced and the chest looks hyper inflated.

EMPHYSEMA

Emphysema is a condition of the lung characterized by an increase in the size of air spaces distal to the terminal bronchiole with destructive changes in the walls of alveoli and reduction in their number. Loss of elasticity and the breakdown of the alveoli walls result in loss of air movement in the air sacs. There is a strong association between cigarette smoking and emphysema. Additionally, chronic bronchitis is often associated with emphysema. Clinical manifestation is undue breathlessness on exertion, and blueness of the lips. Due to the destruction of alveolar walls and blood vessels, the pulmonary artery pressure rises and the right side of the heart works harder to pump the blood. This leads to right ventricular hypertrophy and heart failure (cor pulmonale).

- In emphysema the tiny air sacs or alveoli become permanently swollen with air
- Essential oils such as eucalyptus, lavender, pine, rosemary are helpful for emphysema

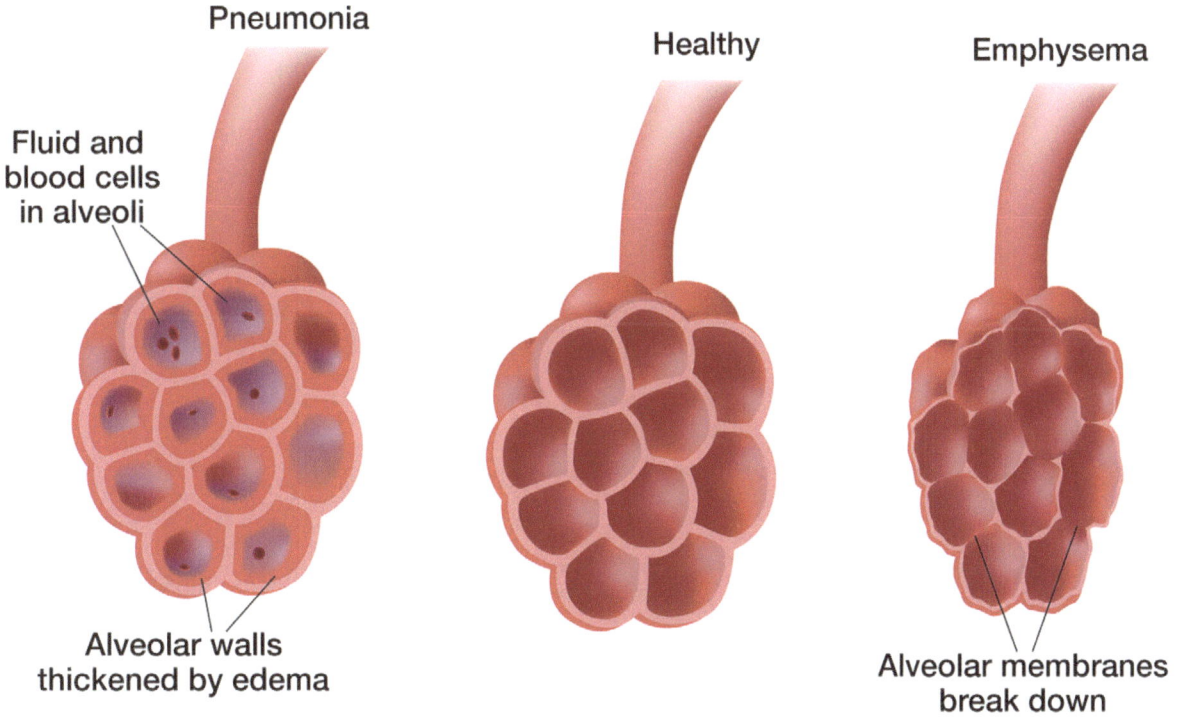

Figure 2-13 Alveoli changes in lung diseases

PLEURISY

Pleurisy is a condition of inflammation of the pleura. Pleurisy frequently occurs as a secondary complication of a respiratory tract infection, such as pneumonia, though other causes may be present.

Pleurisy can take one of the two forms; Dry pleurisy in which the infected pleurae rub against each other or wet pleurisy in which an excess amount of fluid is produced. Both types have similar symptoms such as sharp or stabbing pain in the chest which is clearly related to the movement of breathing. Pain is most severe in dry pleurisy. Accumulation of blood in the pleural space is called hemothorax, which is caused due to injury or infection to the pleura.

PNEUMOTHORAX

Accumulation of air in the pleural space is called pneumothorax. It is caused by the release of air from the lungs through a ruptured emphysematous bulla. It can lead to collapse of the lungs by altering intrapleural pressure. The main symptom of pneumothorax is the sudden onset of sharp pain in the chest aggravated by deep breath or coughing which may radiate to the shoulders. Shortness of breath is also experienced. A fractured rib piercing the lung or any injury that penetrates the wall of the chest may cause pneumothorax, which is an emergency and should be treated promptly.

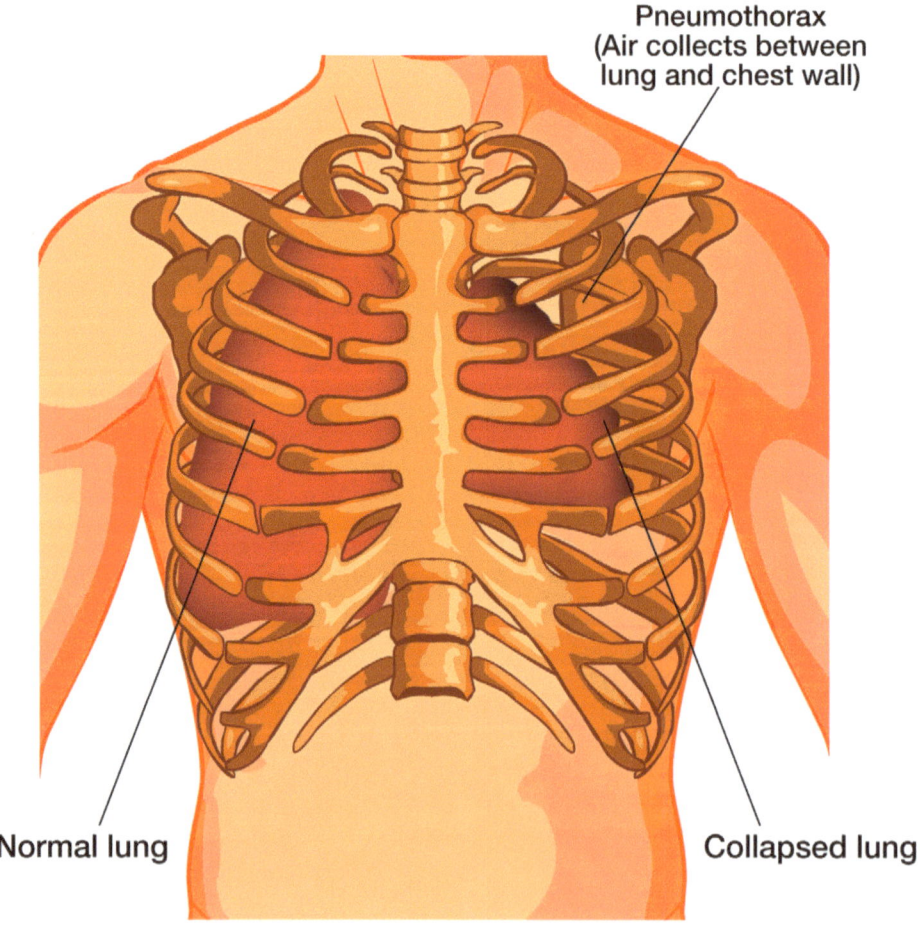

Figure 2-14 Pneumothorax

PNEUMONIA

Pneumonia is any inflammatory condition of the lung caused by bacteria or virus in which some or all of the alveoli are filled with fluid. The infection spreads from the alveolus to larger areas of the lungs, or to the whole lung in some cases. Symptoms may include high fever, persistent dry cough and very rapid rate of breathing. Breathing and coughing often aggravate one-sided chest pain. There may be reddish streaks of blood in the phlegm as well. The symptoms of pneumonia are not always obvious in babies and toddlers. The only obvious signs of serious illness may be a high fever with rapid respirations and in-drawing of the lower ribs while cough may be silent or absent.

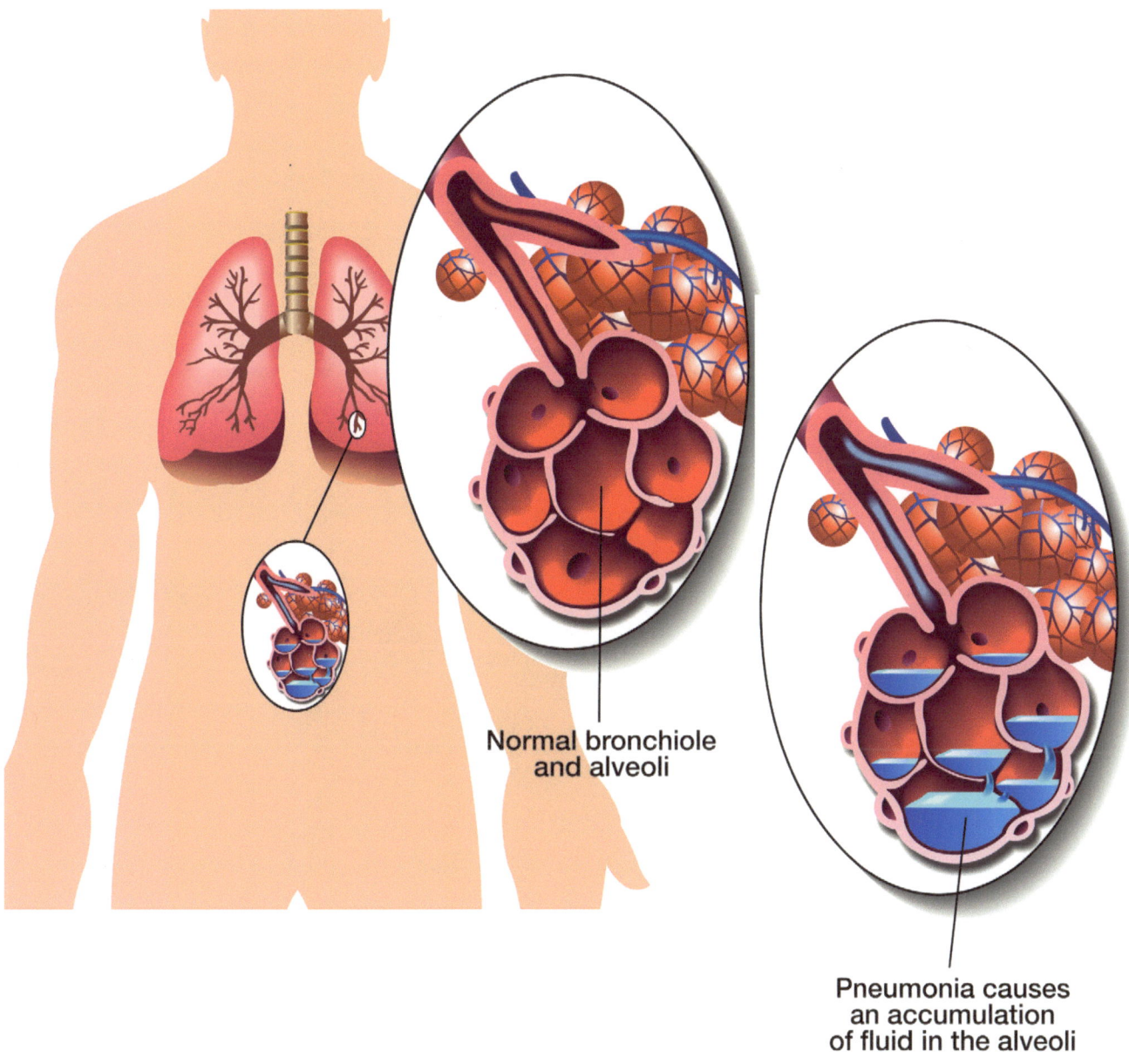

Figure 2-15 Pneumonia

Respiratory System

TUBERCULOSIS

Tuberculosis is a condition caused by a type of bacteria called mycobacterium tuberculosis. The lungs are filled with secretions due to an inflammatory response against the infection. Evening rise of temperature may be experienced and the patient might become very weak with systemic symptoms of malaise. In extreme cases, the infection spreads to other parts of the body like bones, meninges (brain and spinal cord coverings), muscles, etc. Tuberculous infection of spine known as Pott's spine, makes the vertebra very weak and can also lead to fracture.

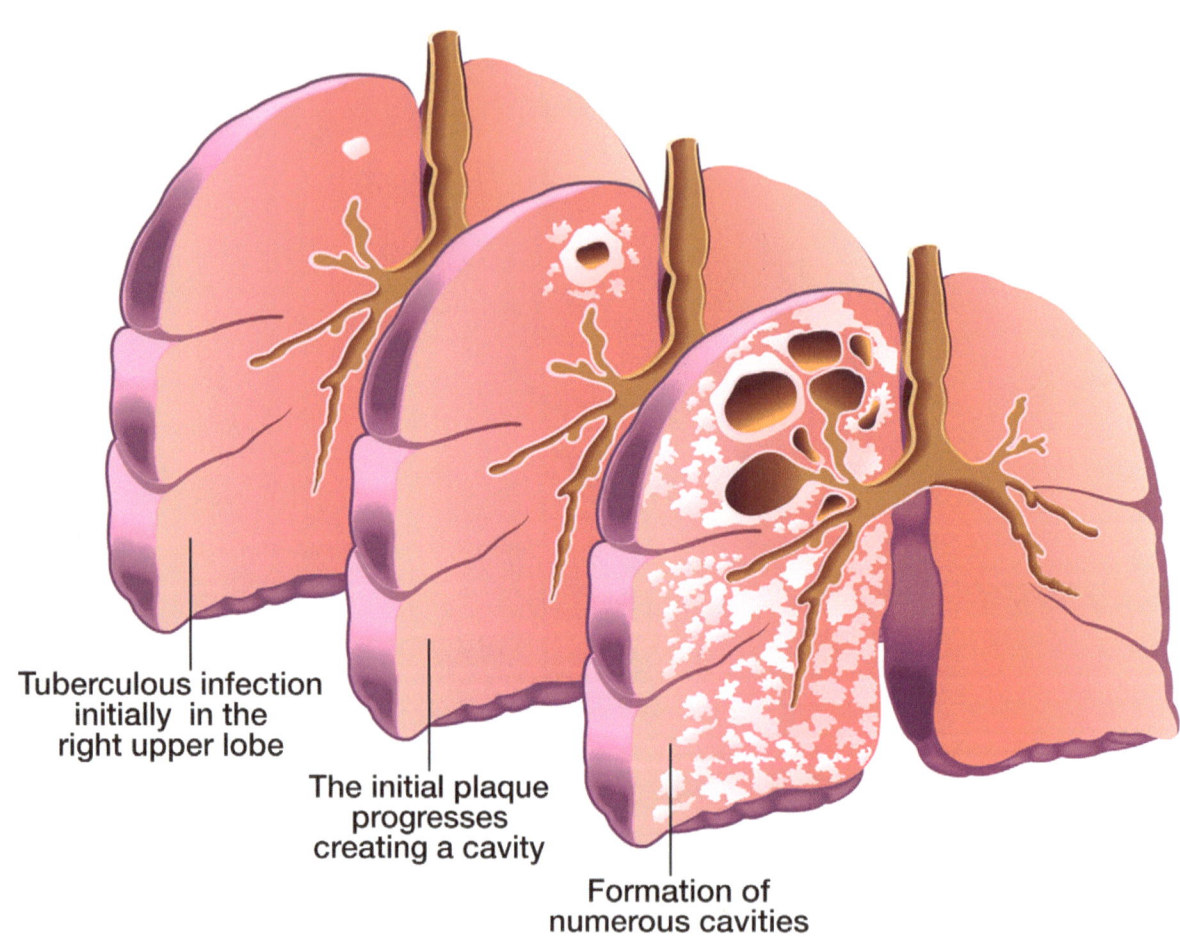

Figure 2-16 Tuberculosis

Chapter 3

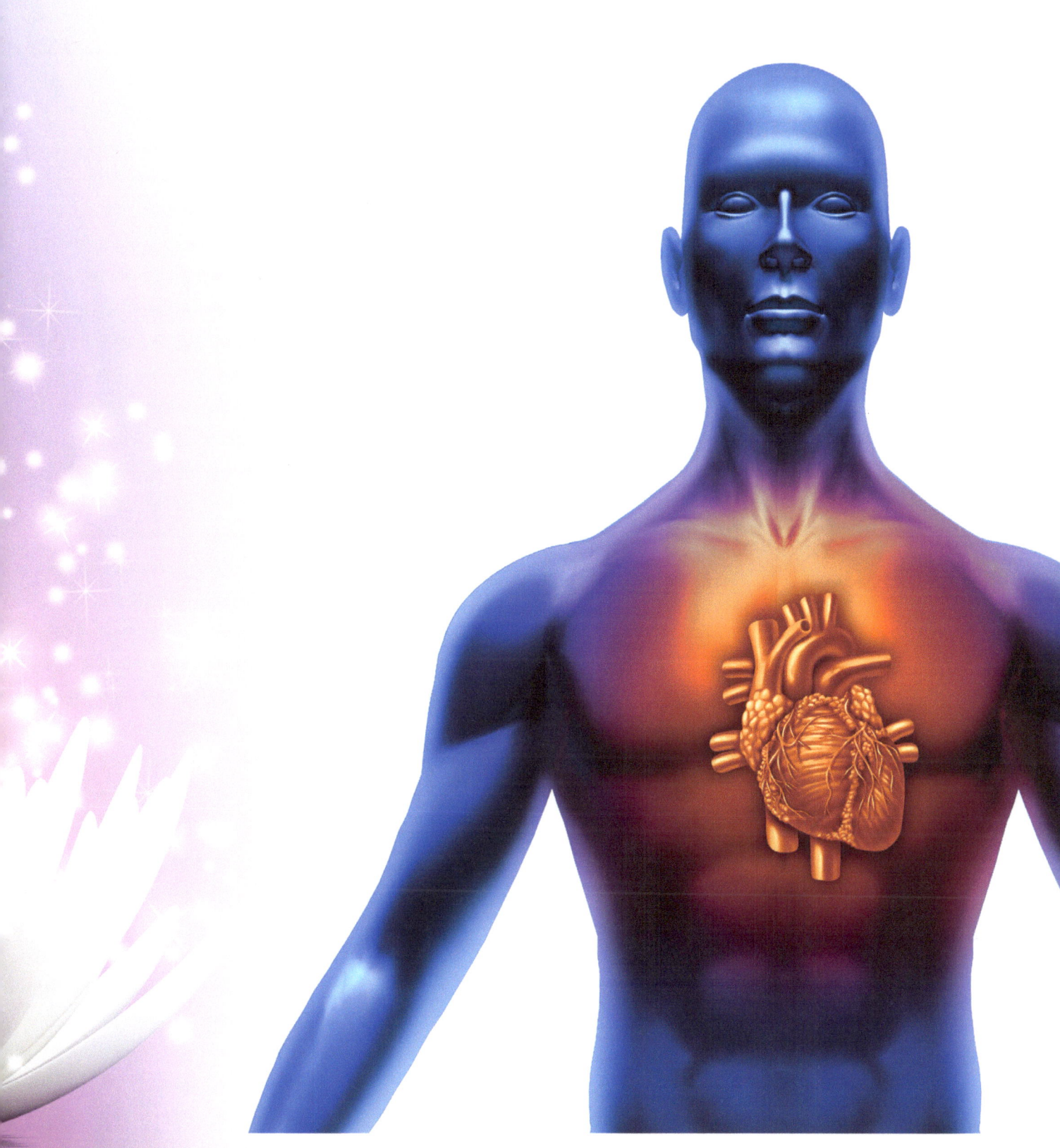

Cardiovascular system

TABLE OF CONTENTS

ANATOMY 48
BLOOD VESSELS 48
ARTERIES 48
VEINS 49
CAPILLARIES 49
HEART 49
HEART VALVES 51
CORONARY CIRCULATION 52
CONDUCTION SYSTEM OF THE HEART 53
ECG AND ELECTRICAL ACTIVITY OF THE MYOCARDIUM 54
    Depolarization and repolarization 55
    P wave 55
    P-R Interval 55
    QRS - Complex 55
    ST segment and T-wave 55
PHYSIOLOGY 56
CIRCULATION 56
    How does myocardial infarction (heart attack) occur? 57
CORONARY ARTERY BYPASS SURGERY 59
    Abnormal circulation due to valve stenosis and
    regurgitation (aortic stenosis and aortic regurgitation) 60
    How does this lead to enlargement or hypertrophy of the left ventricle? 60
    Does the hypertrophied left ventricle affect the lung? 61
BLOOD PRESSURE 61
DISORDERS OF HEART 62
CONGENITAL HEART DISEASE 62
    Coarctation of the aorta 62
    Patent ductus arteriosus 62
    Septal defects 62
    Tetralogy of fallot 63
ARRHYTHMIAS 64
    Heart block 64
    Flutter 64
    Fibrillation 64
ISCHEMIC HEART DISEASES 65
    Angina pectoris 65
    Arteriosclerosis or atherosclerosis 65
    Myocardial infarction 66
    Coronary thrombosis 66

VALVULAR HEART DISEASES 67
- Aortic incompetence or regurgitation 67
- Aortic valve stenosis 67
- Mitral stenosis and mitral regurgitation 67
- Heart failure 67
- Cor pulmonale 67
- Hypertension or high blood pressure 68
- Rheumatic heart disease 69
- Cardiomyopathy 69

PERIPHERAL VASCULAR DISEASES 70
- Aneurysm 70
- Arterial thrombosis 70
- Edema 71
- Causes and types of edema 71
- Buerger's disease 71
- Intermittent claudication 71
- Gangrene 71

CARDIOVASCULAR SYSTEM

ANATOMY

The cardiovascular system is the transport system of the body that comprises of heart and blood vessels. The heart is the central pump and the blood vessels are the series of distributing and collecting tubes. The blood vessels are also in the form of extensive thin walled vascular channels known as capillaries through which the interaction between the cardiovascular system and tissue occurs. The function of the cardiovascular system is to supply oxygen, nutrients, and other essential substances to and removal of metabolic end products from the tissues. A normally functioning body requires continuous transportation of a large number of substances. This is the main function of the circulatory system. The human cardiovascular system is a closed system in which the blood through the vessels flows in one direction only.

BLOOD VESSELS

The 3 types of vessels are arteries which carry blood from heart, veins which carry blood towards the heart, and capillaries which carry blood towards the various parts of the body. These three classes of vessels are further explained herein.

- The blood vessels in the human body are estimated be 60,000 miles which is more than two times the distance around the earth

ARTERIES

Arteries are relatively thick-walled and muscular blood vessels carrying blood away from the heart to the different parts of the body. They divide into branches called arterioles, which further divide and form capillaries. All arteries, except the pulmonary, carry oxygen rich blood. The largest arteries are the aorta which comes out of left ventricle and the pulmonary artery that comes out of the right ventricle.

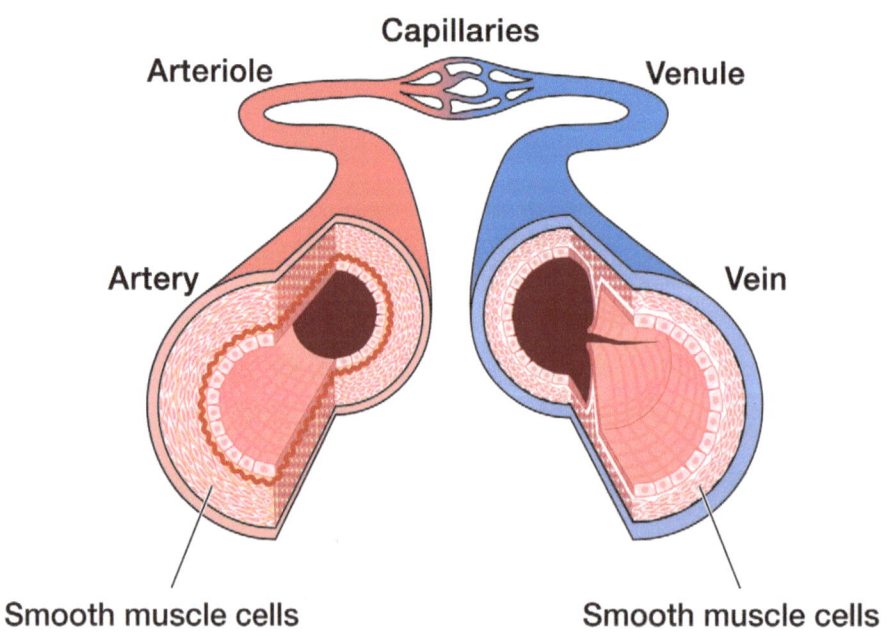

Figure 3-1 Blood vessels

VEINS

Veins are blood vessels that carry the blood to the heart. They transport the blood which contains less oxygen and more carbon dioxide from different parts of the body to heart, the exception being the pulmonary veins. The capillaries lead to venules; the smallest veins which join to form bigger veins. These veins join together to form big trunks of veins called vena cava which drain into the right atrium.

CAPILLARIES

Capillaries are blood vessels with single cell layered walls. They take the role of the communicating links between the arteries and the veins. They receive blood from the arterioles and pass it on to the venules. As the blood passes through the capillaries, the cells absorb oxygen and water, while the waste products such as carbon dioxide are removed from cells into the blood stream.

HEART

Heart is the central organ of the cardiovascular system. The heart is a hollow, muscular organ that contracts at regular intervals, forcing blood through the circulatory system. The heart is cone-shaped, about the size of a fist, and is located in the thoracic cavity between the lungs directly behind the sternum (breastbone). The walls of the heart are made up of three layers of tissue. The inner and outer layers are made up of epithelial layer. The inner layer is called endocardium and the middle muscular layer is known as myocardium. The heart is covered by a double-layered membrane called pericardium. There is a special connection between the cells that allow impulses to travel from one cell to another. The heart is not under voluntary control.

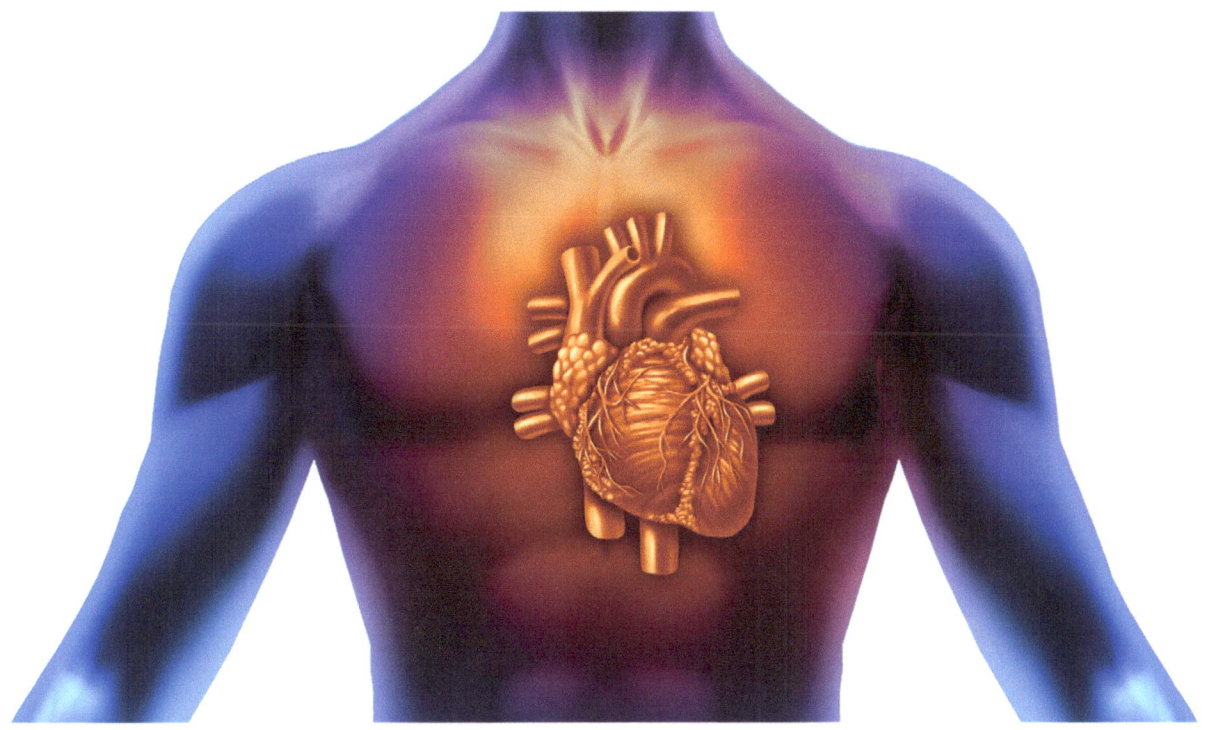

Figure 3-2 Heart

The heart has four compartments: Two upper atrium and two lower ventricles. The atrium and ventricles are divided from the base to apex by a muscular septum or partition into two distinct halves which have no direct communication with each other. Therefore the four chambers are right and left atrium, right and left ventricle.

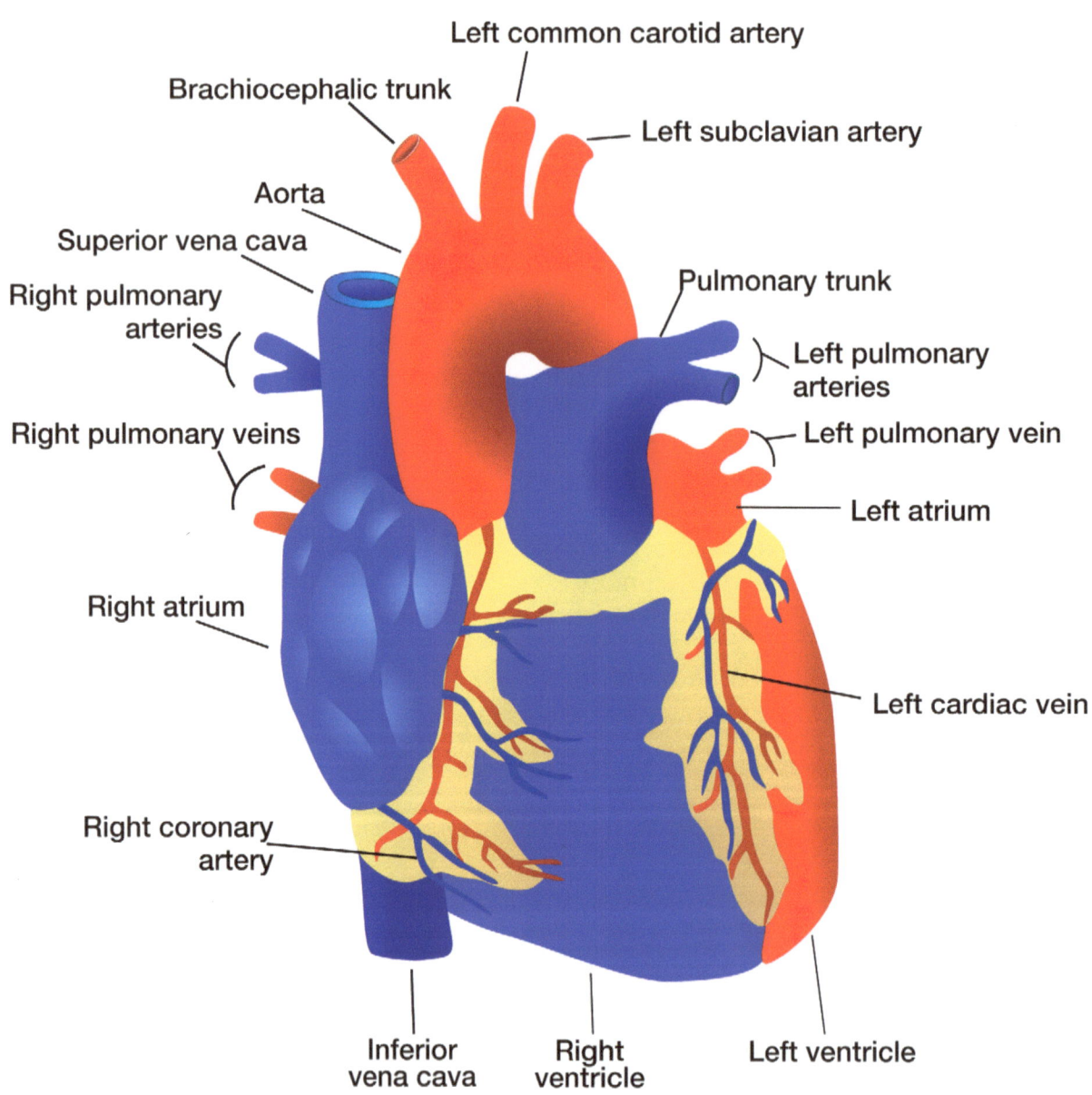

Figure 3-3 Heart anatomy

The atria are the smaller upper chambers of the heart. They are the receiving chambers of the heart. The ventricles are the larger lower chambers and function as the discharging components from which the blood is pumped out of the heart into the arteries. The atrium communicates with the ventricles of the same side. The heart muscles are fed by their own arteries referred to as the coronary arteries.

HEART VALVES

The blood flow is unidirectional in the cardiovascular system and the heart. There are four main valves in the heart to ensure the unidirectional flow, two guarding the atrioventricular junction, and two guarding the ventricular exits.

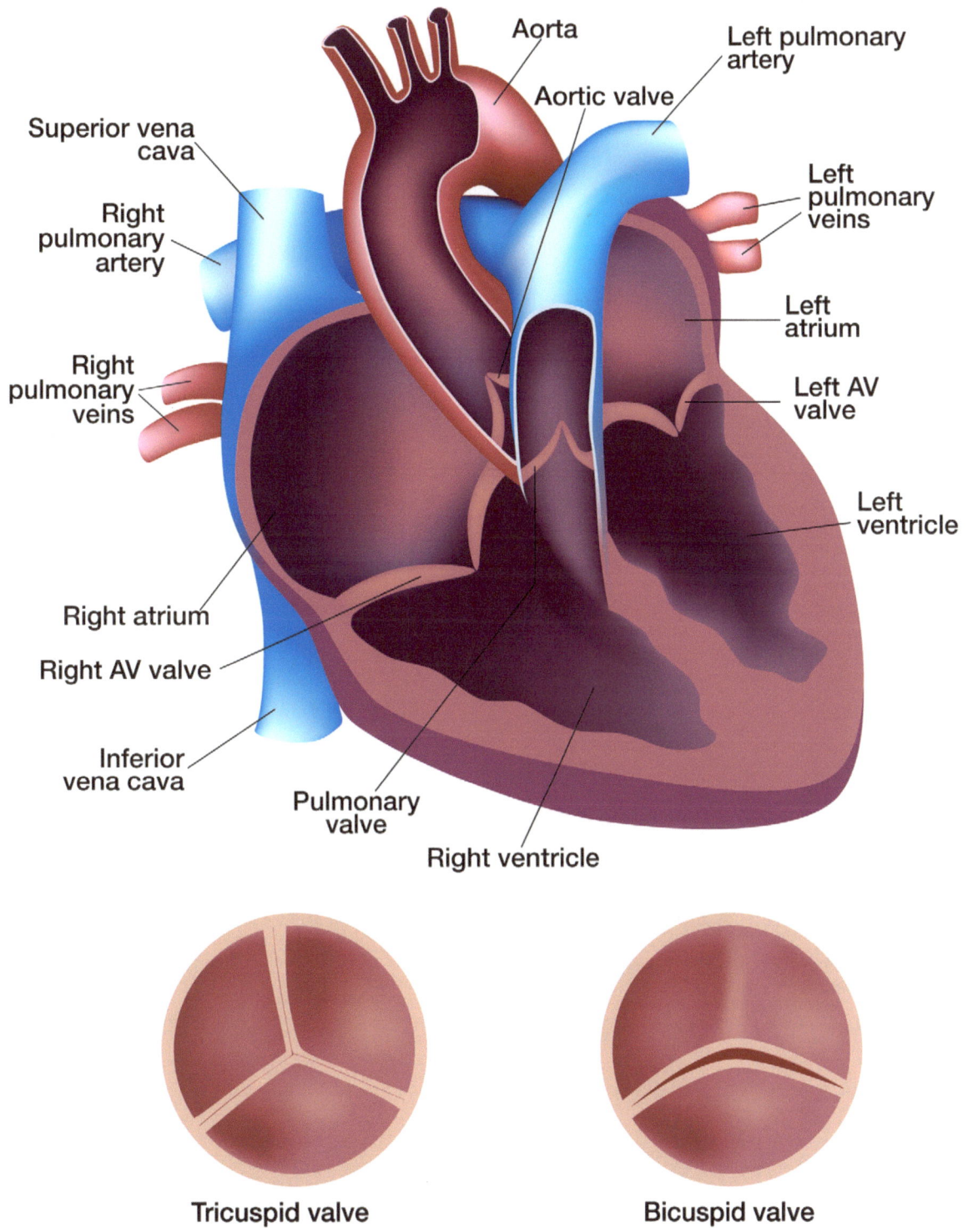

Figure 3-4 Internal anatomy of the heart

Cardiovascular System

1. The left atrioventricular valve (AV) is located between the left atrium and the left ventricle. It is made up of two triangular flaps held in place by papillary muscles. It is also called the bicuspid valve or mitral valve. It allows the blood to flow from the left atrium to the left ventricle.
2. The right atrioventricular valve (AV) is located between the right atrium and right ventricle. It has three triangular flaps and is also called the tricuspid valve. It allows the blood to flow from the right atrium to the right ventricle.
3. The aortic valve guards the exit of the left ventricle into the aorta. It allows the blood to flow from the left ventricle into the aorta and prevents the backflow of blood in the opposite direction.
4. The pulmonary valve guards the exit of right ventricle into the pulmonary trunk. It allows the blood to flow from the right ventricle into the pulmonary trunk and prevents the return of the blood in the opposite direction. The aortic and pulmonary valves have half-moon shaped flaps, and are known as the semilunar valves.

CORONARY CIRCULATION

The heart is supplied by the coronary circulation; the major arteries of the coronary circulation are left and right coronary arteries. The left coronary artery supplies mainly the anterior (front) and lateral (side) portion of the left ventricle.

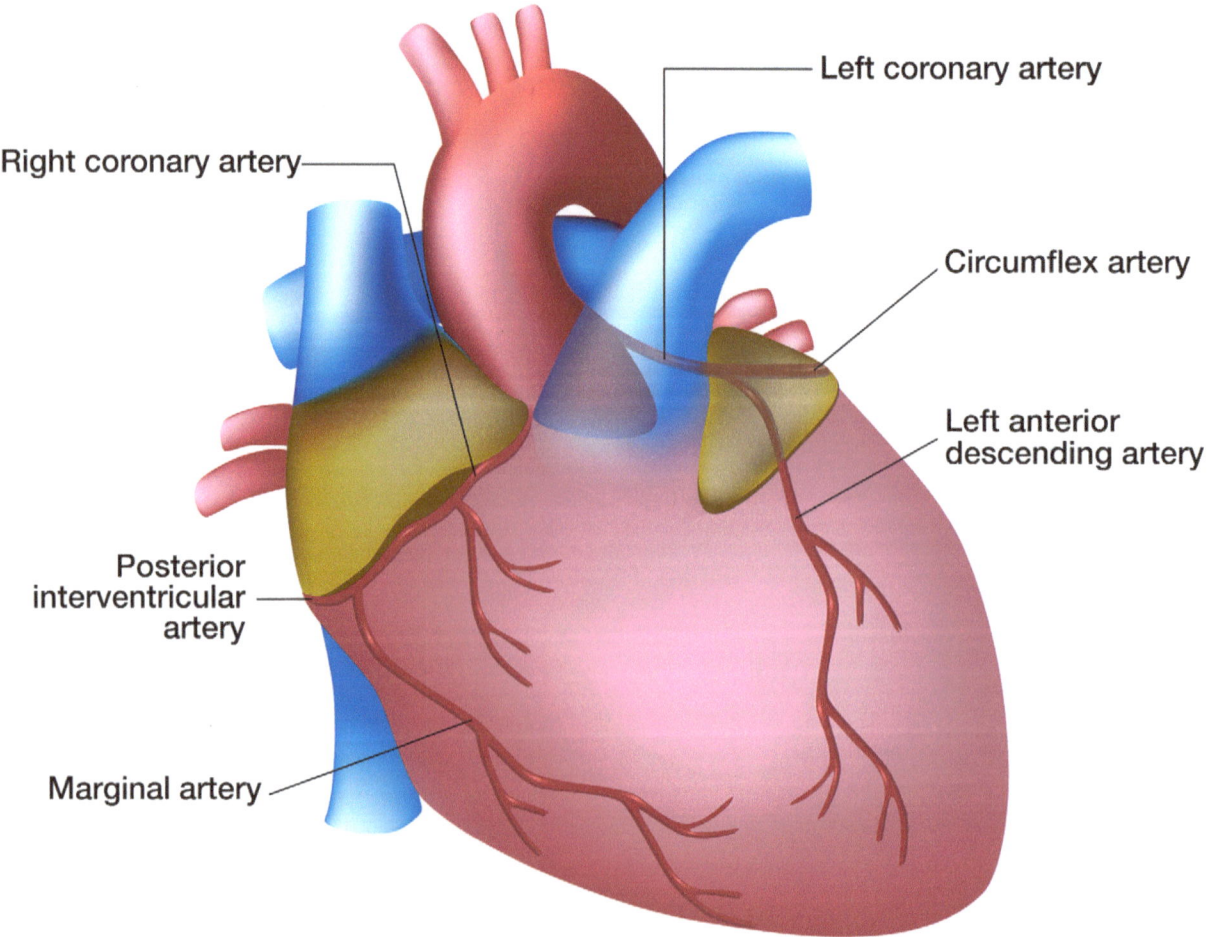

Figure 3-5 Coronary Circulation

52 Cardiovascular System

The right coronary artery supplies most of the right ventricle as well as the posterior (back) left ventricle. The main branches of the left coronary artery include the left anterior descending artery (LAD) and the left circumflex coronary artery (LCA). The main branches of the right coronary artery include the right circumflex coronary artery (RCA) and the right marginal branches.

CONDUCTION SYSTEM OF THE HEART

Although the heart contains nerves that can affect its rate, they are not primarily responsible for its beat. The heart starts beating in the embryo before the heart is supplied with nerves, and it will continue to beat even when the nerve supply is cut.

- In the average person's lifetime the heart beats about 3 billion times

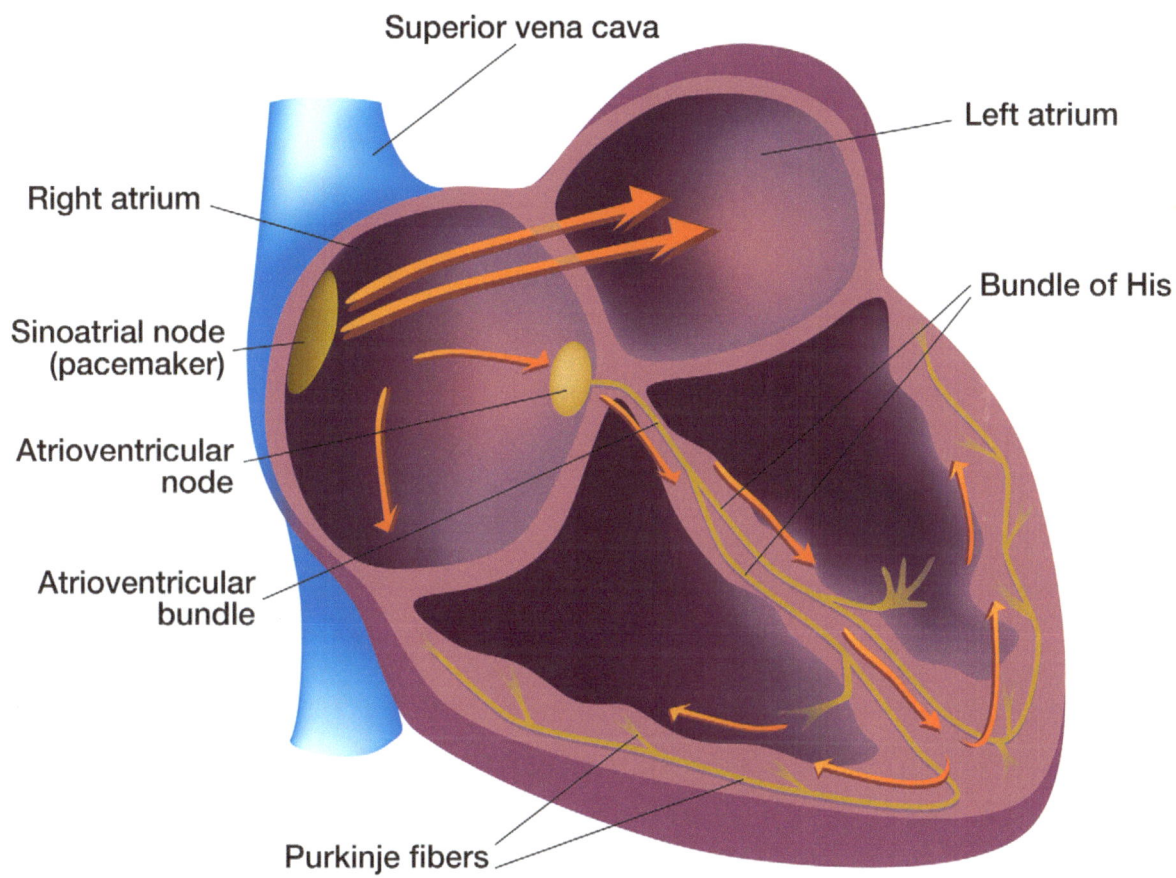

Figure 3-6 Conduction system of the heart

Primary responsibility for initiating the heartbeat rests with a small region of specialized muscle tissue in the right atrium called the sinoatrial node (SA node) or the pacemaker of the heart. The current of electricity generated by the pacemaker causes the walls of the atria to contract and force blood into the ventricles. The wave of electricity passes from the pacemaker to another region of the myocardium at the posterior portion of the interatrial septum known as the atrioventricular node (AV node). The AV node immediately sends the excitation wave to a bundle of specialized muscle fibers called the atrioventricular bundle or bundle of His. The bundle of His divides into right and left bundle branches, which form the conduction fibers that extend through the ventricle walls and stimulate them to contract. Thus, the systole occurs and blood is pumped away from the heart. A short rest period follows, and then the pacemaker begins the wave of excitation across the heart again.

ECG AND ELECTRICAL ACTIVITY OF THE MYOCARDIUM

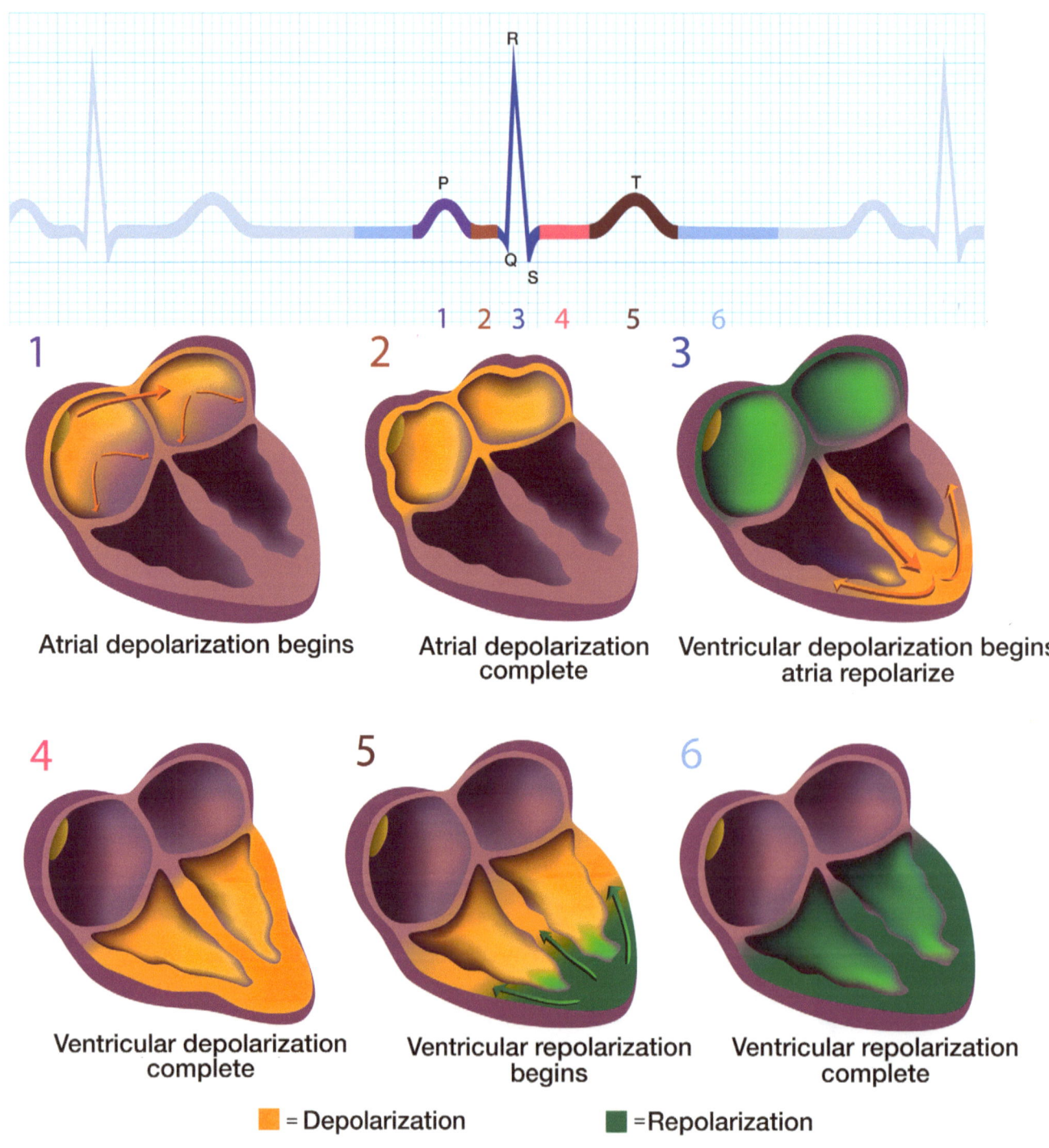

Figure 3-7 ECG and electrical activity of myocardium

54   Cardiovascular System

An electrocardiogram (ECG) records the electrical activity of the heart. Just like the spark-plug of an automobile which generates a number of "sparks" per minute, in the heart the electrical activity or "sparks" are generated by the sino-atrial (SA) node which is the pacemaker of the heart. Similar to increasing the the sparks per minute when we press the accelerator of the automobile , the adrenalin acts as an accelerator of the heart which increases the number of "sparks" or electrical impulses per minute.

This electrical impulse starts at the atrium of the heart and then spreads down to the ventricles and makes the heart muscles contract. This allows the atrium to contract first followed by the ventricles. This contraction causes the blood to be pumped to different parts of the heart. Otherwise if the entire heart contract at the same time, blood cannot be pumped to the different parts of the heart.

The ECG provides important information about the patient's heart rhythm, a previous attack, thickness of the heart muscle etc. It also helps to find various conditions such as arrhythmia or irregular heartbeat, cardiac infarction, or the cause of symptoms such as palpitations or chest pain. For instance, in cardiac infarction the electrical signal cannot travel in the area of the dead tissue and is detected by ECG.

DEPOLARIZATION AND REPOLARIZATION

During depolarization negatively charged ions inside the cell travel out of the cell. Repolarization occurs when positively charged ions travel inside the cell through the cell membrane.

P WAVE

The electrical impulse first travels through the right and the left atrium. The conduction of the electrical impulse throughout the atrium makes the atrium contract which is seen on the ECG as the P wave. This represents atrial depolarization.

P-R INTERVAL

The electrical impulses from the sino-atrial are picked up by the atrio-ventricular (AV) node and held for a brief period of time. This critical delay in the conduction system allows the atrium and the ventricle to contract at different times. This delay also allows the blood to flow effectively from the atrium to the two ventricles. This delay is recorded by the ECG machine as the P-R interval.

QRS- COMPLEX

The electrical impulse then travels through the ventricular muscles via the Bundle of HIS. This allows the ventricles to contract and pump the blood into the pulmonary artery and aorta. This represents the ventricular depolarization.

ST SEGMENT AND T-WAVE

This is a period following the entire ventricular depolarization and roughly corresponds to a plateau. The T-wave represents ventricular repolarization meaning that there is no associated activity of the ventricles indicating the resting phase during the cardiac cycle.

PHYSIOLOGY

The heart contracts or beats about 72 times per minute. The heart beats about 3 billion times in an average life span. The only time the heart gets a rest is between the beats. The cardiac muscle tissue has a rich supply of blood, which ensures that it gets plenty of oxygen. The contraction of the heart muscle is called the systole in which the blood is pumped and the relaxation is known as the diastole during which the blood enters the heart chambers. This is the phase during which the heart receives its blood supply from coronary circulation. The blood pressure is the pressure exerted by the flowing blood on the arterial walls. It has a systolic and a diastolic component. The amount of the blood pumped out by every left ventricular systole is 70 ml, which is known as the stroke volume. The sounds of heart are called the pulse, which are the characteristic of a lub and dub sound in a successional order. The number of beats per minute is known as the pulse rate, which can be measured by feeling the radial artery especially at the wrist. Pulse can further be defined as the lateral force exerted by the flowing column of the blood.

CIRCULATION

Oxygen-poor blood from all parts of the body is collected up into the two large veins, the superior and inferior vena cava and enters the right atrium. The blood passes through the right atrium to the right ventricle due to the contraction of the right atrium. The right ventricle in turn

- The blood travels a total of 19,000 km (12,000 miles) in a day

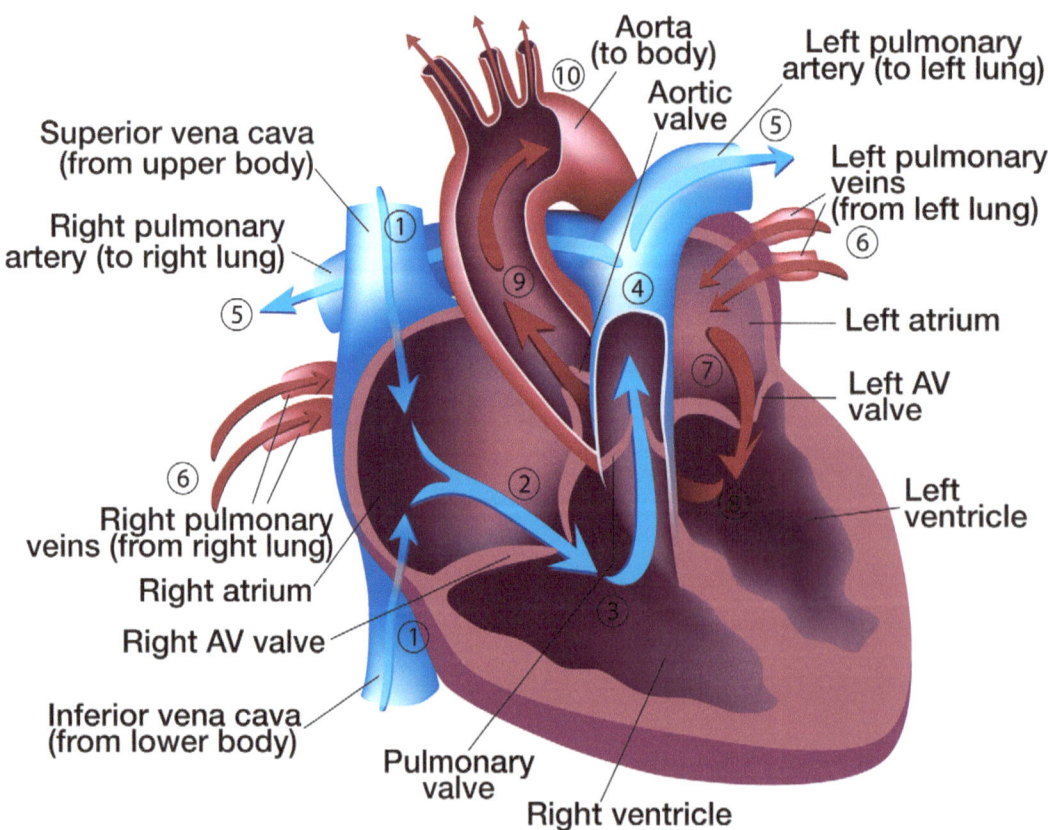

Figure 3-8 The pathway of blood flow through the heart

56 **Cardiovascular System**

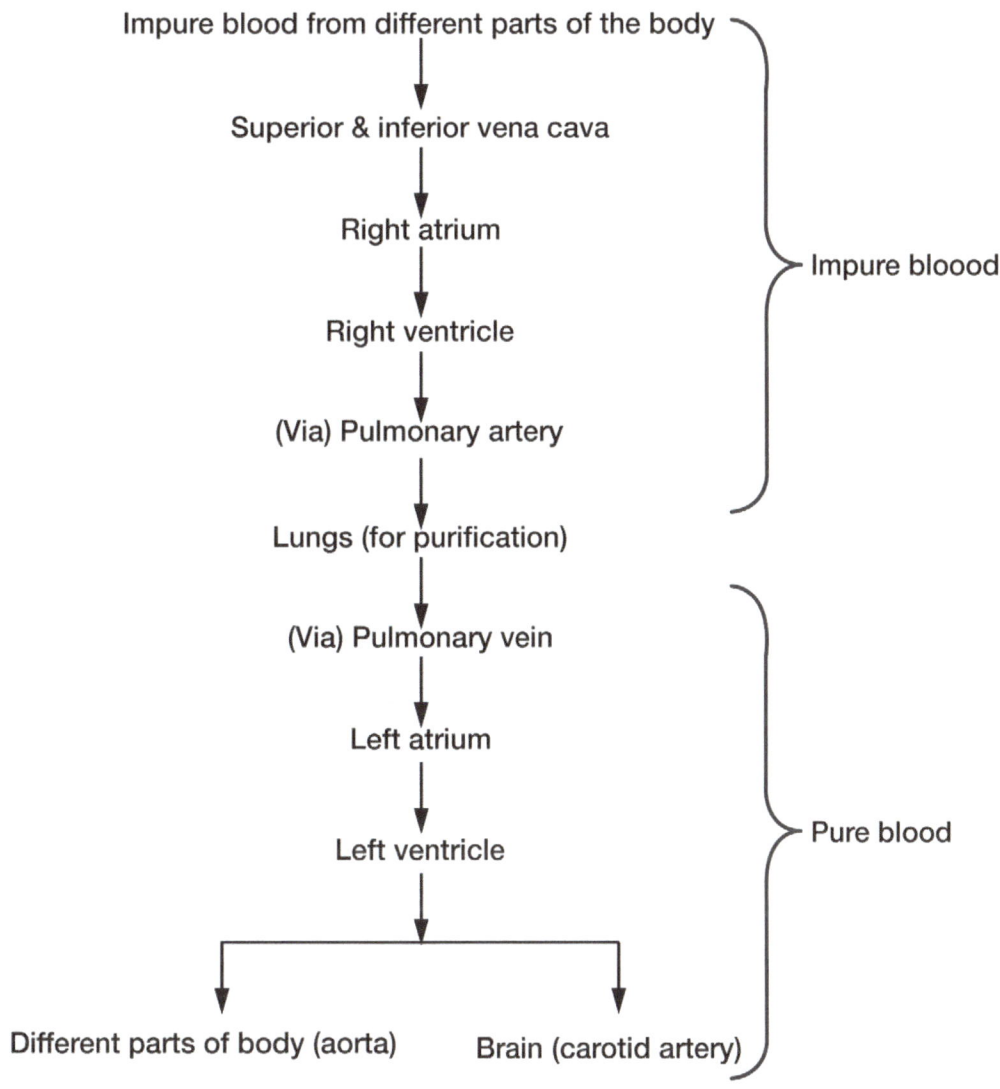

contracts and drives the blood into the lungs via the right and left pulmonary arteries, which carry impure blood to the lungs for purification. Here, the blood takes in oxygen and gives off carbon dioxide. The oxygenated or pure blood is collected up into the left atrium of the heart via the pulmonary veins (the pulmonary artery and the vein are two exceptions in their function). The left atrium contracts and drives the blood into the left ventricle. The left ventricle in turn contracts and pushes the blood into the aorta, which distributes the blood to all parts of the body. The blood passes to the brain through a pair of carotid arteries.

HOW DOES MYOCARDIAL INFARCTION (HEART ATTACK) OCCUR?

When there is a sudden coronary occlusion or a constriction of coronary artery, the blood flow ceases in the coronary vessels beyond the occlusion, except for small amount of collateral flow from surrounding vessels. The blood supply to the muscles of the heart in that area becomes either zero or so little that it cannot sustain cardiac muscle function. As a result, the cardiac muscles become infarcted or dead. The overall process is called a myocardial infarction, commonly known as the heart attack. The muscle injury can range from a small marble to the size of a tennis ball. The seriousness depends on the size and portion of the plugged artery.

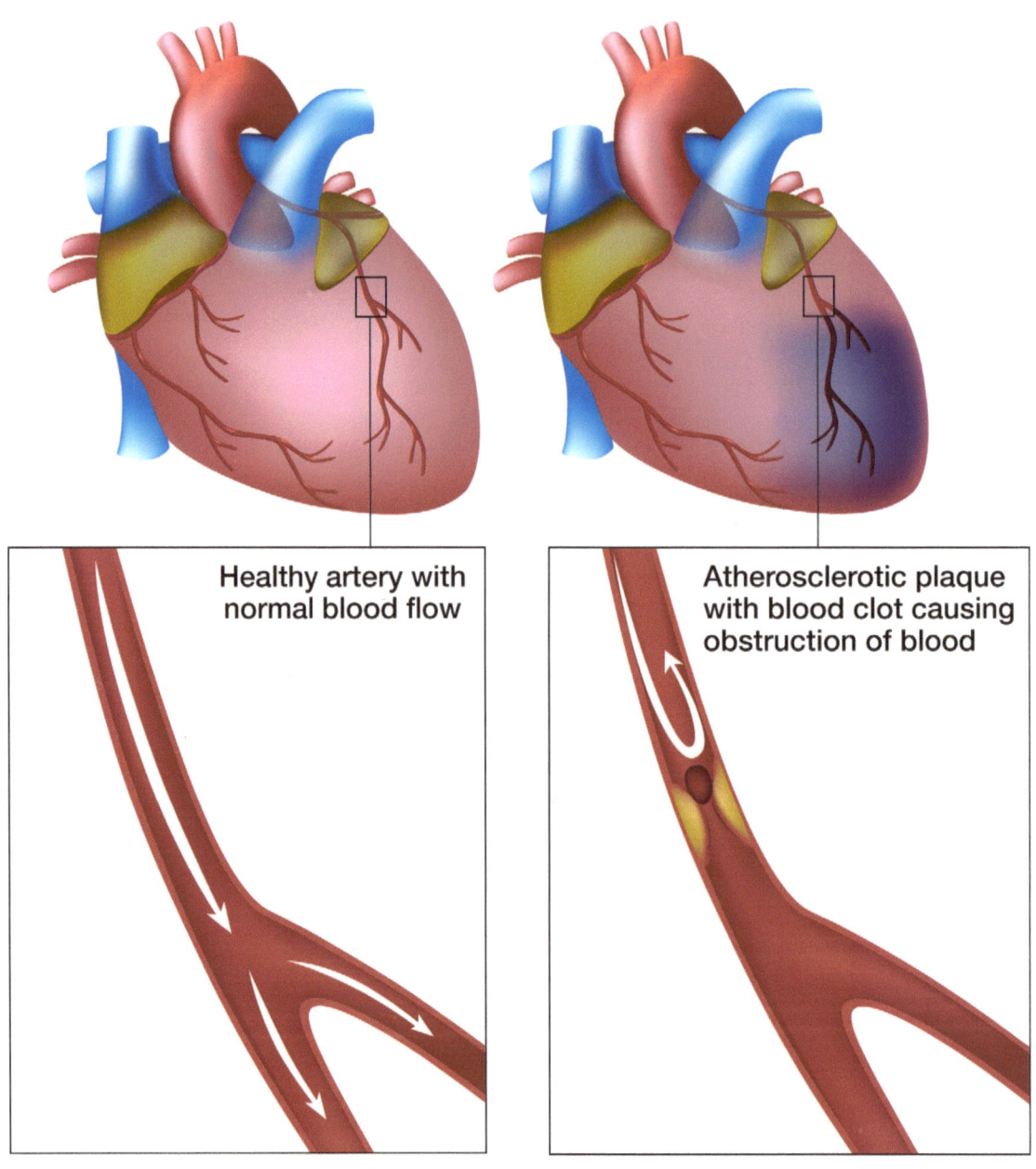

Figure 3-9 Anatomy of heart attack

As the coronary arteries start hardening and constricting, cardiac pain called angina pectoris begins to appear whenever the work load on the muscles of the heart becomes too great in relation to the decreased coronary blood flow. This pain is usually felt beneath the upper sternum (breast bone) and often spreads to surface areas of the body, most commonly to the left arm and left shoulder and also sometimes to the neck and sides of the face. The pain is frequently described as hot, pressing and constricting. It is of such a degree that it usually makes the patient stop all activity and come to a complete state of rest. Angioplasty is a procedure used to open a blocked or a narrow coronary artery.

- According to a ten year study in Scotland 20% more people die of heart attacks on Mondays.

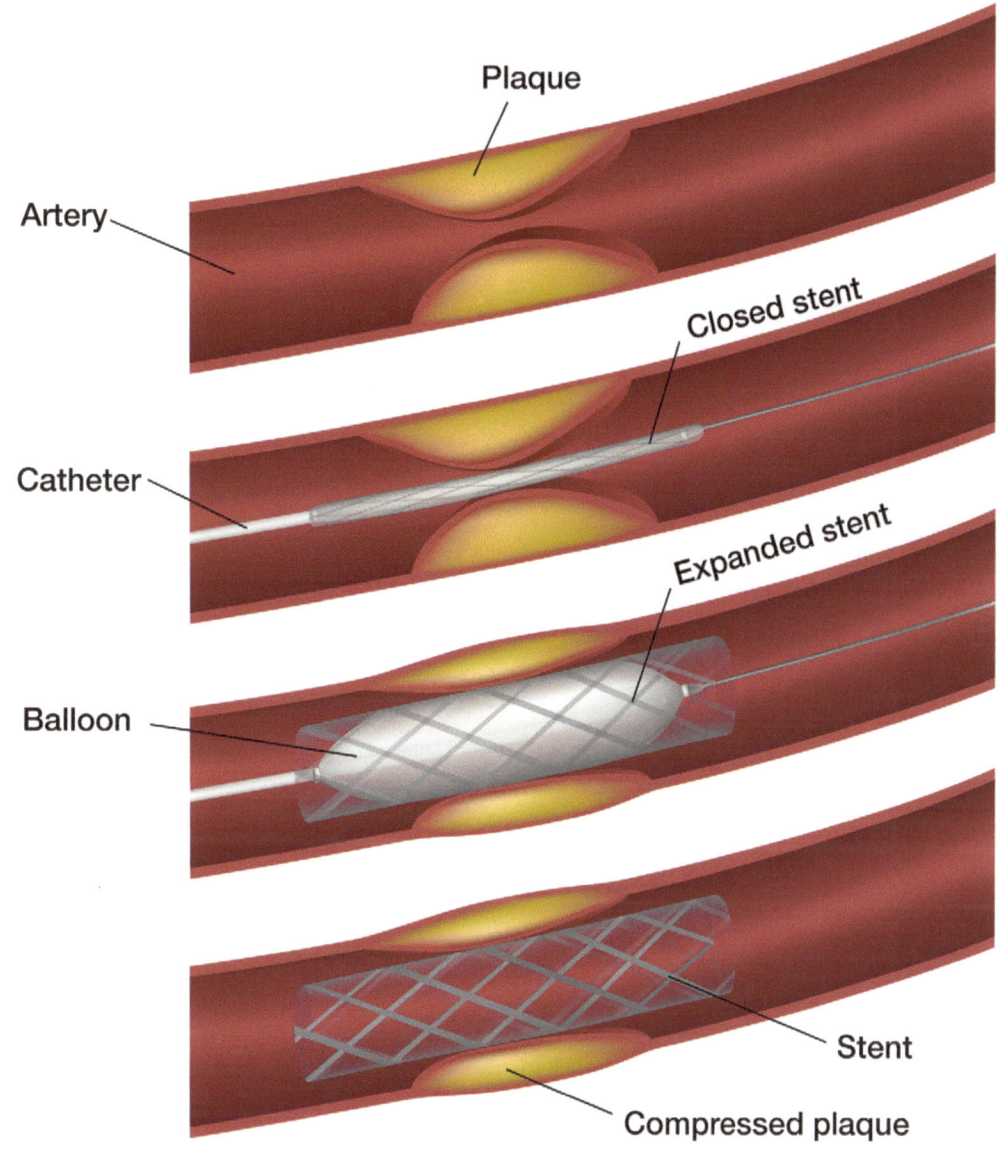

Figure 3-10 Angioplasty

CORONARY ARTERY BYPASS SURGERY

Coronary artery bypass surgery or coronary artery bypass graft (CABG) surgery is a procedure performed to relieve angina (pain that occurs when the heart muscle is not receiving enough oxygen) or coronary artery disease. These problems may appear due to occlusion (obstruction) in the coronary artery or due to atherosclerosis which is caused by cholesterol and fat depositing on the inner wall of the coronary artery.

The goal of the surgery is to restore normal blood flow to the heart by bypassing the blocked coronary artery and create new pathways for blood flow to the heart. There can be single or more bypass grafts performed during a single surgery depending on the condition of the heart. The graft is usually taken from the patient's own artery or veins either from the chest, leg or arm. This surgery is performed when a patient presents with a significant risk of a heart attack or during or after a heart attack.

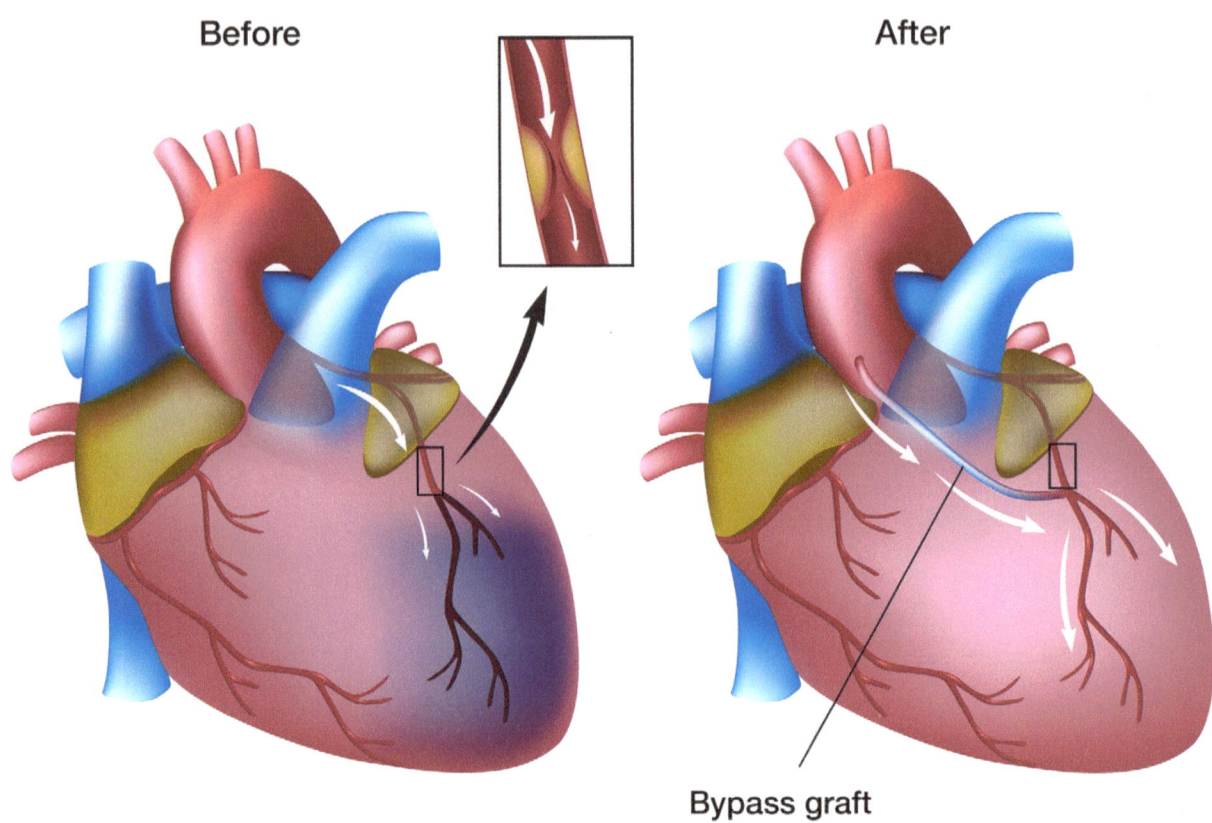

Figure 3-11 Coronary artery bypass surgery

Abnormal circulation due to valve stenosis and regurgitation (aortic stenosis and aortic regurgitation)

A valve in which the leaflets stick to one another so extensively that blood cannot flow through satisfactorily is said to be stenosed. A valve, in which the edges are so destroyed that they cannot close as the ventricle contract or back-flow of blood occurs, is known as regurgitation. Let us recall that pure blood passes from the left ventricle to the aorta through the aortic valve. In aortic stenosis, the blood is ejected from the left ventricle to the aorta through only a very small opening of the aortic valve. Therefore the blood has to force its way out. In Aortic regurgitation there is back flow of blood into the left ventricles even after the left ventricle has pumped the blood into the aorta.

- The aorta is the largest artery in the body and it is approximately the size of a garden hose. The thickness of a human hair is equal to the thickness ten capillaries

How does this lead to enlargement or hypertrophy of the left ventricle?

In both the conditions, there is an excess workload on the left ventricle, to pump out the blood. The extra workload causes a compensatory enlargement and thickens the left ventricular muscles, creating a tremendously large left side of the heart.

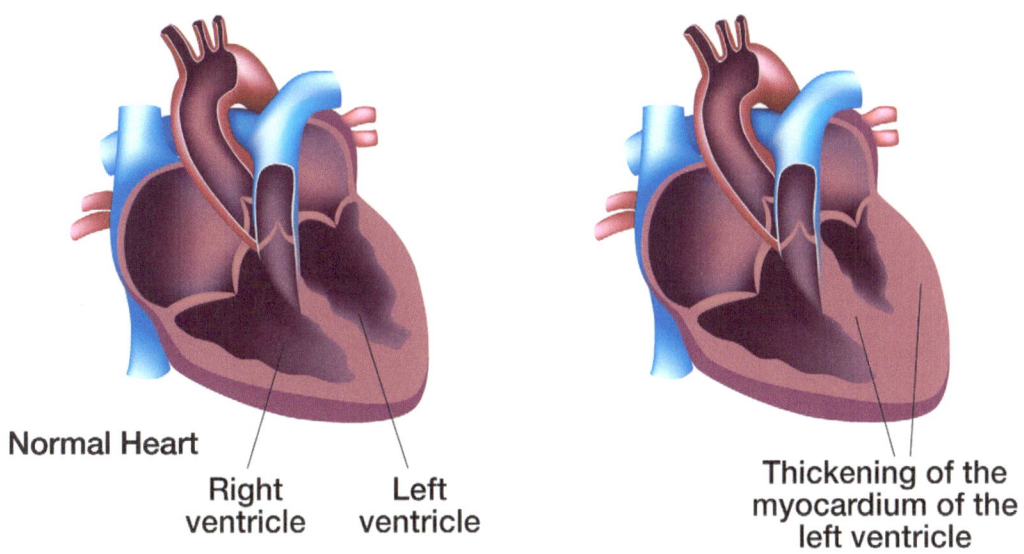

Figure 3-12 Left ventricular hypertrophy

Does the hypertrophied left ventricle affect the lung?

Yes, beyond critical stages in these two aortic valve lesions, i.e. aortic stenosis and regurgitation, the ventricle finally fails to withstand the workload. As a consequence, the left ventricle enlarges and cannot pump out sufficient blood. Blood simultaneously dams up in the left atrium and lungs due to the failing left ventricle. This leads to excess accumulation of blood in the lung. Pulmonary edema occasionally occurs so rapidly that it causes death by suffocation in 20 to 30 minutes.

BLOOD PRESSURE

The lateral pressure exerted by blood on the blood vessel usually is referred to as blood pressure which is commonly the arterial blood pressure. Systolic pressure is the pressure recorded during systole which indicates the forceful contraction of the heart pushing the blood into the blood vessels. Diastolic pressure is the pressure recorded during diastole and indicates the minimum work of the heart or the relaxation phase of the heart.

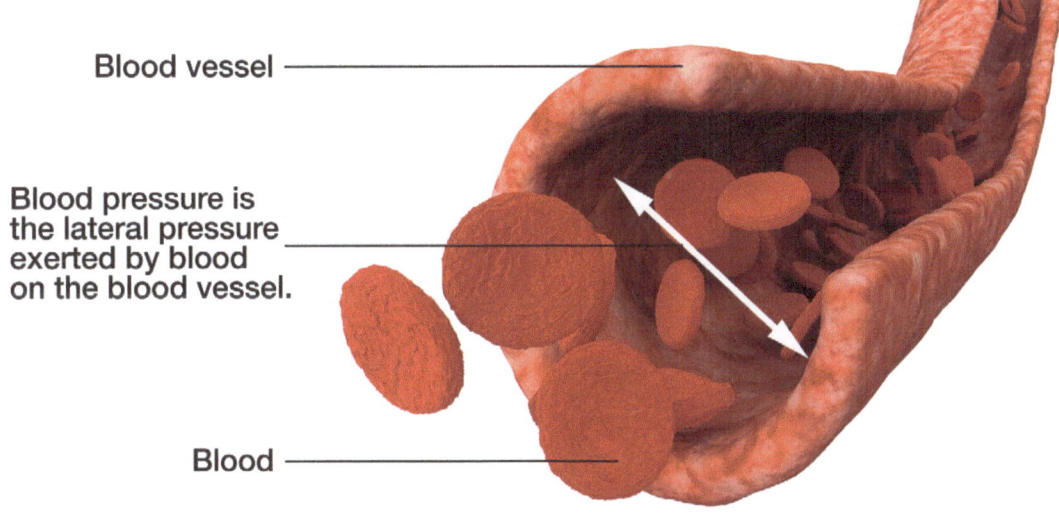

Figure 3-13 Blood pressure

Normal blood pressure is around 120/80 mmHg, 120 is the systolic blood pressure and 80 is the diastolic blood pressure. The rise in the diastolic indicates increased load on the heart.

DISORDERS OF HEART

CONGENITAL HEART DISEASE

Abnormalities of the heart during birth are referred to as the congenital heart diseases. Some congenital heart diseases are minor and go unnoticed until a routine medical examination, but others may be too serious for the child to live a normal life. The congenital heart diseases include Atrial septal defect, Ventricular septal defect, Patent ductus arteriosus, Coarctation of aorta, Fallot's tetralogy etc.

COARCTATION OF THE AORTA

It is a condition where there is a congenital narrowing of the aorta that supplies the blood to the entire lower part of the body. Due to this issue, there is a reduced blood circulation to the lower part of the body.

PATENT DUCTUS ARTERIOSUS

A small duct is present between the aorta and the pulmonary artery during the fetal stages, which normally closes soon after birth. If this duct remains open (patent) even after birth it results in mixing of venous and arterial blood. This mixture of blood leads to decreased oxygenation in the body and a bluish discoloration called the cyanosis. This will result in breathlessness, shortness of breath, and crying spells whenever the activity of the child increases.

SEPTAL DEFECTS

Improper closure of septum during its formation in fetal stages leads to small holes in the septa known as the septal defects. It is referred to as the atrial septal defect (ASD) when occurring between the atria and ventricular septal defect (VSD) when taking place between ventricles. Although many septal defects will close spontaneously, others may require surgery.

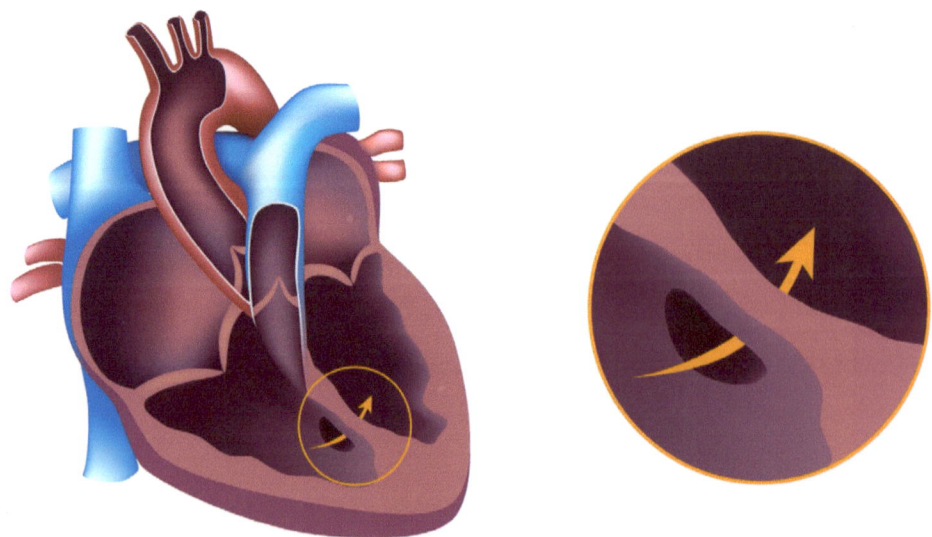

Figure 3-14 Ventricular septal defect

TETRALOGY OF FALLOT

As the name indicates it is a congenital malformation of the heart involving four distinct defects. The four defects are described below:

1. Pulmonary artery stenosis: Narrowing of the pulmonary artery resulting in an inadequate blood flow to the lungs for oxygenation.
2. Ventricular septal defect: The gap in the ventricular septum which allows deoxygenated blood to pass into the left ventricle and from there to the aorta.
3. Shift of the aorta to the right: Here, due to the ventricular septal defect and close proximity of aorta to the septal defect, the aorta overrides the interventricular septum resulting in the passage of deoxygenated blood from the right ventricle to the aorta.
4. Hypertrophy of the right ventricle: The myocardium has to work harder to pump blood through a narrowed pulmonary artery, and thus it enlarges in size.

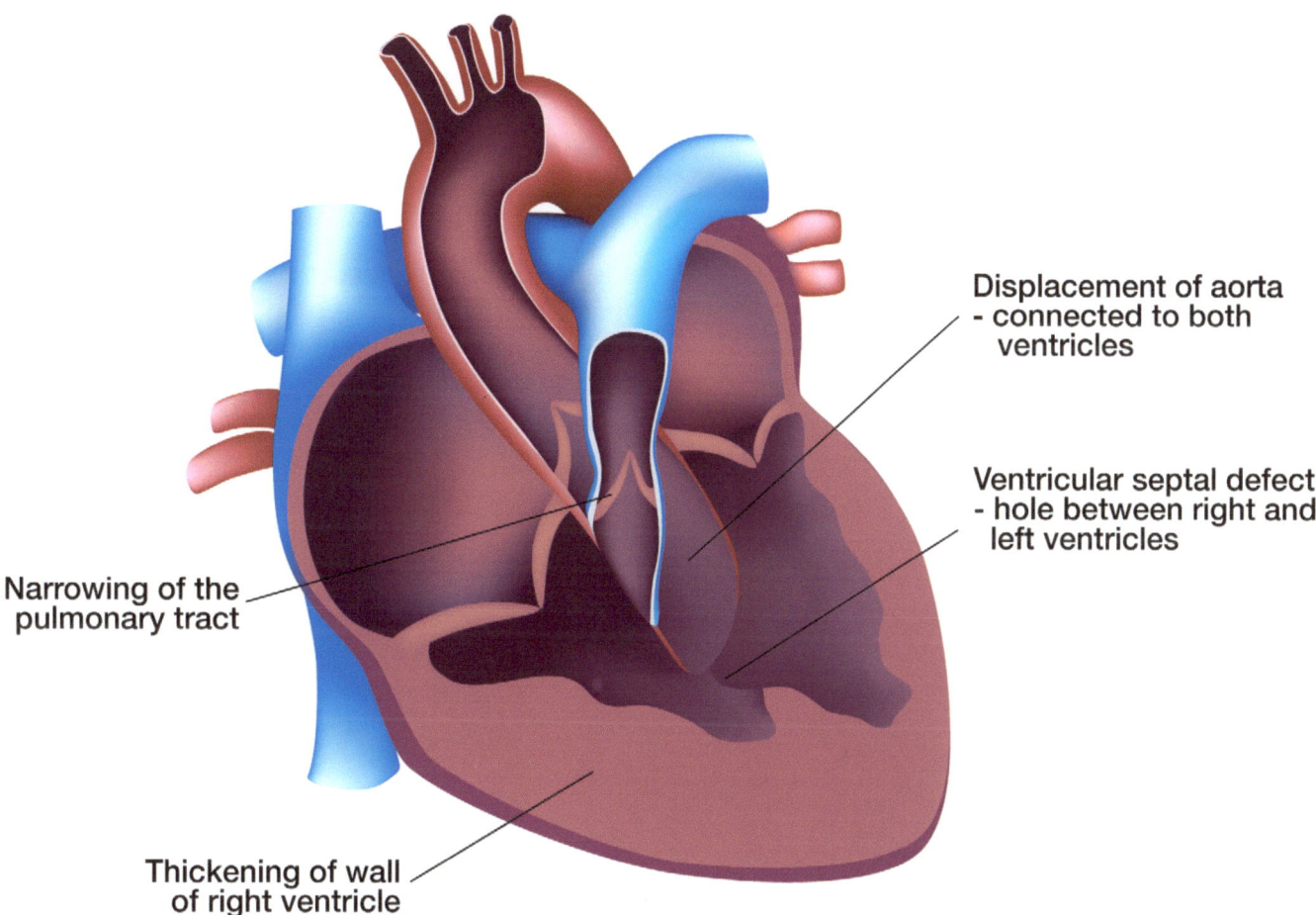

Figure 3-15 Tetralogy of fallot

The Fallot's tetralogy results in decreased oxygenation of the blood. This causes cyanosis which is a bluish coloration of skin, lips, oral mucosa etc. These babies become bluish in color when they exert like crying, or trying to crawl a distance. The babies affected by Fallot's tetralogy are called "blue babies". The congenital heart diseases when minor will be corrected as the child grows, but there are a few major defects which the body cannot correct on its own and they need surgical correction.

Cardiovascular System

ARRHYTHMIAS

Arrhythmia refers to the irregularity of the heartbeat. The arrhythmia includes heart block, fibrillation, and flutter.

HEART BLOCK

Failure of proper conduction of impulses through the AV node to the atrioventricular bundle or bundle of His is referred to as the heart block. The heart block is caused as a result of damage to SA node, where the impulses from SA node become too weak to activate the AV node and fail to reach the ventricles. If the failure occurs occasionally, the heart will miss a beat in a rhythm at regular intervals which is called a partial heart block. If no impulses reach the AV node from the SA node, the ventricles contract slower than the atria and are not coordinated, a complete heart block occurs. Implantation of a cardiac pacemaker can overcome heart block and establish a normal rhythm.

FLUTTER

Rapid but regular contractions of atria or ventricles are referred to as the flutter. This condition can occur in patients with heart diseases and the heart rhythm may reach up to 300 beats per minute. Symptoms include palpitation, breathlessness, and chest pain on exertion, myocardial infarction, congenital abnormalities of the heart, ischemic heart diseases, and rheumatic fever.

FIBRILLATION

Rapid but irregular heartbeat of atria or ventricles is termed as fibrillation. Symptoms are palpitation, shortness of breath, and feeling of being unwell or general tiredness. Ventricular fibrillation is a serious disturbance of the normal heart rhythm where the ventricles beat very fast, irregularly and inefficiently. It is caused by myocardial infarction or ischemic heart disease. The symptoms include missing heartbeat and sometimes the patient may suddenly collapse and become unconscious without any warning.

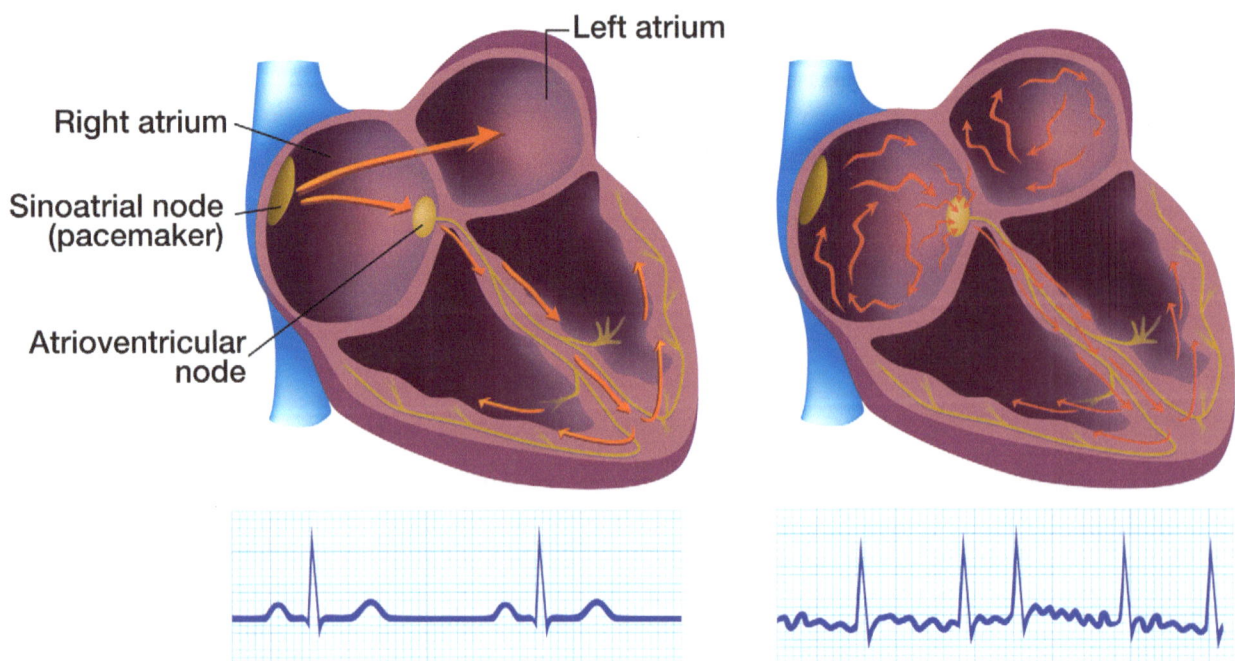

Figure 3-16 Fibrillation

The fibrillation is treated by defibrillator, which uses high voltage electrical energy to break the irregular rhythm during fibrillation and bring it back to normal rhythm. It is also called the cardioverter.

ISCHEMIC HEART DISEASES

ANGINA PECTORIS

As discussed earlier, this is the pain occurring in the heart when sufficient blood is not supplied to the heart muscles. A severe pain is usually experienced across the upper chest. Narrowing of the coronary arteries is the most common cause. The literal meaning of angina is "I cry".

- It is common for people who have chronic kidney disease to also have heart disease

The muscles of heart cry for the want of blood. The patient experiences pain across the upper part of the front of the chest and sometimes the pain spread to jaw, down the left arm, and to the sides of the face. The patient may experience a constricting, tight and burning pain lasting for a few minutes. Uncontrolled negative lower emotions, chronic smoking and overweight are among the major causes.

ARTERIOSCLEROSIS OR ATHEROSCLEROSIS

It refers to the narrowing or hardening of arteries due to deposition of fat in the inner wall. As the arteries narrow, the resistance to the blood flow increases, due to which there is an extra workload on the pumping system of the heart in order to distribute the blood to different parts of the body via the arteries.

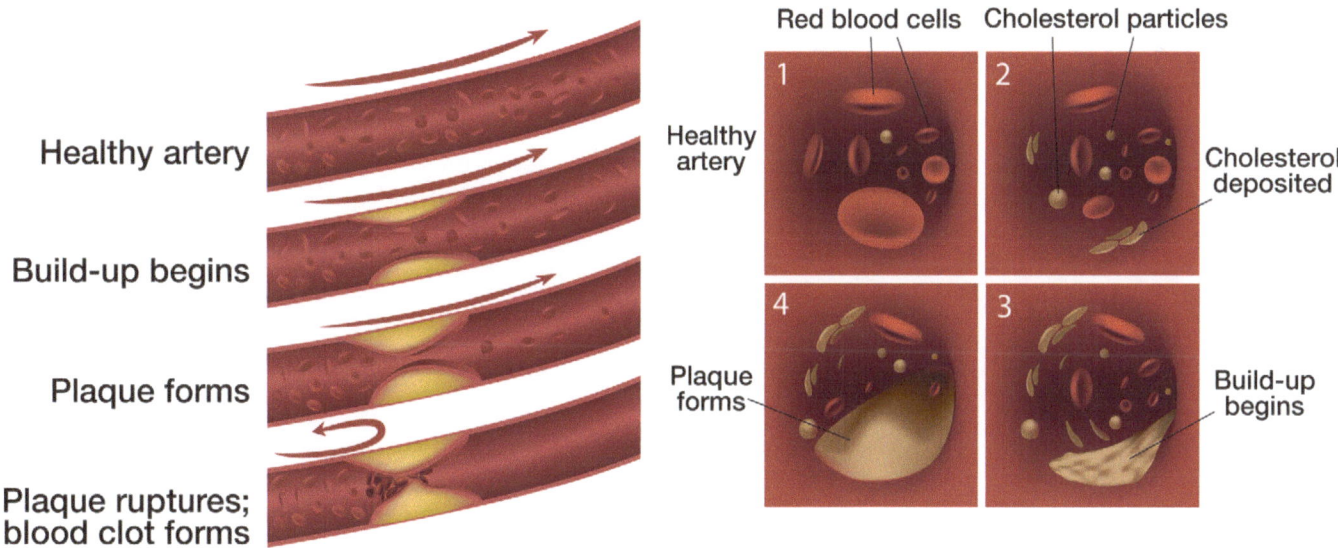

Figure 3-17 Stages of atherosclerosis

In some cases, minute blood clot formation (thrombus) within the arteries due to arteriosclerosis can dislodge itself from the site and pass in the blood stream and obstruct some other artery such as cerebral arteries in the brain or coronary arteries in the heart, and thereby reduces or completely blocks blood supply to their respective organs, leading to lethal diseases. This is what happens in myocardial infarction (heart attack) or in stroke/hemiplegia (one side paralysis of body). When a blood clot blocks the arteries of the brain or the heart, it deprives that particular portion of the organ of blood.

MYOCARDIAL INFARCTION

The most common problems of the heart and circulation are caused by hardening of the arteries (arteriosclerosis), high blood pressure and heart attack (myocardial infarction). A complete block in the brain or heart can lead to stroke or heart attack while angina, dizziness and disturbances of vision occur when the blockage is partial. In some conditions the mechanism controlling the rhythm of the heart may be disturbed due to congenital abnormality leading to very fast and irregular heartbeat. In adults this problem may occur due to deterioration in the nerves controlling the heartbeat or in their blood supply.

Those with a high risk are as follows:

Smokers: Smoking has very harmful effects on arteries, both within the heart and in the general circulation.

Babies: Drugs taken by the pregnant mother, certain diseases contracted during pregnancy, smoking, can all result in congenital abnormalities in the heart of babies.

The middle aged and elderly: Diseases elsewhere in the body such as serious lung diseases like chronic bronchitis and an obstructive airway disease that strains the heart may affect the heart. Stress is the major culprit. Improper diet, obesity, lack of exercise can also lead to heart trouble.

CORONARY THROMBOSIS

A 'heart attack' from a layman's point of view usually means a coronary thrombosis. Thrombus is a local clot in an artery and a coronary thrombosis is the most common cause of heart attacks. In a coronary thrombosis an artery supplying blood to the heart is obstructed leading to myocardial infarction. Myocardial infarction is a condition where the heart muscle of a particular area dies due to the lack of blood supply as a result of the blockage in the coronary artery. The patient experiences severe constricting pain behind the sternum or breast bone, often spreading to one of the arms, neck, jaw and sides of the face. The onset of pain is sudden and although it feels like anginal pain, it does not reduce during rest unlike anginal pain.

There may be undue tiredness, shortness of breath, unaccustomed indigestion experienced a few weeks before an attack. The chances of developing a coronary thrombosis are more increased by smoking, obesity, diabetes, high blood pressure, lack of exercise and a faulty diet.

VALVULAR HEART DISEASES

AORTIC INCOMPETENCE OR REGURGITATION

As discussed previously in this text, to outline the condition, the aortic valve prevents the backward flow of blood into the heart after being pumped. In some conditions like rheumatic heart disease, the valve becomes thickened and does not close adequately, thereby allowing backward flow of blood into the heart and causing pressure in the heart. Shortness of breath is the main symptom of this condition. Hardening of the valve or arteriosclerosis, congenital abnormalities of heart, rheumatic fever, infection and stress are among the causes.

AORTIC VALVE STENOSIS

Due to disease, the leaflets of the aortic valve become thick and hard and stick to one another. This narrowing impairs the blood flow from the heart to different part of the body via the aorta. In some people this condition is present at birth. Symptoms of this condition include the shortness of breath, dizziness especially when standing up from a sitting or lying portion and fainting on exertion. The major cause is rheumatic fever in early life, which may go unnoticed. As years go by the valves become inflamed, thick and become fused.

MITRAL STENOSIS AND MITRAL REGURGITATION

Mitral valve (left atrioventricular valve) helps in blood flow from the left atrium to the left ventricle. In mitral stenosis, the blood flow from the left atrium into the left ventricle is impeded. In mitral regurgitation much of the blood that has been pumped into the aorta from the left ventricle flows back into the left ventricle after being pumped.

HEART FAILURE

Inability of the heart to pump enough blood out of the heart is referred to as the heart failure. Blood accumulates in the lungs in the left-sided heart failure causing pulmonary edema. The right-sided heart failure results in accumulation of fluid in the abdominal organs like liver, spleen and subcutaneous tissue of the legs. Congestive heart failure often develops gradually over several years, although it can be acute in some cases. Therapy includes lowering dietary intake of sodium, and diuretics to promote loss of fluids. When the left heart failure is very severe a surgical procedure is pursued, where a pump in the left heart LVAD (Left ventricular assist device) is placed.

COR PULMONALE

Failure of the right side of the heart is referred to as cor pulmonale. This condition occurs due to long-standing lung-conditions that strain the heart causing the heart failure. The impure blood passes from the right ventricle of the heart to the lungs for purification. Due to a poor uptake of oxygen by the lungs the small arteries in the lungs get constricted, thus reducing blood flow from the right ventricle to the lungs. Therefore, the right ventricle pumps with greater pressure and is strained in the long run. Since the blood does not reach sufficiently from the right ventricle to the lung, the right atrium is also affected and the impure blood gets stagnated there. Consequently, the impure blood from the rest of the body is not pumped properly into the right atrium. The symptoms or cor pulmonale include shortness of breath, blueness of lips and face and swelling of the ankles. The causes are chronic bronchitis, asthma, fibrosis of the lung, structural deformities of the chest and spine.

HYPERTENSION OR HIGH BLOOD PRESSURE

In adults, a blood pressure equal to or greater than 140/90 mmHg is considered high blood pressure and is termed as hypertension. Diuretics, beta-blockers, ACE inhibitors, and calcium channel blockers are the various classes of drugs used to treat the hypertension. Losing weight, limiting sodium (salt) intake, stopping smoking, and reducing fat in the diet are also important in therapy.

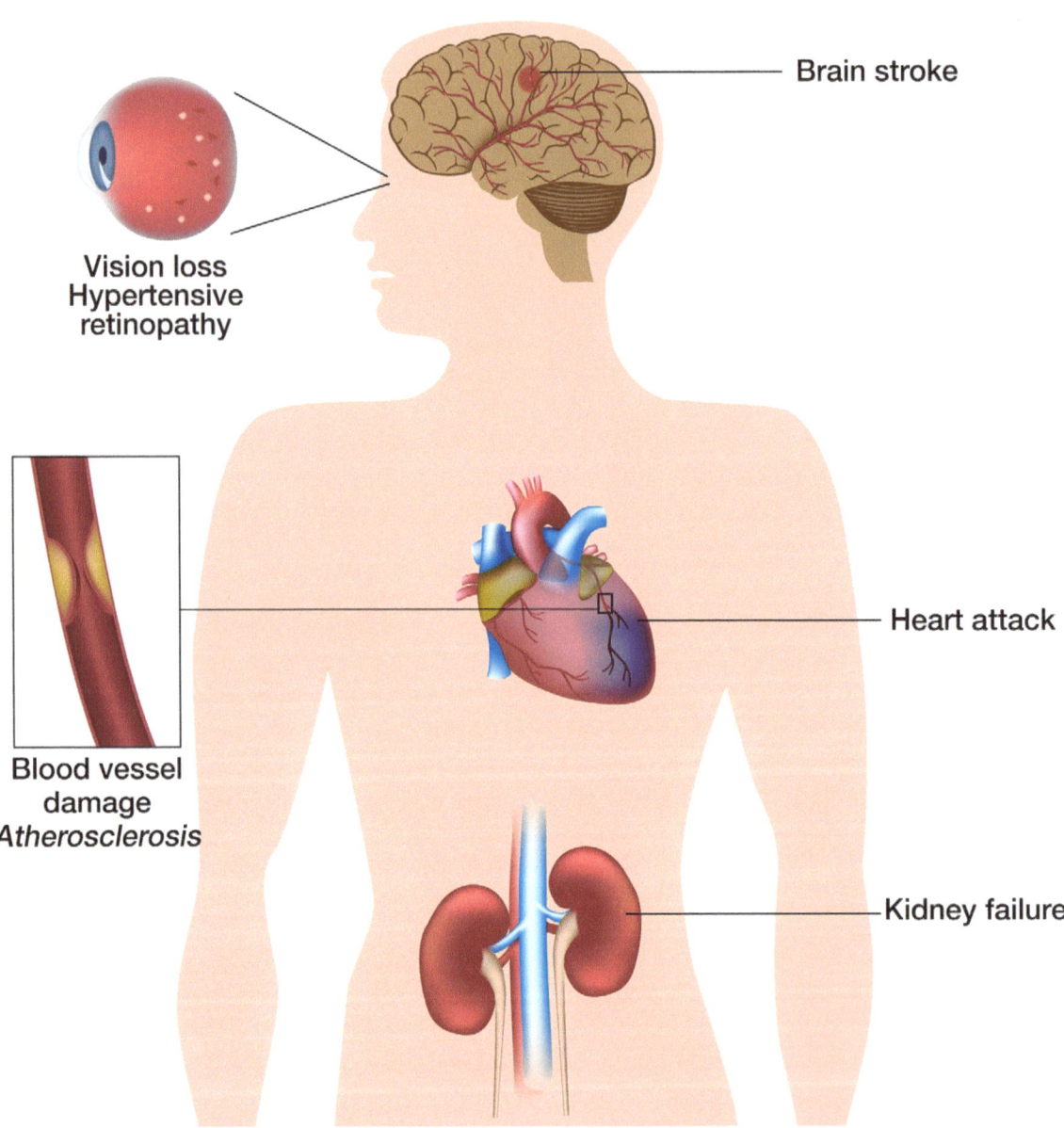

Figure 3-18 Main complications of hypertension

In secondary hypertension, there is always some associated lesion in other organs such as glomerulonephritis, pyelonephritis, or disease of the adrenal glands, that is responsible for the elevated blood pressure. There are various complications of hypertension. Uncontrolled high blood pressure can lead to hardening and thickeneing of arteries (atherosclerosis) which can lead to brain stroke and heart attack. It can cause kidney failure, damage to the blood vessels in the retina of the eye and other complications.

RHEUMATIC HEART DISEASE

Rheumatic heart disease is a condition of the heart resulting from rheumatic fever, chiefly manifested by abnormalities of the valves. This results after a streptoccocal infection of throat or a middle ear. The antibodies produced by the body to destroy the invading organism continue to destroy the heart valves and the joint cartilage. It is commonly said that the rheumatic fever "licks the joints and bites the heart" because the injury is maximal to the heart valves. The repaired valves need to be surgically corrected if the damage is severe.

CARDIOMYOPATHY

Cardio refers to heart and myo refers to muscles. The term cardiomyopathy refers to a group of disorders of heart muscles, which lead to progressive weakness of the heart, disturbance of rhythm and eventual heart failure. The coronary arteries are not usually affected by this group of disorders. Symptoms are shortness of breath, cough, and angina (pain in the chest). The exact cause is not known, though some types have a hereditary basis.

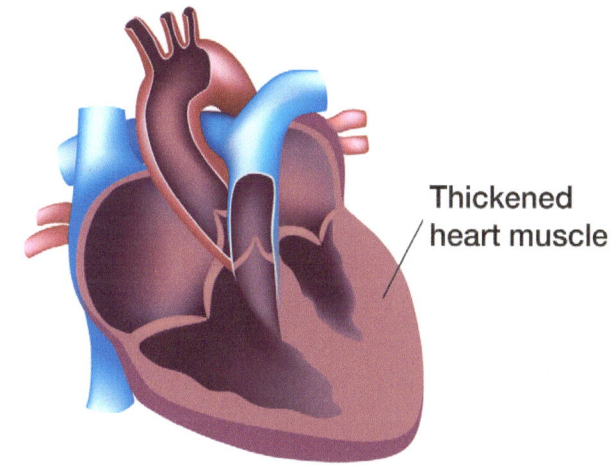

Hypertrophic cardiomyopathy

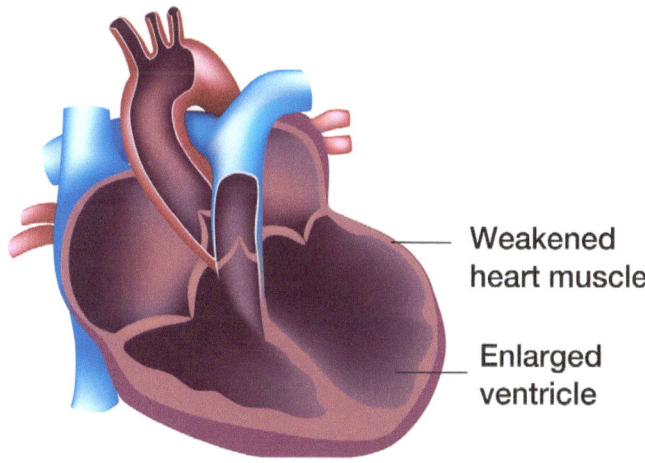

Dilated cardiomyopathy

Figure 3-19 Cardiomyopathy

PERIPHERAL VASCULAR DISEASES

ANEURYSM

Aneurysm means the local swelling of an artery. This can develop if the artery is diseased or weakened, especially when the blood pressure is high. Aorta is the most commonly affected artery (the main artery of the chest and abdomen). Sometimes small congenital aneurysms (those at birth) can occur in otherwise healthy arteries supplying the brain.

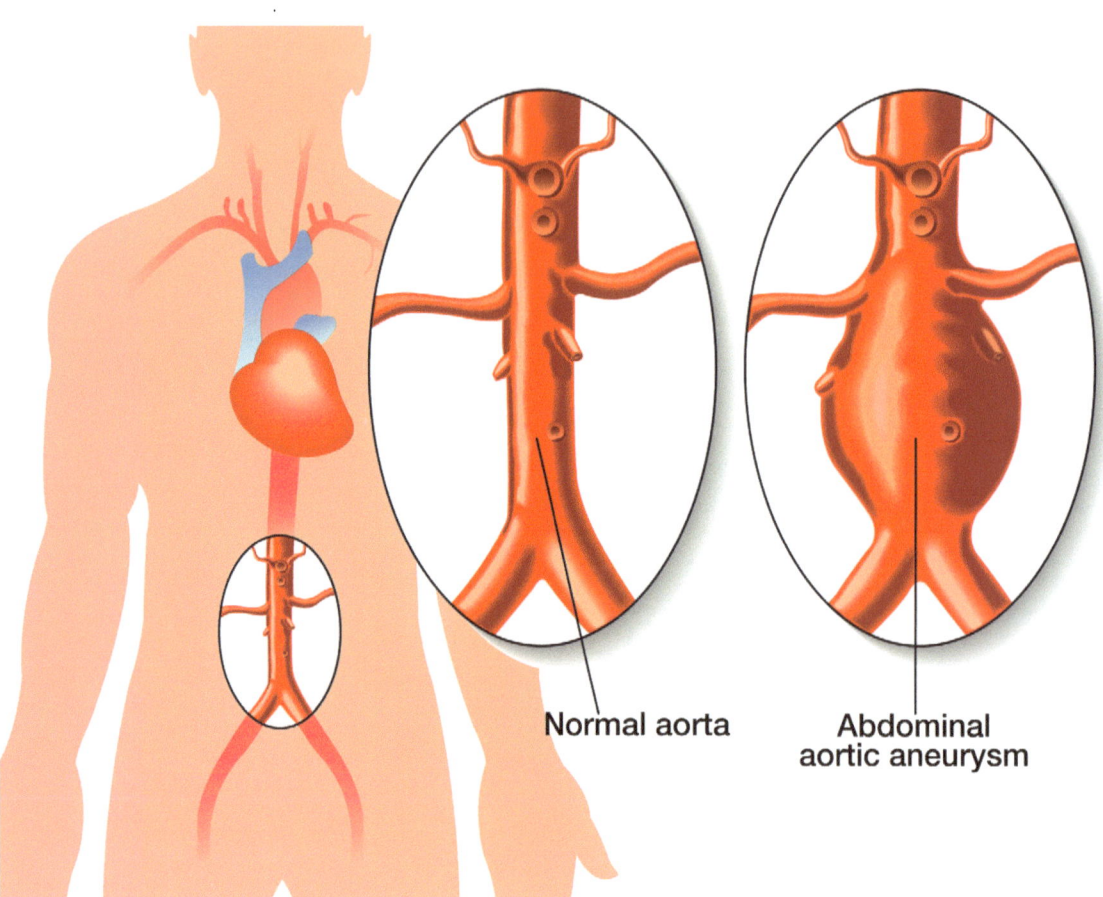

Figure 3-20 Aneurysm

Due to aneurysm there may be a rupture of the artery. These ruptures, which develop in the chest, are more likely to interfere with the proper function of the heart, causing chest pain and shortness of breath. Aneurysm may be caused by atheroma (degenerative change of the wall of the artery).

ARTERIAL THROMBOSIS

Arterial thrombosis refers to clotting of the blood in the artery, obstructing the normal flow of the blood. Arteries of heart, brain and legs are mostly involved, but any artery may be affected. The major symptom of this disease is a sudden onset of pain at rest usually in the leg, which may be colder or paler than the other leg. The cause is most likely to be degenerative changes in the arteries.

EDEMA

Edema is a medical terminology commonly used to describe a swelling containing fluid. Plasma protein or protein in the blood has the property of holding fluid in the blood. Due to diminished plasma protein content, more fluid from the blood escapes into tissue spaces and stretches the tissue spaces, which looks swollen. Therefore, an abnormal accumulation of tissue fluid in the intercellular spaces occurs. The reason attributed is the large quantities of proteins passing from the capillaries and escaping into the tissue fluid.

CAUSES AND TYPES OF EDEMA

1. Any obstruction in the veins raises the venous and capillary pressure and thus increases the filtration of fluid out of the vessels.
2. Cardiac edema is caused in cases of the right-sided heart failure (congestive heart failure). The edema is noticed in the most dependent parts e.g. in the ankles, if the person is walking about.
3. Renal edema is seen in nephritis. When kidney does not function properly, the nephrons which are the functional units in the kidney do not reabsorb the proteins. Thus the proteins are wasted in urine and thus, edema occurs.
4. Nutritional edema is due to low protein content in diet and this in turn leads to lowering of plasma protein levels.
5. Lymphatic obstruction may occur due to parasitic worms and may lead to edematous condition of the affected parts e.g. filariasis.
6. Inflammatory edema is accompanied by local heat, redness, swelling and pain. In this type of edema, an increased reactive capillary dilatation and permeability occurs.

BUERGER'S DISEASE

In this condition, the arteries and veins become clogged and inflamed. This occurs mainly in the lower limbs, though the hands are often involved as well. It is seen mostly among the heavy smokers under the age of 40 years. The symptoms are inflammation and pain in the leg veins, discoloration of feet and burning feeling of the feet. Muscular activity of the lower limbs worsens the perceived symptoms. Sometimes there may be pins and needles in the feet. The exact cause is unknown though the disease is associated with heavy smoking.

INTERMITTENT CLAUDICATION

Refers to the pain in the legs while walking. Symptoms are tightness of calf muscles and gripping pain in the calves, which usually occur on walking a certain distance, and is relieved by rest. When the severity of disease is advanced, pain is not relieved even on rest. Causes of this disease include degenerative changes of the main arteries supplying blood to the legs and blood clot or thrombosis of the artery supplying blood to the calf.

GANGRENE

Death and decay of a part or whole of the limb, or other parts of body that occurs when their blood supply is cut off is referred to as gangrene. The causes are, constriction or blockage of the arteries from any cause, diabetes, arteriosclerosis of arteries, pressure- such as bedsores or tight bandage and frostbite. The cause has to be addressed in order to treat this disease.

Chapter 4

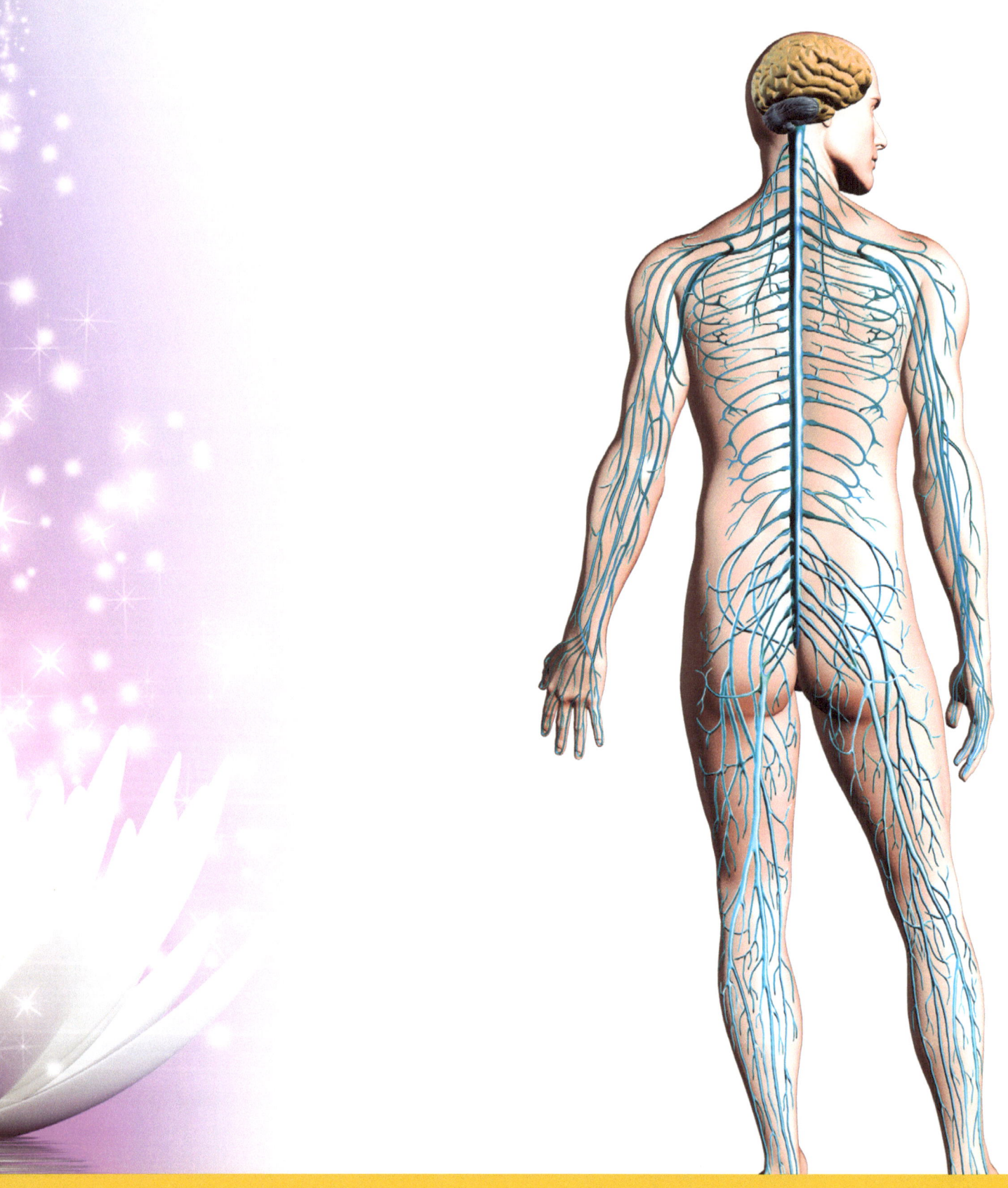

Nervous system

TABLE OF CONTENTS

- NERVOUS SYSTEM 74
- CEREBRUM 77
- HYPOTHALAMUS 78
- THALAMUS 79
- BRAIN STEM 79
- CEREBELLUM 79
- BASAL GANGLIA 80
- AUTONOMIC NERVOUS SYSTEM 80
- SPINAL CORD 81
- NEURONS 84
- DISORDERS OF NERVOUS SYSTEM 85
  - Athetosis 85
  - Bell's palsy 85
  - Cerebral palsy 85
  - Chorea 85
  - Dementia 86
  - Encephalitis 86
  - Epilepsy 86
  - Hemiplegia / hemiperesis / stroke 87
  - Meningitis 88
  - Migraine 90
  - Multiple sclerosis 90
  - Myasthenia gravis 91
  - Paraplegia and quadriplegia 91
  - Parkinson's disease 91
  - Transverse myelitis 91
  - Trigeminal neuralgia 92

NERVOUS SYSTEM

The nervous system controls all the activities of the body. It is divided into two parts; the central nervous system and the peripheral nervous system.

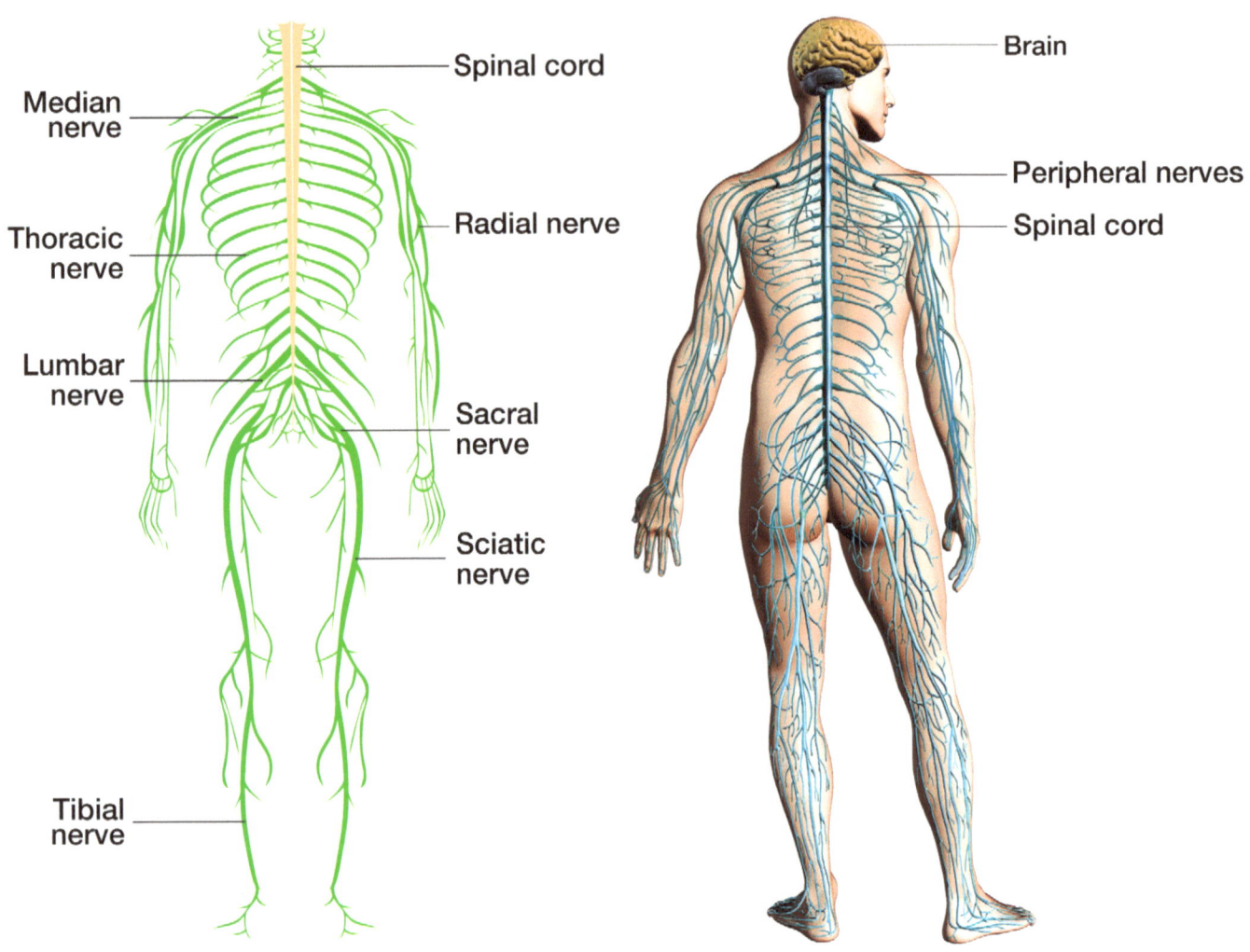

Figure 4-1 Central & peripheral nervous system

The central nervous system includes the brain and the spinal cord. The brain is situated in the skull. The brain has a soft-jelly like structure, bathed in a watery fluid called the cerebrospinal fluid (CSF), which is produced in the brain and passes down the spinal cord. CSF helps in exchange of nutritive and waste materials between blood and brain. It also acts as a shock absorber protecting the brain.

- The cerebrospinal fluid acts as a shock absorber protecting the brain
- The net weight of the brain is reduced from 1400 gm to about 50 gm because the brain is immersed in the CSF, thereby reducing the pressure at the base of the brain

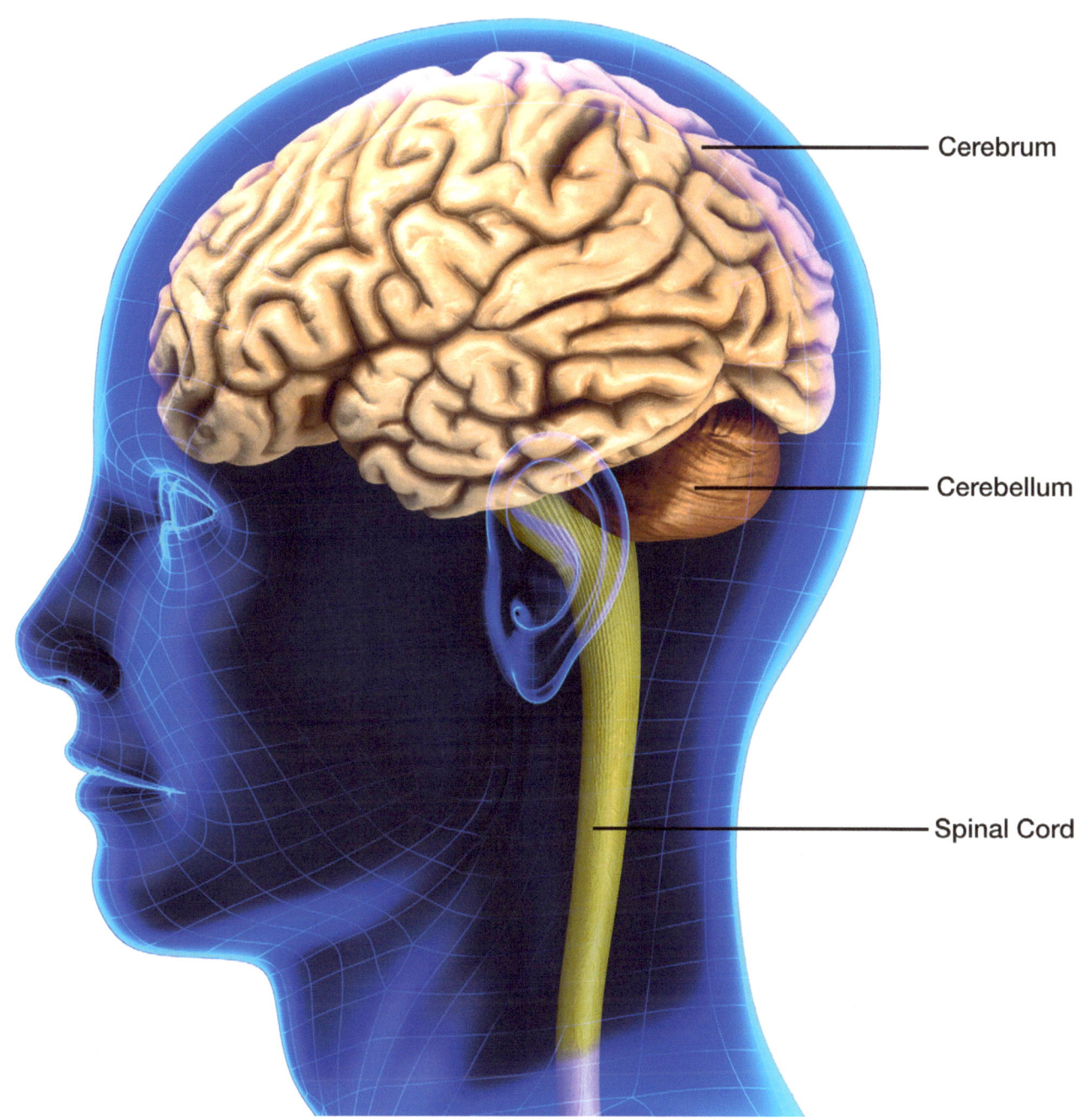

Figure 4-2 Brain anatomy

The brain is divided into the forebrain, the midbrain and the hindbrain. The forebrain consists of cerebrum, hypothalamus and thalamus. The midbrain is a small portion between the forebrain and hindbrain. The cerebellum, the pons and the medulla constitute the hindbrain (fig 4-4, page 77). The brain and the spinal cord are covered by meninges.

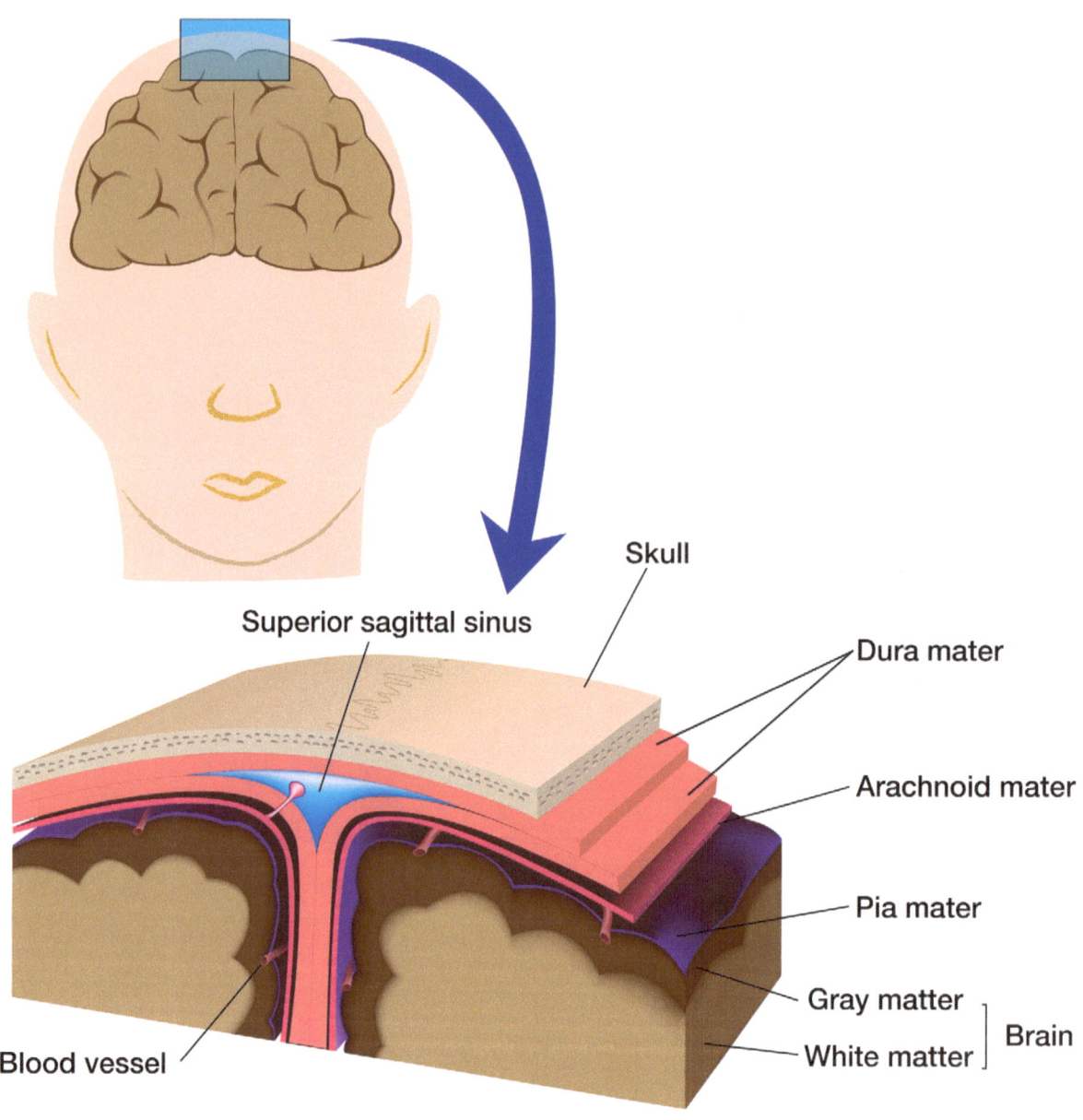

Figure 4-3 The meninges of the brain

The brain requires oxygen for its survival which is supplied by the blood pumped by the heart. If the oxygen supply is cut for few minutes it results in paralysis, coma or death.

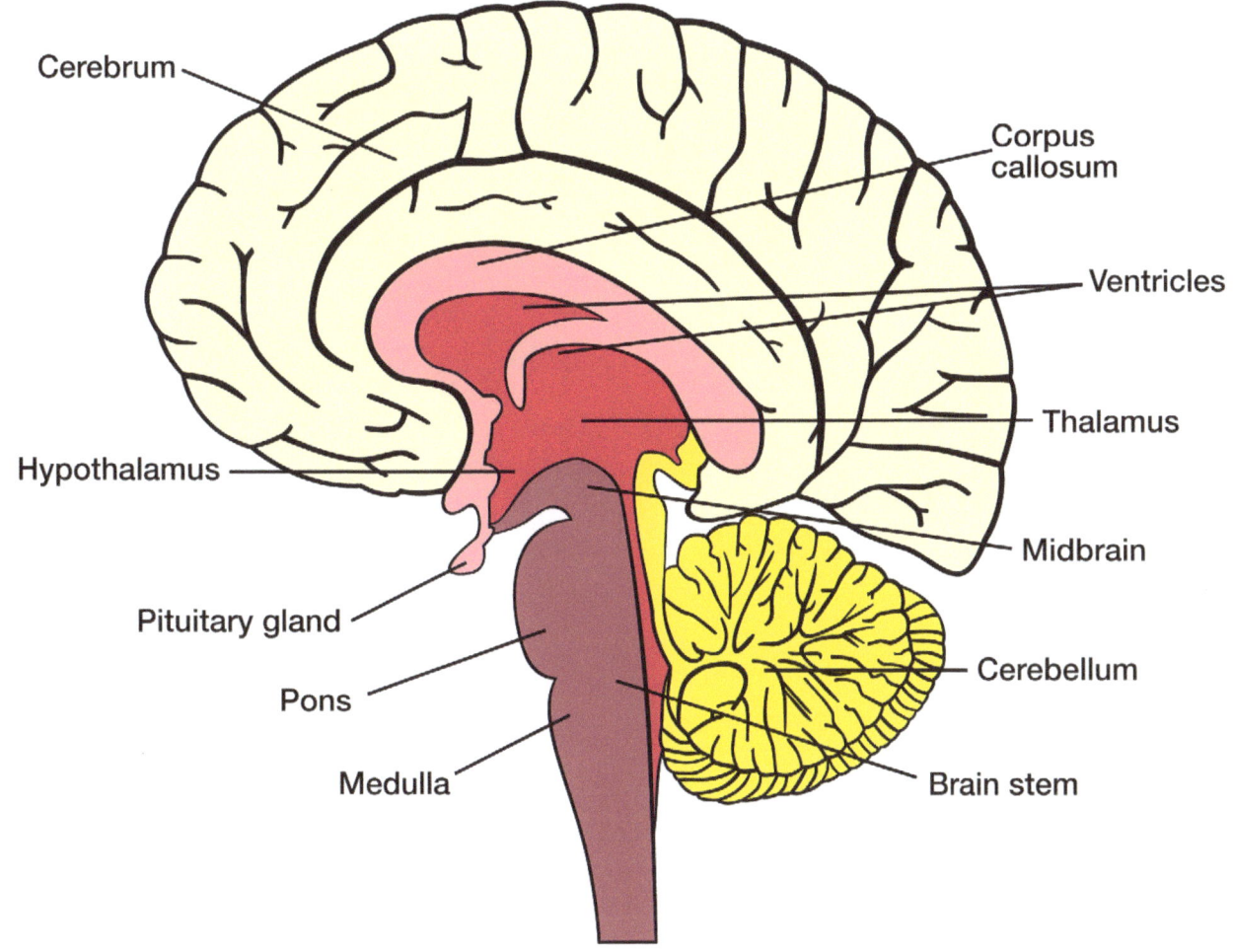

Figure 4-4 Human brain - side view

The peripheral nervous system consists of a network of nerves, which carries information to and from the central nervous system.

CEREBRUM

Cerebrum is a highly developed part of the brain. It is divided into two hemispheres, each of which consist of four lobes namely frontal, parietal, occipital and temporal lobes. These hemispheres control the opposite side of the body, therefore, any dysfunction of the right side of the cerebrum affects the left side of the body and vice versa. The frontal lobe is concerned with initiation of voluntary movements and speech. It helps in coordination of movements such that the skilled movements are done in a smooth and accurate manner. It is also the center for higher functions like emotion, learning, memory and social behavior. In addition, it is the area for planned actions and intelligence. The parietal lobe is responsible for sensation of the skin and to a lesser extent for muscles, bones and joints. It also helps in timing and programming of movements.

- Compared to other mammals of similar body size the human brain is three times bigger in size
- The human skull which protects the brain is made of 22 bones that are joined together

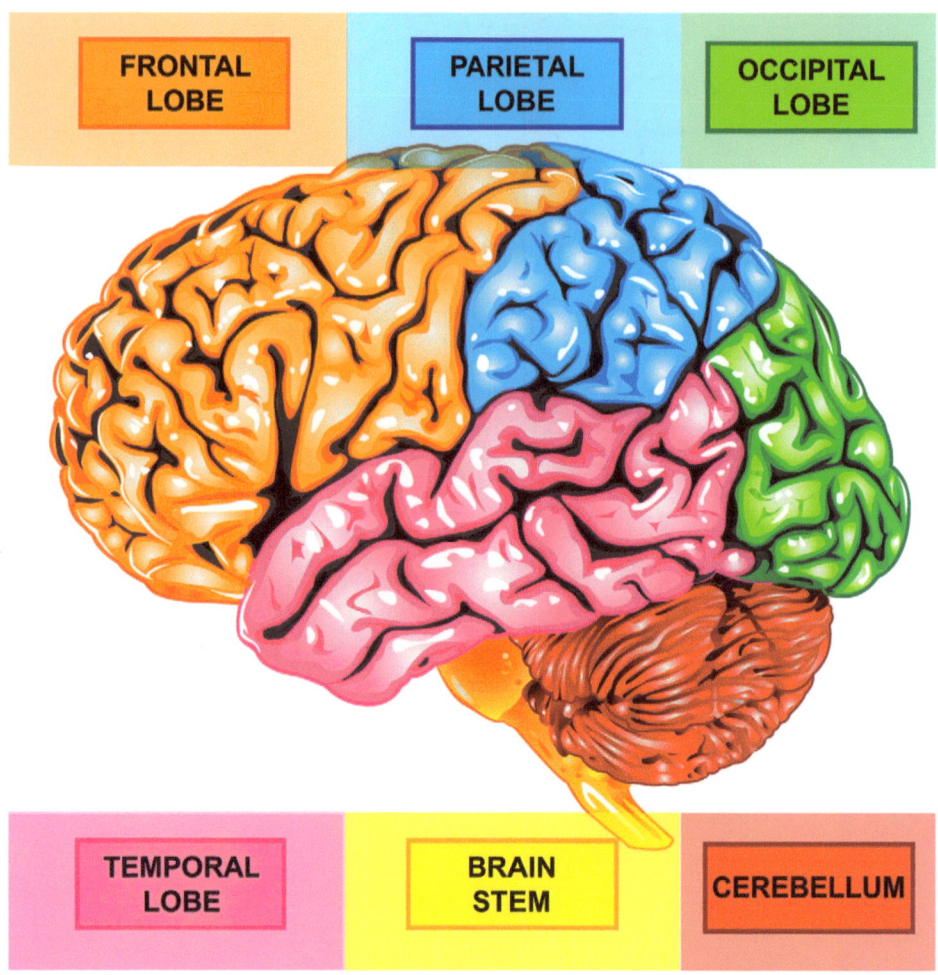

Figure 4-5 The lobes of the cerebrum

The temporal lobe is responsible for hearing, smelling and tasting and the occipital lobe is responsible for vision. Damage to the cerebrum results in emotional instability, lack of concentration, loss of voluntary movements, lack of initiation for planning of any action, impairment of memory, numbness, tingling sensation, hallucinations etc.

HYPOTHALAMUS

The hypothalamus is a part of the forebrain which represents less than 1 percent of the brain mass and plays a key role in controlling endocrine functions, hunger, thirst, sleep, emotional and sexual functions. Various functions of the hypothalamus are presented in more detail herein.

1. Regulation of endocrine functions

    All secretions by the pituitary are controlled by signals from the hypothalamus. This is because the pituitary gland receives its blood supply mainly from the blood passing through the lower border of the hypothalamus. Therefore, hypothalamus indirectly controls the thyroid, adrenal and the reproductive glands.

2. Helping in the regulation of body temperature

    The hypothalamus can increase the sweat secretion by stimulating the sweat glands and thus controls the body heat.

3. The hypothalamus is involved in regulation of cardio-vascular responses. Therefore stimulations of different parts of hypothalamus cause increase (or) decrease in heart rate. It also regulates the blood pressure.
4. The hypothalamus can also control the feeding center based on which a person may experience uncontrolled hunger (or) loss of appetite.
5. The hypothalamus regulates the fluid volumes in the body by either increasing the sensation of thirst or controlling the urine output through thermoregulatory and hormonal mechanisms.
6. The hypothalamus also regulates the sleep and the wakefulness.
7. The hypothalamus helps in regulation of behavioral patterns. Various experiments in the past have proven that the stimulation of different areas of hypothalamus has had an effect over the behavioral function, such as positive and negative emotions, increased sexual urge, fear, thirst etc.
8. The hypothalamus helps in regulating the milk secretion by the breast and contraction of uterus during child birth. The hypothalamus secretes a hormone called oxytocin which expels the milk through the nipples so that the baby can nourish itself. In addition, it helps in contraction of the uterus during pregnancy to expel the baby.

THALAMUS

The thalamus is a small organ located in the forebrain which acts as a relay center for all sensations. It also controls sexual sensations and helps in integration of motor functions.

BRAIN STEM

The brain stem is formed by the medulla oblongata, the pons and the midbrain. The midbrain is the portion between the forebrain and the hindbrain. The pons forms a bridge between the midbrain and the medulla. The medulla oblongata is continued in the form of the spinal cord downwards.

The brain stem controls the major centers such as respiratory center for breathing, the cardiac center controlling the heart performance, the vasomotor center that regulates the blood pressure. They are responsible for controlling the food and air passages. This center regulates swallowing, induces vomiting, sneezing, coughing and also controls salivation. Even during sleep and unconsciousness, the lower center of medulla continues to function. Any injury to these vital centers is often fatal and results in coma, paralysis and death.

CEREBELLUM

Cerebellum is smaller than the cerebrum and lies below it. The cerebellum is under the control of the cerebrum through the nerve fibers. It is responsible for maintaining tone, posture, equilibrium and muscle coordination. It also helps in coordination of the movements, which are initiated by the cerebrum. It assists in doing skilled movements like typing, dancing, walking etc., as well as helping in timing and programming of movements. Lack of coordination of movements, weakness of muscle, tremor while attempting do a voluntary act, to and from movement of the eyeball, difficulty in speech are all the signs noticed

- The cerebellum is responsible for maintaining tone, posture, equilibrium and muscle coordination

when the cerebellum is damaged. As a result of this damage, a disturbance in the range of voluntary movements may also appear. In some cases, the patient may be unable to determine the strength that is required to accomplish an act; for instance, they might apply too much pressure to take a light weight object like a sponge.

BASAL GANGLIA

The basal ganglia are scattered masses in the central hemisphere which contain motor and sensory nerve fibers making a connection between the cerebral cortex, other parts of the brain and the spinal cord. One of their principal roles is to control the complex patterns of motor activity such as writing which are initiated by the cerebrum. A serious damage to the basal ganglia can turn the individual's writing crude, as if one is learning how to write for the first time. They also help in controlling the tone of the muscle and automatic associated movements such as swinging of the arms during walking. In addition, they play a major role in arousal mechanism. Any damage to the basal ganglia can lead to drowsiness.

AUTONOMIC NERVOUS SYSTEM

The autonomic nervous system is primarily concerned with regulation of the internal organs of the body such as heart, lungs, blood vessels and other glands such as lacrimal glands and salivary glands.

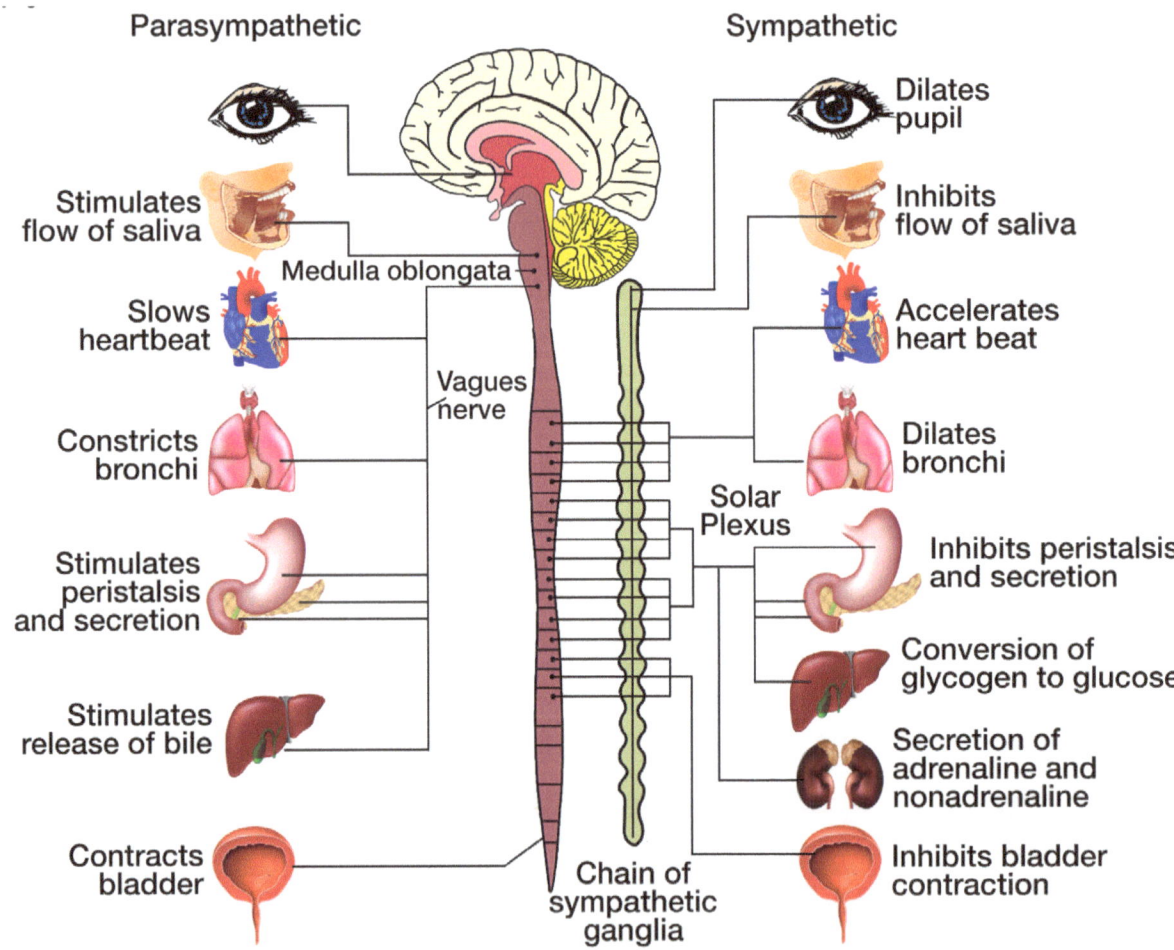

Figure 4-6 Sympathetic and parasympathetic nervous system

It is divided into the sympathetic and the parasympathetic systems. The sympathetic system consists of nerve fibers coming from the thoracic and lumbar portions of the spinal cord. Their function is to reduce the secretions of the lacrimal and salivary glands. They also decrease the secretions of the stomach and the intestine. When stimulated, an increase in heart beat rate and sweating is experienced. They also play a major role in filling of the bladder.

The parasympathetic system consists of nerve fibers coming from the cranial nerves of the brain and the sacral portion of the spinal cord. Stimulation of the parasympathetic nerves results in increased secretion of the lacrimal and the salivary glands. They also increase the secretion of the stomach and the intestine. Contrary to the sympathetic system, the parasympathetic system helps in emptying the bladder. Its main action on the heart is to reduce the heart rate.

Apart from the above mentioned functions and responsibilities, both sympathetic and parasympathetic play an essential role in maintaining the constant internal environment in the body.

SPINAL CORD

The spinal cord is a continuous structure, which extends from the medulla oblongata on the backside of the brain to the first lumbar vertebra underneath. It is a cord of nervous tissue occupying the spinal canal. The spinal cord is covered by meninges which are dura mater, arachnoid and pia mater. They are responsible for protection and nourishment of nervous tissue. The spinal cord is cylindrical in shape. It has two expansions, one in neck and one in low back region which are called cervical and lumbar enlargements, respectively. The spinal cord rapidly narrows down to a cone shaped structure called conus medullaris.

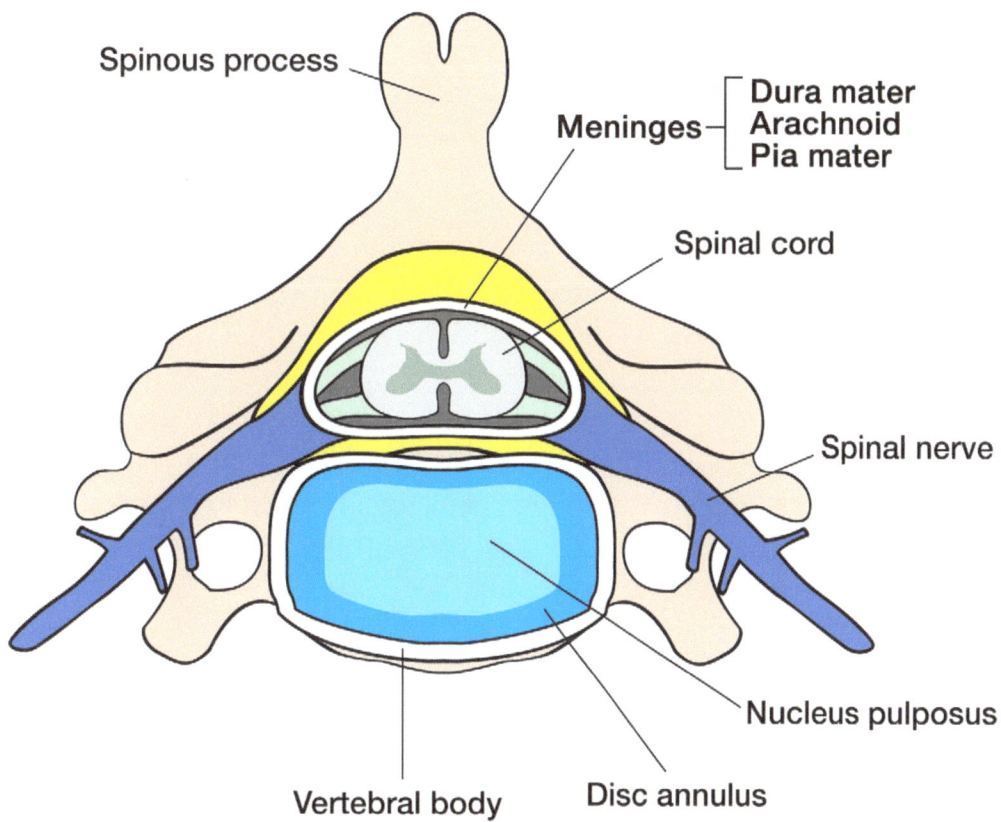

Figure 4-7 Spine – cross section

The spinal cord is made of 31 spinal segments according to the corresponding vertebrae namely 8 cervical segments, 12 thoracic segments, 5 lumbar, 5 sacral segments and 1 coccygeal segment. The appearance of a segment is given by 31 pairs of spinal nerves arising from either side of the spinal cord from the corresponding vertebrae. The spinal nerves are mixed nerves that contain both motor and sensory nerves.

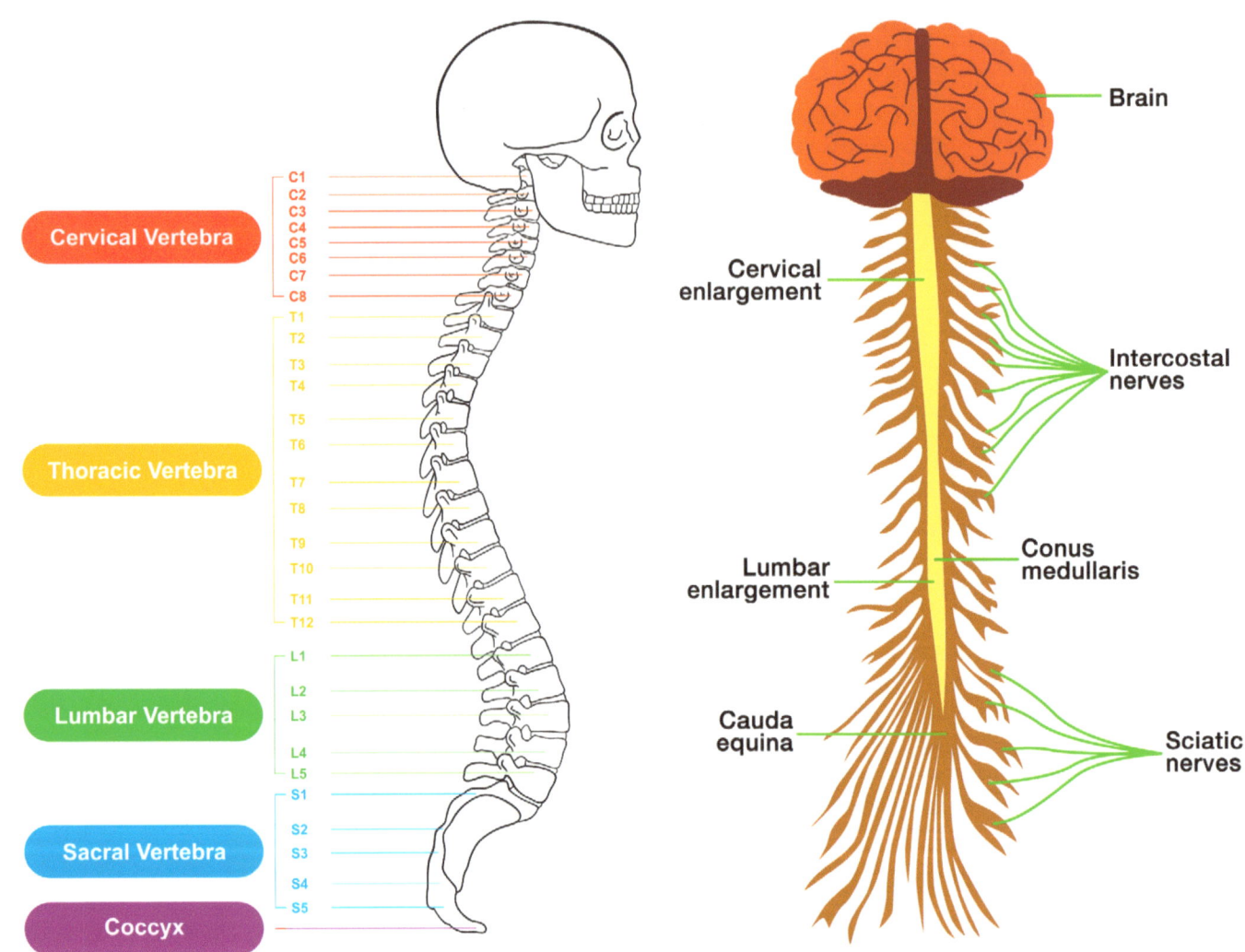

Figure 4-8 Spinal nerves

The spinal cord is connected to the brain through spinal tracts. Sensory information from the distal parts of the body is transmitted to the spinal cord through the peripheral nervous system. The information is sent from the spinal cord to the brain through the ascending tracts. The received signals are processed in the brain and then these signs from the motor areas of the brain travel back down to the cord through the descending tracts.

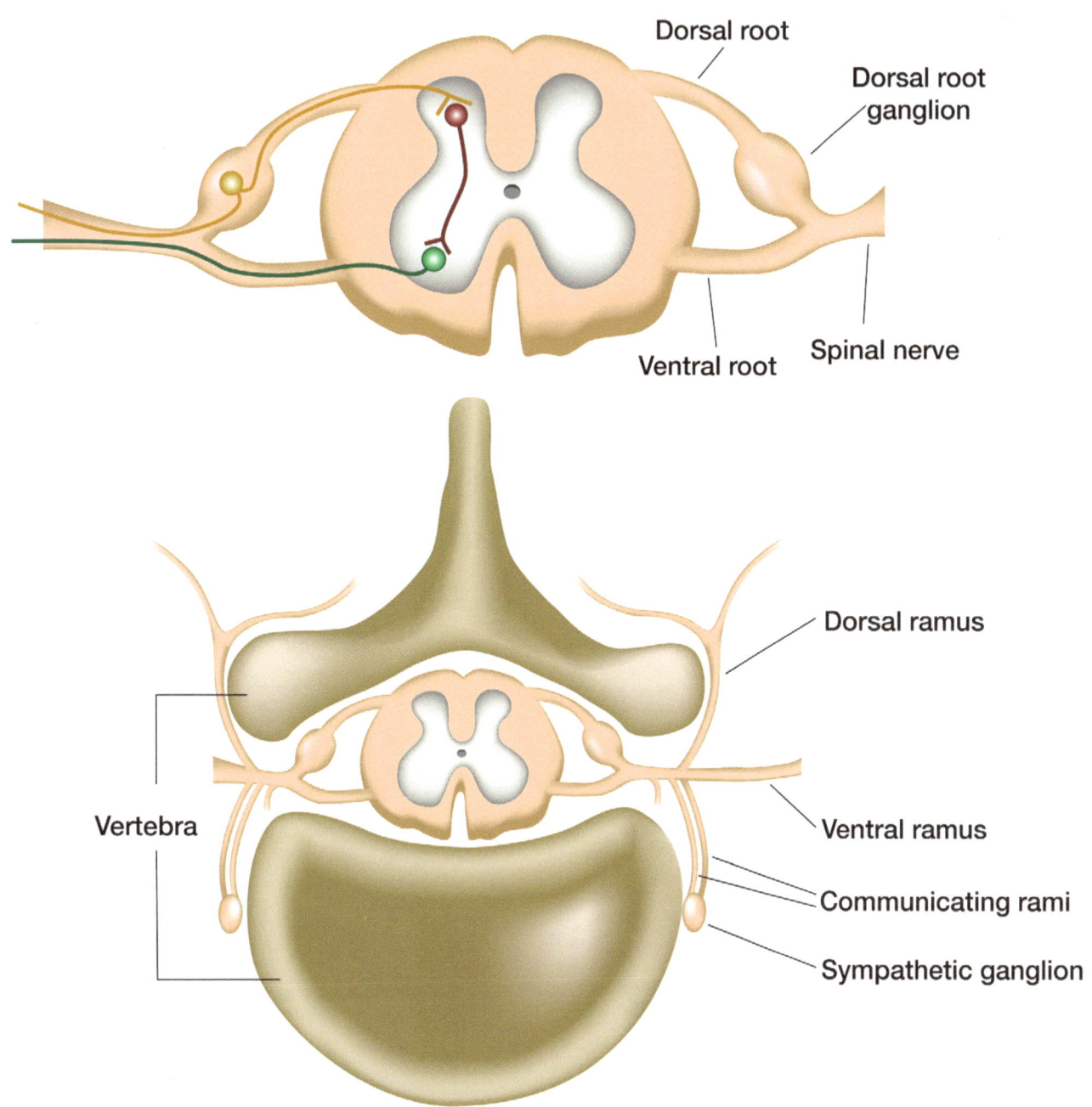

Figure 4-9 Cross section of the spinal cord

The ascending tracts maintain the crude touch sensation, the pain and the temperature sensation, consciousness and awareness. They also help in determining the vibratory sensation and sensation of awareness of various muscular activities of the body. In addition, they are responsible for recognizing the known objects by touching with closed eyes.

The descending tracts are mainly concerned with co-ordination of voluntary movements, muscle tone, respiration and position of the head and the body during movements. Any damage to the spinal cord results in paralysis of the limbs with loss of motor and sensory functions.

NEURONS

The neuron is the structural and functional unit of the nervous system. A neuron is made up of 3 structures namely nerve cell body, dendrites, and axon. The nerve cell body is responsible for the synthesis of protein which helps in forming the structure of the nerves. It also provides energy for the nerves to function.

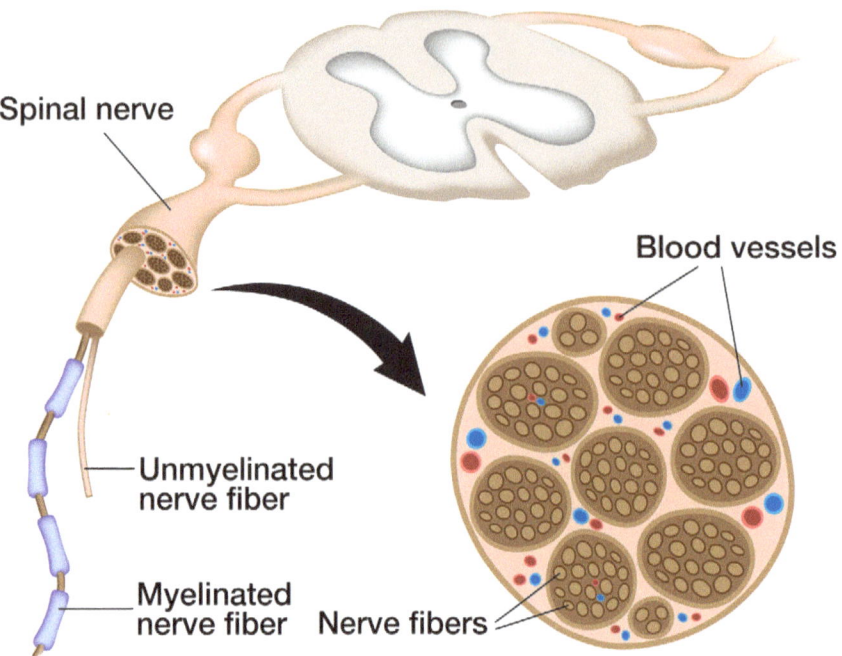

Figure 4-10 Spinal nerve-cross section

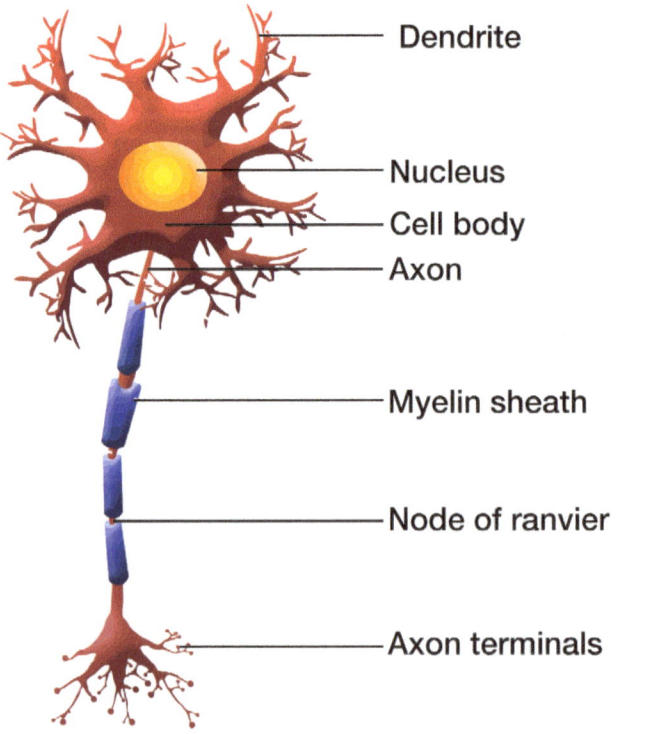

Figure 4-11 Neuron

The dendrites are the repeatedly branched process of the neurons which help in conduction. Axons are the longest process of the nerve cells. There are certain types of chemicals called the neurotransmitters, which are transported from the nerve cell body to the muscles via the axons. They transmit the signals to the organs on the receiving end. A sheath called myelin covers and protects the neurons and helps with their functioning. The myelin sheath acts as insulator and boosts faster conduction of signals from one part of the body to the other. The neurons supply skeletal and visceral organs. The neurons have both sensory and motor functions. Damage of the neurons makes it difficult for the body to carry out any kind of activity; however, in some cases, the damaged neurons can be regenerated and the functions can be restored.

- The nerve signals travel at a speed of 100 meters or more a second
- There are approximately 100 billion neurons in the human brain

DISORDERS OF NERVOUS SYSTEM

ATHETOSIS

Athetosis refers to abnormal involuntary movements which are slow, rhythmic and twisting. There is usually a constant succession of slow, involuntary movements of the fingers and hands, and sometimes of the toes and feet. Athetosis is mostly caused by the damage of basal ganglia.

BELL'S PALSY

Bell's palsy is an acute onset due to the inflammation of the facial nerve, the cause of which is unknown. It sometimes initiates as a result of exposure to cold (or) viral infection. It may also occur because of a tumor or due to trauma of the facial nerve. It is a one sided paralysis of the face in which the voluntary, emotional and associated movements of the upper and the lower facial muscles are involved. The disease is characterized by upward and inward movement of the eyeball on closing the eyes. The nasal folds become less prominent on the affected side and a deviation of the angle of mouth towards the opposite side is observed. Loss of taste sensation on the affected side is experienced and the patient will be unable to raise the eyebrow on the affected side.

CEREBRAL PALSY

Defect of motor power and coordination related to damage of the brain is known as cerebral palsy. It occurs due to birth injuries, maternal infections or because of insufficient oxygen supply to the fetus. The child's limbs are clumsy. The lower limbs are affected more than the upper limbs. This condition is associated with mental retardation and difficulty in speech. Bowel and bladder are also affected and convulsions are produced. Physiotherapy and rehabilitation are treatment of choice.

CHOREA

Chorea refers to abnormal involuntary movements which are rapid and jerky. The movements are spasmodic and occur in the limbs or facial muscles, often accompanied by hypotonia. The location of the responsible cerebral lesion is not known.

DEMENTIA

Progressive loss of recent memory is called dementia. As the condition progresses, the psychiatric symptoms such as loss of motor functions and personality changes appear. The patient begins to lead a vegetative life without any thinking power. Dementia may be caused by infections such as syphilis, tuberculosis, degenerative disorders like Parkinson's, raised intracranial tension like tumors and senile dementia like alzheimer's disease. Dementia can also occur due to drugs, toxins, hormonal changes, vitamin deficiencies etc. The dementia occurring in people over the age of 65 years is called alzheimer disease. In this condition, the central cortex is atrophied and the patient may develop psychiatric symptoms. In this stage, both motor and sensory nerves become damaged.

ENCEPHALITIS

Encephalitis is an inflammatory process of central nervous system coupled with the dysfunction of the brain. It occurs due to infections, injury, toxins, tumors and imbalance of fluid and electrolyte in the body. The patient may experience irritability, confusion, vomiting, loss of memory, cardiorespiratory insufficiency, seizures, ultimately coma and even death. Therefore, emergency treatment is required and the airway should be maintained open.

EPILEPSY

Epilepsy is an intermittent disorder of the nervous system presumably due to a sudden, excessive or disorderly discharge of cerebral neurons. There is an uncontrolled excessive activity of either all or a part of the central nervous system. It is characterized by recurrent seizures that are caused by abnormal electrical activity in the brain. Seizures can occur for many reasons, including damage to the brain due to infection, injury, birth trauma, tumor, stroke, drug intoxication, and chemical imbalance. Epilepsy is also characterized by instantaneous disturbance of sensation, loss of consciousness, convulsive movements, or some combination of these symptoms. Sometimes it is an obvious symptom of a brain disease that also manifests itself in other ways, and at times it is the solitary expression of deranged cerebral function in an individual who otherwise maintains perfect health. Epilepsy can be classified into four major types namely grand mal epilepsy, petit mal epilepsy, partial epilepsy, focal epilepsy.

Grand mal epilepsy-

In grand mal epilepsy there is an extreme neuronal discharge in the cerebrum, brainstem and thalamus and all the way into the spinal cord. Since the spinal cord is involved generalized tonic seizures and spasm of the muscles are experienced. It has the two following phases: the tonic phase and the clonic phase. In the tonic phase the patient experiences a tonic spasm in which all the muscles of the body are tightly contracted including the muscles of the airway. The patient may get irritated and stressed. Often the person bites the tongue and may have difficulty in breathing. The patient may cry loudly and fall on the ground which may lead to serious injury. The attack lasts from a few seconds to 3 to 4 minutes. This is followed by a clonic phase in which all the muscles of the body are relaxed. After this stage patient may have a loss of consciousness which lasts for 30 minutes. There is an increase in the pulse rate, the blood pressure, sweating and urination. The patient is often confused and does not remember this episode once recovered.

Petit mal epilepsy-

Petit mal epilepsy usually appears in the late childhood and resolves by age. A loss of consciousness or diminished consciousness during the attack is experienced by the patient. This lasts for about half a minute and is characterized by twitch-like contractions of the muscles, usually on the head region, especially blinking of the eyes after which the patient returns to consciousness. The patient never falls down. The attack may be once in many months or seldom in a rapid series one after the other.

Partial epilepsy-

Partial epilepsy may occur in a simple and complex type. In simple partial epilepsy there is no loss of consciousness and only twitching movements of the lips are present. In complex partial epilepsy there is an alteration in the state of consciousness.

Focal epilepsy-

Focal epilepsy can result from some organic lesions in any particular part of the brain or functional abnormality, such as scar tissue in the brain, a tumor that compresses an area of the brain or a destroyed area of brain tissue involving any part of the brain. It is characterized by muscle contraction through out the opposite side of the body. Sometimes the patient cannot remember their activities during the attack. In other cases they are aware of everything they have been doing during the attack. Sometimes the focal epilepsy can become generalized which is called Jacksonian march.

HEMIPLEGIA / HEMIPERESIS / STROKE

Hemiplegia, hemiparesis or stroke, refers to the paralysis of one side of the body, which includes both hands and legs. This can occur due to a clot in the artery obstructing the blood flow to the brain or the rupture of the artery called hemorrhage that reduces the blood supply to the brain. The internal capsule is a structure located in the brain containing dense nerve fibers which become damaged due to insufficient blood supply. This damage results in paralysis of the opposite half of the body; for example, the paralyzed left side indicates that the right internal capsule is affected.

The severity of symptoms of the stroke varies depending on the extent of the damage of arteries or the extent of the block. Depending on the part of the brain which is involved, a stroke can cause paralysis, dementia, blindness or other serious brain disorders. The following clinical features are observed as a result of a stroke.

- Paralysis of the lower two thirds of the face on the opposite side.
- Difficulty of speech and swallowing.
- Paralysis of the upper and the lower limbs on the opposite side.

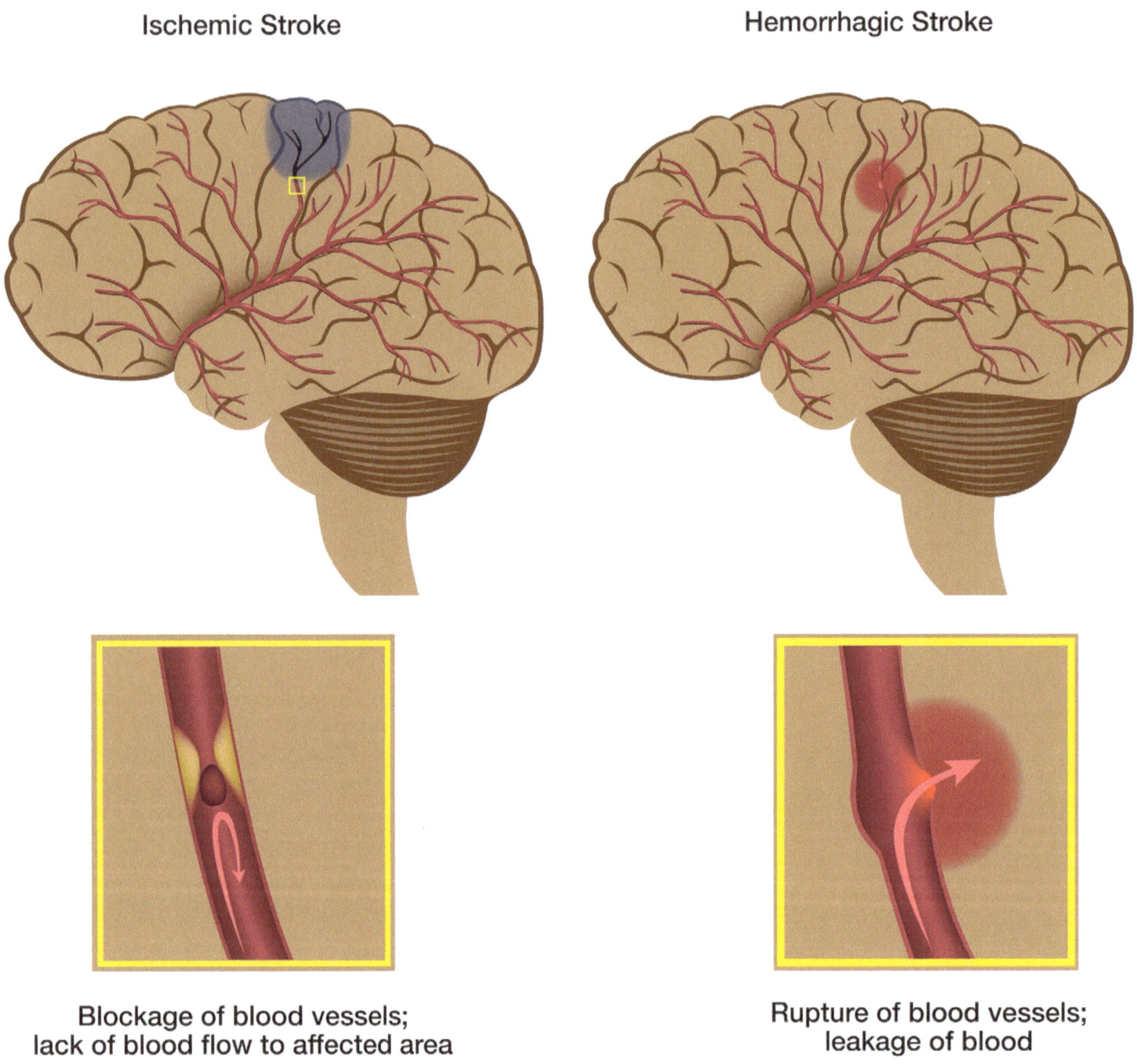

Ischemic Stroke

Hemorrhagic Stroke

Blockage of blood vessels;
lack of blood flow to affected area

Rupture of blood vessels;
leakage of blood

Figure 4-12 Brain stroke

- Bowel and bladder involvement. The patient will not be able to control his urination.
- Spasticity (tightness) or flaccidity (loss of tone) of the affected muscles.

MENINGITIS

Meningitis is a condition occurring due to the inflammation of meninges and could be bacterial, viral or tuberculosis.

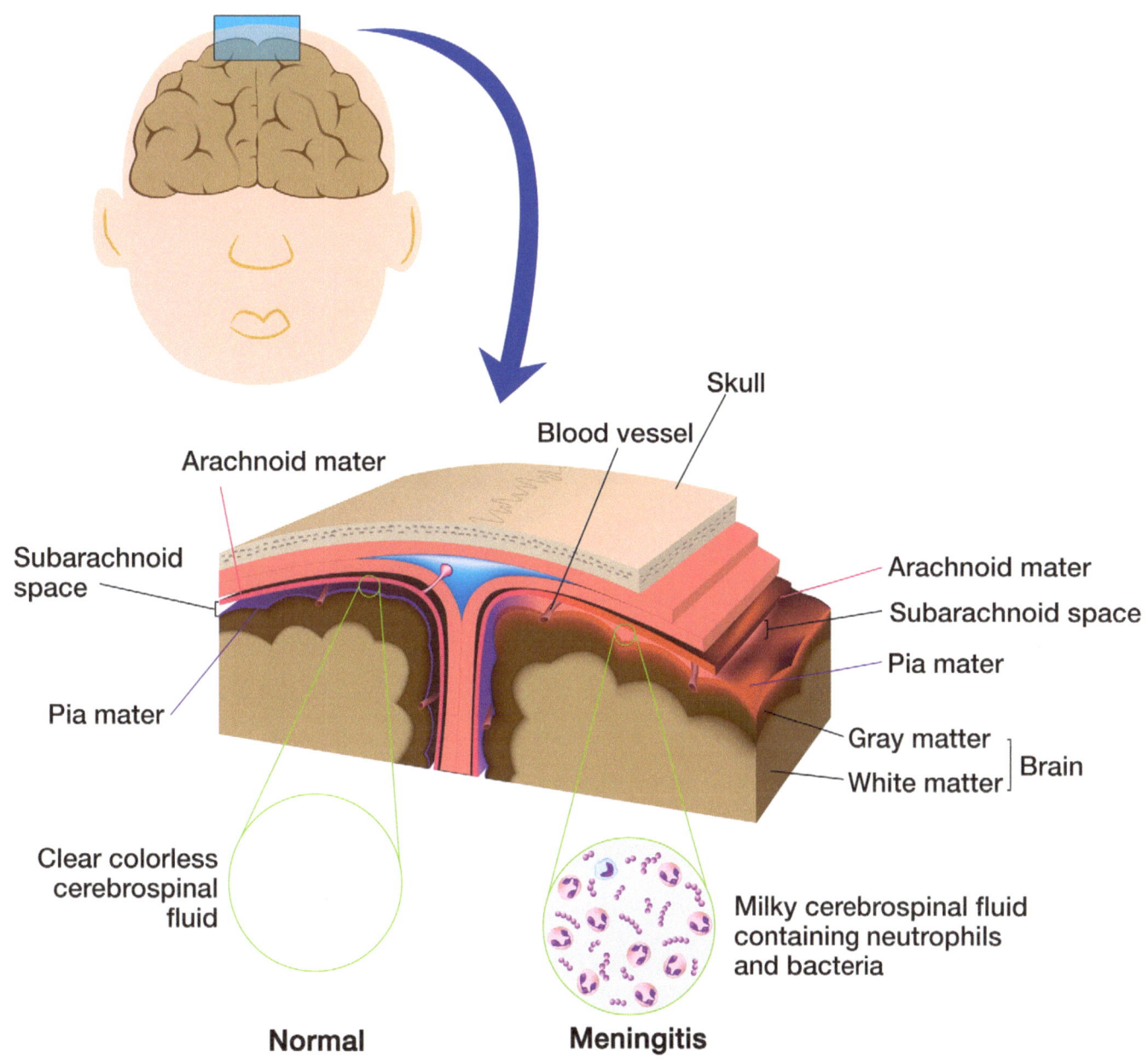

Figure 4-13 Meningitis

Bacterial meningitis

The bacteria may spread via the blood to the meninges from the distal foci of infection in the body like pus or pneumonia. The onset is acute; in the initial phases, the patient becomes irritable and experiences severe headache accompanied with vomiting. Seizures are common and photophobia is more marked along with difficulties in breathing. Bacterial meningitis is more serious with complications like shock and epilepsy.

Viral meningitis

Viral meningitis is usually relatively mild. It is caused by herpes virus and mosquito-borne viruses. It clears up within a week or two without specific treatment. Viral meningitis is also known as the aseptic meningitis.

Nervous System

Tuberculous meningitis

The infection of meninges occurs due to the secondary spread of tuberculosis bacteria from lungs. The onset is sudden and associated with vomiting, irritability, seizures and progressive loss of consciousness.

MIGRAINE

Migraine is a one-sided headache most common in females accompanied with headache, nausea and vomiting. It is usually episodic in nature. Migraine attack starts with malaise, irritability and is followed by an aura. The aura could be either visual, auditory or some form of sensations. The patient will then experience severe headache associated with vomiting and photophobia (fear of light). Migraine commonly occurs due to psychological stress and depression.

MULTIPLE SCLEROSIS

Multiple sclerosis is an autoimmune disease where the antibodies are produced against the myelin sheath of the central nervous system, the covering that wraps around the axon is destroyed with inflammation and scarring, ultimately producing inflammation of meninges.

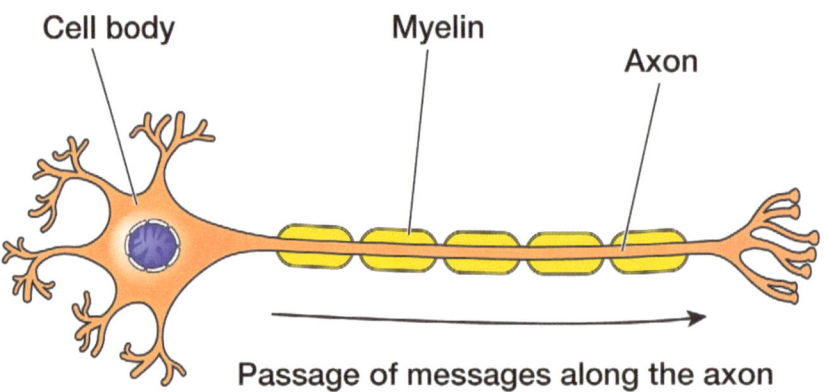

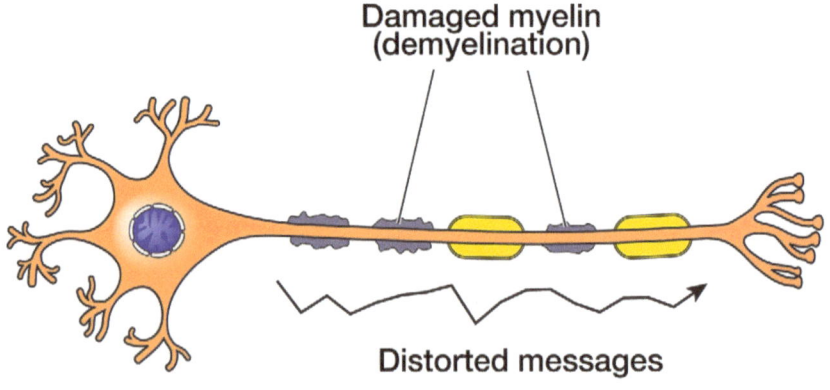

Figure 4-14 Multiple sclerosis

Multiple sclerosis could arise because of environmental reasons or due to genetic factors. The clinical course of the diseases includes relapses and remissions. The gap between the two attacks ranges from weeks to years. The disease is characterized by tingling in spine and limbs, tremor, facial palsy, optic neuritis, para paresis, and trigeminal neuralgia. In the later stages of multiple sclerosis, the bowel and the bladder are involved, spasticity of muscles is experienced by the patient.

MYASTHENIA GRAVIS

Myasthenia gravis is a neuromuscular disorder characterized by weakness and fatigability of muscles due to antibodies produced against the muscle receptors which are necessary for muscle contraction. This disease is more common in females. It can also affect the muscles of the eyes, the jaws, the face, the pharynx and the larynx. The disease is characterized by abnormal fatigability of muscles, diplopia in addition to weakness in chewing, swallowing and speaking. When the patient is asked to count aloud, the voice gradually weakens. The muscles of respiration are affected and the patient may require assisted ventilation.

PARAPLEGIA AND QUADRIPLEGIA

Paraplegia is the condition of partial or complete paralysis of both lower limbs. Quadriplegia is the condition of partial or complete paralysis of all four limbs. These conditions occur due to traumatic injuries of spinal cord resulting from accidents, which can cause complete or incomplete transactions of the spinal cord. Paraplegia occurs due to injury at the thoracic or lumbar level and quadriplegia occurs as a result of injury at the cervical level. The following three stages are involved in the above mentioned conditions.

1. Stage of spinal shock.
2. Stage of reflex activity
3. Stage of reflex failure.

In the stage of spinal shock the limbs become paralyzed and are flaccid and a loss of sensation occurs. Bowel and bladder become paralyzed in this stage and there is a fall in the blood pressure, the heart rate and the pulse. The stage of spinal shock can last for 3 weeks. This stage is followed by the stage of reflex activity also called the stage of recovery. The functional activities return. The tone of the muscle also starts to improve. This stage is then followed by a stage of reflex failure where the patient's condition starts deteriorating and the muscles becomes flaccid and undergoes wasting.

PARKINSON'S DISEASE

Parkinson's disease occurs due to the damage of the basal ganglia. The various possible causes include the viral infection of the brain like encephalitis and injury to the basal ganglia due to certain drugs. It is mostly idiopathic and appears in the old age. It is characterized by tremor during rest, rigidity, absence of automatic associated movements resulting in mask like face, inability to do voluntary movements, and emotional instability.

TRANSVERSE MYELITIS

Transverse myelitis is an acute onset disease with total transaction of the spinal cord which occurs due to infection of the spinal cord. The disease is associated with back pain, bladder involvement, loss of power and sensation of both the lower limbs. 70 percent of patients recover within 3 months.

TRIGEMINAL NEURALGIA

Trigeminal neuralgia is a painful condition of the face. The trigeminal nerve contains mainly the sensory nerve fibers in the three following groups.

1. The ophthalmic nerve supplying the upper part of the face.
2. The maxillary nerve supplying the upper jaw.
3. The mandibular nerve supplying the lower jaw.

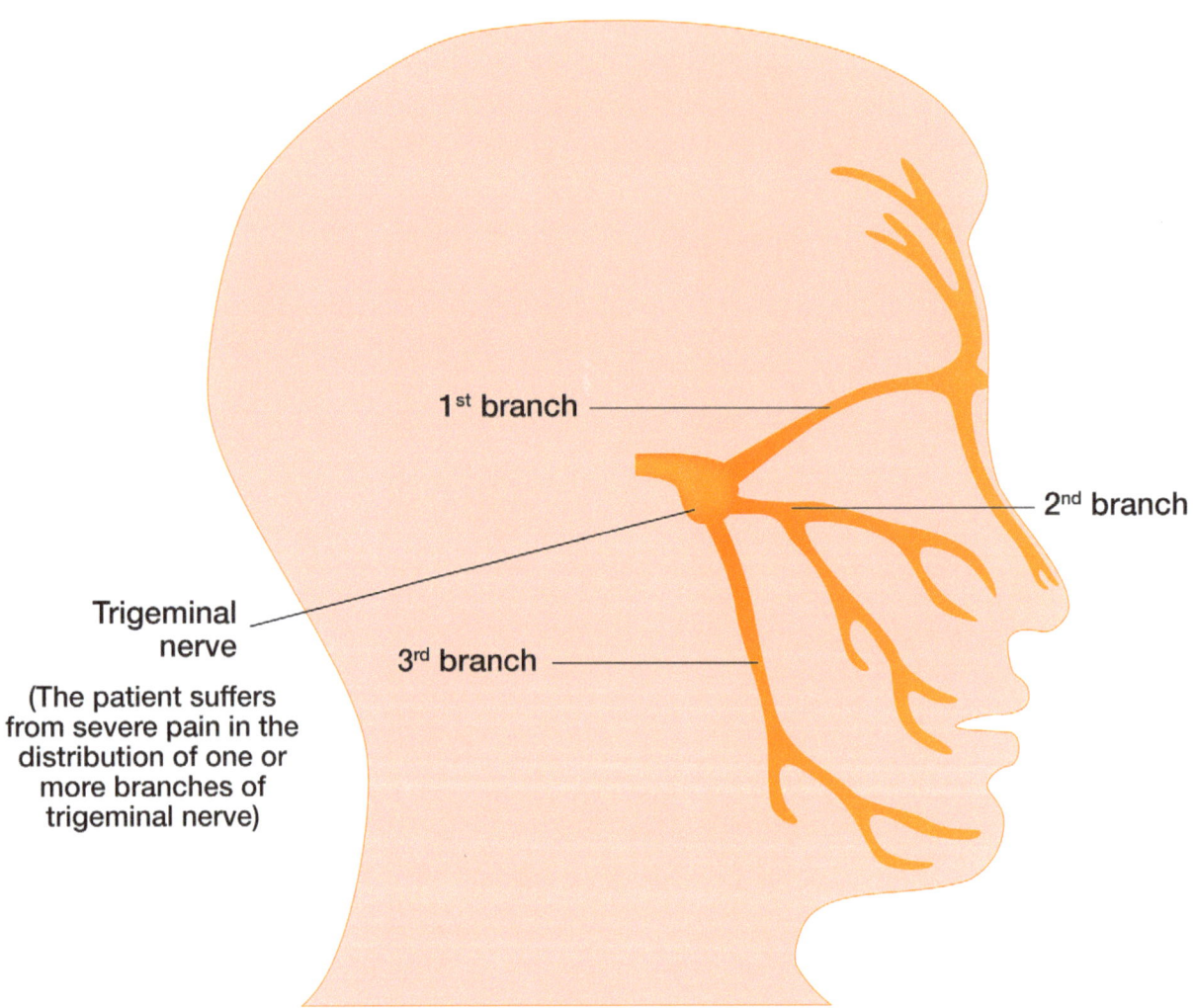

Figure 4-15 Trigeminal nerve

In trigeminal neuralgia, the patient suffers from severe pain in the distribution of one or more branches of trigeminal nerve. It is mostly associated with twitching of the facial muscles, an aura before the pain starts experienced in most cases. Remissions and exacerbations are common as well in this disease. It is a sharp, sudden, severe stabbing pain initiated by stimulation of trigger points by washing face, chewing, brushing teeth, laughing etc.

Chapter 5

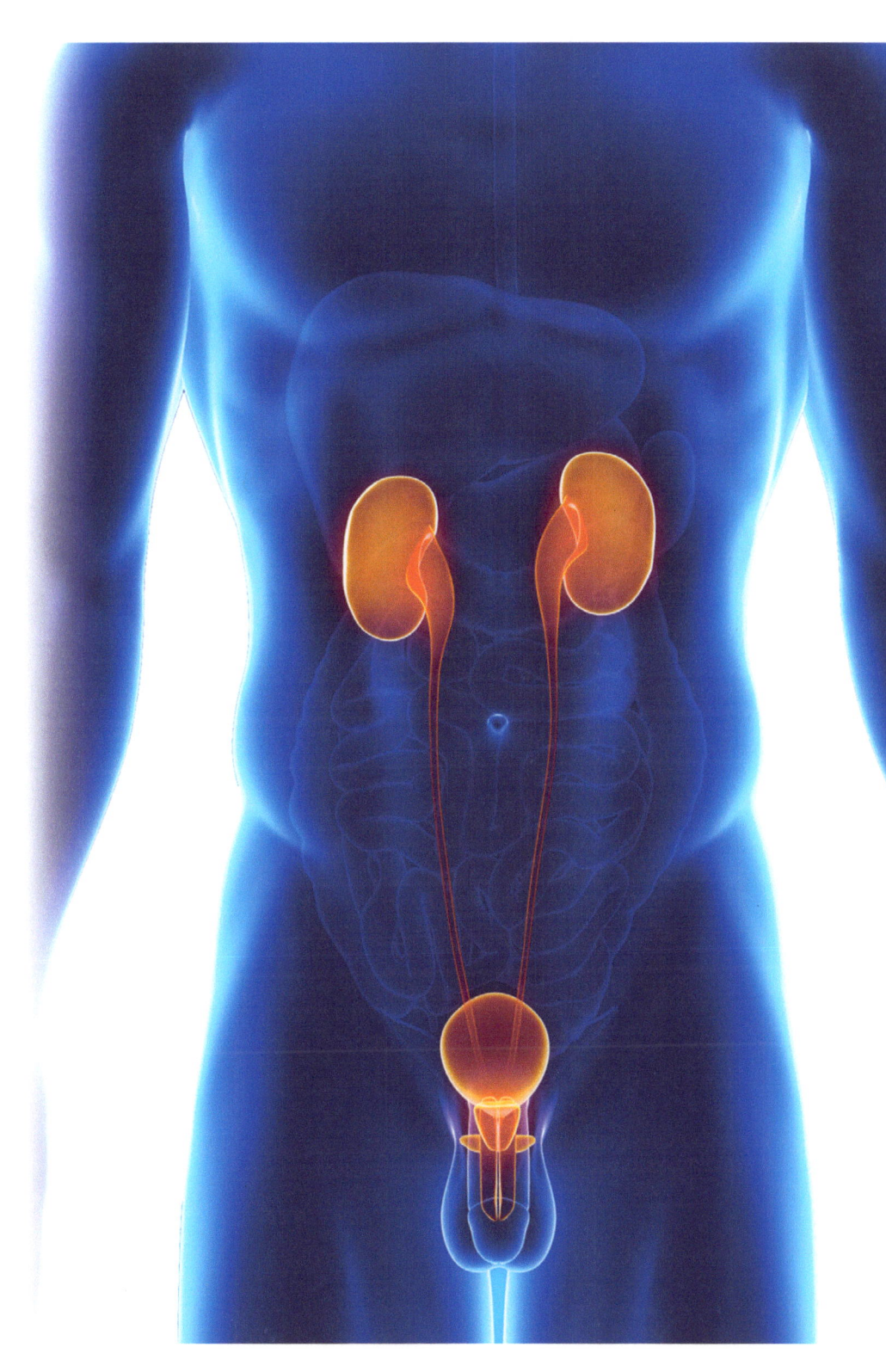

Urinary system

TABLE OF CONTENTS

ANATOMY	95
KIDNEYS	96
URETERS	97
BLADDER	97
URETHRA	97
PHYSIOLOGY	97
FORMATION OF URINE	98
Regulation of water and electrolyte balance	99
DISORDERS OF KIDNEY	99
Glomerulonephritis	99
Nephrotic syndrome	99
Kidney stones	99
Polycystic kidneys	100
Pyelonephritis	101
Renal failure	101
Renal hypertension	101
Uremic poisoning	101
Cystitis	102
ASSOCIATED PROBLEMS	102
Diabetes insipidus	102
Diabetes mellitus	102

URINARY SYSTEM

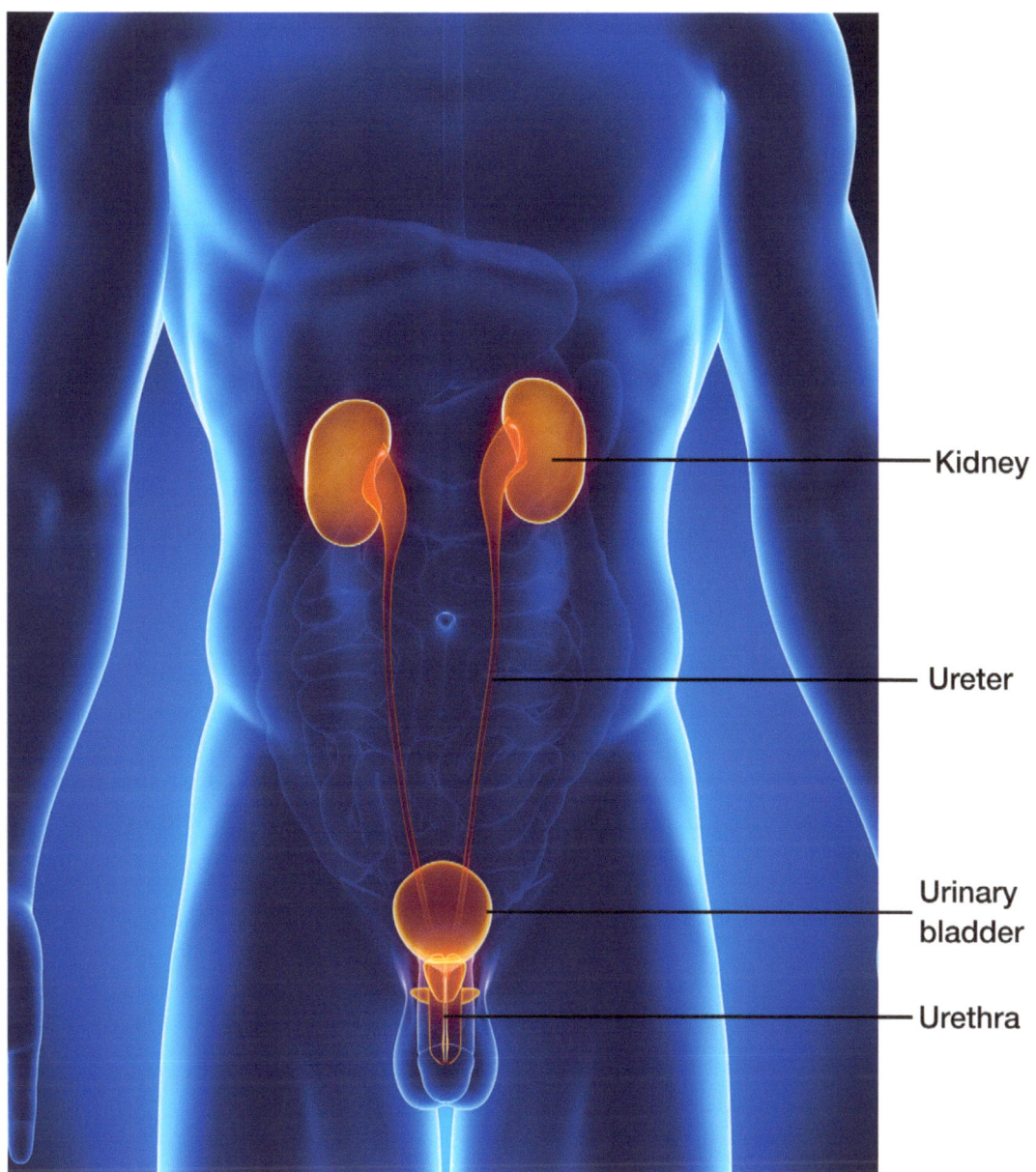

Figure 5-1 Urinary system

ANATOMY

The body breaks down the complex food materials that we take into simple nutrients. The nutrients are absorbed and are transformed into energy and waste products. The unwanted material if not removed will create an imbalance in the body. The urinary system is responsible for maintaining the balance of chemicals and water by removing the waste products such as urea, uric acid, ammonia, creatinine and bilirubin which are formed as a result of the metabolism. In addition to these chemicals substances such as alcohol, drugs, and toxins are also removed through the urinary system.

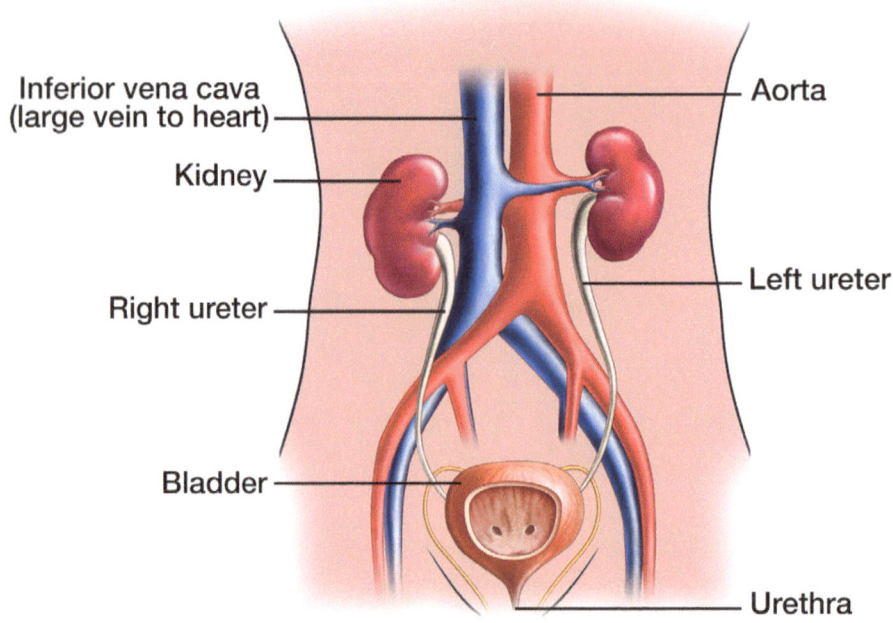

Figure 5-2 Anatomy of urinary system

Urinary system consists of two kidneys, two ureters, a muscular urinary bladder, and the urethra.

KIDNEYS

The kidneys are a pair of purplish-brown organs located below the ribs towards the middle of the back. They are bean shaped structures that weigh about 150 g each. The right kidney is slightly lower than the left kidney in order to accommodate the liver.

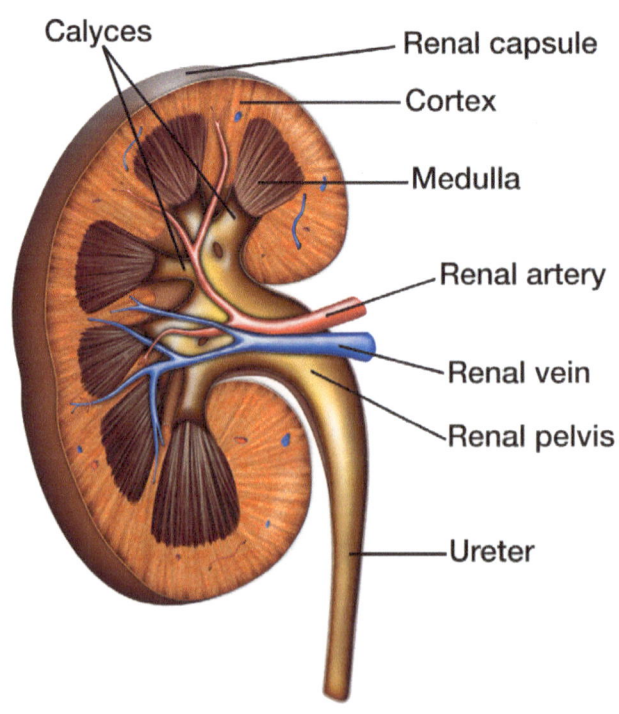

Figure 5-3 Anatomy of kidneys

Each kidney contains about 2 million filtering units called nephrons which are the structural and functional unit of kidney. Each nephron consists of a ball formed of small blood capillaries called glomerulus. The glomerulus is encircled by a cup-shaped part of nephron known as bowman capsule which is connected to a small tube called the renal tubule. Water with other waste substances forms the urine and passes through the nephrons down the collecting tubules of the kidney. Thousands of such collecting tubules lead to the renal pelvis, a basin-like area in the central part of the kidney. Small, cup-like regions of the renal pelvis are called calices or calyces. There are major and minor calyces based on their size. The inner concave surface of the kidney has a region called hilum where the renal vessels and the ureter connect to the kidney.

- The right kidney is slightly lower than the left kidney in order to accommodate the liver
- To locate the kidneys put your hands on your hips and they are located just about where your thumbs are
- Each kidney contain upto two million nephrons which are responsible for filtering the blood and removing waste products

URETERS

The ureters are narrow tubes that carry urine from the kidneys to the bladder. Muscles in the ureter walls continually tighten and relax forcing urine downward, away from the kidneys. About every 10 to 15 seconds, small amounts of urine are emptied into the bladder from the ureters.

BLADDER

The bladder is a triangle-shaped hollow muscular organ located in the lower abdomen. It is held in place by the ligaments that are attached to other organs and the pelvic bones. The bladder walls relax and expand to store urine, and contract and flatten to empty urine through the urethra. A healthy adult bladder can store up to 700 ml of urine for two to five hours. The outlet of the bladder is equipped with two circular sphincter muscles that help keep urine from leaking by closing tightly like a rubber band.

- A healthy adult bladder can store up to 700 ml of urine for two to five hours

URETHRA

Urethra is a tube that allows urine to pass outside the body. In a male body, it passes through the prostate gland and is a common passageway for both semen and urine. In females, the urethra opens at the vulva as the urethral orifice is not connected to the reproductive system.

PHYSIOLOGY

The kidneys play an important role in filtering the harmful substances from the blood. The important functions of kidneys include the following:

- Removal of waste products of metabolism from the blood in the form of urine.
- Keep a stable balance of salts and other substances in the blood.
- Produce erythropoietin, a hormone that aids the formation of red blood cells.

FORMATION OF URINE

Blood enters each kidney through the right and left renal arteries. After the renal artery enters the kidney, it branches into smaller and smaller arteries. The smallest arteries are called the arterioles, and are located throughout the outer cortex of the kidney. Each arteriole in the cortex of the kidney leads to the capillaries which form a tiny ball called the glomerulus. The kidneys produce urine by a process of filtration. As blood passes through the glomeruli, the walls of each glomerulus are thin enough to permit water, salts, sugar, urea and other nitrogenous wastes such as creatinine and uric acid to leave the bloodstream. These materials are collected in a tiny, cup-like structure called the bowman capsule, which surrounds each glomerulus. The walls of the glomeruli prevent large substances such as proteins and blood cells from filtering into the bowman capsule. Large substances remain in the blood and normally do not appear in urine.

- The volume of blood that passes through the kidneys every day is over 180 liters (50 gallons)
- Only 0.1% of blood that the kidney filters is converted to urine

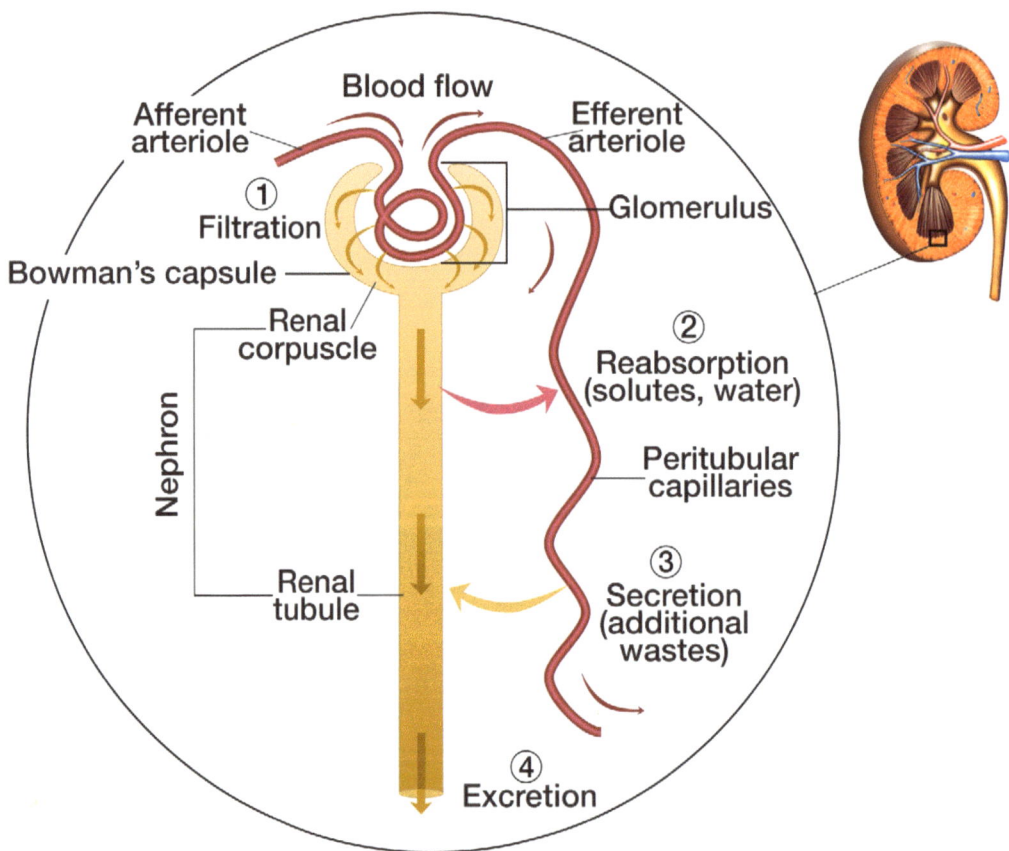

Figure 5-4 Formation of urine

Attached to each bowman capsule is a long, twisted tube called the renal tubule. As water, sugar, salts, urea, and other wastes pass through the renal tubule, most of the water, all of the sugar, and some salts such as sodium return to the bloodstream through the tiny capillaries surrounding each tubule. This reabsorption ensures that the body retains essential substances such as sugar, water, and salts. The final process in the formation of urine is the secretion of some substances from the bloodstream into the renal tubule most of which are waste products of metabolism that become toxic.

Therefore, only wastes, water, salts, acids, and some drugs remain in the renal tubule. Each renal tubule, which at this stage contains urine, ends in a larger collecting tubule. Through the collecting tubules, urine reaches the renal pelvis. The renal pelvis narrows into the ureter, which carries the urine to the urinary bladder where the urine is temporarily stored. As the bladder fills up, pressure is placed on the base of the bladder, which causes the desire to urinate. When an individual feels the need to urinate, the brain signals the bladder muscles to tighten, which squeeze urine out of the bladder and also signals the sphincter muscles to relax to let urine exit the bladder through the urethra. When all the signals occur in the correct order, normal urination occurs.

REGULATION OF WATER AND ELECTROLYTE BALANCE

The balance between the intake and the output of water and electrolytes is maintained largely by the kidney. Therefore, for maintenance of homeostasis (the state of equilibrium of bodily fluids) the intake of water and electrolytes must be precisely matched. The kidneys adjust their excretion rates to match intake of water and electrolytes. This is governed mainly by a person's eating and drinking habits. The kidney eliminates foreign chemicals and most toxins that are ingested and produced by the body. Additionally, the kidney has other functions such as regulation of blood pressure, regulation of the acid-base balance, production of blood and absorption of vitamins D. There is a disruption of these homeostatic function and abnormalities of body fluid volumes and composition in chronic kidney diseases or acute failure of kidneys.

DISORDERS OF KIDNEY

GLOMERULONEPHRITIS

Inflammation of the glomerulus is referred to as glomerulonephritis. It may develop as a part of a systemic disorder or may be idiopathic (unknown cause). It can also occur after an acute infection, as in poststreptococcal glomerulonephritis. Most patients recover spontaneously, but in some cases the disease becomes chronic which can result in high blood pressure, albuminuria (protein seeps through damaged glomerular walls), renal failure, and uremia. This condition can be treated with drugs when mild, but dialysis or transplant may be necessary in chronic cases.

- Diabetes and high blood pressure are the most common causes of kidney diseases.
- Most kidney diseases affect the nephrons and destroy them, but this will be apparent after many years as the process is very slow

NEPHROTIC SYNDROME

Nephrotic syndrome is a condition where there is excessive protein loss in the urine (proteinuria). It is also referred to as nephrosis. In addition to proteinuria, symptoms include edema and susceptibility to infections. Drugs may be useful to heal the leaky glomerulus.

KIDNEY STONES

Condition of stone formation in kidneys is referred to as nephrolithiasis. Kidney stones are usually composed of uric acid or calcium salts. Conditions associated with an increase in the concentration of calcium like parathyroid gland tumors or high levels of uric acid in the blood as in gouty arthritis

- Kidney stones are usually composed of uric acid or calcium salts

may contribute to the formation of calculi. Stones often lodge in the ureter or bladder as well as in the renal pelvis and may require removal. Treatment is usually done by noninvasive means like extracorporeal shock wave lithotripsy where the large stones are broken down to smaller ones and are passed along with urine.

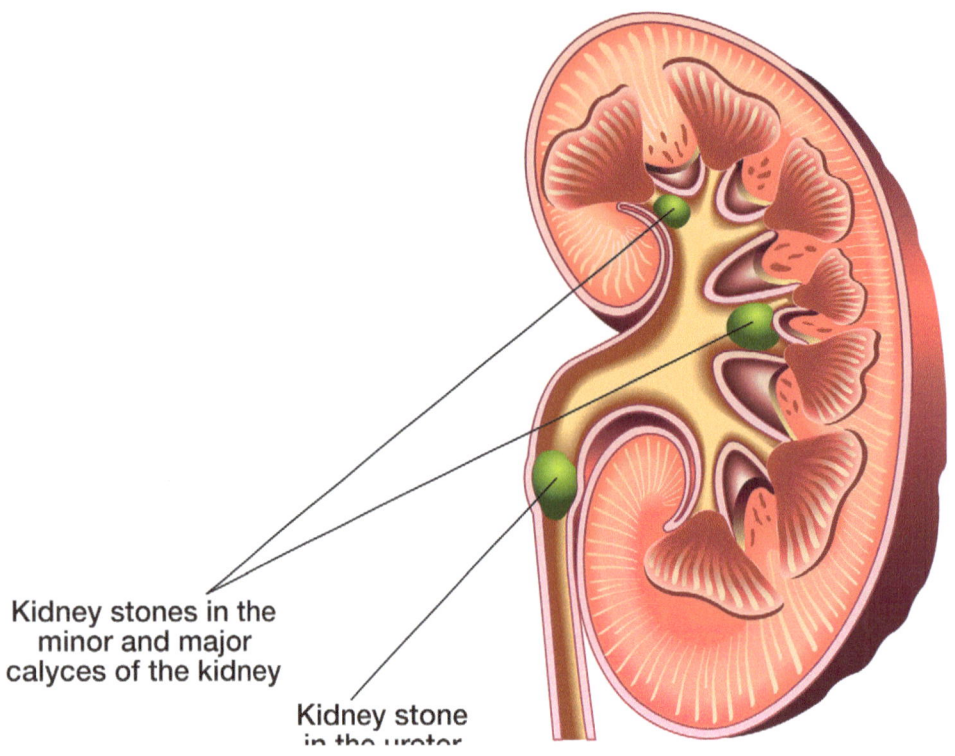

Figure 5-5 Kidney stones

POLYCYSTIC KIDNEYS

Polycystic kidneys refers to a condition where multiple fluid-filled sacs in the kidney are formed. This is a hereditary condition that usually remains asymptomatic until adult life. Cysts progressively develop in both kidneys leading to nephromegaly and renal failure.

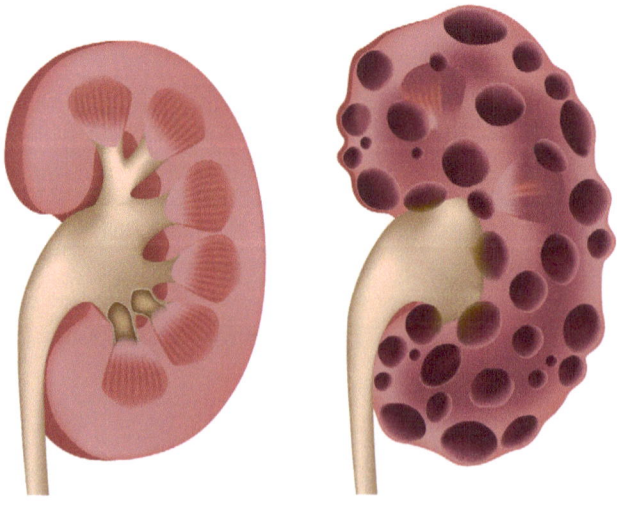

Figure 5-6 Polycystic kidneys

PYELONEPHRITIS

Inflammation of the renal pelvis and renal medulla is called pyelonephritis. It is caused by bacterial infection. In acute pyelonephritis pus is found in the urine (pyuria). Treatment consists of antibiotics and surgical correction of any obstruction to urine flow.

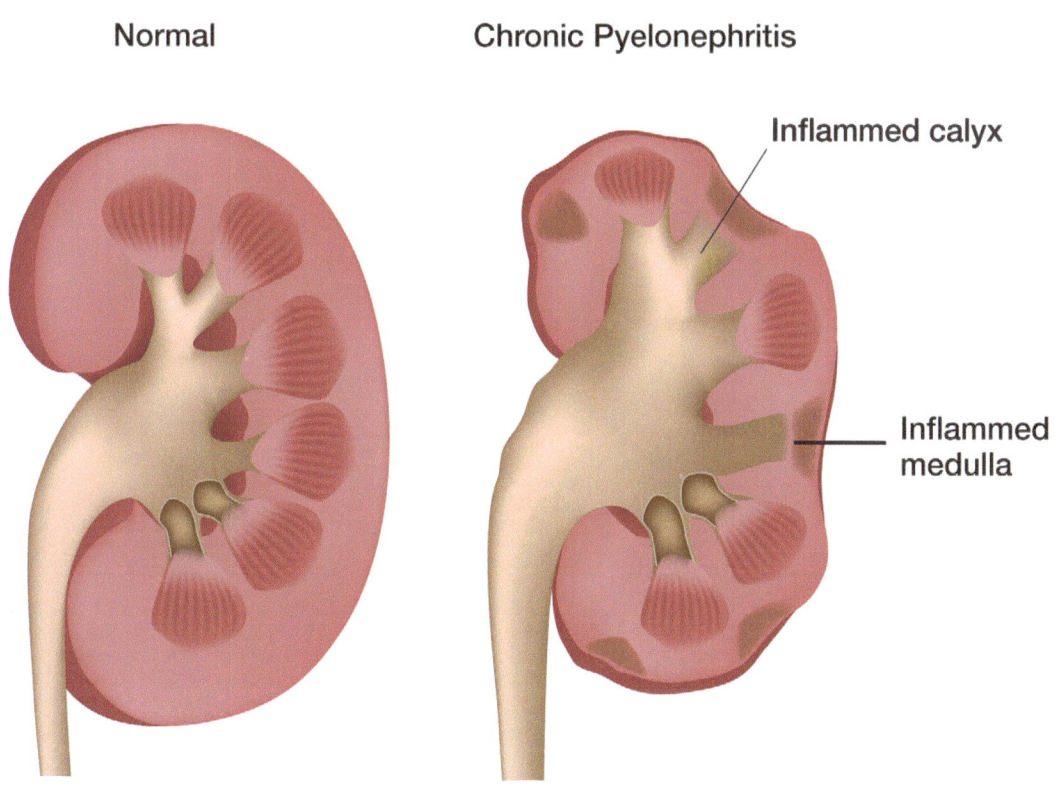

Figure 5-7 Pyelonephritis

RENAL FAILURE

Failure of the kidney to excrete urine is referred to as renal failure. In this condition, the kidney stops excreting waste products of metabolism. Renal failure may be acute or chronic, reversible or progressive and mild or severe. The final phase of chronic renal failure is called the end-stage renal disease (ESRD). If untreated, the condition is fatal. In chronic cases it is treated with dialysis until the kidneys can be replaced from suitable donors.

RENAL HYPERTENSION

Renal hypertension is a condition where there is an increase in the blood pressure resulting from a kidney disease. Renal hypertension is the most common type of secondary hypertension. If the cause of high blood pressure is not known, it is called the essential hypertension. Chronic essential hypertension can damage the kidney tissue.

UREMIC POISONING

Uremic poisoning is a condition where the kidneys fail to eliminate excess urea in the blood. The name simply means the urine in the blood. Whitish crystals of urea may even appear as stain, a mechanism by which the sweat glands try to discard the urea.

CYSTITIS

Infection and inflammation of the bladder is called cystitis. It is often asymptomatic; however, most of the time symptoms such hematuria, polyuria, burning in genitals on voiding can occur. A rise in temperature is also experienced.

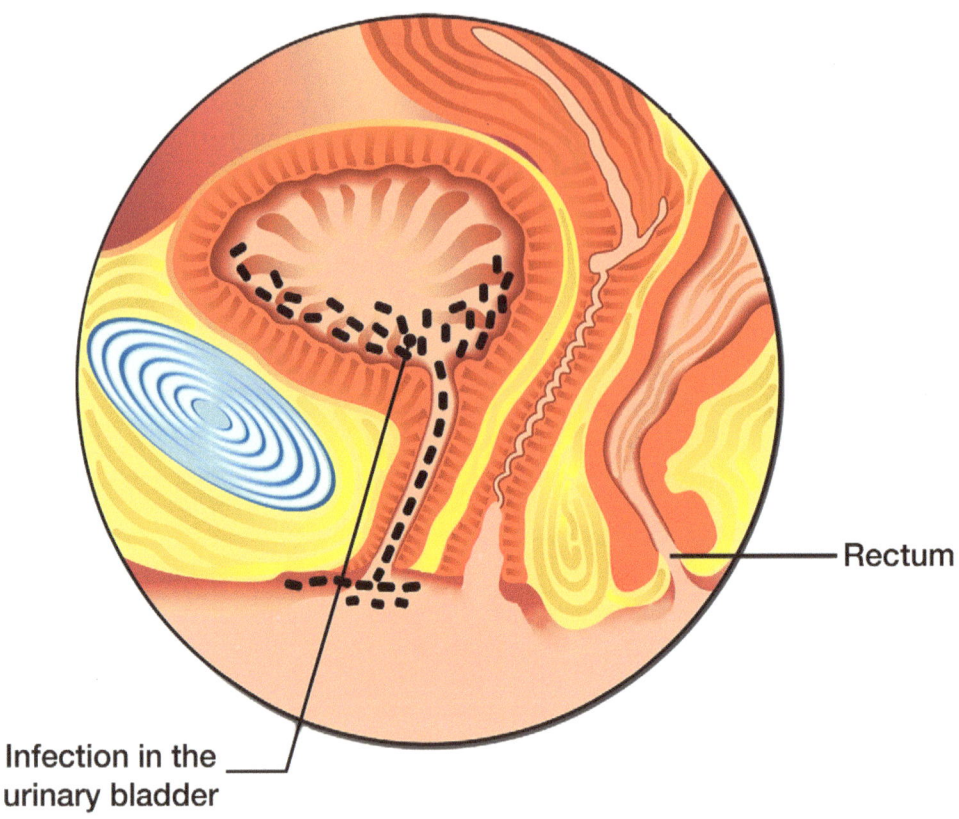

Figure 5-8 Cystitis

ASSOCIATED PROBLEMS

DIABETES INSIPIDUS

Inadequate secretion or resistance of the kidney to the action of antidiuretic hormone where there is excess elimination of water in urine. Insipidus means tasteless, reflecting that the urine is very dilute and watery. The endocrine disorder is treated to address this condition.

DIABETES MELLITUS

In diabetes mellitus there is inadequate secretion or improper utilization of insulin. Major symptoms of diabetes mellitus are glycosuria (glucose in urine), hyperglycemia (increased blood sugar), polyuria (increased urination), and polydipsia (increased thirst), polyphagia (increased eating). Mellitus means sweet, reflecting the content of the urine. The term diabetes is commonly used to refer to diabetes mellitus, rather than diabetes insipidus.

Chapter 6

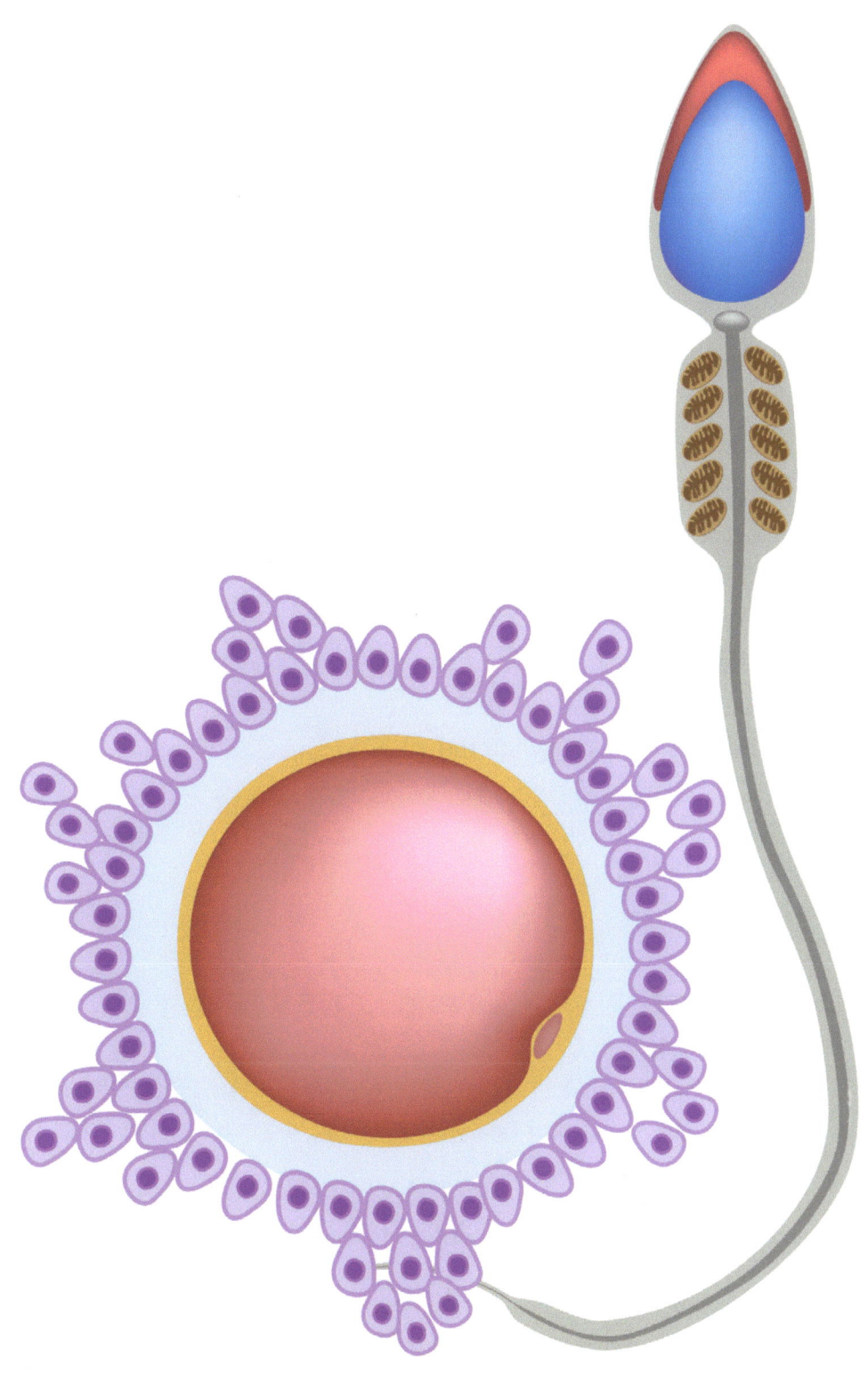

Reproductive system

TABLE OF CONTENTS

- [FEMALE REPRODUCTIVE SYSTEM](#) 106
- [OVARIES](#) 106
- [FALLOPIAN TUBES](#) 107
- [UTERUS](#) 107
- [EXTERNAL GENITALIA](#) 108
- [BREAST](#) 108
- [MENSTRUAL CYCLE](#) 109
- [PREGNANCY](#) 111
- [HORMONAL INTERACTIONS](#) 114
- [DISORDERS OF FEMALE REPRODUCTIVE SYSTEM](#) 114
    - Amenorrhea 114
    - Dysmenorrhea 114
    - Leukorrhea 115
    - Osteoporosis 115
    - Salpingitis, anexitis, cervicitis, vaginitis 116
    - Uterine fibroids 116
    - Uterine prolapse 116
    - Polycystic ovary syndrome (PCOS) 117
- [MALE REPRODUCTIVE SYSTEM](#) 118
- [TESTIS](#) 118
- [EPIDIDYMIS](#) 119
- [VAS DEFERENS](#) 119
- [PROSTATE GLAND](#) 120
- [DISORDERS OF MALE REPRODUCTIVE SYSTEM](#) 121
    - Phimosis 121
    - Hydrocele 121
    - Sexually transmitted diseases 121
    - Chlamydial infection 121
    - Gonorrhea 121
    - Herpes genitalis 121
    - Syphilis 121
    - Benign prostatic hypertrophy (Prostate enlargement) 122

REPRODUCTIVE SYSTEM

The process by which organisms produce their offspring is referred to as reproduction. The complex system consisting of the male or female reproductive organs, associated ducts, and external genitalia dedicated to the function of reproduction is called the reproductive system.

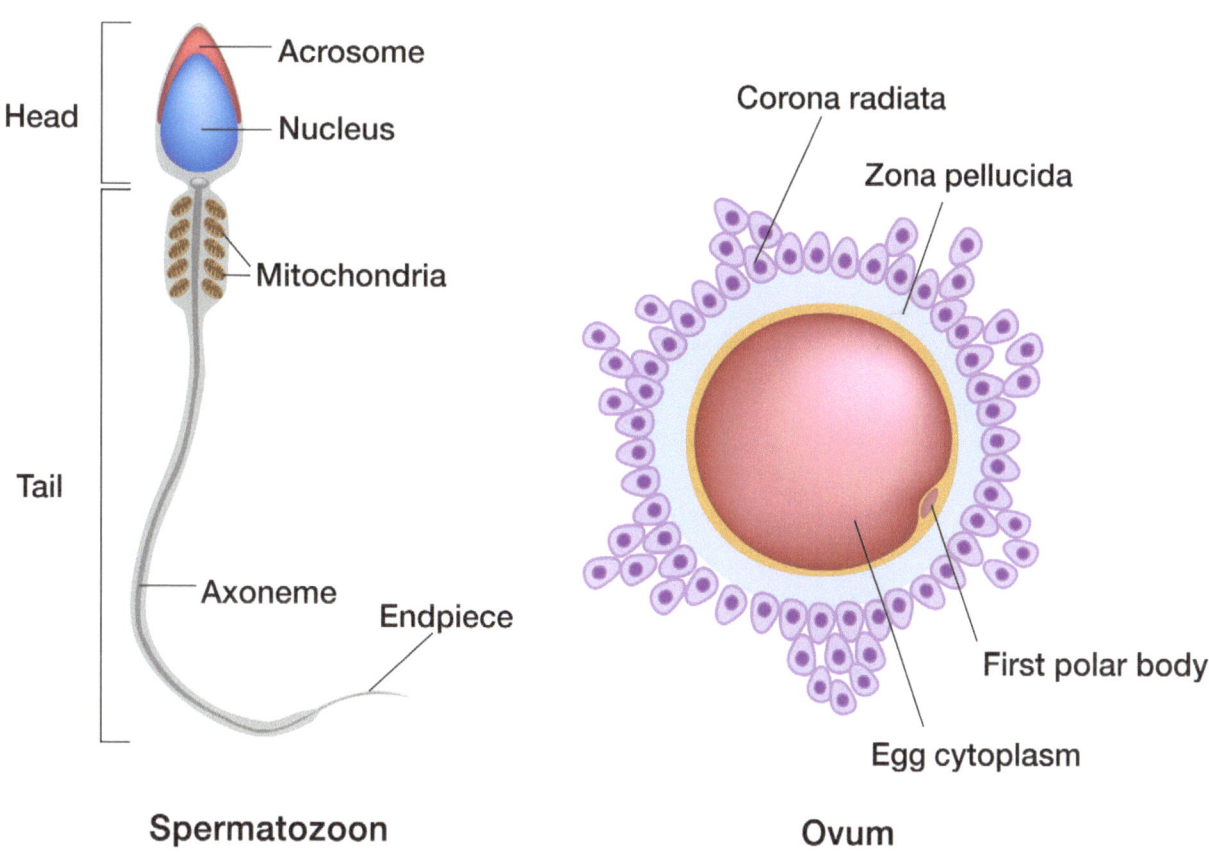

Figure 6-1 Spermatozoon & Ovum

The sexual reproduction is the union of the nuclei of the female sex cell (ovum) and the male sex cell (sperm) that results in the creation of a new individual. Each sex cell, also called a gamete, contains exactly half the number of chromosomes that a normal body cell contains. When the nuclei of ovum and sperm cell unite, it contains a full, normal complement of hereditary material. Gametes are produced in special organs called gonads in both males and females. The female gonads are called ovaries, and the male gonads are called testes.

FEMALE REPRODUCTIVE SYSTEM

The female reproductive system consists of organs that produce ovum and provide a place for the growth of the embryo into a normal infant. It consists of organs including external genitalia, vagina, uterus, two fallopian tubes, and two ovaries. The breasts are accessory sex organs.

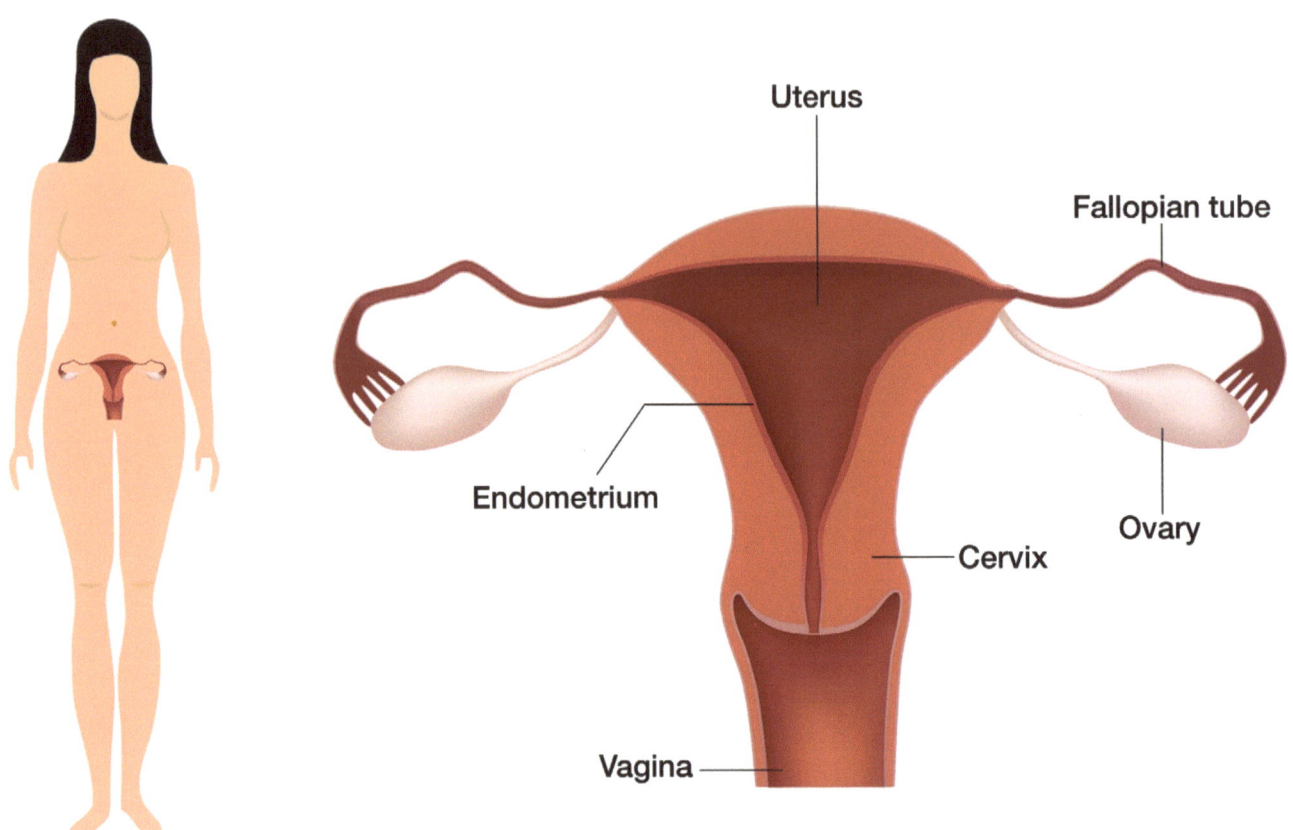

Figure 6-2 Female reproductive system

OVARIES

The ovaries are a pair of small, almond-shaped organs located in the lower abdomen. They produce the female reproductive cell called ovum or egg from the graafian follicle cell. It also produces hormones namely estrogen and progesterone. An ovary barely weighs seven grams. At birth there are about 1,000,000 ova or eggs, by puberty there are only about 400,000 ova, and at menopause there may be few or none remaining.

- The female egg is the largest cell in the human body and male sperm is the smallest cell in the body

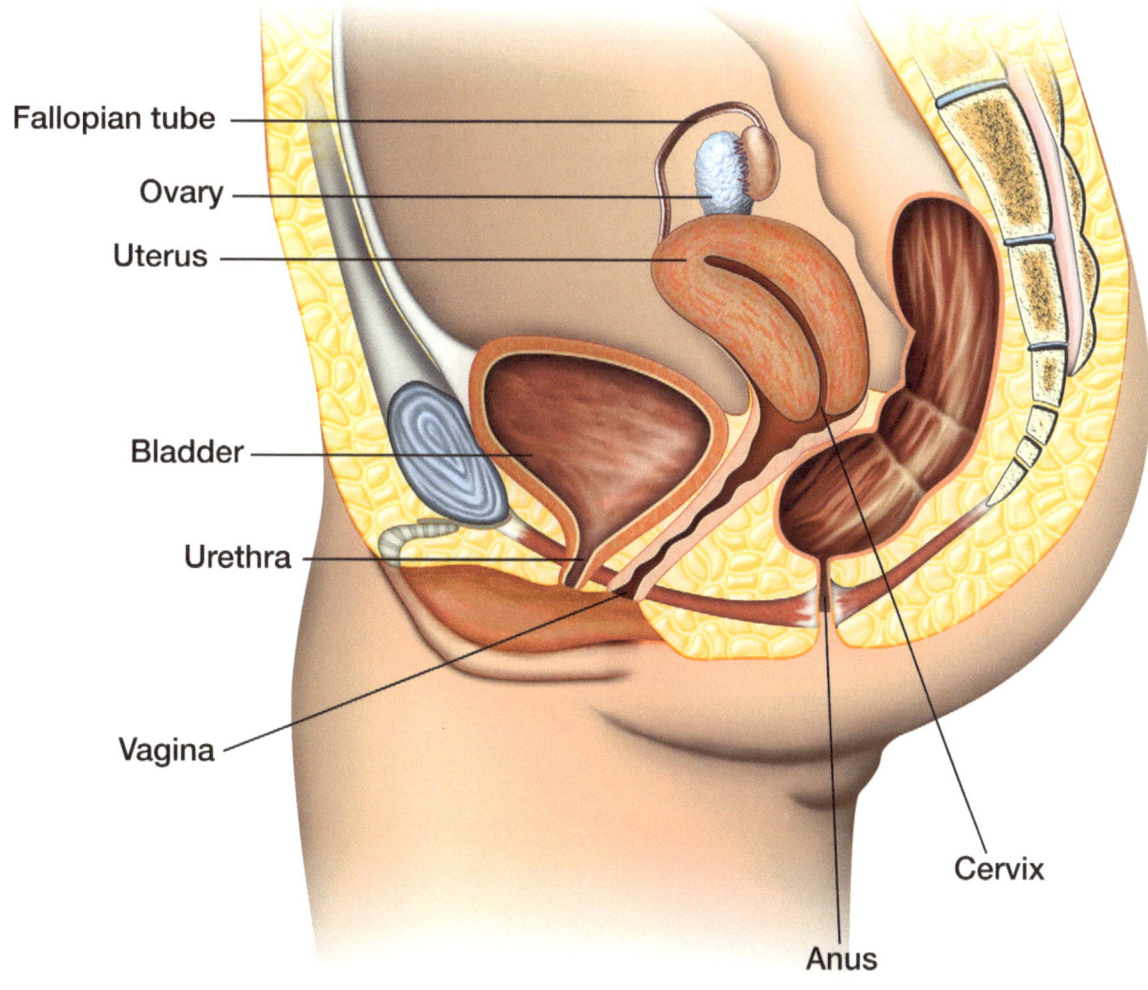

Fig 6-3 Female reproductive system- side view

FALLOPIAN TUBES

The fallopian tubes are tubes that lead from each ovary to the uterus, which is a muscular organ situated between the urinary bladder and the rectum. They have finger-like projections at the end of ovaries, which collect the ovum when they are mature and move them to the uterus.

UTERUS

The uterus is a pear-shaped organ with muscular walls and a mucous membrane lining filled with a rich supply of blood vessels. The rounded upper portion of the uterus is called the fundus, and the larger central section is called the body of uterus. The inner specialized epithelial mucosal layer of the uterus is called the endometrium, the middle muscular layer is called the myometrium, and the outer membranous tissue layer is referred to as uterine serosa.

The narrow, lower portion of the uterus is the cervix which means neck. The cervical opening leads into a 3-inch-long tube called the vagina, which opens to the outside of the body. The uterus is normally in a bent-forward position and about 3 inches in length in a nonpregnant woman. The uterus performs the supreme wonder of the universe by transforming a few cells into a complex new human being.

EXTERNAL GENITALIA

The external genitalia (external organs of reproduction) of the female are collectively called the vulva. The labia majora are the outer lips of the vagina, and the labia minora are the smaller, inner lips. The hymen is a mucous membrane that normally partially covers the entrance to the vagina. The clitoris and bartholin glands are also parts of the vulva.

The vagina is a tube extending from the uterus to the exterior of the body. Bartholin glands are two small, rounded glands on either side of the vaginal orifice. These glands produce a mucous secretion that lubricates the vagina. The clitoris is an organ of sensitive, erectile tissue located anterior to the vaginal orifice and in front of the urethral meatus.

BREAST

The breasts, other wise called mammary glands, are located in the upper anterior region of the chest. They are composed of glandular tissue, containing milk glands that develop in response to hormones produced from the ovaries during puberty. The breasts also contain fibrous and fatty tissue, special lactiferous or milk-carrying ducts and sinuses which are cavities that carry milk to the opening, or nipple. The breast nipple is otherwise called the papilla which is surrounded by a dark-pigmented area called the areola.

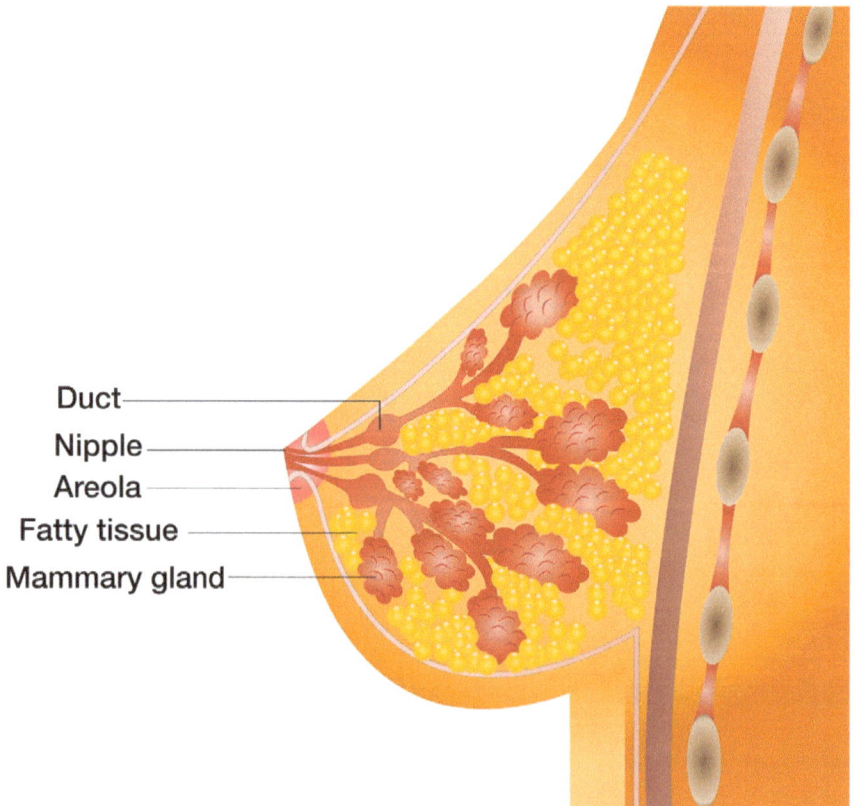

Fig 6-4 Healthy breast

MENSTRUAL CYCLE

The cyclic endometrial shedding and discharge of a bloody fluid from the uterus is referred to as menstrual cycle. The beginning of menstruation at the time of puberty is called menarche. Each menstrual cycle is of 28 days. These days can be grouped into four time periods, which are useful in describing the events of the cycle.

- There are nearly 400,000 egg cells in a female ovaries but only around 400 will get an opportunity to create a new life.

Days 1-5: This period is also called as menstrual period. During these days bloody fluid containing disintegrated endometrial cells, glandular secretions, and blood cells are discharged through the vagina.

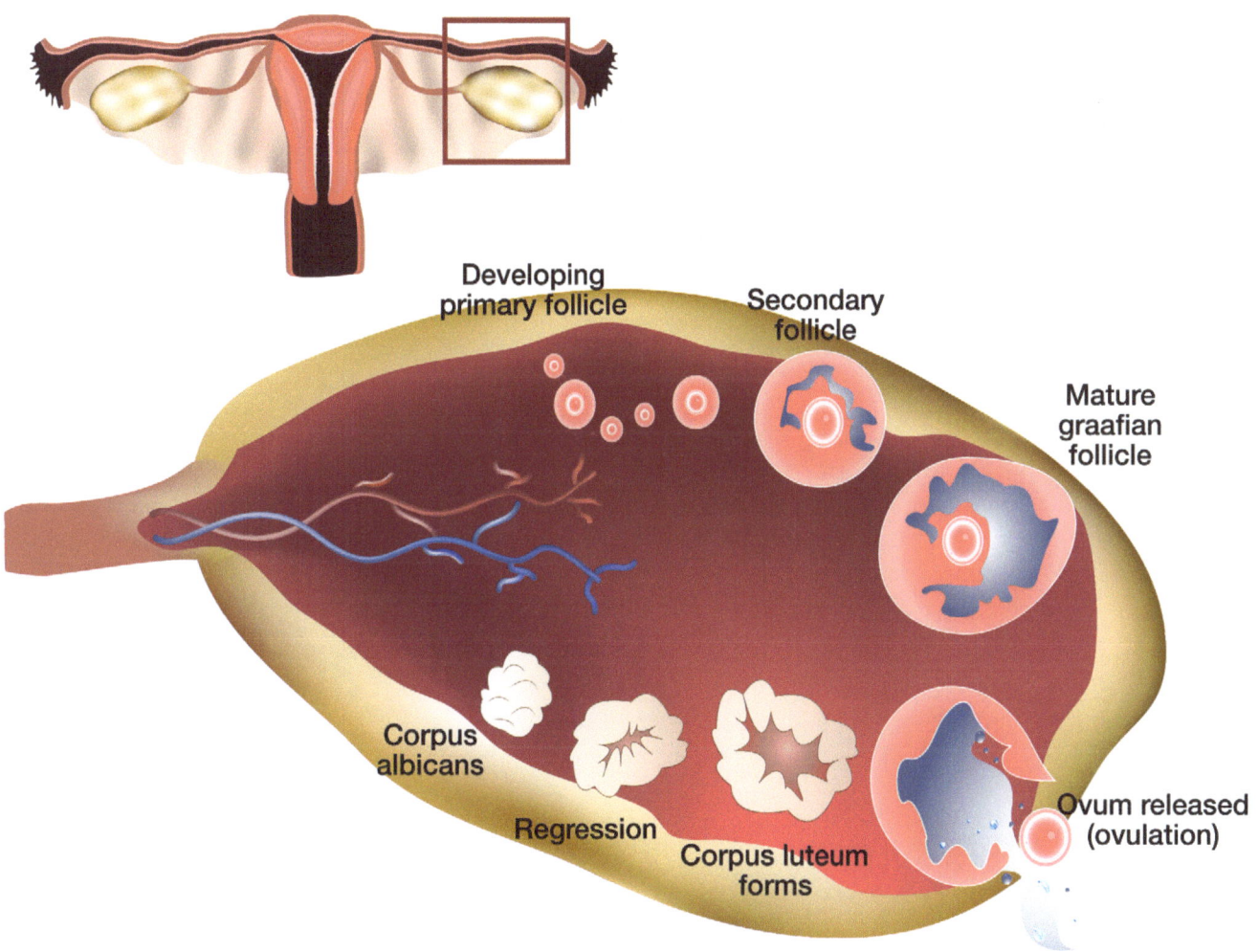

Fig 6-5 Stages of follicular development

The diagram represents various stages of follicular development. The primary follicles begins to mature to form graffian follicle. Simultaneously the ovum also increases in size.

Reproductive System

Days 6-12: After the menstrual period, the endometrium begins to repair itself as the hormone estrogen is released by the maturing graafian follicle in the ovaries. At this stage the primary follicles begins to mature to form Graafian follicles. This is also the period of the growth of the ovum in the graafian follicle.

Days 13-14: It is also referred to as ovulatory period, around the 14th day of the cycle, the graafian follicle ruptures and the egg leaves the ovary to travel slowly down the fallopian tube. The release of the ovum is called ovulation.

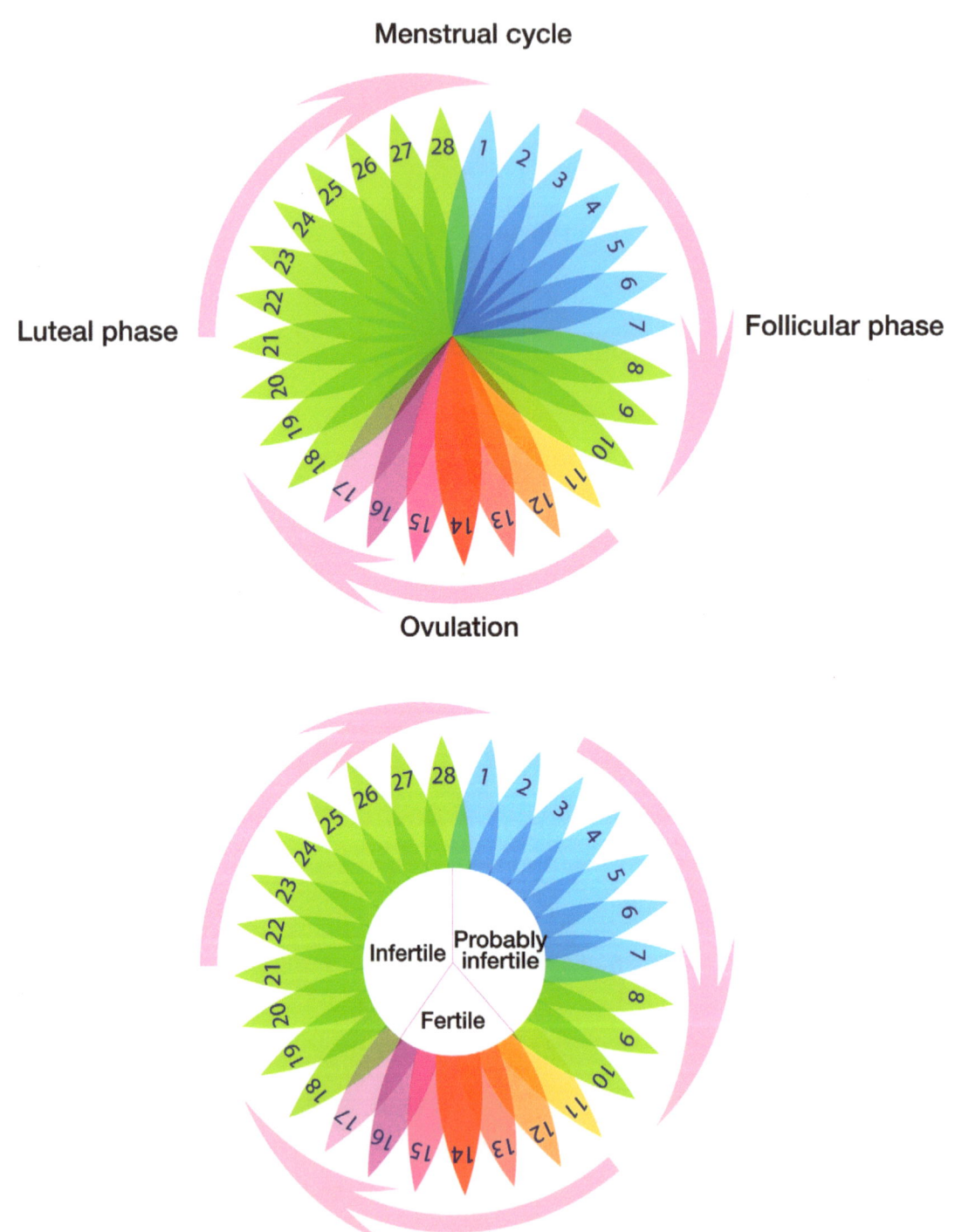

Fig 6-6 Phases of menstrual cycle

110   Reproductive System

Days 15-28: The empty graafian follicle fills with a yellow material and becomes known as the corpus luteum. The corpus luteum secretes two hormones, estrogen and progesterone. If pregnancy occurs, the corpus luteum functions as an endocrine organ during the entire pregnancy. If the pregnancy does not occur the corpus luteum in the ovary stops producing hormones. At this time, some women have symptoms of depression, breast tenderness, and irritability prior to menstruation. These symptoms are known as premenstrual syndrome. About 5 days after the fall in hormones, the uterine endometrium breaks down and the menstrual period begins .The corpus luteum remains active for two weeks and then degenerates forming a white scar called corpus albicans.

PREGNANCY

The condition of a female after conception until the birth of the baby is referred to as pregnancy or gestation.

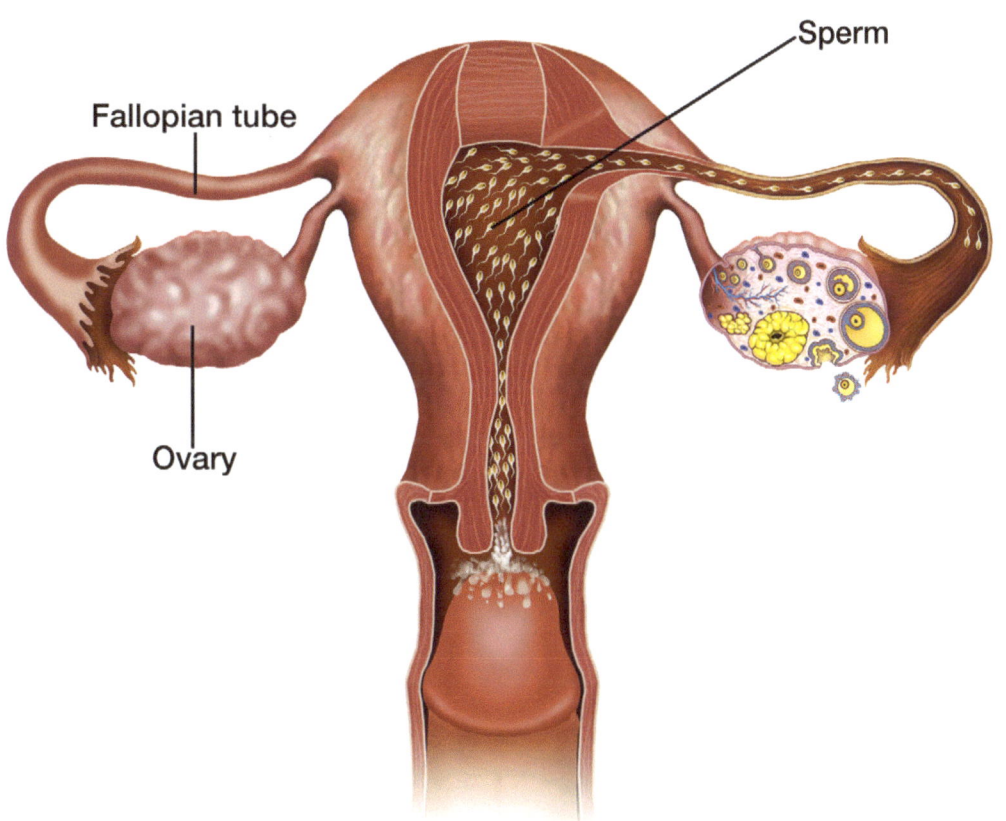

Fig 6-7 Fertilization

The process leading to pregnancy occurs when the female sex cell or oocyte and male sex cell spermatozoon merges. This is called conception or fertilization. The fused oocyte and spermatozoon is referred to as a zygote or fertilized egg. This fertilized egg travels to the uterus in six days and during this process rapid cell division begins. It continues to develop into what is known as blastocyst. The blastocyst finally attaches to the uterine wall and this process is known as implantation. Pregnancy begins with implantation.

- Our body was the size of the head of the pin when we were a fertilized egg.

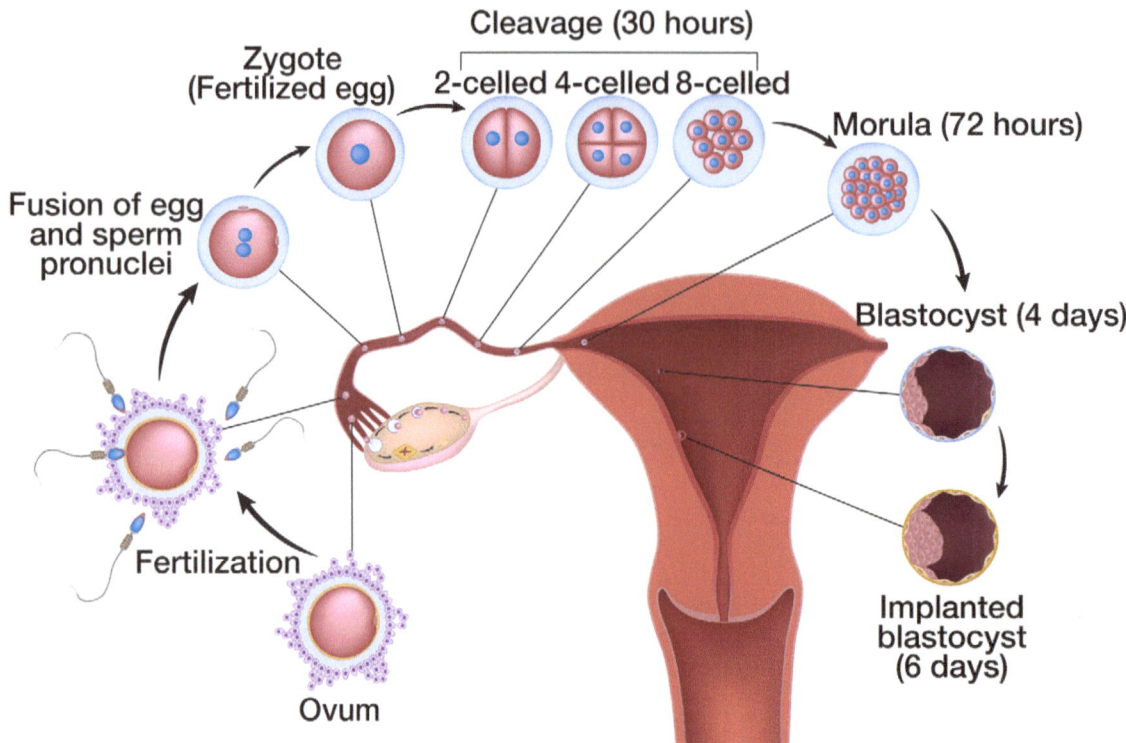

Fig 6-8 Implantation

The corpus luteum in the ovary continues to produce progesterone and estrogen, which support the vascular and muscular development of the uterine lining.

The placenta, a vascular organ, now forms within the uterine wall. The placenta is derived from maternal endometrium and from the chorion, which is the outermost membrane that surrounds the developing embryo. The amnion is the innermost of the embryonic membranes, and it holds the fetus suspended in an amniotic cavity surrounded by a fluid called the amniotic fluid, which usually ruptures or breaks during labor.

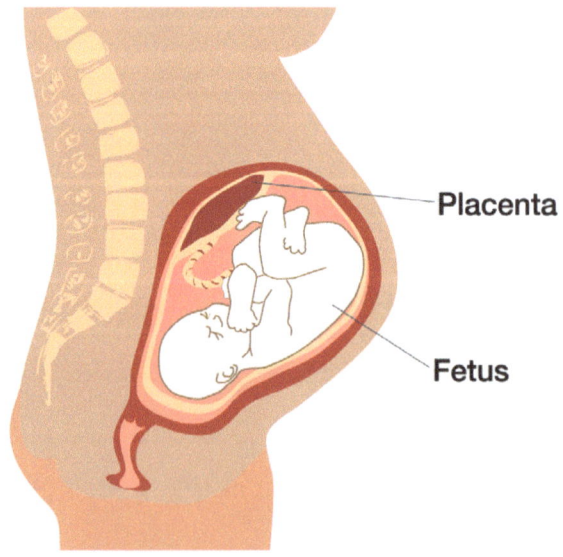

Fig 6-9 Pregnancy

The maternal blood and the fetal blood never mix during pregnancy, but important nutrients, oxygen, and wastes are exchanged as the blood vessels of the baby lie side by side with the mother's blood vessels in the placenta. The placenta produces its own hormone as it develops in the uterus. This placental hormone is called human chorionic gonadotropin (HCG). HCG is the hormone tested for in the urine of women who suspect that they are pregnant. HCG stimulates the corpus luteum to continue producing hormones until about the 3rd month of pregnancy, when the placenta itself takes over the endocrine function and releases estrogen and progesterone. Progesterone maintains the development of the placenta. Low levels of progesterone can lead to spontaneous abortion in pregnant women and menstrual irregularities in nonpregnant women.

The uterus normally lies in the pelvis. During pregnancy, the uterus expands as the fetus grows, and the superior part rises out of the pelvic cavity. By about 28-30 weeks, it occupies a large part of the abdominopelvic cavity.

The onset of true labor is marked by rhythmic contractions, dilation of the cervix, and a discharge of bloody mucus from the cervix and vagina. In a normal delivery position, the head appears first and is called cephalic presentation and helps to dilate the cervix. After the baby is delivered, the umbilical cord is expelled and cut.

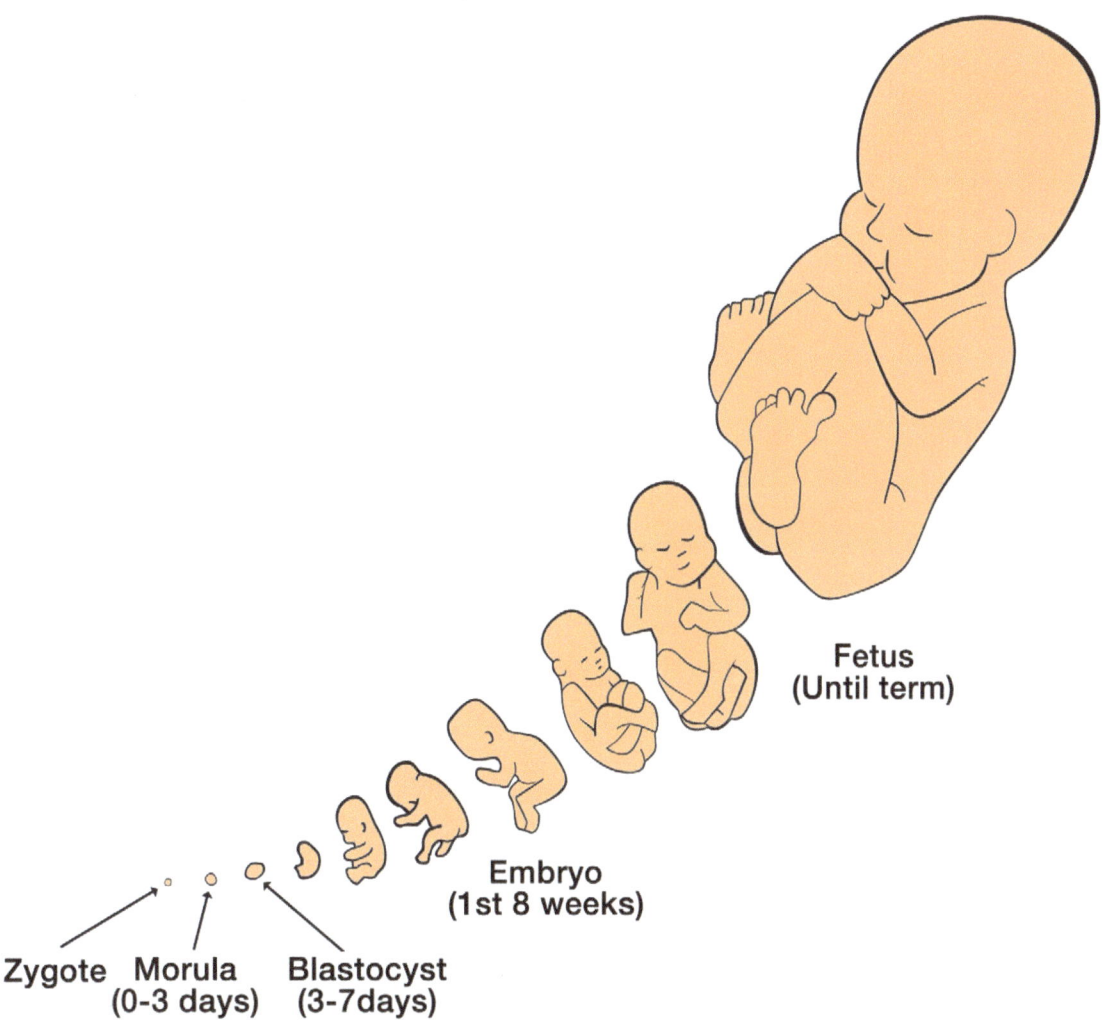

Fig 6-10 Development of fetus in the womb

Reproductive System

HORMONAL INTERACTIONS

The events of menstruation and pregnancy are dependent not only upon hormones from the ovaries but also on hormones from the pituitary gland. These pituitary gland hormones are follicle-stimulating hormone (FSH) and luteinizing hormone (LH). After the onset of menstruation, the pituitary gland begins to secrete FSH and LH, which stimulate the maturation of the ovum and ovulation. After ovulation, LH in particular influences the maintenance of the corpus luteum and its production of estrogen and progesterone.

During pregnancy, the high levels of estrogen and progesterone affect the pituitary gland itself by shutting off its production of FSH and LH. This means that while a woman is pregnant, additional eggs do not mature and ovulation cannot occur. This negative feedback is the principle behind the action of birth control pills. The pills contain varying amounts of estrogen and progesterone. As they are taken, the level of hormones rises in the blood. Negative feedback occurs, and the pituitary does not release FSH or LH. Without FSH or LH, ovulation cannot occur and the woman does not become pregnant.

Other female contraceptive measures include the IUD (intrauterine device) and the diaphragm. When the secretion of estrogen from the ovaries lessens and fewer egg cells are produced, menopause begins. Menopause is the gradual ending of the menstrual cycle and is a natural process resulting from the normal aging of the ovaries.

DISORDERS OF FEMALE REPRODUCTIVE SYSTEM

AMENORRHEA

Amenorrhea is a condition where there is absence of menstrual periods. Primary amenorrhea refers to the condition where menstruation has not begun, although the female has reached or passed the age when it should have commenced. It may be an indication of hormonal imbalance. Secondary amenorrhea is a condition where a woman of childbearing age, who previously had periods, has now stopped having them.

After menopause, between 40 and 53 years, which marks the end of a normal woman's reproductive cycle, there is a sequence of changes taking place because ovaries secrete less estrogen. There are fatty deposits in the arteries and, therefore, there are chances of heart attack, skin may become dry, muscles may stiffen and the female may become prone to osteoporosis (a condition where the bones become brittle due to reduction of calcium in the long bones). Irritability, depression, sleeping difficulty, headaches, palpitation, and fatigue are common; all these occur as a result of lack of hormones, which were present previously.

DYSMENORRHEA

The most familiar problem is dysmenorrhea, a term to denote painful menstruation. It is caused due to an imbalance of the sex hormones.

In some condition, exercise and movement aggravates the pain while rest improves the condition, which may be due to some mechanical abnormality or inflammation of pelvic organs.

Sometimes the dysmenorrhea may be spasmodic in nature characterized by disorderly spasmodic muscular contractions of the uterus. The pain usually develops on the 1st day of the period and resembles colic or spasm or a continuous ache. (In spasmodic dysmenorrhea it has been found out that pregnancy cures this condition. Many married women have not suffered as much from dysmenorrhea since pregnancy.)

LEUKORRHEA

This is an excessive discharge of a white or colorless secretion from the vagina. It is usually caused by an underlying infection. White discharge may be either physiological during periods of ovulation, coitus, etc or it can be pathological where usually an infective organism is isolated. Pathological discharge is usually excessive, foul smelling with associated lower abdominal pain or discomfort. Failure to recognize and treat this condition may lead to pelvic inflammatory disease and infertility.

OSTEOPOROSIS

Post-menopausal osteoporosis has become an increasing medical and social problem. Osteoporosis is the most widespread of all metabolic bone disorders. It is a condition in which bone mass is diminished to a point where fracture of skeleton can result either spontaneously or after minor trauma. It is a major cause of fractures is postmenopausal women and in the elderly. The condition is often without any symptom until a fracture occurs. Sometimes the first symptom is usually lumbar pain caused by vertebral compression fracture and is often the result of some minor incident.

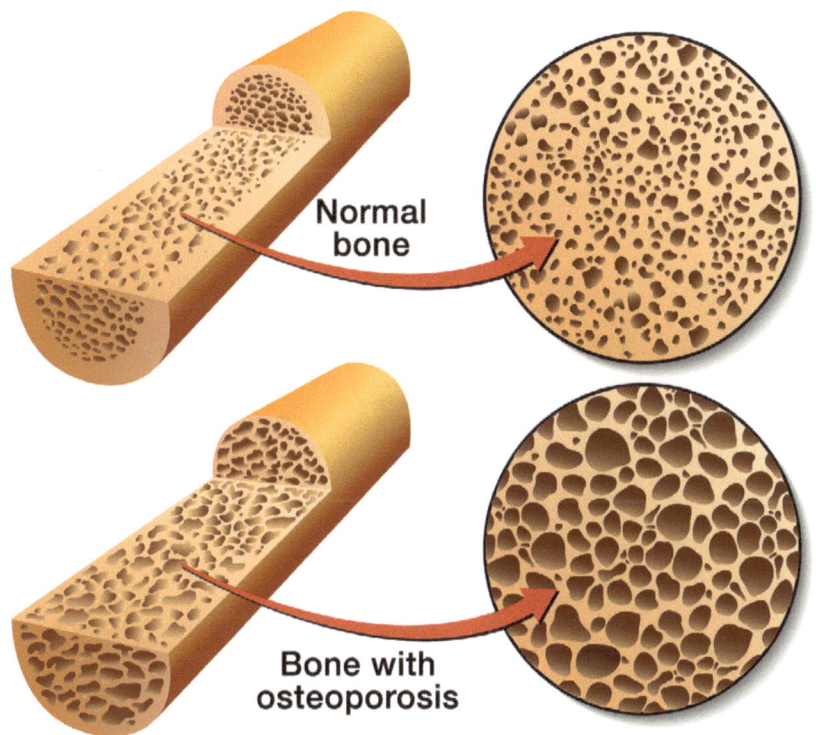

Fig 6-11 Osteoporosis

Many factors are associated with osteoporosis. These include estrogen deficiency, scoliosis, a sedentary lifestyle, and low calcium intake, early menopause, moderate to heavy alcohol consumption, smoking and stress. Women are much more prone to osteoporosis than men and bone loss accelerates in postmenopausal period.

However the major cause that attributes to osteoporosis include an age-related decrease in intestinal calcium absorption. Since there is inadequate calcium absorption, there is an increased dependence on calcium in the bone for maintenance of serum calcium in the body.

Directing the treatment towards improving calcium absorption is highly important in the treatment of postmenopausal osteoporosis.

SALPINGITIS, ADNEXITIS, CERVICITIS, VAGINITIS

Acute or chronic inflammation of the fallopian tubes is called salpingitis. The structures in close proximity to the uterus are called adnexa and inflammation of these structures is called Adnexitis. The inflammation of the neck of the uterus is called cervicitis. Inflammation of vaginal wall is called vaginitis. They are all the result of infection, usually by bacteria, which usually spreads upwards from the vagina.

UTERINE FIBROIDS

Uterine fibroids are the noncancerous tumors present in the muscle wall of the uterus, usually present in women above 35 years. Due to this, the periods are painful and heavy. This is accompanied by backache and in some cases swelling of lower abdomen occurs. This may also result in infertility, anemia and rarely degeneration of the muscle wall causing more pain. The uterine fibroids can be surgically removed.

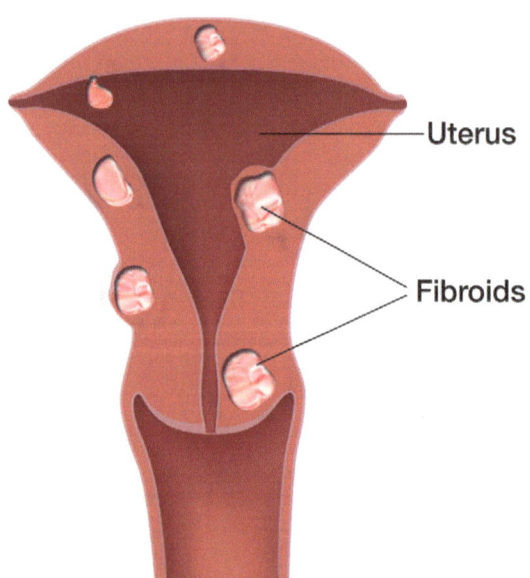

Fig 6-12 Uterine fibroids

UTERINE PROLAPSE

In this condition the uterus prolapses or slips through the vaginal orifice. It is a common disorder of elderly women due to the weakening of the supporting ligaments. There will be pain in the pelvis. Repeated or difficult childbirths are the major cause what attributes to this condition. The patient experiences a sensation that the contents of the uterus are dropping down or falling out of the vagina. Sometimes urine automatically flows out on coughing.

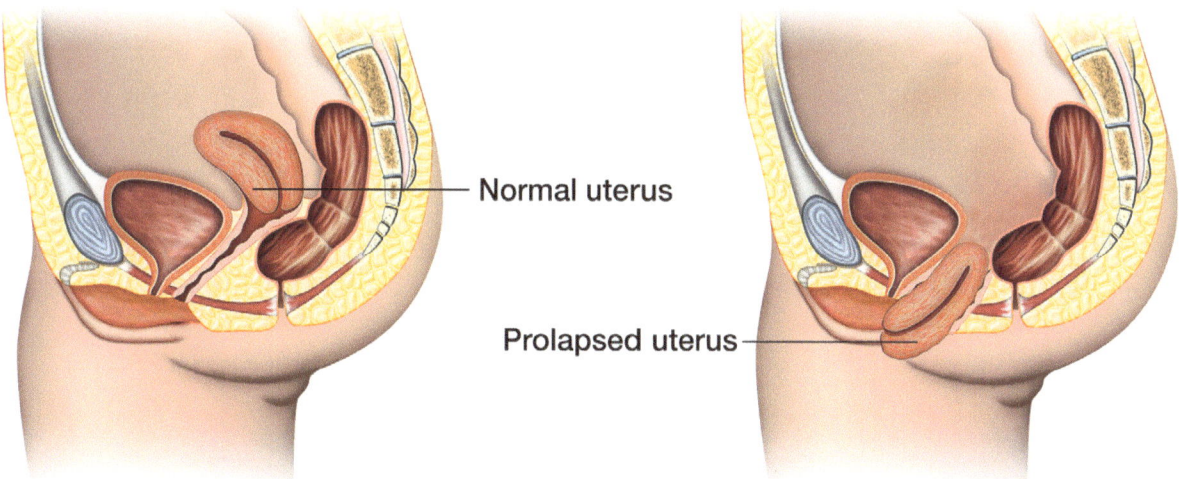

Fig 6-13 Prolapsed uterus

POLYCYSTIC OVARY SYNDROME (PCOS). PCOS is one of the most common female endocrine disorder in which there is hormonal imbalance due to the production of a hormone called androgen. Androgens are male hormones that females also make.

The ovaries produce higher than normal amounts of androgens which interfere with egg development and release. In PCOS the egg in these follicles do not mature and are not released. Instead they form small cysts in the ovary.

Girls with PCOS have irregular or missed periods because they are not ovulating every month nor releasing an egg every month. Women with PCOS have higher rates of miscarriage, premature delivery.

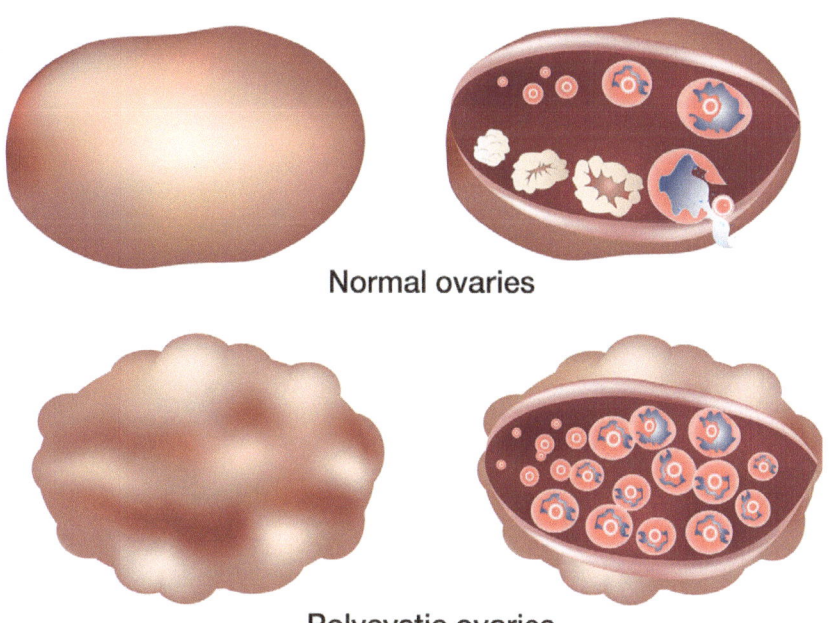

Fig 6-14 Polycystic ovaries

Reproductive System

MALE REPRODUCTIVE SYSTEM

The male reproductive system consists of organs that produce male gamete sperm. They also secrete hormones that support the formation and maturation of sperm and bring about male secondary sexual characteristics.

The primary male reproductive organs are testicles, the accessory organs include vas deferens, prostate gland, bulbourethral glands, penile urethra and penis.

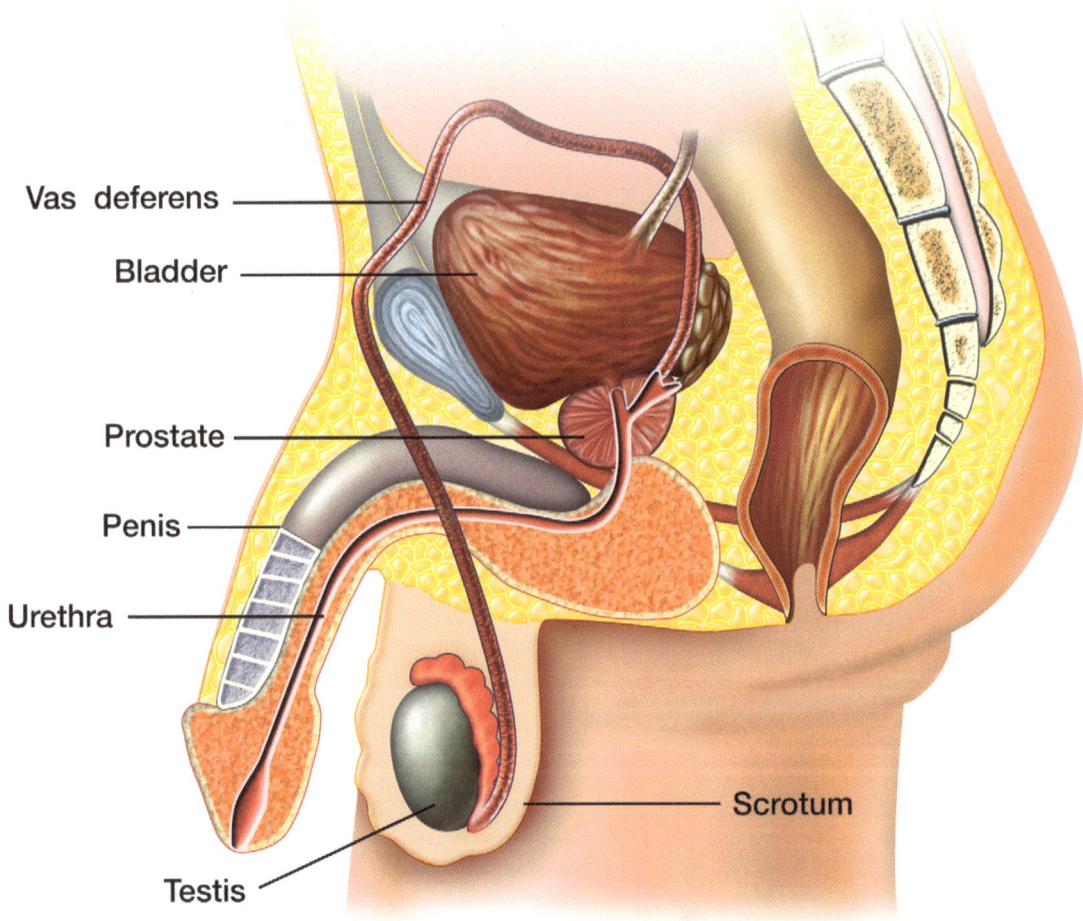

Fig 6-15 Male Reproductive System

TESTIS

The male gonads consist of a pair of testes also called testicles which are oval shaped organs that develop in the abdomen before descending during embryonic development into the scrotum. Scrotum is the sac that encloses the testes outside of the body.

The interior of a testis is composed of a large mass of narrow, coiled tubules called the seminiferous tubules. These tubules contain cells that manufacture spermatozoa. The seminiferous tubules are the functional tissue of the testis. Other cells in the testis, called interstitial cells, manufacture an important male hormone, testosterone.

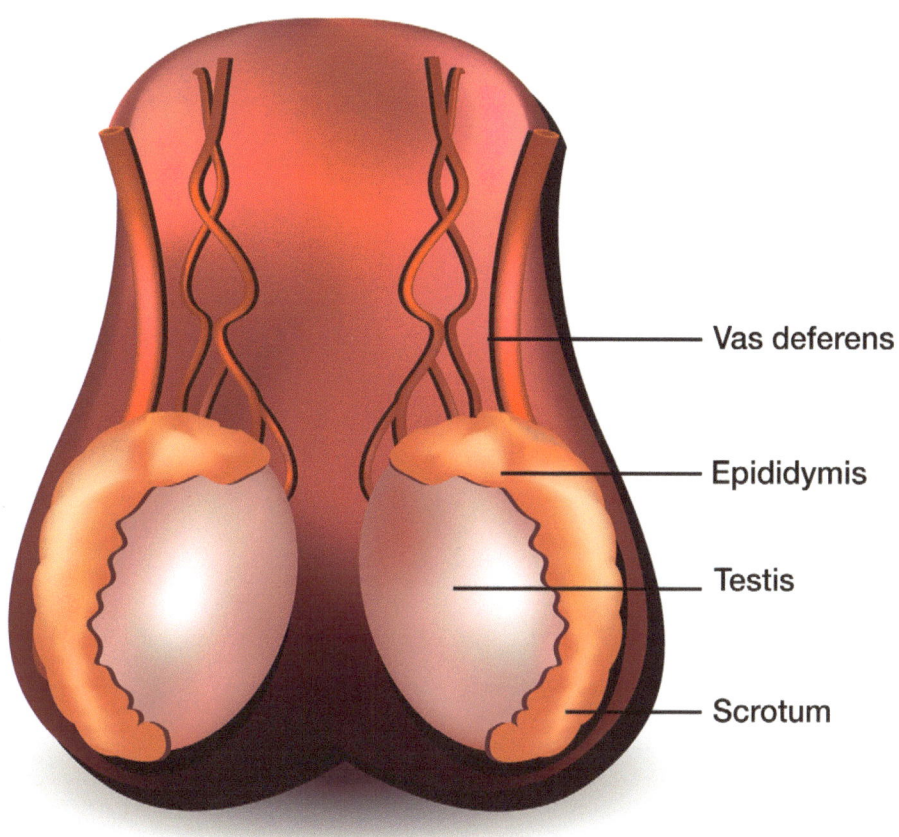

Fig 6-16 Testis

EPIDIDYMIS

After formation of the sperm cells, they move through the seminiferous tubules, which then move to the upper part of each testis. The testis is outlined by a highly coiled tube about 16 feet long called epididymis. The spermatozoa mature and become motile and are temporarily stored there. The epididymis leads to a straight tube called the vas deferens.

VAS DEFERENS

The vas deferens carries the sperm up into the pelvic region, at the level of the urinary bladder, merging with ejaculatory duct leading toward the urethra. Situated in the base of the urinary bladder are two glands, which open into the ejaculatory duct as it joins the urethra. They secrete a thick, sugary, yellowish substance that nourishes the sperm cells and forms much of the volume of ejaculated semen.

Semen is a combination of fluid and sperm cells that is ejected from the body through the urethra. In the male, as opposed to in the female, the genital orifice combines with the urinary opening.

Reproductive System

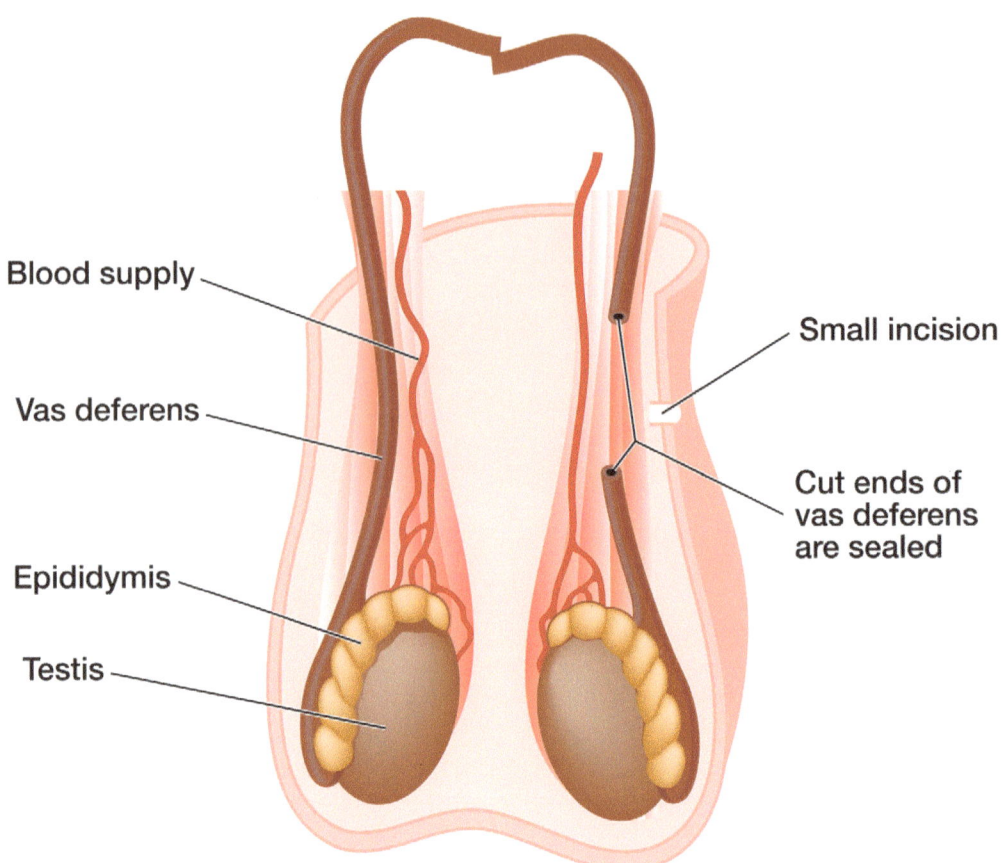

Fig 6-17 Vasectomy

Vasectomy is a permanent birth control surgical procedure in which the vas deferens of a man severed, and then tied or sealed. By doing this the sperm cannot pass through and enter into the seminal fluid to fertilize a women's egg during sexual intercourse.

PROSTATE GLAND

The prostate gland is at the base of the urinary bladder in the region where the vas deferens enters the urethra. The prostate gland secretes a thick fluid that, as part of semen, aids the motility of the sperm. This gland is also supplied with muscular tissue that aids in the expulsion of sperm during ejaculation. Cowper, otherwise called bulbourethral gland, is present just below the prostate gland and also secrete fluid into the urethra.

The urethra passes through the penis to the outside of the body. The penis is composed of erectile tissue and at its tip expands to form a soft, sensitive region called the glans penis. A fold of skin called the prepuce, or foreskin covers the glans penis. Circumcision is the process whereby the foreskin is removed, leaving the glans penis visible at all times.

DISORDERS OF MALE REPRODUCTIVE SYSTEM

PHIMOSIS

A condition where there is narrowness of the opening of the prepuce preventing from it being drawn back over the glans. This condition can interfere with urination and cause secretions to accumulate under the prepuce, leading to infection. Treatment is circumcision.

- Every day a mans testicles manufactures 10 million new sperm cells-enough to repopulate the entire planet in just 6 months.

HYDROCELE

A collection of serous fluid in muscular layers of scrotum is referred to as hydrocele. Hydroceles may occur as a response to infection or tumors, or they may occur as a result of generalized edema. If the hydrocele does not resolve on its own, hydrocelectomy may be necessary. The sac is aspirated via needle and syringe or surgically removed through an incision in the scrotum.

SEXUALLY TRANSMITTED DISEASES

The diseases that are transmitted by sexual contact are referred to as sexually transmitted diseases. Common sexually transmitted diseases include chlamydia, gonorrhea, herpes genitalis, syphilis and AIDS etc.

CHLAMYDIAL INFECTION

Chlamydia trachomatis invade the urethra and reproductive tract of men, and the vagina and cervix of women. Within 3 weeks after becoming infected, men may experience dysuria and a white or clear discharge from the penis. Women may develop a yellowish endocervical discharge, but often the disease is asymptomatic. This condition is treated with antibiotics.

GONORRHEA

Inflammation of the genital tract mucous membranes, caused by infection with gonococci. Symptoms include dysuria and a yellow, pus-filled discharge from the urethra. Many women carry the disease asymptomatically, and others have pain, vaginal and urethral discharge, and salpingitis. This condition is present in men too.

HERPES GENITALIS

Infecting organism in this condition is herpes simplex virus (HSV). Symptoms include reddening of skin with fluid-filled blisters and ulcers.

SYPHILIS

It is caused by a spiral-shaped bacterium (spirochete). A hard ulcer usually appears on the external genitalia a few weeks after bacterial infection. Swelling of lymph nodes follows as the infection spreads to internal organs. It could cause damage to the brain, spinal cord, and heart.

BENIGN PROSTATIC HYPERPLASIA (PROSTATE ENLARGEMENT)

Benign prostatic hyperplasia (BPH) or enlargement of the prostate, is one of the most common conditions affecting middle aged or older men. This condition commonly occurs in men who are over 50 years of age. The prostate gland doubles in size during early puberty and begins to grow again

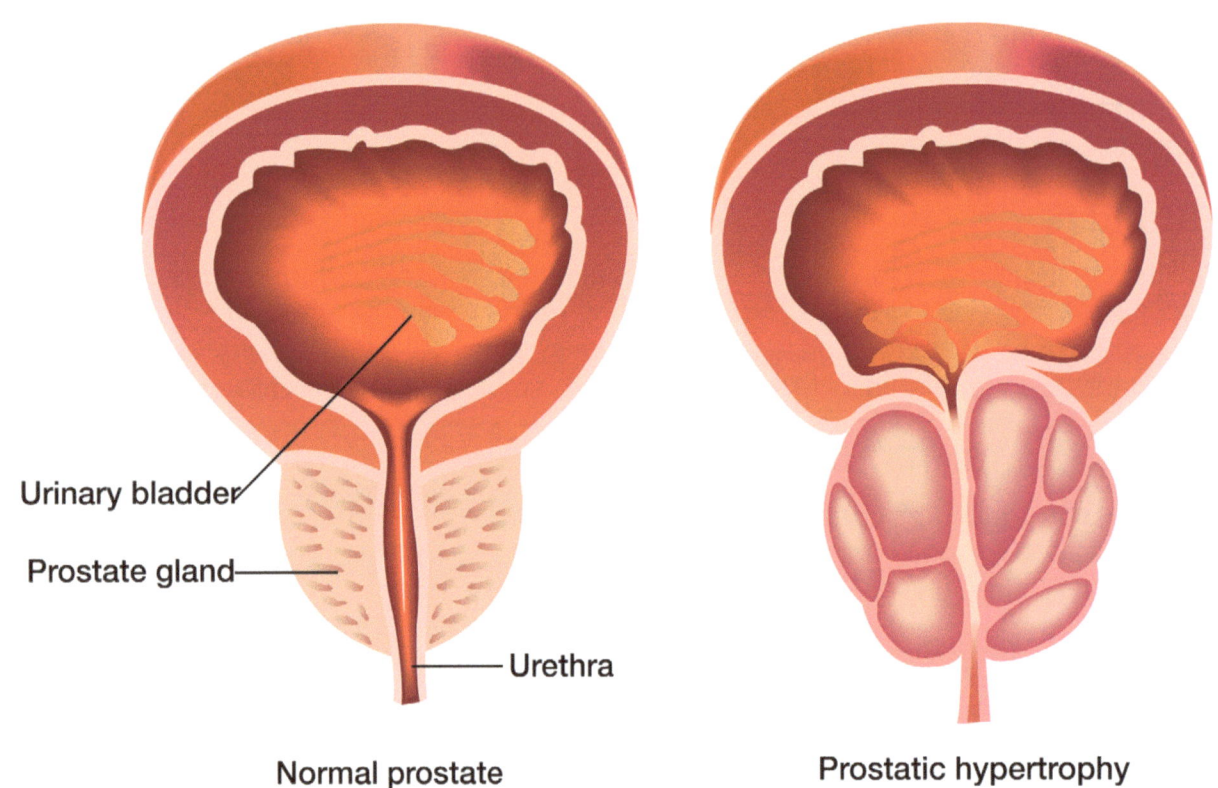

Fig 6-18 Prostate enlargement

around the age of 25 years. This second phase of growth results in BPH after middle age. As the prostate gland enlarges it presses against the urethra. Due to this the bladder muscles begin to contract even when there is a small amount of urine. This results in frequent urination. Frequency of urination, burning sensation, retarded flow, the feeling after urinating that the bladder has not been completely emptied, and dribbling, are the classic symptom of enlarged prostate.

Chapter 7

Musculoskeletal system

TABLE OF CONTENTS

MUSCULOSKELETAL SYSTEM 125
BONES 126
JOINTS 127
BURSA 130
DISORDERS OF BONES AND JOINTS 131
    Fracture 131
    Ankylosing spondylitis (AS) 132
    Bursitis 132
    Osteoarthritis 133
    Osteomyelitis 134
    Rheumatoid arthritis 134
    Gout 136
    Carpal tunnel syndrome (CTS) 136
    Frozen shoulder 137
MUSCLES AND LIGAMENTS 137
DISORDERS OF MUSCLES & LIGAMENTS 140
    Sprain 140
    Strain 140
    Tennis elbow 141
    Plantar fasciitis 142
SKULL, SPINE, THORAX AND PELVIS 143
DISORDERS OF SKULL, SPINE, THORAX AND SPINE 148
    Spondylosis 148
    Spondylolysis and spondylolisthesis 149
    Sciatica 149
    Herniated intervertebral disc 150
    Kyphosis 151
    Scoliosis 151

MUSCULOSKELETAL SYSTEM

The musculoskeletal system formed by bones, joints, muscles and ligaments provides the essential framework of the body. It is vital for protection of the internal organs and important for locomotion and movements.

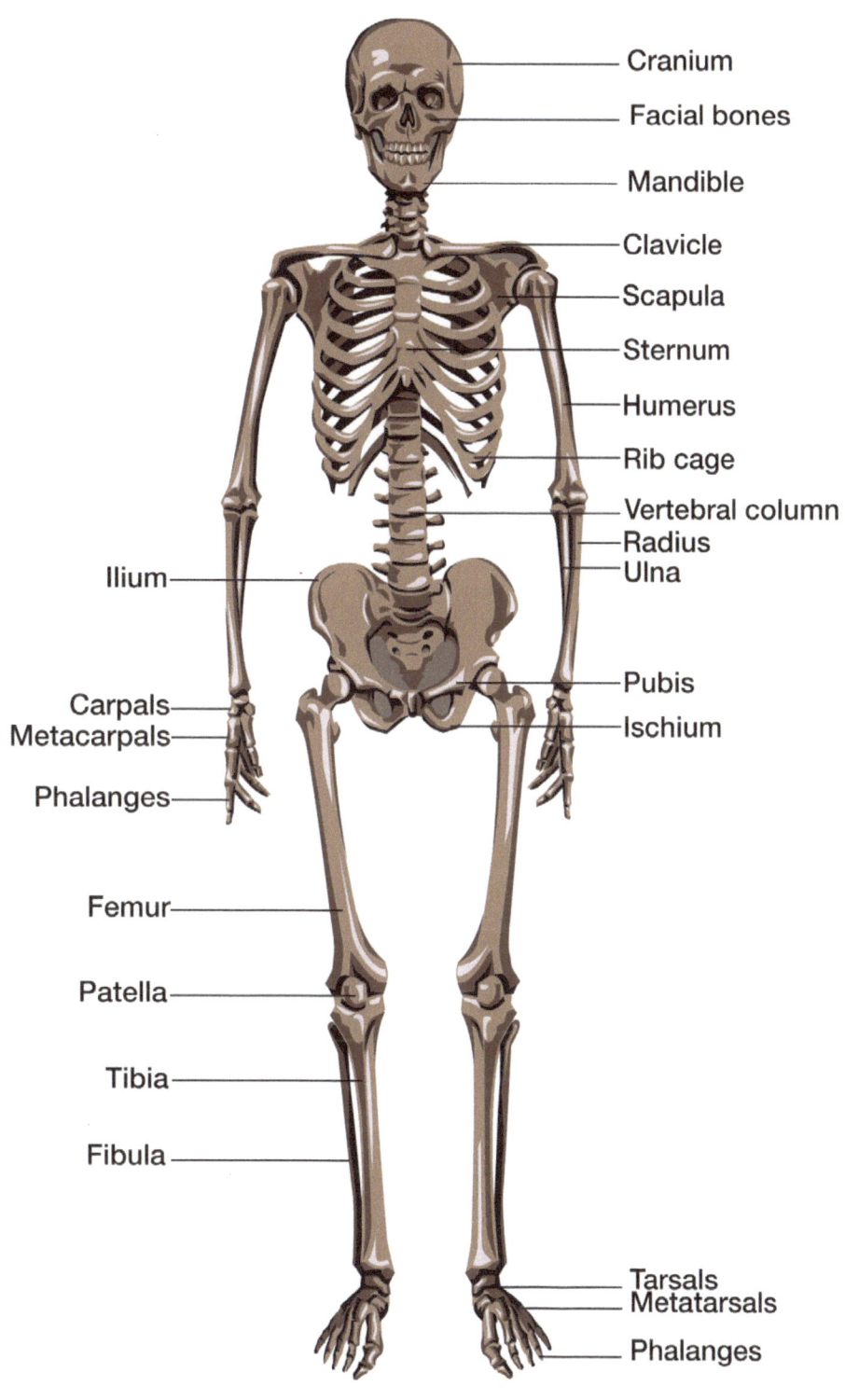

Figure 7-1 Skeletal system

Musculoskeletal System 125

BONES

Bones are hard connective tissue consisting of cells embedded in a matrix of mineralized ground substance and collagen fibers. Bone is composed of 75% inorganic material such as calcium, magnesium, carbonates and sodium, and 25% organic material like collagen and fibrous tissue. In males, there are 206 distinct bones in the skeleton. Bone consists of a dense outer layer of a compact or cortical substance covered by the periosteum, and an inner loose, spongy substance. The central portion of a long bone is filled with marrow.

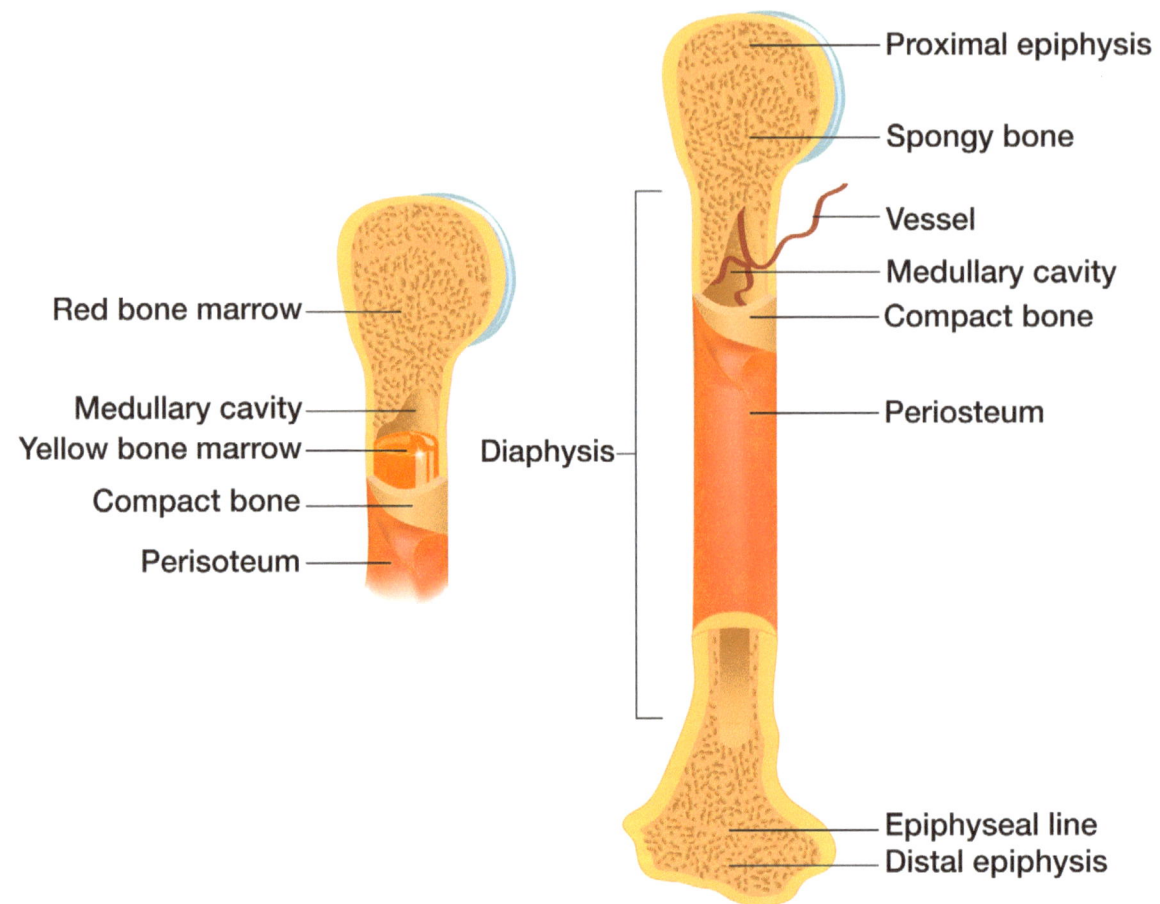

Figure 7-2 Bone Anatomy

The bones can be classified as long bones, short bones, flat bones and sesamoid bones, based on their size and structure. The long bones form the limbs. The bones in arms (humerus), forearms (radius and ulna), thighs (femur), and legs (tibia and fibula) are long bones. A long bone consists of three components; one middle region with two ends. The middle region or shaft of a long bone is called the diaphysis while each end of a long bone is known as an epiphysis. The epiphyseal line or plate which is an area of cartilage tissue present between the diaphysis and the epiphysis is the point where new bony tissue forms as the bone grows. It is also commonly known as the growth plate.

- A fully grown adult has 206 bones while an infant has 350 bones
- The jawbone is the hardest bone in the human body
- The jaw muscles can exert a force of 219 kgs

126 Musculoskeletal System

The periosteum is a strong fibrous membrane covering the surface of a long bone, except at the ends of the epiphysis. The ends of long bones and the surface of any bone that meets another bone to form a joint are covered with articular cartilage. In fact, the bones do not touch in a joint, and the articular cartilage that covers the end of one bone comes in contact with that of the other bone. Articular cartilage cushions the joint and allows it to move smoothly and efficiently.

The bones are made up of hard compact and soft cancellous bone layers. Compact bone is a layer of hard dense bone that lies under the periosteum in all bones. Within the compact bone, there is a system of small canals called the haversian canals. The haversian canals contain the blood vessels that bring oxygen and nutrients to the bone and remove waste products such as carbon dioxide. The compact bone has a central cavity that contains the yellow bone marrow which is mostly fat.

- The thigh bone is the longest bone in the body

Cancellous bone, also called spongy bone, is much more porous and less dense than the compact bone. This type of bone is present in almost all the bones of the body. Spaces in cancellous bone contain red bone marrow which is the site of blood cells production.

JOINTS

All the bones of our body are joined or articulated together to form the skeletal system. A joint is made by the articulation of two or more bones. Some joints are immovable, such as the suture joints between the skull bones. Other joints, such as those between the vertebrae, are partially movable. Most joints, however, allow considerable movement and flexibility. These freely movable joints are called the synovial joints.

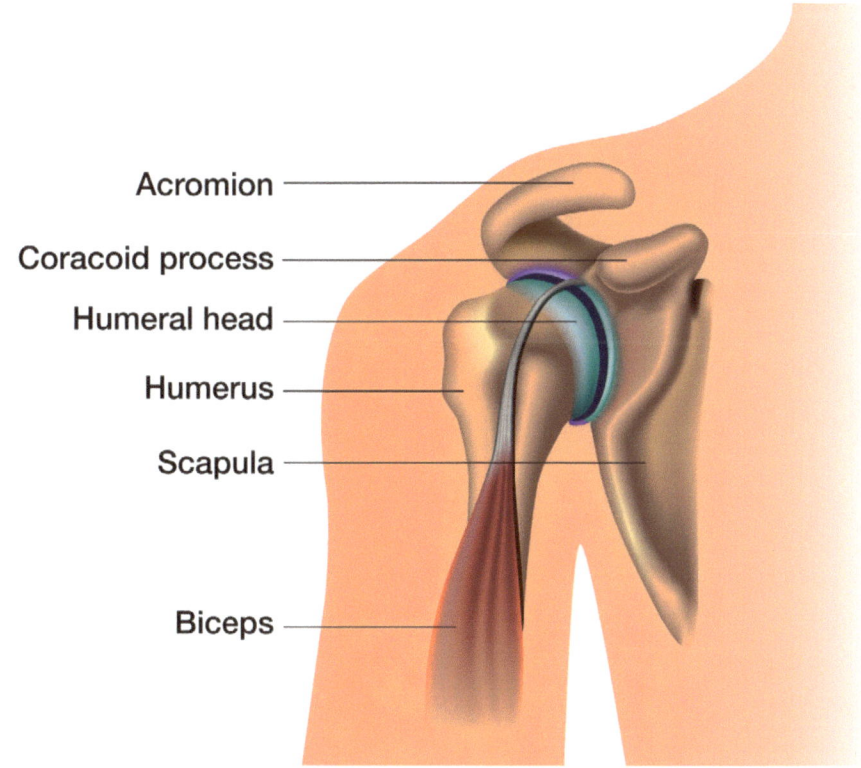

Figure 7-3 Shoulder joint

Musculoskeletal System

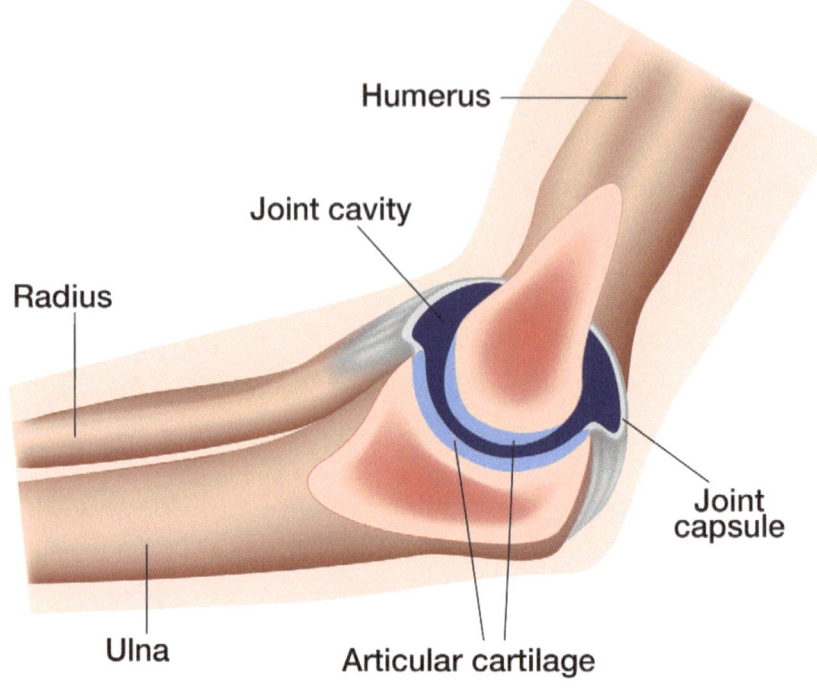

Figure 7-4 Elbow joint

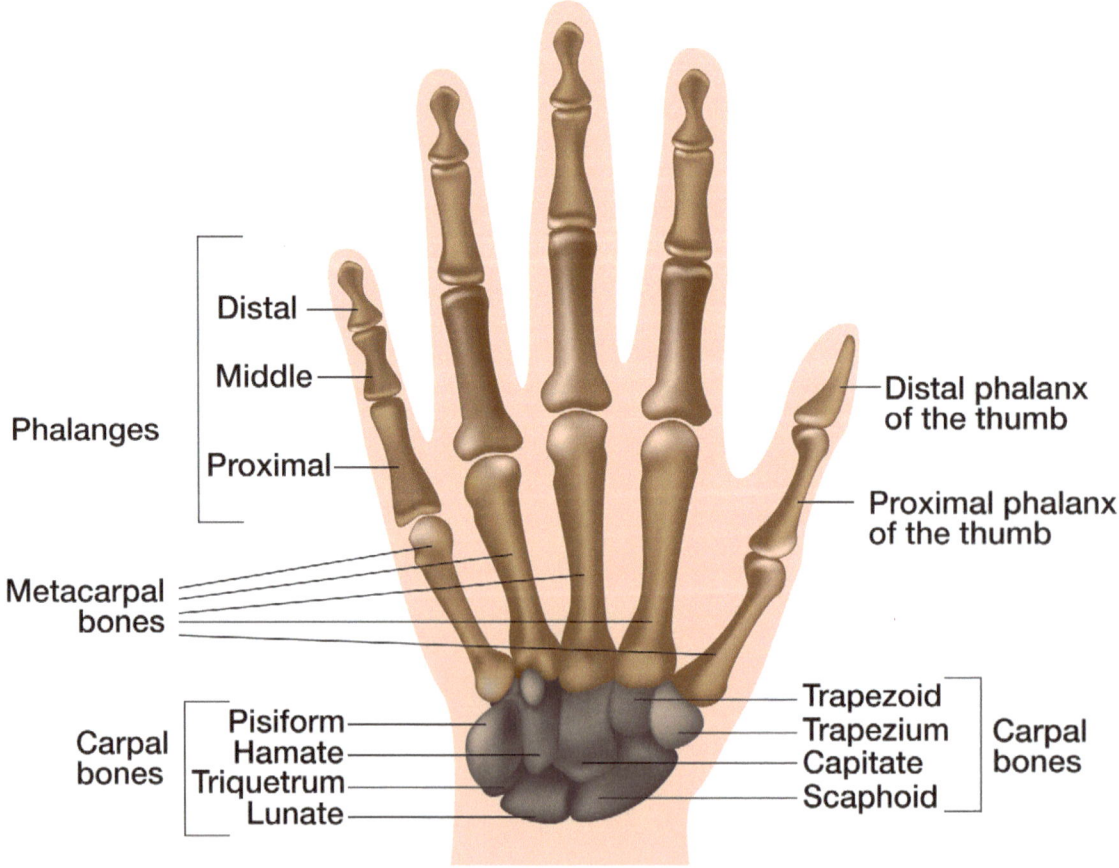

Figure 7-5 Wrist joint

128 Musculoskeletal System

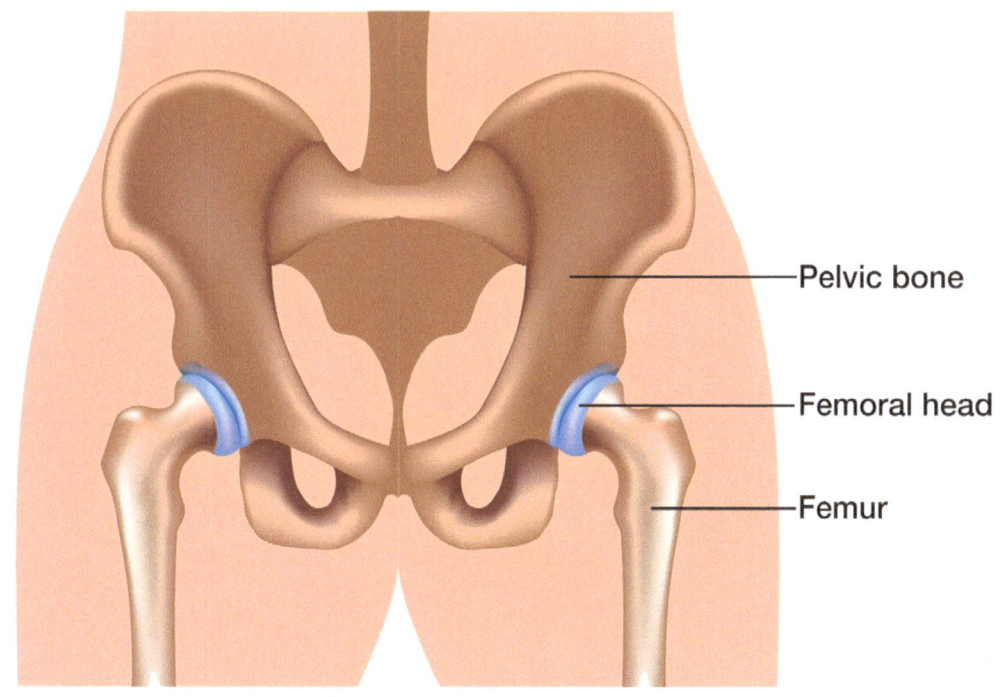

Figure 7-6 Hip joint

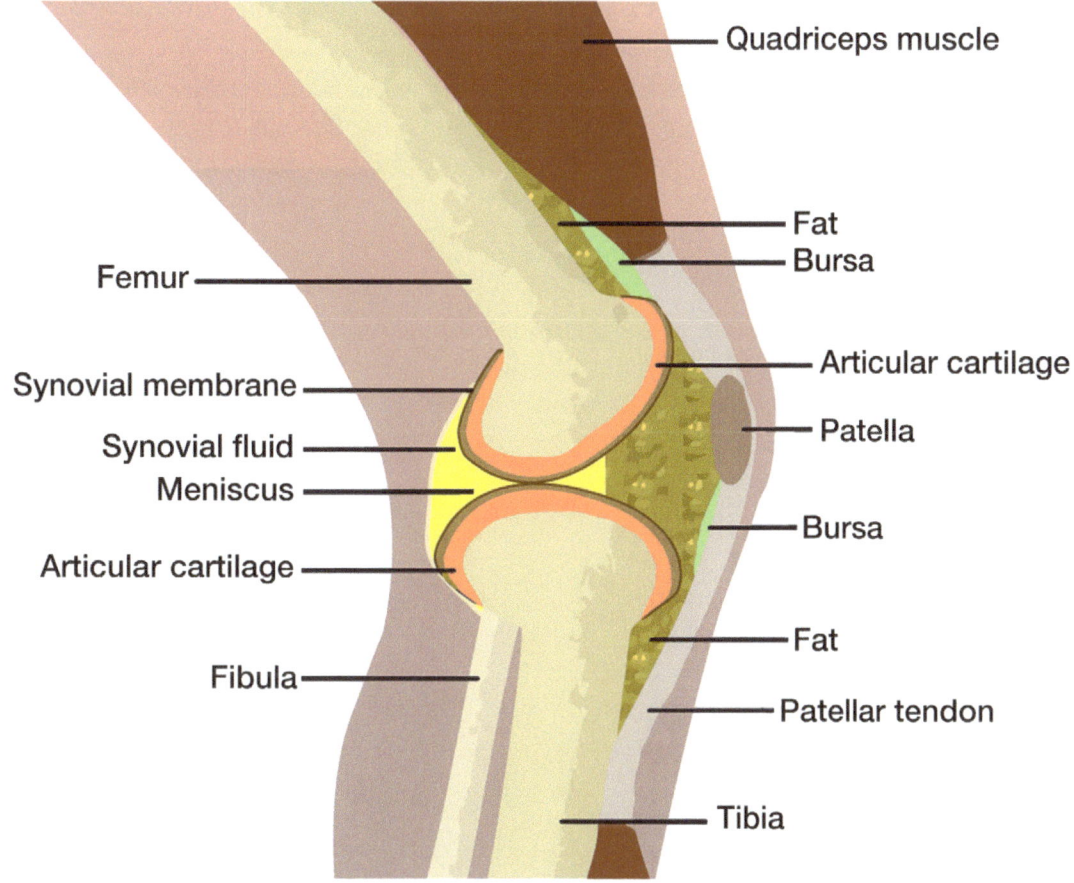

Figure 7-7 Knee Joint

Musculoskeletal System

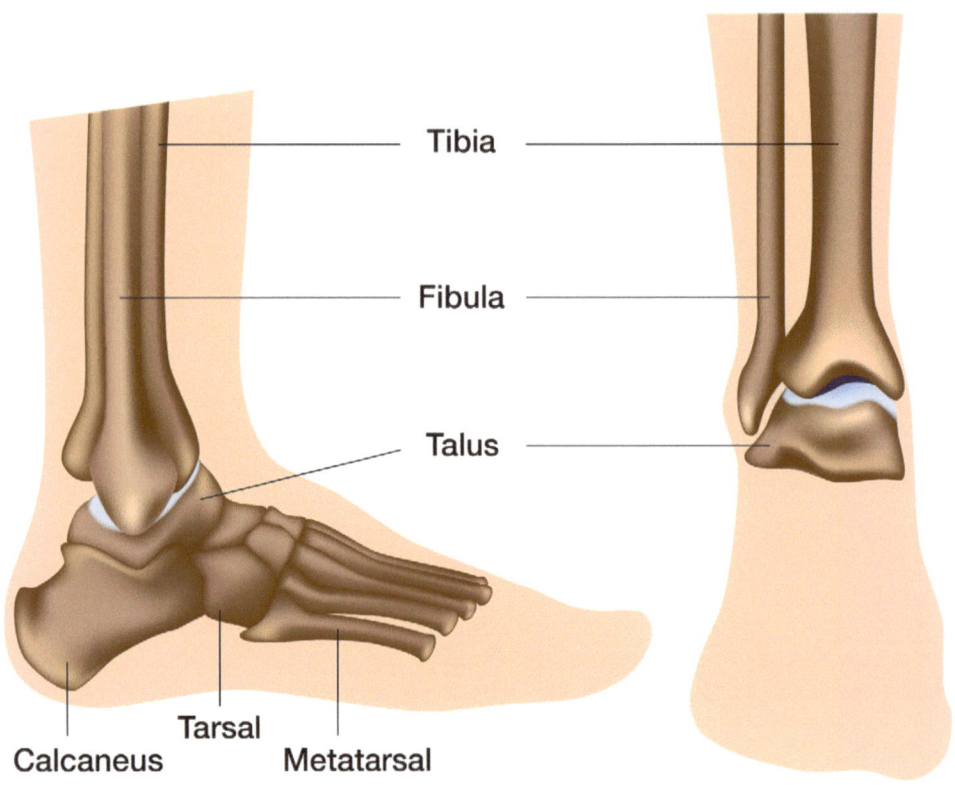

Figure 7-8 Ankle Joint

The articulating surfaces of the bones are covered by the articular cartilage, which help in friction-free movements of the joints. The joints are also covered by a fibrous capsule called the synovial membrane which contains the synovial fluid. The synovial fluid acts as a lubricant and reduces wear and tear in the joints.

BURSA

Bursae are little sacs formed by the synovial membrane which secretes a very thick fluid and acts as a water cushion, facilitating the movements of one part on another. Bursae are present wherever two types of tissue are closely opposed and need to slide past one another with as little friction as possible. Bursae serve as layers of lubrication between the tissues. Common sites of bursae are between tendons (a connective tissue that connects muscle to bone) and bones, between ligaments (connective tissue binding bone to bone) and bones, and between skin and bones in areas where bony anatomy is prominent.

Common locations of bursae include the elbow joint (olecranon bursa), knee joint (patellar bursa), and shoulder joint (subacromial bursa).

DISORDERS OF BONES AND JOINTS

FRACTURE

A sudden breaking of a bone is referred to as a fracture. A closed fracture means that a bone is broken but there is no open wound in the skin, whereas an open fracture refers to a broken bone accompanied by an open wound in the skin. A pathological fracture is caused by the weakening of the bone by a bone disease or a change in the tissue surrounding the bone. A tumor in a bone, for instance, can make a bone weak and lead to a pathological fracture.

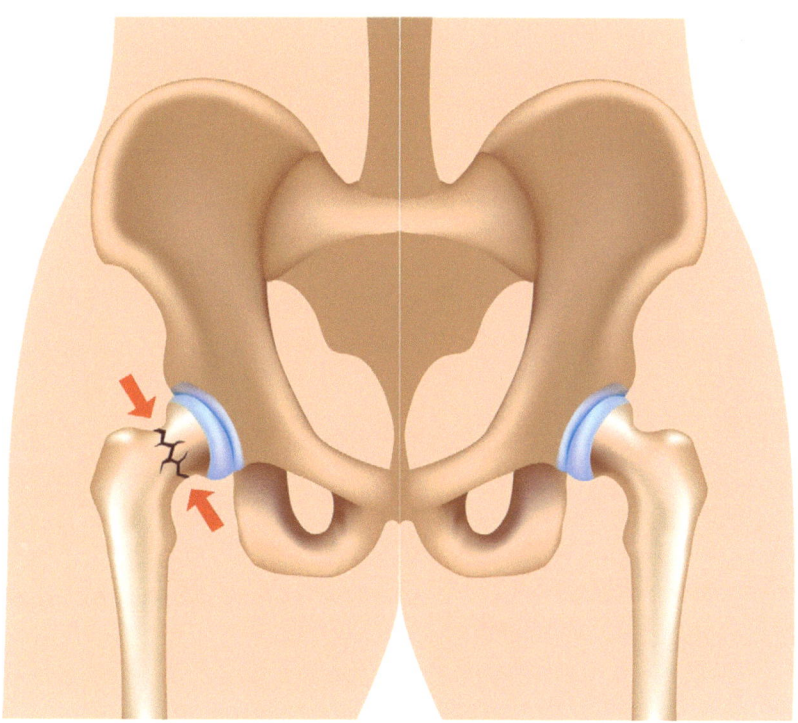

Figure 7-9 Hip Fracture

Different types of fractures based on their severity are presented herein:

- Hairline fracture: There is no bony discontinuity in this type of fracture except a simple hairline crack that may lead to swelling at the fracture site.
- Simple fracture: It is a fracture in the bone with an intact skin at the site of fracture and there is no external injury.
- Compound fracture: It is a type of fracture in which the skin is perforated and there is an open wound down to the fracture.
- Comminuted fracture: In this type of fracture, the bone is splintered or crushed into several pieces. A severe soft tissue injury also occurs in this type of fracture.
- Compression fracture: In this type of fracture the bone is compressed and broken, it occurs usually in vertebrae. It is also known as burst fracture.
- Greenstick fracture - Bone is partially broken but its continuity is not lost, i.e. the bone is angulated but intact on the opposite side, as when a green stick breaks. This type of fracture usually occurs in children's bones.

Treatment of fractures involves reduction, which is the restoration of the bone to its normal position. A closed reduction is manipulative reduction without a surgical incision. After reduction a cast is applied for immobilization of the bone involved to allow for fracture healing. In an open reduction, an incision is made into the fracture site, the fracture fragments are brought into alignment and fixed using external or internal fixators (plates, screws, rods, etc.) and a cast is applied to fractures to immobilize the injured bone.

ANKYLOSING SPONDYLITIS

Ankylosing spondylitis (AS) is a painful, progressive form of inflammatory arthritis where some or all of the joints of the spine fuse together (bamboo spine). The symptoms include onset of a gradual back pain or stiffness and pain in early morning which wears off or reduces during the day with exercise or movement, stooping over time, weight loss, tiredness, experiencing night sweat, feeling feverish, etc. When AS affects the thoracic spine the vital capacity of the lungs is also significantly reduced.

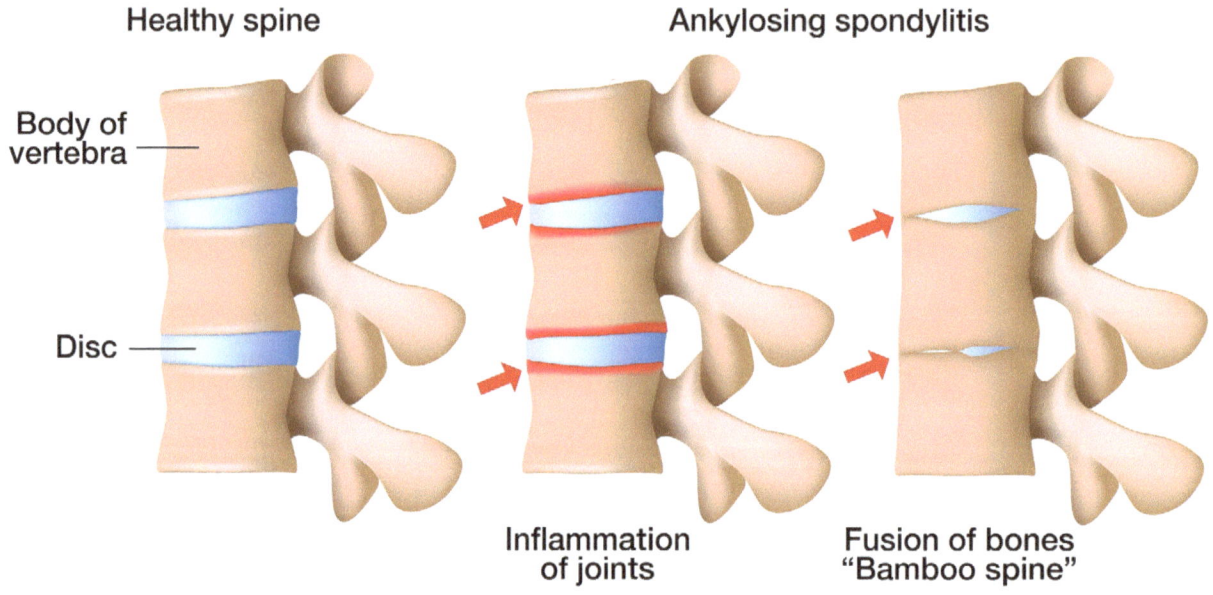

Figure 7-10 Ankylosing spondylitis

The treatment of AS is often preventive and palliative rather than corrective. Medication is usually prescribed to ease the pain associated with inflammation and stiffness. Exercise is excellent for this condition since muscles need to be kept strong, and those that have become shortened need to be stretched. Special exercises can be developed by a physiotherapist.

BURSITIS

Bursitis is inflammation of the bursae which may appear because of an injury or repeated strain. The patient experiences acute pain and sometimes, stiff shoulder due to mild bursitis. Pain in knee joint may also occur due to bursitis. This is also known as housemaids knee since it is common in maids who bear weight on their knees to clean the floor.

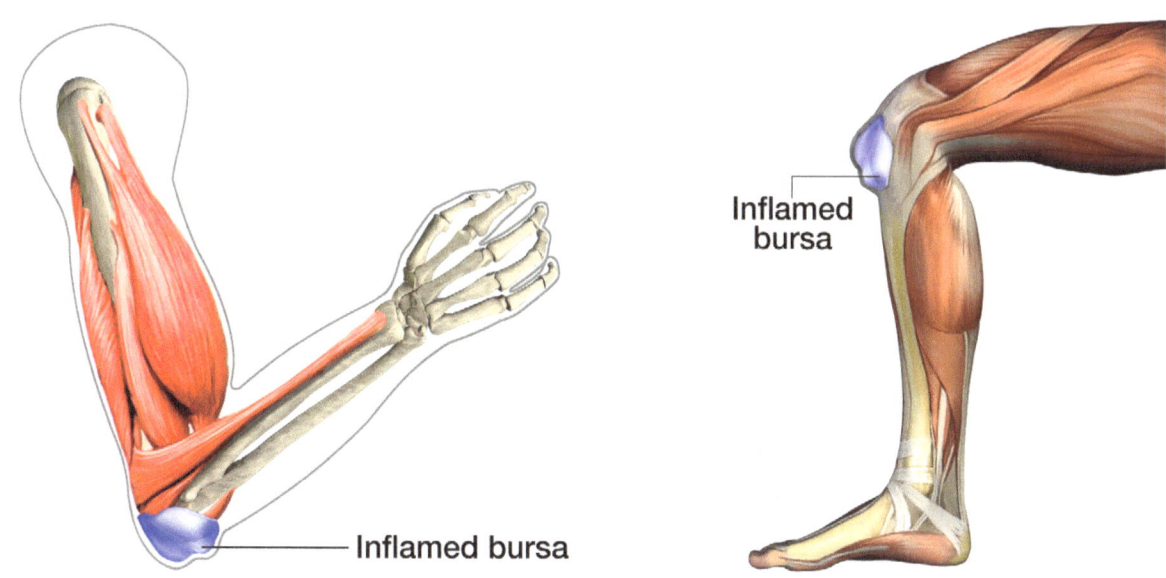

Figure 7-11 Bursitis

OSTEOARTHRITIS

Osteoarthritis is a condition where the articular cartilage loses its ability to repair itself and recover from repeated small injuries and starts to degenerate.

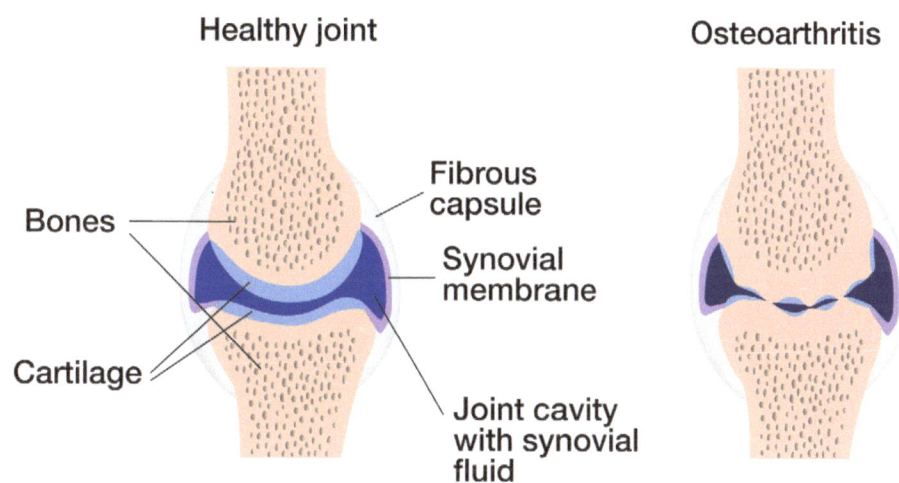

Figure 7-12 Osteoarthritis

This is the most common joint disorder in the world and the number one cause of disability. Often described as "wear and tear", osteoarthritis involves a complex degeneration of the joints. It develops gradually over a period of several years. As the cartilage starts eroding, the disease progresses and bony "out growths" form at the outer edges of the joints. The synovial membrane and the capsule also thicken and are inflamed in later stages of osteoarthritis. All these changes and deformations lead to painful movements and stiffness. As the disease progresses, the cartilage becomes significantly worn out, cracks and fissures start appearing and the cartilage becomes thinner as a result the bones come in contact with each other. The ligaments also become strained and weakened and limitation of movements with a lot of pain is experienced. The pain increases on movements and reduces by rest. Osteoarthritis affects mainly the weight bearing joints like knees and hip joints.

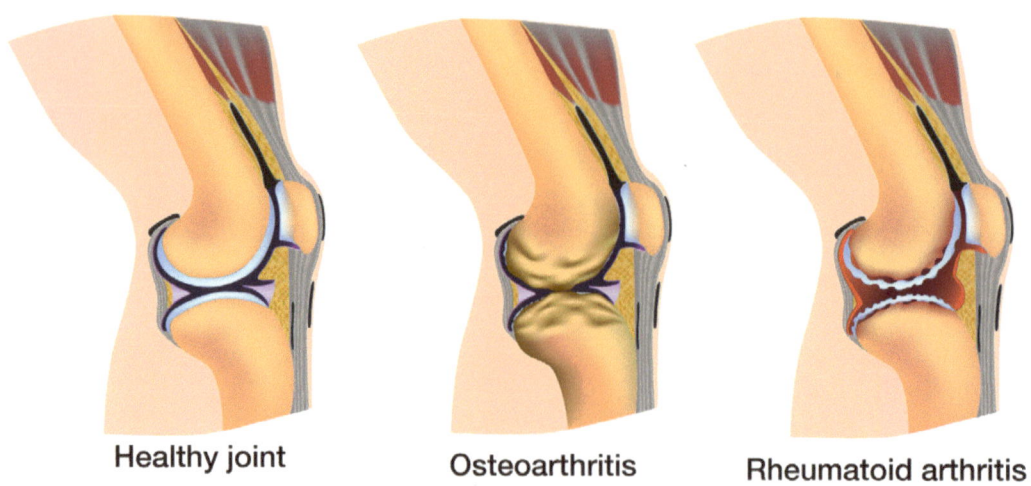

Figure 7-13 Arthritis in the knee joint

Osteoarthritis involving hips and knees can often be helped by weight loss to reduce the load on joints and slow progression. Increasing the strength of muscles around joints can also enhance joint protection. Osteoarthritis can be helped dramatically by an artificial joint replacement; however, this treatment is usually considered as a final resolution for end-stage osteoarthritis.

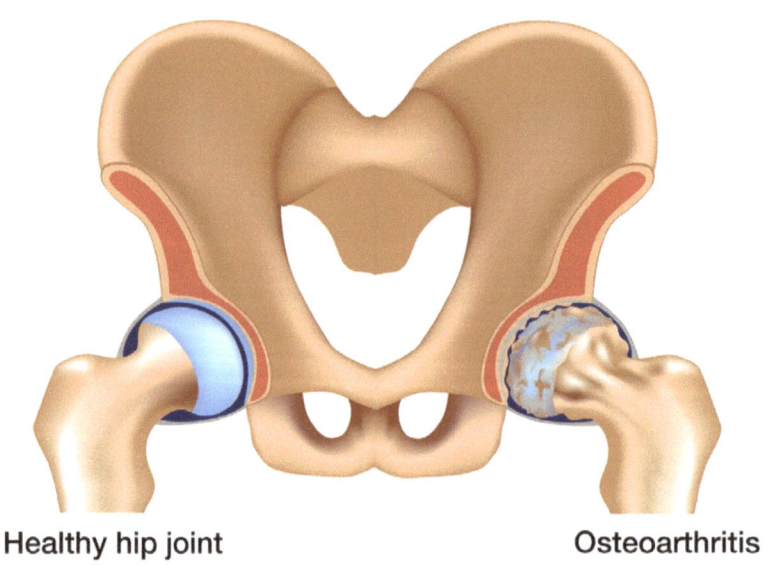

Figure 7-14 Osteoarthritis in the hip joint

OSTEOMYELITIS

Osteomyelitis is an inflammation of the bone and bone marrow which may spread from an infection near the bone, in the skin or throat. It usually affects the long bones of the legs and arms. This is more common in children. It can also affect the jaw bone from infections in the throat (or) mouth.

RHEUMATOID ARTHRITIS

Rheumatoid arthritis occurs due to inflammation in the joints. It first affects the small joints like finger and then spreads to bigger ones. The characteristic features are shifting of pain from one joint to another and early morning stiffness in all joints. Pain reduces on movement and increases during rest.

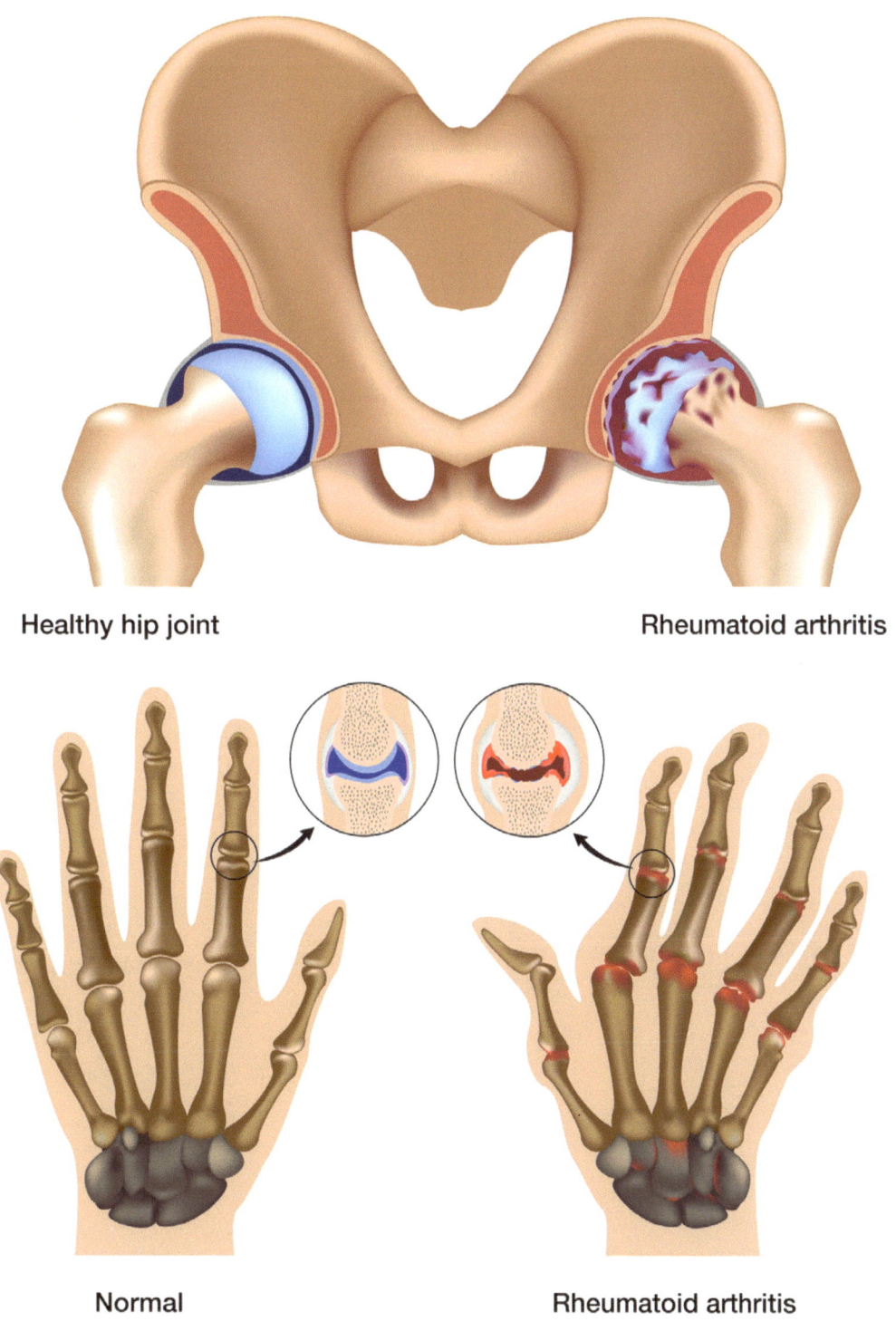

Figure 7-15 Rheumatoid arthritis

GOUT

Gout is a disorder characterized by severe recurrent acute arthritis of sudden onset resulting from deposition of crystals of sodium urate in connective tissues and articular cartilage. Uric acid is a breakdown product of metabolism and at normal levels stays dissolved in the bloodstream as it travels to the kidney and passes out in the urine. However, when the levels get too high, it settles and forms crystals around joints. Most cases of gout are inherited, resulting from a variety of abnormalities of urine metabolism. The symptoms of gout include sudden severe joint pain, joint swelling and shiny red skin around the joint and extreme tenderness in the joint area. Its treatment includes nonsteroidal antiinflammatory drugs, steroids, and avoiding foods that increase the uric acid.

CARPAL TUNNEL SYNDROME

Carpal tunnel syndrome (CTS) is an inflammatory disorder affecting the soft tissue structures in the fibroosseous tunnel formed by flexor retinaculum (a fibrous band in the anterior aspect of wrist) and the carpal bones. It is caused by repetitive stress, physical injury, or medical conditions. It is often very difficult, however, to determine the precise cause of carpal tunnel syndrome.

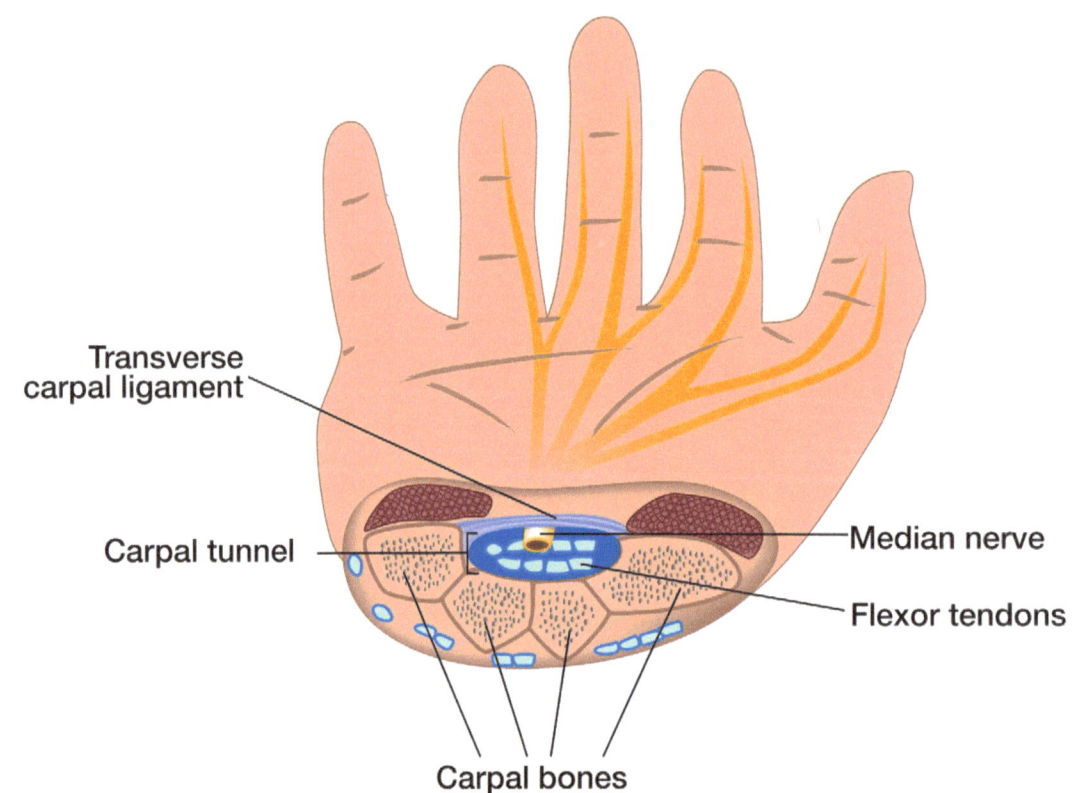

Figure 7-16 Carpal tunnel

Carpal tunnel syndrome can range from a minor inconvenience to a disabling condition. In severe cases, the muscles at the base of the thumb may wither and sensation may be permanently lost. CTS can get so crippling that the patient becomes unable to do their jobs or even perform simple tasks at home. When mild the CTS can be treated by pain relievers and treating the involved soft tissue structures symptomatically. However, severe cases require a surgical release of the flexor retinaculum to relieve the pressure inside the carpal tunnel.

FROZEN SHOULDER

Adhesive capsulitis or 'frozen shoulder' is a disorder in which there is inflammation in the shoulder joint, resulting in adhesions within the joint and contraction of its 'capsule'. Adhesive capsulitis occurs secondary to the condition that results in prolonged immobilization of the arm, including shoulder muscle injuries, tendinitis, mastectomy, or even fractures of the forearm. It can also occur in individuals with diabetes mellitus and periarthritis shoulder (Inflammation of the parts surrounding the shoulder joint). Symptoms of frozen shoulder include limitation of both active and passive movement of the shoulder, pain in the extremes of motion, and problems with activities of daily living. Night pain and joint restriction are also common.

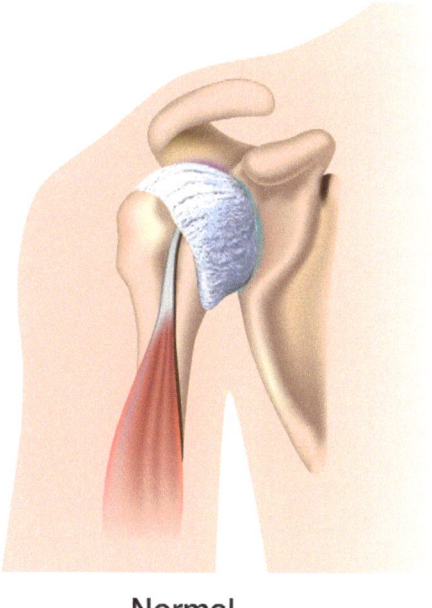
Normal

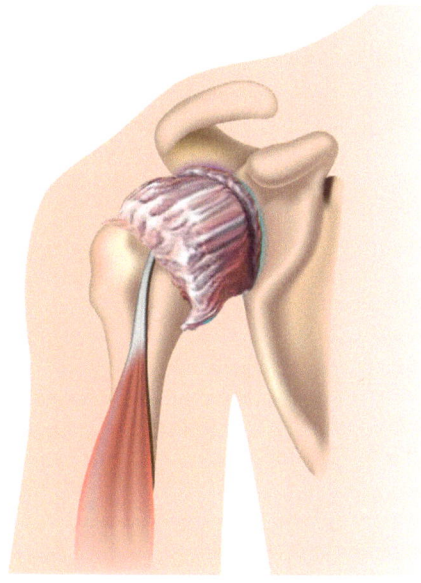
"Frozen"

Figure 7-17 Frozen shoulder

Adhesive capsulitis is treated initially with non-steroidal anti-inflammatory drugs, and a gentle exercise program of stretching once the pain is controlled. A corticosteroid injection or a short course of oral corticosteroids may be prescribed to control the pain. The affected joint is manipulated under anesthesia to improve the range of movement.

MUSCLES AND LIGAMENTS

Muscle is a tissue consisting predominantly of highly specialized contractile cells which contracts to bring about movement. The muscles may be classified as skeletal muscles, cardiac muscles and smooth muscles microscopically. The skeletal muscles are voluntary muscles that move the bones resulting in movement of the body. They are attached to each extremity by means of tendons, to a bone or other structures. The fixed attachment of the muscle is called the origin, and the distal or movable attachment of the muscle is known as the insertion. The central fleshy part of the muscle connected to tendons at either side is called the muscle belly. The muscle belly contains contractile muscle fibers which are covered by fibrous sheath called perimysium.

- It is easier to smile than to frown because it only takes 17 muscles to smile but it takes 40 muscles to frown

The skeletal muscles constantly remodel in response to use, disuse, and other factors. The total mass of the muscle increases by constant use in specific sports or body building which is referred to as the muscle hypertrophy. If a muscle is not used for a long period of time as in fractures or prolonged bed rests, it becomes weaker and smaller and consequently muscle atrophy occurs.

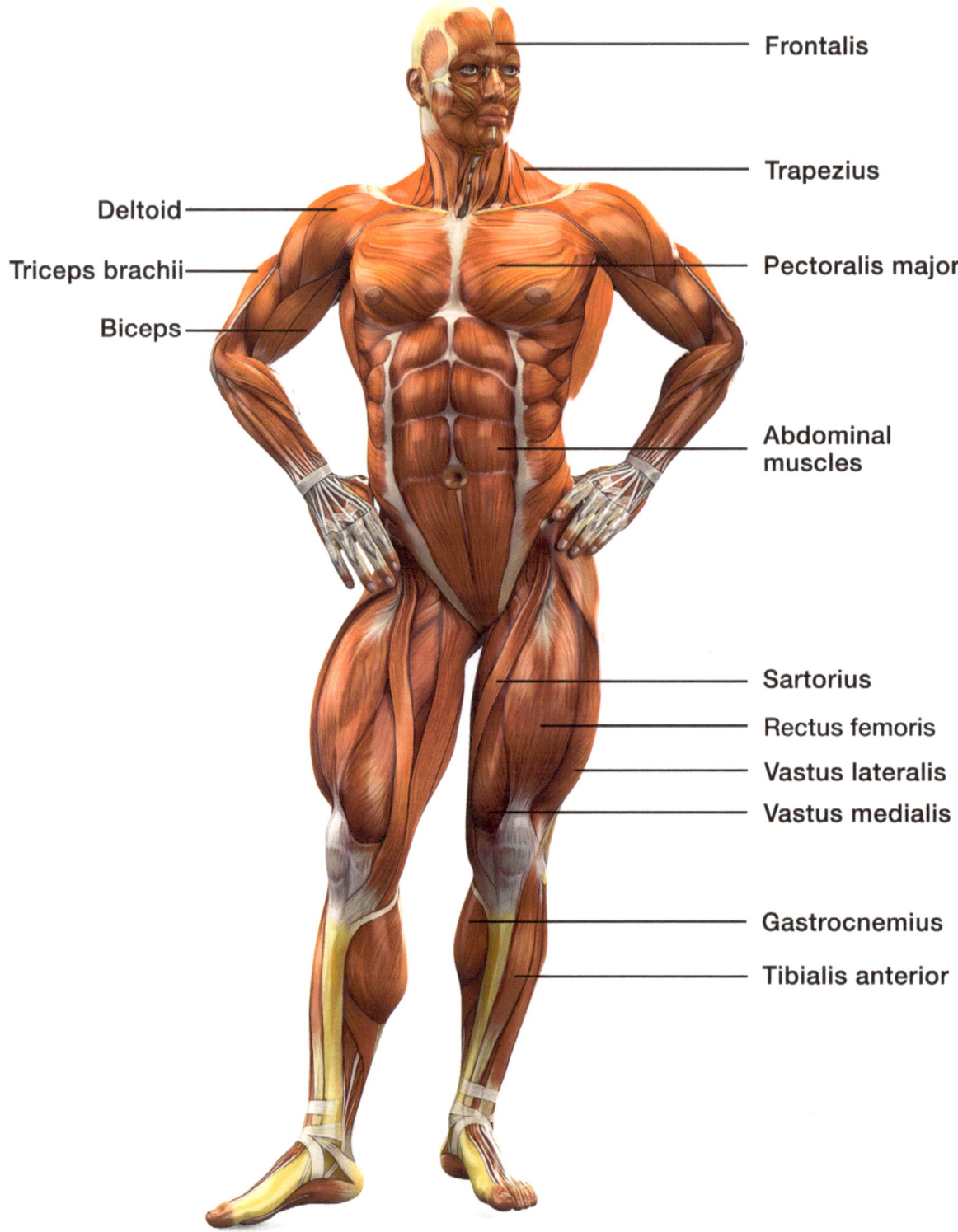

Figure 7-18 Muscular system - Anterior view

Atrophy can also begin immediately if a muscle loses its nerve supply, in a stroke or nerve injury. The muscle functions can return if there is a regeneration of the nerve within three months. After that period of time there is less return of function. The muscles can be injured when stretched beyond limits or stressed with excessive loads. The muscle injury is referred to as strain.

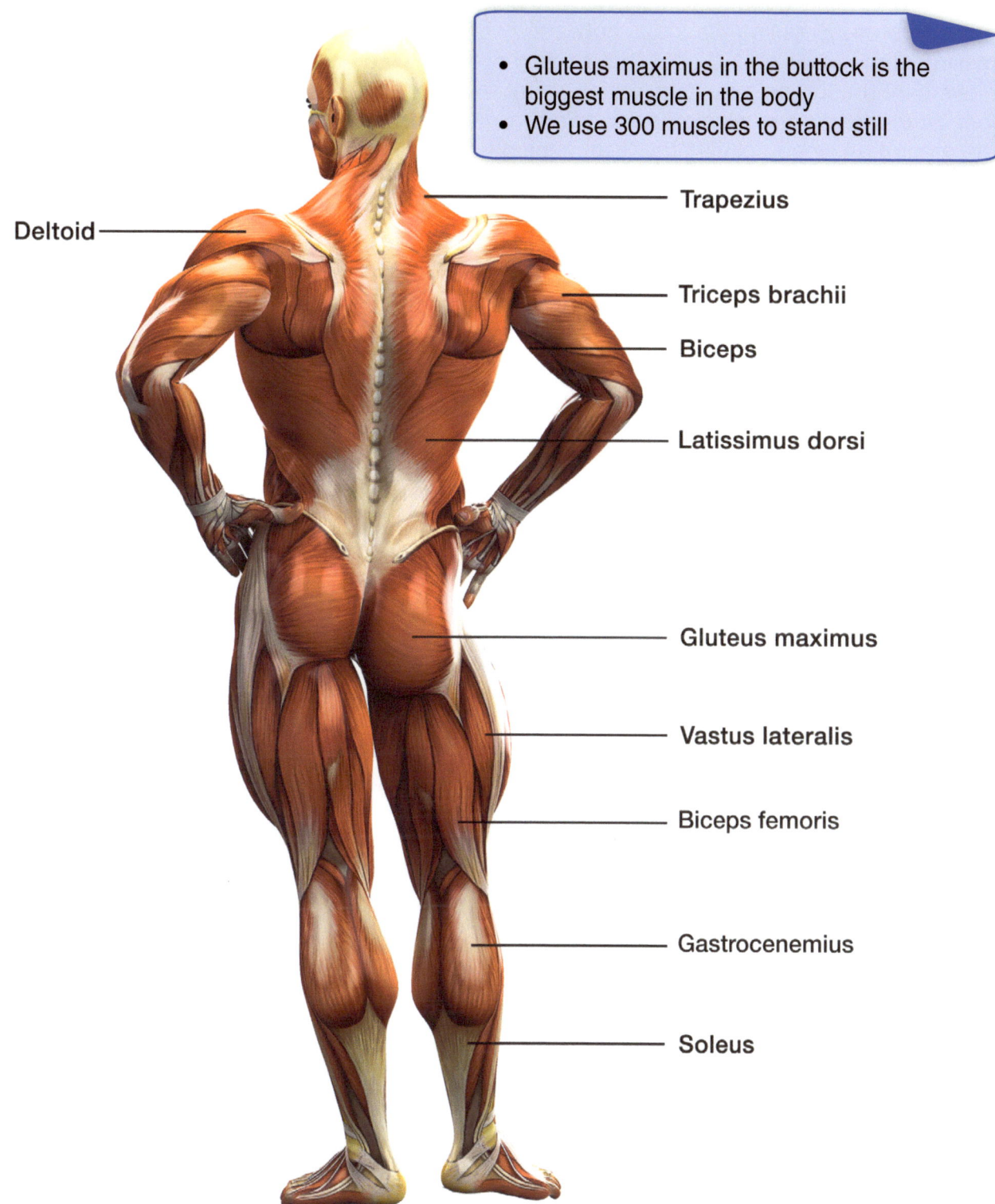

Figure 7-19 Muscular system - Posterior view

Musculoskeletal System

A ligament is a band of elastic fiber in parallel bundles which hold two or more bones together. It is present in all joints and adds to the strength of the movable joint without restricting the movements. Due to injuries, a partial or complete tear of the ligament may occur, referred to as sprain. Various movements brought about by contraction of the muscles are as follows: Flexion is the movement involving decreasing the angle between two bones; i.e. bending a limb and extension is straightening out a limb or increasing the angle between two bones, abduction is the movement away from the midline of the body, adduction is the movement toward the midline of the body, rotation is a circular movement around an axis. Dorsiflexion refers to decreasing the angle of the ankle joint so that the foot bends backward, plantarflexion refers to the motion that extends the foot downward toward the ground as when pointing the toes, supination is the act of turning the palm forward, or up and pronation is the act of turning the palm backward, or down.

DISORDERS OF MUSCLES & LIGAMENTS

SPRAIN

A sprain is the rupture or tear of the ligament. It does not directly involve a muscle, as some people think, but instead occurs due to the stretching or tearing of ligaments that hold joints together. The tear may be partial or complete and is usually associated with swelling and pain.

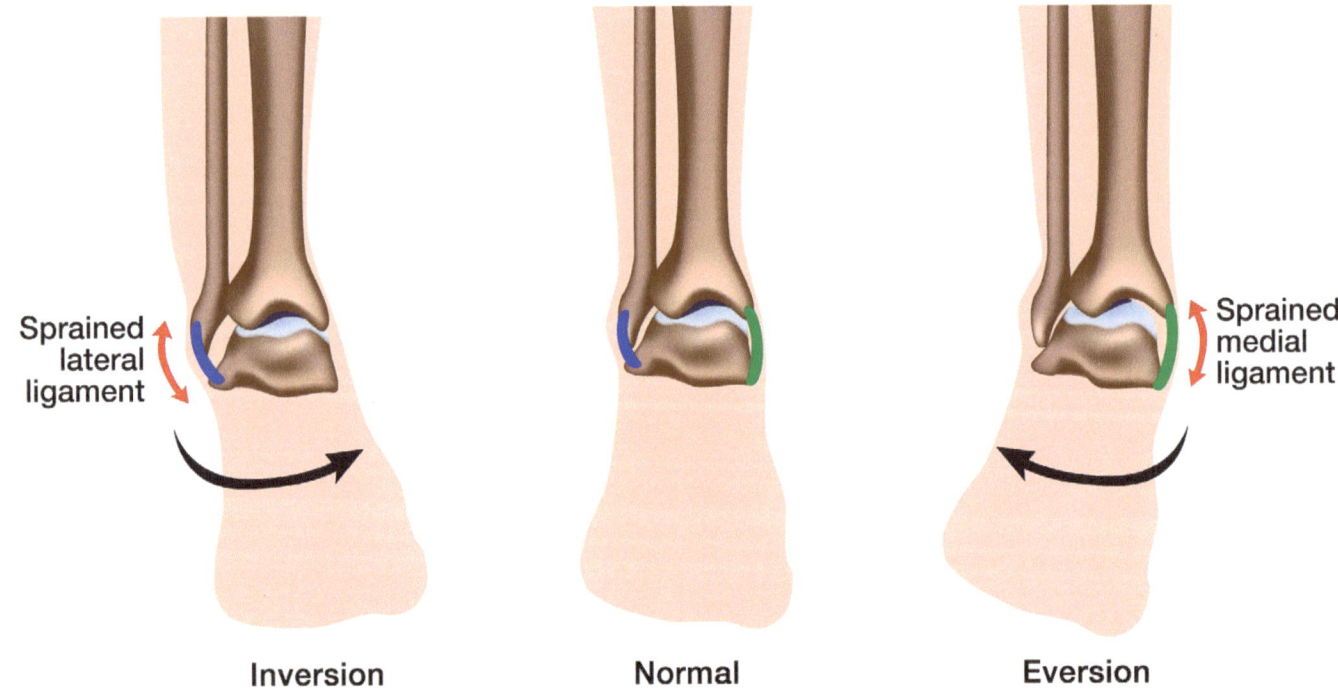

Figure 7-20 Ankle sprain (left foot)

STRAIN

A strain is defined as the rupture or tear of the muscle, commonly referred to as the muscle pull. A strained or pulled skeletal muscle results from stretching the muscle beyond its limit or applying excess pressure; for instance a strained calf muscle could result from running a long distance without proper conditioning or warm-up.

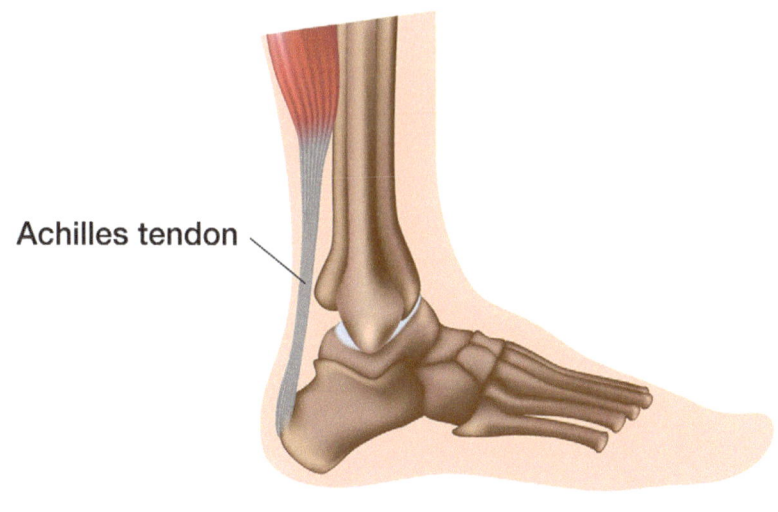
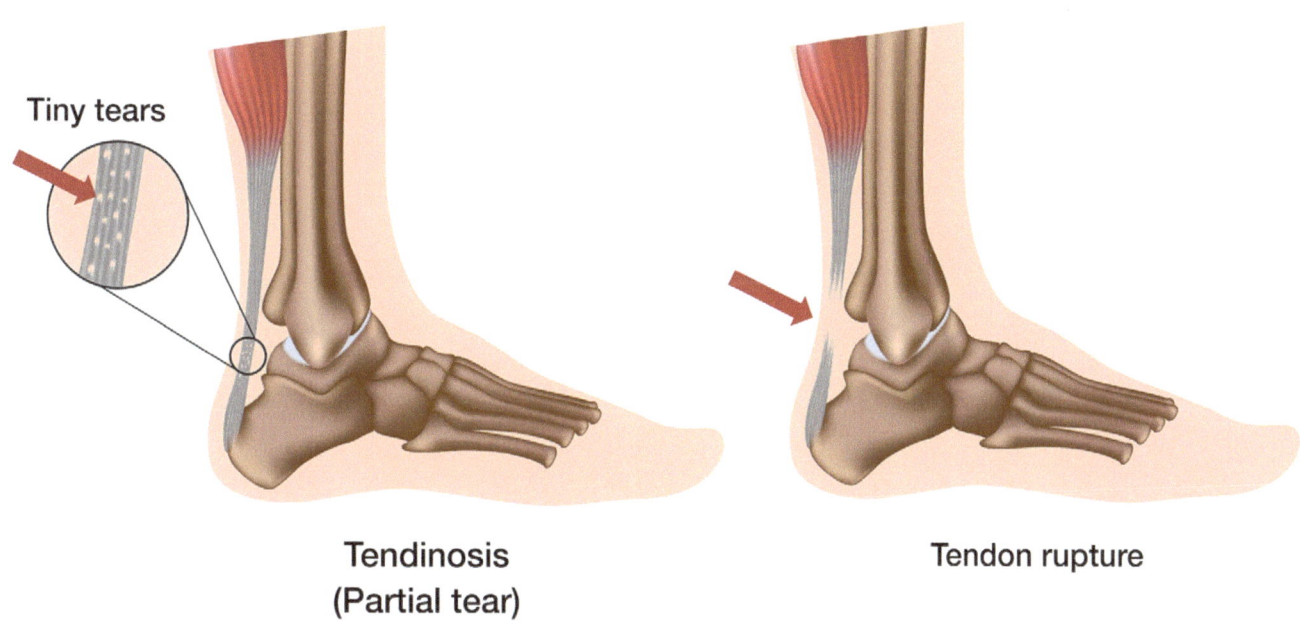

Figure 7-21 Strain

TENNIS ELBOW

Tennis elbow is a painful condition on the lateral aspect (outside) of the elbow, involving the tendons that are attached to the bone of the elbow. This condition is also referred as the lateral epicondylitis. It is usually accompanied with degeneration of the tendon attachment due to overuse and trauma.

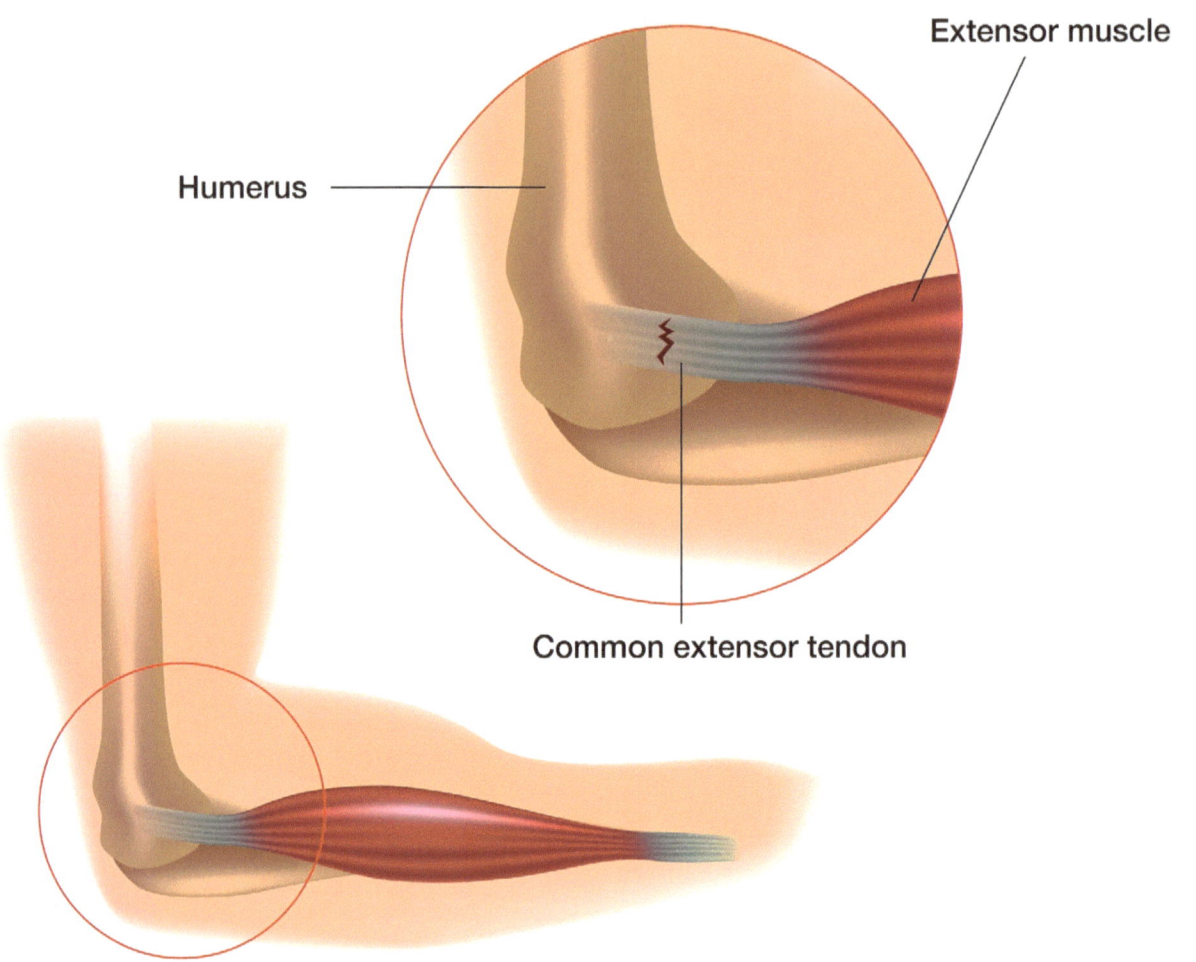

Figure 7-22 Tennis elbow

Some daily activities such as gripping, lifting and meat cutting can cause this condition. It is called "tennis elbow" since it is very common among tennis players. Activity modification and physiotherapy are helpful to relieve the pain.

PLANTAR FASCIITIS

Plantar fasciitis is a painful inflammatory condition of the plantar fascia, the thick tissue on the bottom of the foot. The plantar fascia runs from the heel to the ball of the foot. The plantar fascia overstretches and tears when placed under excessive stress resulting in inflammation.

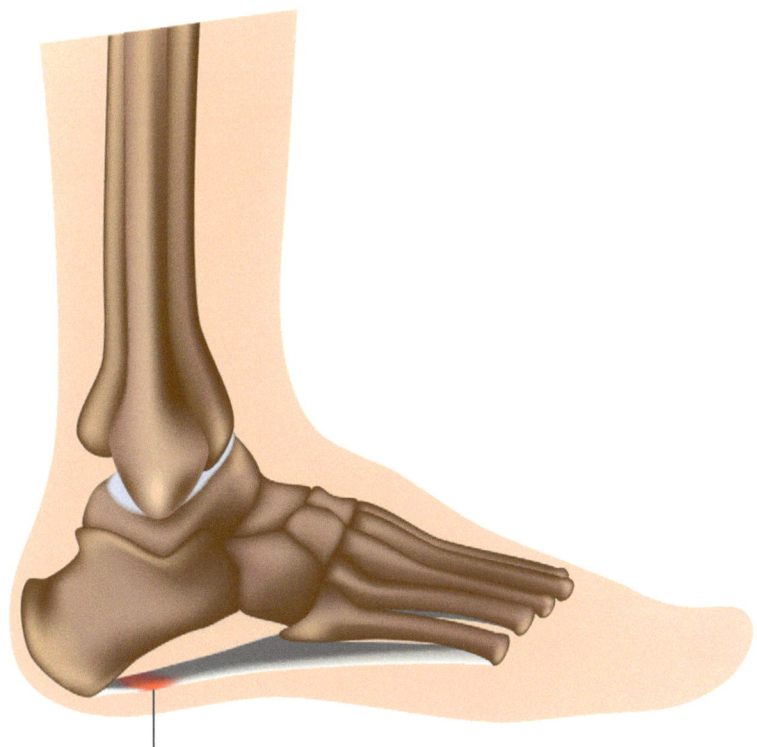

Inflammation of the plantar fascia

Figure 7-23 Plantar fasciitis

Obesity, pregnancy, flat feet, high arches, increases activity and improper foot wear may cause the plantar fasciitis. The pain may be more severe in the morning because the fascia is in shortened position due to rest and gets stretched suddenly as one stands up. Rest, massage therapy, weight loss, using proper foot wear and physical therapy are among the treatment options.

SKULL, SPINE, THORAX AND PELVIS

The skull or the bony part of the head is divided into two parts; the cranium which has 8 bones, and protects the brain and the skeleton of the face which consists of 14 facial bones. The spinal or the vertebral column consists of 33 irregular bones called the vertebrae. The spine is divided into five divisions based on the location.

1. The cervical or neck region of the spine has 7 vertebrae which are called cervical vertebrae. They are capable of a good range of movement and they transfer the weight of head to the spine underneath.

2. The thoracic or chest region has 12 vertebrae and are connected to the ribs which form a thoracic cage by connecting to the chest bone (sternum) anteriorly. The thoracic vertebrae have twelve ribs attached to them on either side. The first eight ribs are directly connected to the sternum or chest bone and are called the true ribs. The ninth and tenth ribs are connected to the sternum by cartilage and are called false ribs. The last two ribs are not connected to the sternum and are known as the floating ribs. The thoracic spine has a less range of motion.

Musculoskeletal System

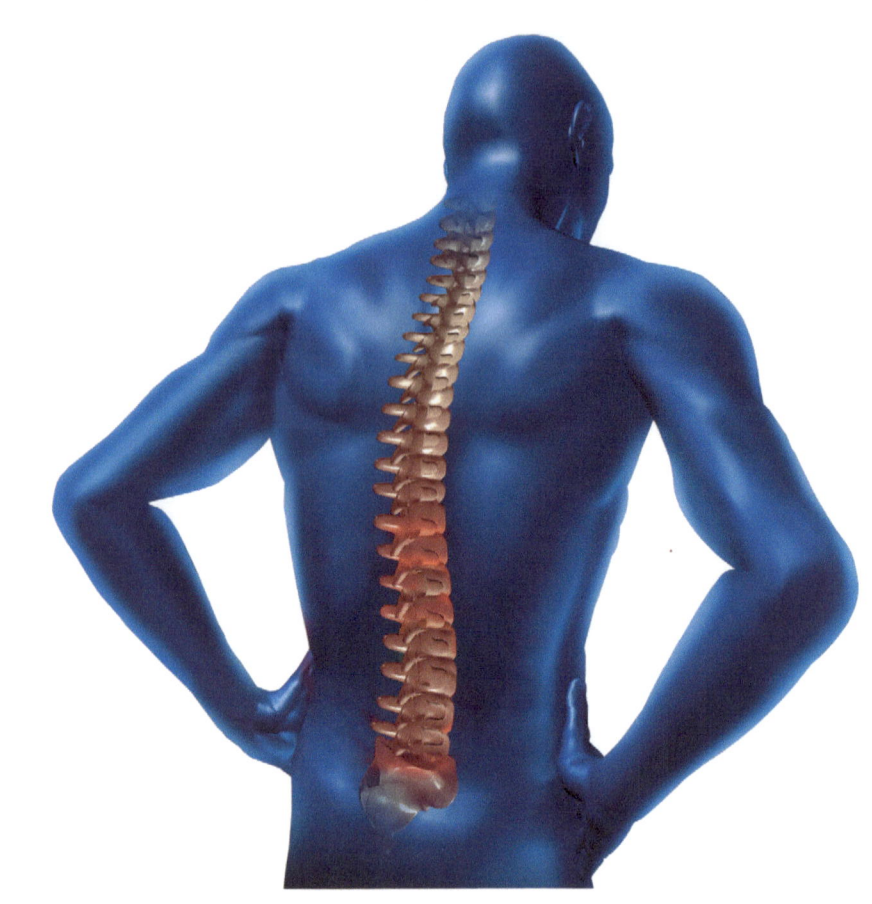

Figure 7-24 Spine

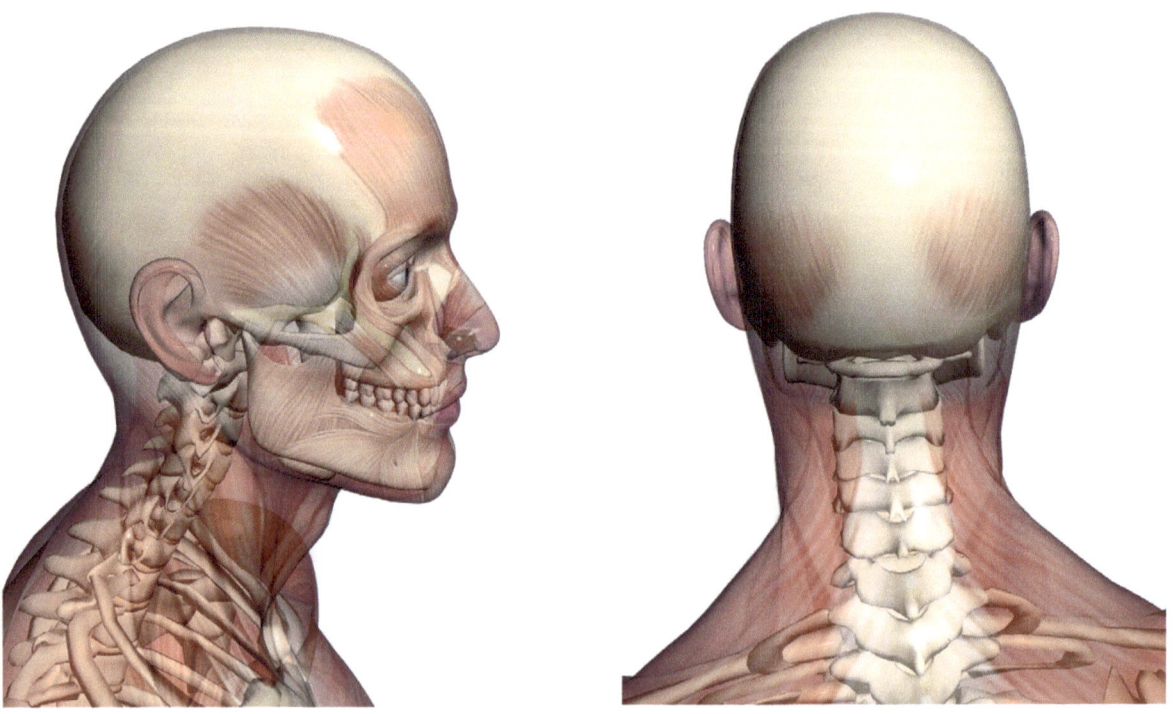

Figure 7-25 Cervical spine

144 Musculoskeletal System

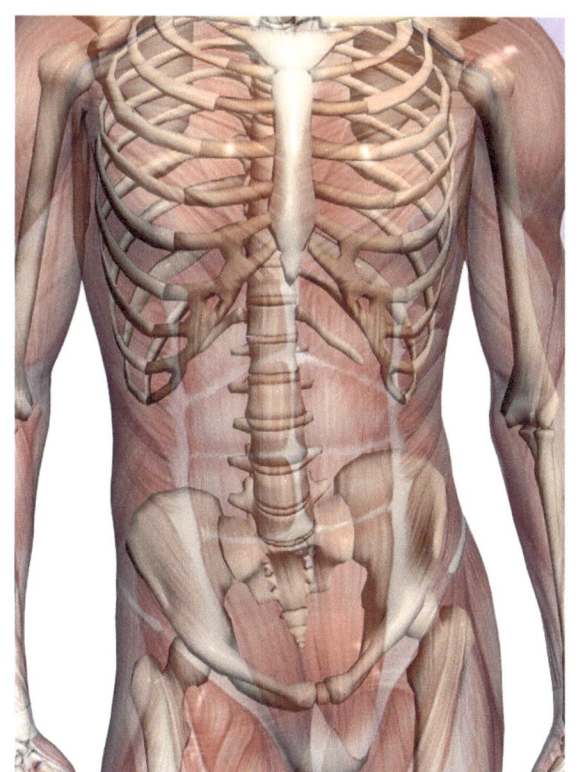
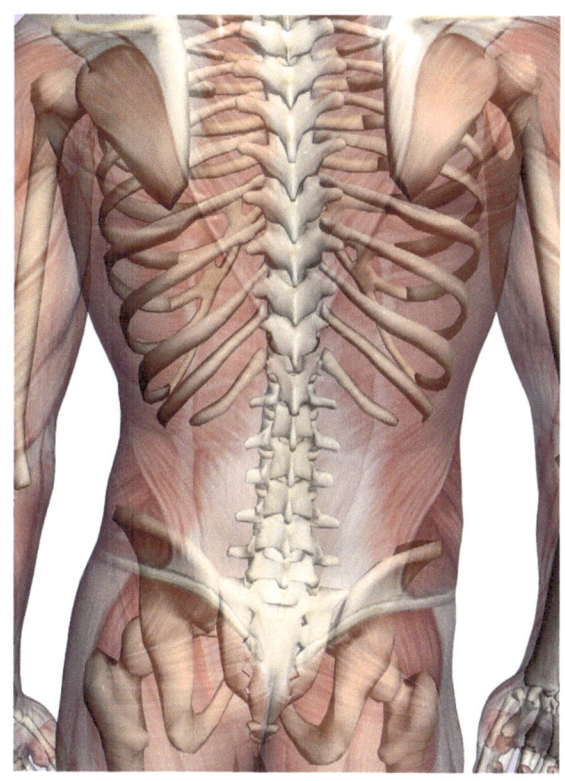

Figure 7-26 Skeletal system - Anterior and posterior view

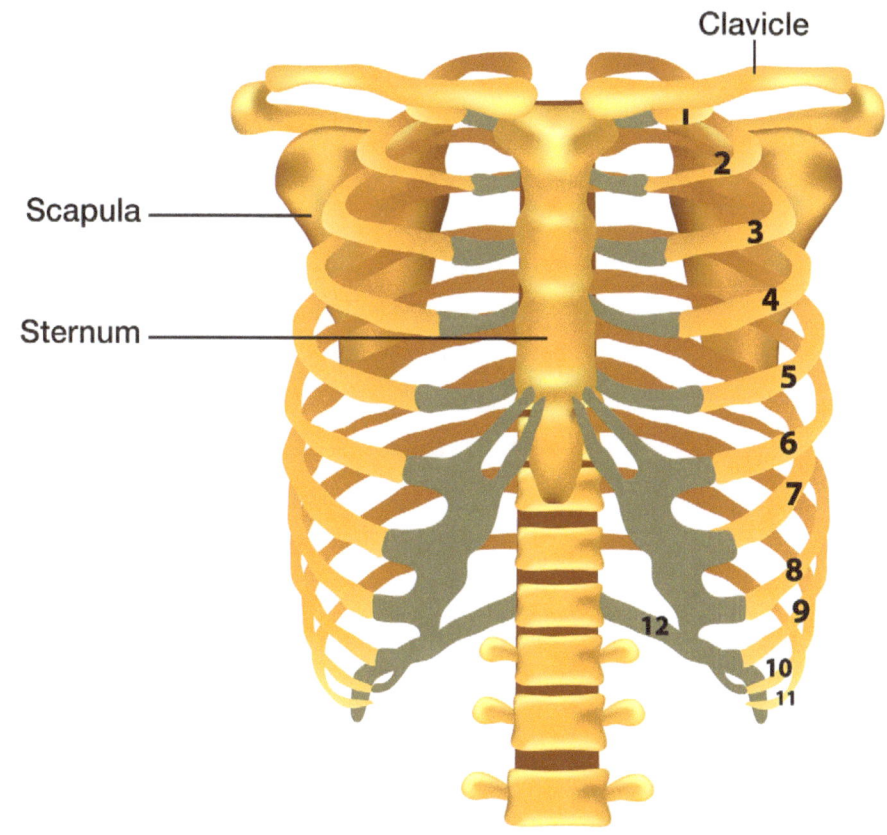

Figure 7-27 Rib cage

Musculoskeletal System 145

3. The lumbar or low back region has 5 vertebrae which are larger than other vertebrae which transfer the load of head, neck, thorax and upper limbs to the sacrum below. This region has also a good range of mobility.
4. Below the lumbar region, the 5 sacral vertebrae are fused together to form a sacrum, which transfers weight of the whole body to the lower limbs. No movements occur in this region as it is fused.
5. The last region or tip of the spine is called the coccyx, here 4 vertebrae are fused together to form one bone, it is also called tail bone.

Each spinal bone or vertebrae has a central ring called the vertebral foramen. Anterior bony body and posterior connecting arch called the vertebral arch, which contains transverse and spinous processes.

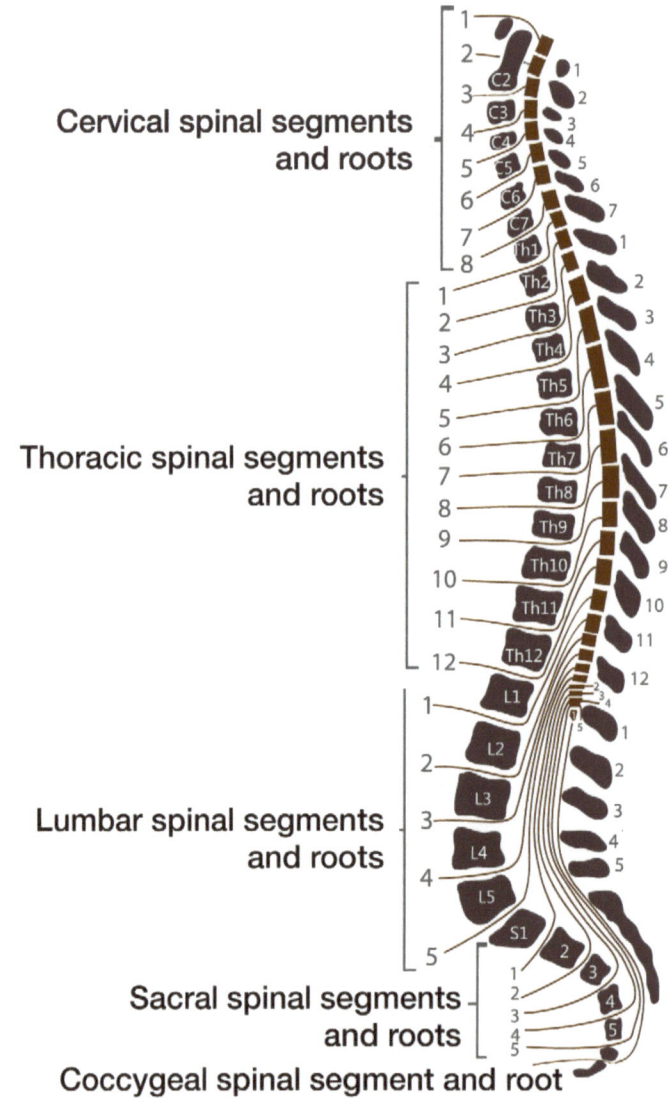

Figure 7-28 Spine, spinal segments and roots

146 **Musculoskeletal System**

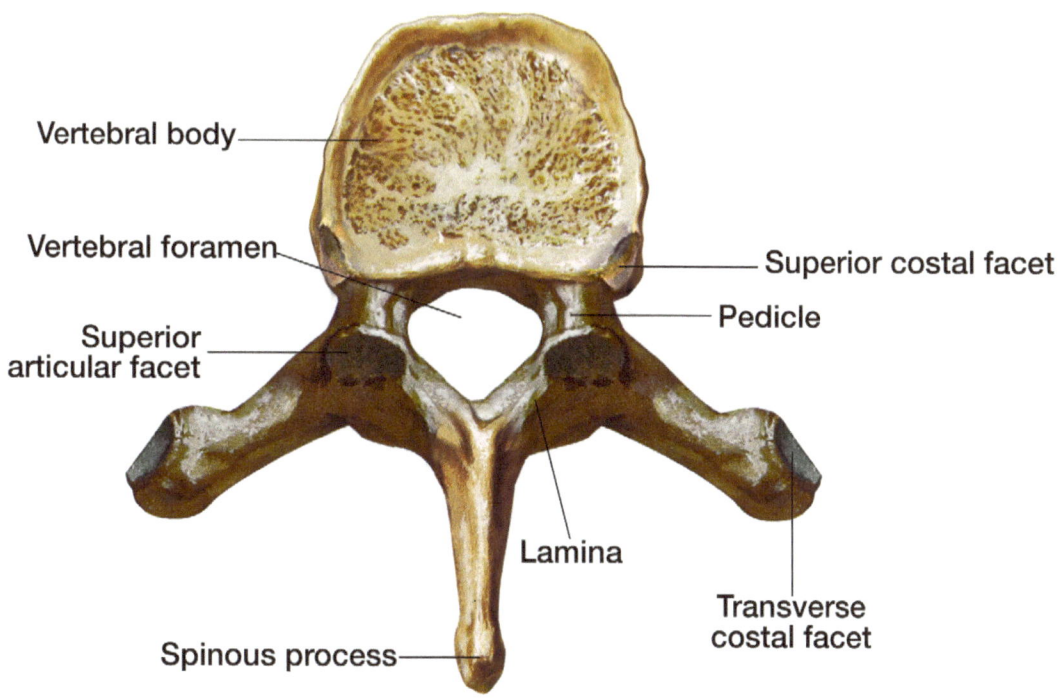

Figure 7-29 Vertebrae anatomy

Cushion-like cartilaginous structures called the intervertebral discs are present between the adjacent vertebral bodies. They contain a fibrous outer ring known as the annulus fibrosis and a jelly-like inner substance called the nucleus pulposus. This gives the cushioning effect to the spine and helps in mobility of the spine.

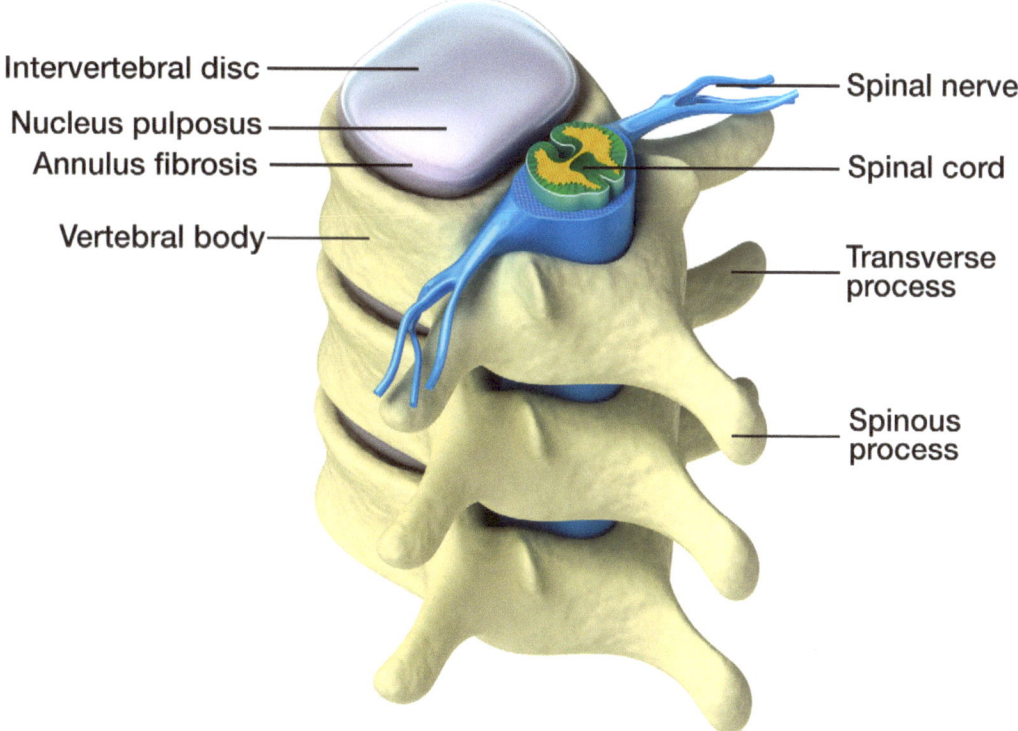

Figure 7-30 Spine anatomy

Musculoskeletal System

Considering the extremities, the lower and the upper extremities bear a close resemblance. We can divide the lower extremity into thigh, lower leg and foot. The thigh is made up of **thighbone or femur** which is the longest and largest bone of the body. The lower leg has two bones: tibia and fibula. The tibia is thicker and on the inner side while the fibula is thinner and located on the outer side. The knee has a cap called the patella. The bones of the foot are divided into tarsal bones, metatarsal bones and phalanges. The upper extremity can be divided into arm, forearm and hand. The humerus is present in the arm and the forearm consists of ulna in the inner side and radius on the outer side. The bones in the hands can be divided into carpal bones, metacarpal bones and phalanges.(Refer fig 7-1, page 125)

DISORDERS OF SKULL, SPINE, THORAX AND SPINE

SPONDYLOSIS

Degenerative arthritis of the apophyseal joints or facet joints of the spine may result in problems with ligaments and discs and is referred to as spondylosis. The spinal canal may narrow and compress the spinal cord and the spinal nerves. It occurs in highly mobile regions of the spine. Cervical and lumbar regions are usually affected.

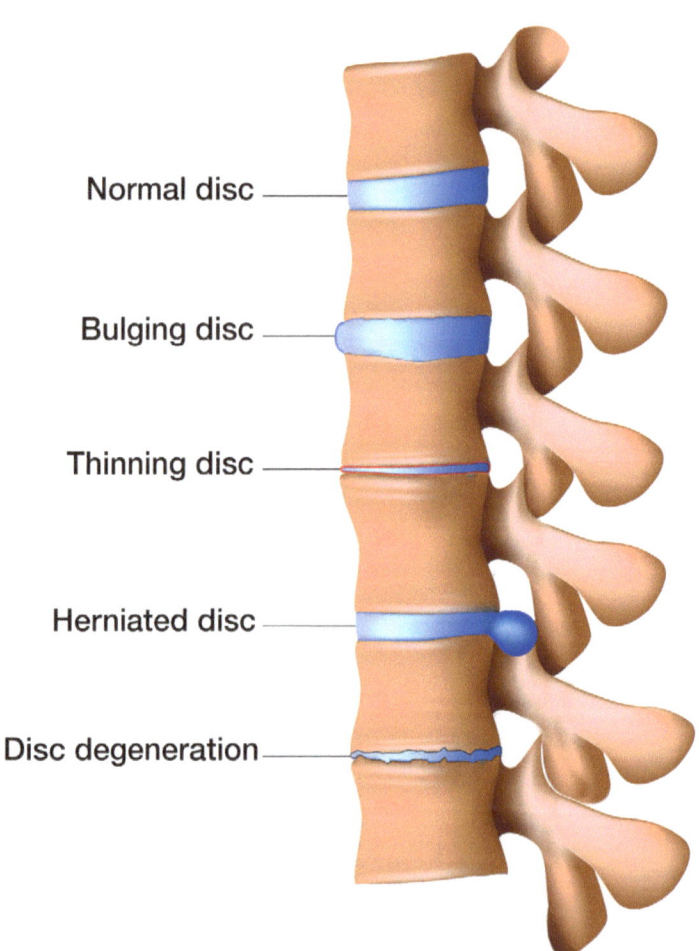

Figure 7-31 Spondylosis

The pain may range from mild discomfort to severe crippling dysfunction. Cervical spondylosis can lead to chronic pain and stiffness in the neck that may also radiate to the upper extremities. Similarly it can affect the lumbar region and the pain can radiate down to the lower limbs. Pain and stiffness may become more severe with activity. Numbness and weakness of the regions involved are also common in this case. Spondylosis can be treated conservatively using physical therapy modalities or injection to the involved regions.

SPONDYLOLYSIS AND SPONDYLOLISTHESIS

A stress fracture in the vertebrae is called spondylolysis. It usually occurs in the fifth lumbar vertebrae and less commonly affects the fourth lumbar vertebrae. *Spondylos* in Greek means spine and *lysis* means a break. The fracture of the pars vertebra connecting the vertebral arch with body resulting in shift of vertebra from its place is referred to as spondylolisthesis. If too much slippage occurs, the bones may begin to press on nerves and surgery may be necessary to correct the condition. Some sports such as gymnastics, weight lifting and football constantly over stretches the spine and can result in a stress fracture causing spondylolisthesis.

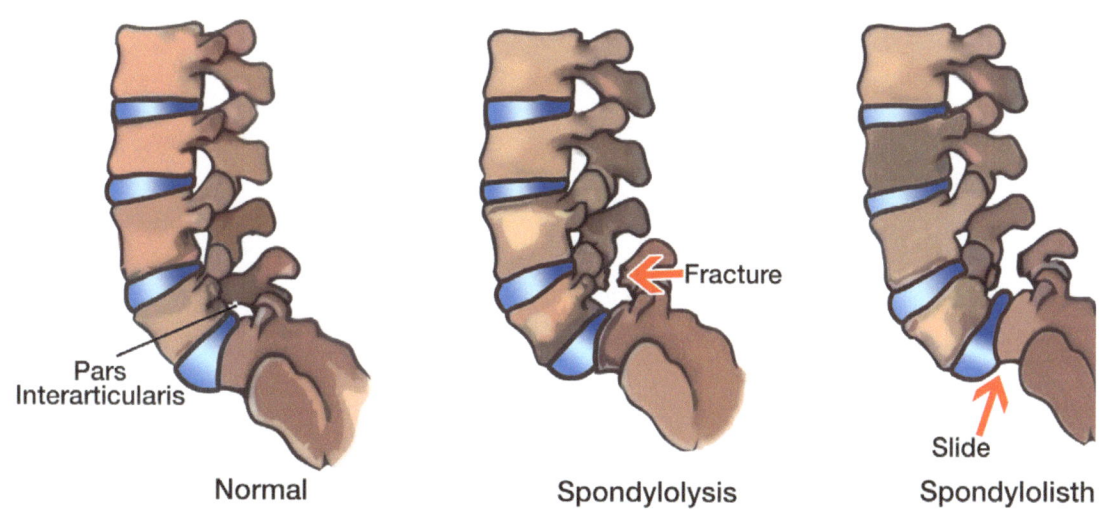

Figure 7-32 Spondylolysis and Spondylolisthesis

Many people remain asymptomatic with spondylolysis and spondylolisthesis without any obvious symptoms. Pain usually spreads across the lower back, and may feel like a muscle strain. Spondylolisthesis can cause spasms that stiffen the back and tighten the hamstring muscles, resulting in changes to posture and gait. If the slippage is more severe, surgical treatment is required.

SCIATICA

Pain in the lower back and hip radiating down the back of the thigh into the leg is commonly referred to as sciatica. The sciatic nerve arises from the lumbar and sacral vertebra (L4, L5, S1, S2, S3). A ruptured disc, a bony spur or a growing tumor can irritate the sciatic nerve which extends to the legs. Pain then radiates at the back of the thigh all the way down to the toes from the lumbar and sacral vertebrae. Though the pain is distributed in the leg along the nerve course, the actual cause is in the lumbar and the sacral vertebrae. In some cases, the pain is only related to the lumbar spondylosis and the sciatic nerve may not even be involved. Treatment of sciatica includes probable rest for at least a few days while the inflammation goes away, along with possible prescription of nonsteroidal anti-inflammatory medications (NSAIDs). Physical therapy modalities like TENS are also of great help. However, in severe cases surgical decompression of the nerve is important.

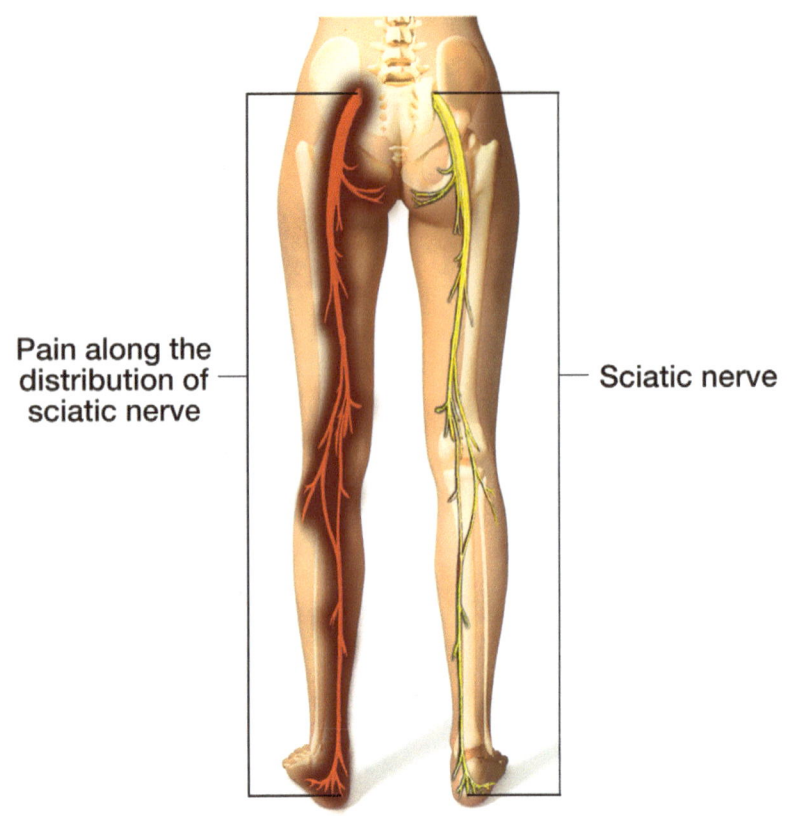

Figure 7-33 Sciatica

HERNIATED INTERVERTEBRAL DISC

Most people have encountered patients complaining about their slipped disc or ruptured disk in their neck or lower back. What they actually describe is a herniated disc. It occurs when a part of the center, nucleus pushes through the outer edge of the disc and results in pressure on the nerves. Spinal nerves are very sensitive to even slight amounts of pressure and pain, numbness or weakness may be felt in one or both arms or legs.

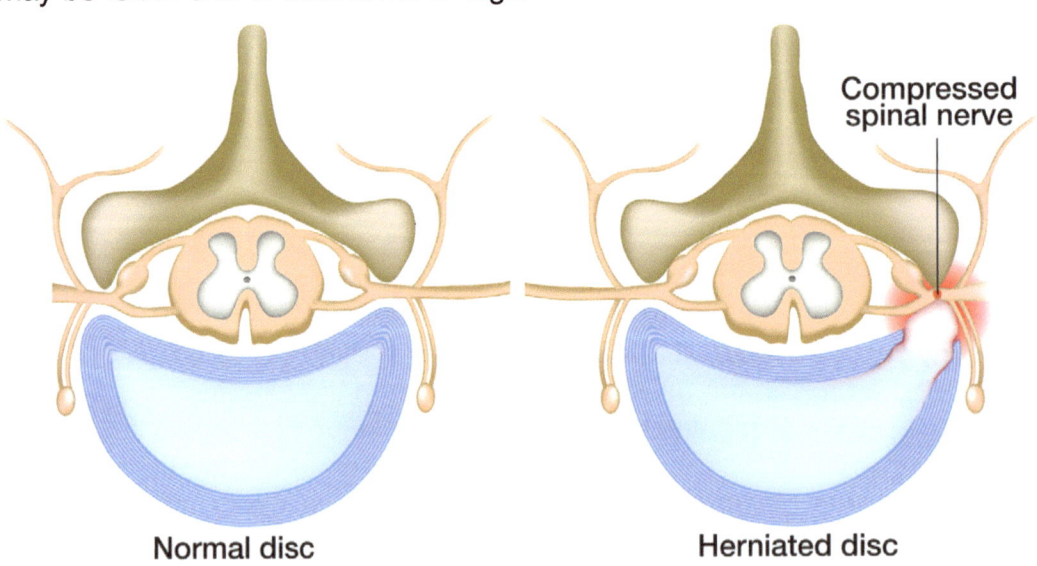

Figure 7-34 Spinal disc herniation

Musculoskeletal System

The symptoms might also include weakness in one leg or one arm, tingling sensation or numbness in limbs, loss of bladder or bowel control, a burning pain centered in the neck or back. Conservative treatment includes bed rest, anti-inflammatory medication and muscle relaxers. Cold compresses or ice may also be effective; however, in severe cases surgical reduction of the herniated disc is necessary.

KYPHOSIS

Kyphosis is an abnormal curvature of spine where there is an exaggerated rounding to the back. A variety of disorders may be responsible for this condition; it can be postural which is often attributed to "slouching" or congenital where spinal column does not develop properly while the fetus is still in the womb. Treatment will depend on the reason for the deformity. Most teens with postural kyphosis will do well throughout their lives. An exercise program may help with back pain, if present.

SCOLIOSIS

Scoliosis is a condition where there is side-to-side spinal curvature. The spine of an individual with scoliosis looks more like an "S" or a "C" rather than a straight line, making the person's waist or shoulders appear uneven. Other symptoms include prominent shoulder blade, elevated hips and leaning to one side. They are usually asymptomatic but in severe cases can cause breathing difficulties. Most spine curves in children with scoliosis will remain small. If a curve does progress a brace can be used to prevent it from getting worse. Children with braces can continue to participate in the full physical and social activities.

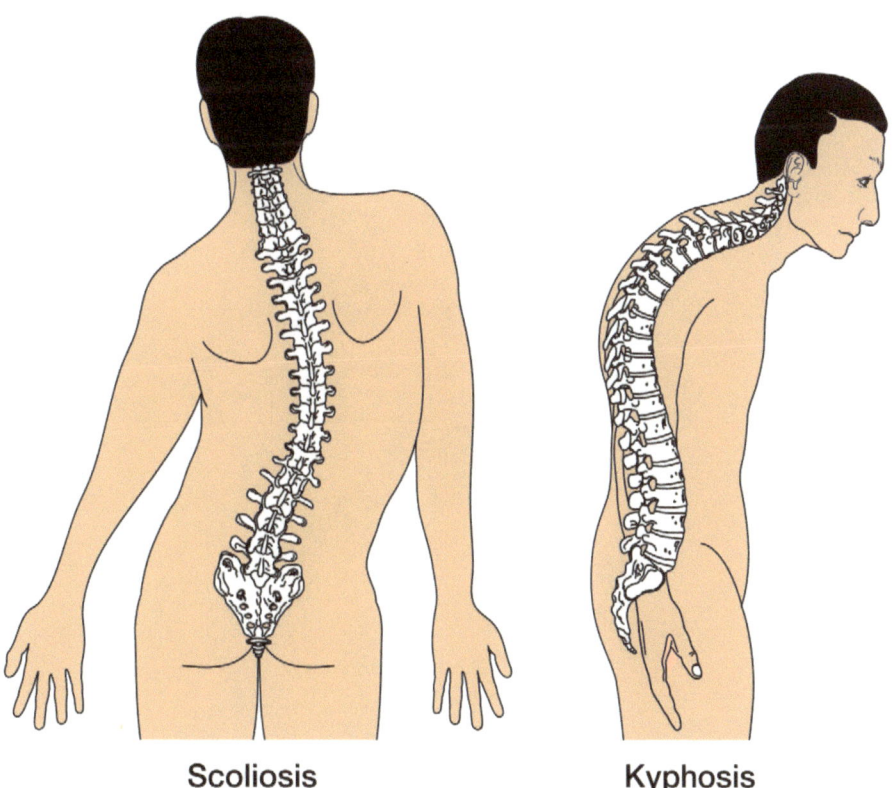

Figure 7-35 Scoliosis & Kyphosis

Musculoskeletal System

Chapter 8

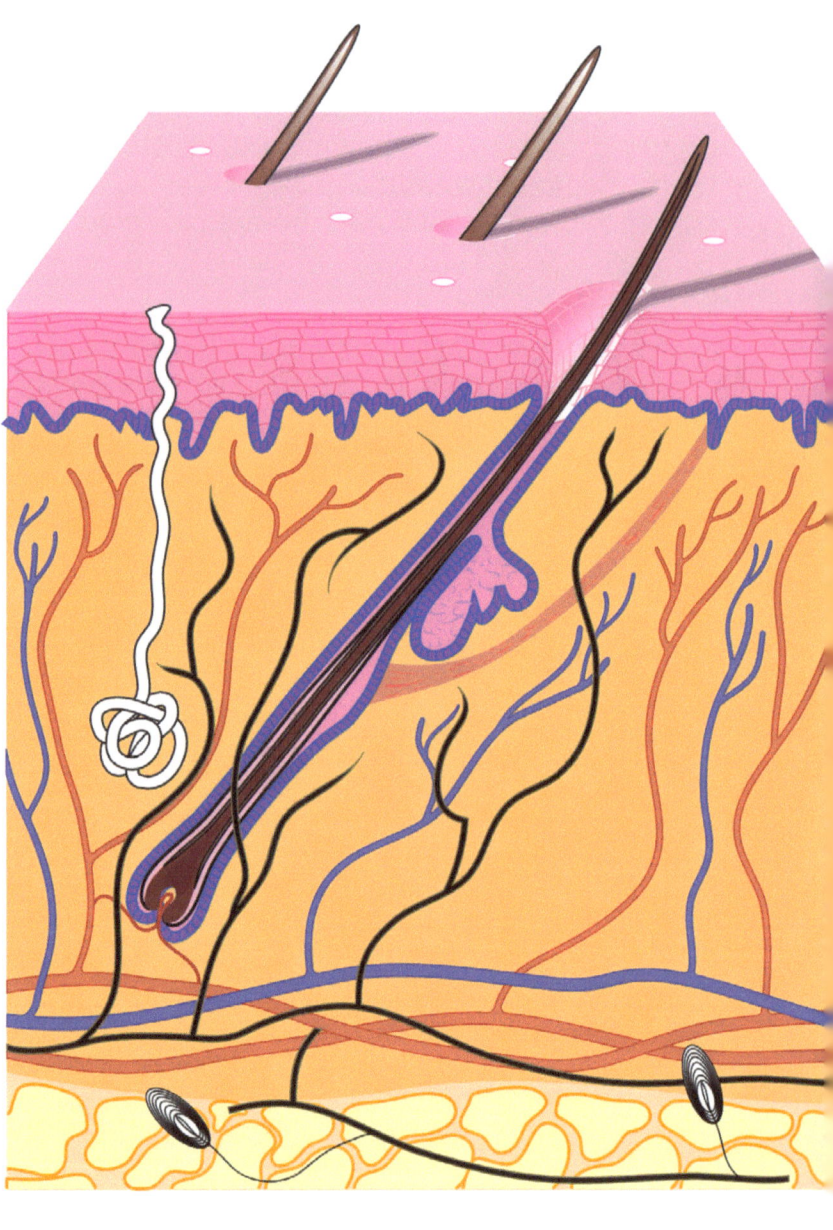

Skin

TABLE OF CONTENTS

INTRODUCTION 154
DISORDERS OF SKIN 155
    Scabies 155
    Psoriasis 155
    Eczema 156
    Impetigo 156
    Ring worm 157
    Warts 158
    Alopecia 158
    Leprosy 159
    Shingles (or) Herpes zoster 159
    Acne vulgaris (or) Pimples 160
    Wound healing 161

SKIN

INTRODUCTION

Skin is the largest organ of the body. It is not uniformly thick, at some places it is thick and at some places it is thin. The average thickness of skin is 1 to 2 mm. It is thickest in the sole of the foot and palms of the hand. It is thinnest in the eyelids and penis.

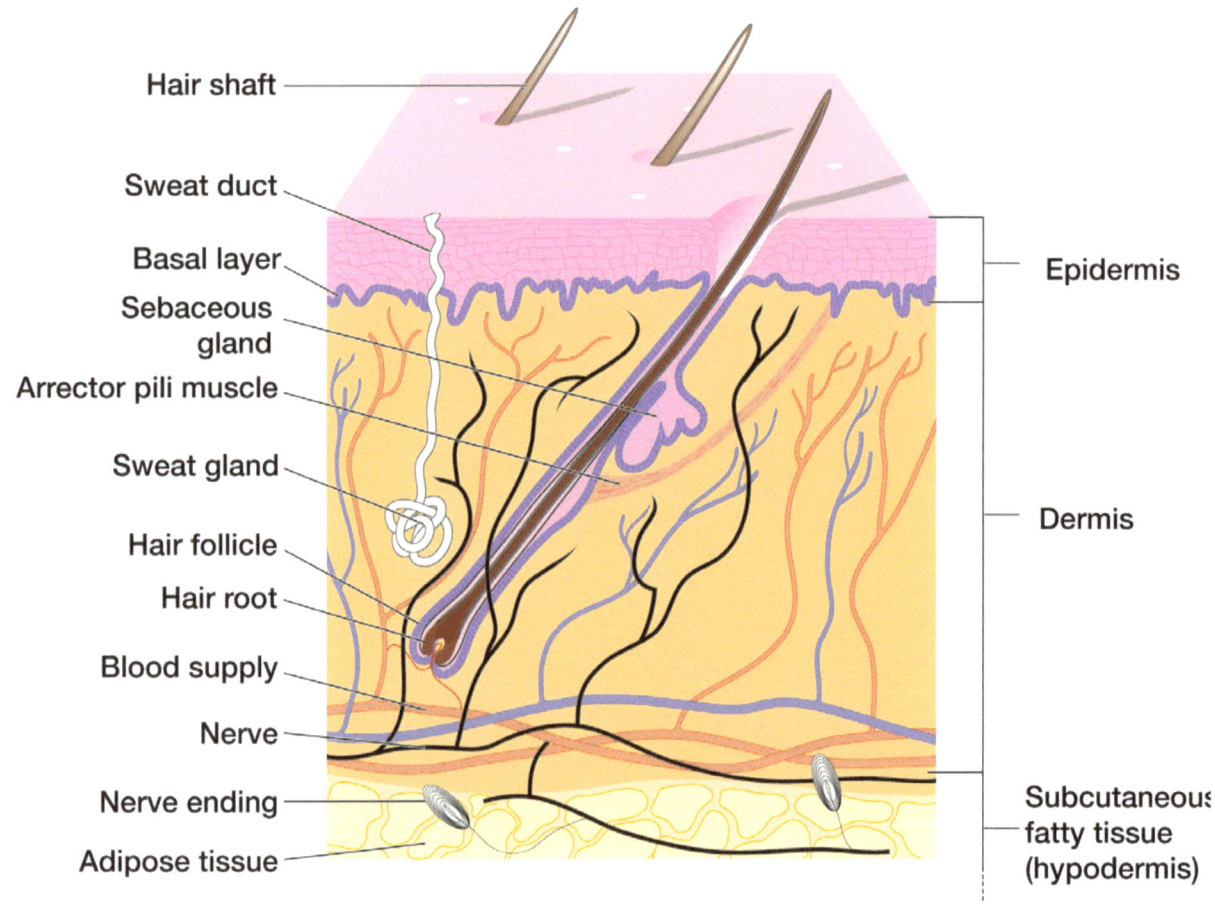

Fig 8-1 Skin anatomy

It has two layers:
- Outer epidermis
- Inner dermis

Epidermis has five layers. They are as follows:

Stratum corneum (first) has dead cells. Stratum lucidum (second) is shiny in character. Stratum granulosum (third) secretes keratin. The lower most two layer has melanocytes which secretes melanin. They are responsible for the pigmentation of skin.

- Skin is the body's largest organ
- The epidermis around the palms and soles is the thickest -measuring 1.5 mm and thinnest in the eyelids and penis

The inner dermis has collagens which is responsible for the elastic property of skin and storing and holding of water. The dermis has hair follicles, sweat glands and sebaceous glands.

Below the skin is the subcutaneous tissue which connects the skin to the internal structures of the body.

DISORDERS OF SKIN

SCABIES

Scabies is a parasitic infection caused by a mite and it is a common worldwide public health problem. This mite creates mini tunnels underneath the skin which are called burrows. Eggs are deposited in the burrow which develop into larvae within a few days and the cycle begins again. The body reacts to this organism and produces papules (a distinct elevated lesion up to 0.5 cm in diameter).

The main symptom is itching and the common sites involved are palms, soles and genital area in boys. It is common in unhygienic conditions and spreads due to intimate personal contact.

PSORIASIS

Psoriasis is a common scaling skin disease, non-infectious probably genetic in origin which runs in families. It is a chronic inflammatory disease of the skin. Apart from genetic predisposition, it is also caused by certain drugs, stressful living conditions, and lack of sun exposure.

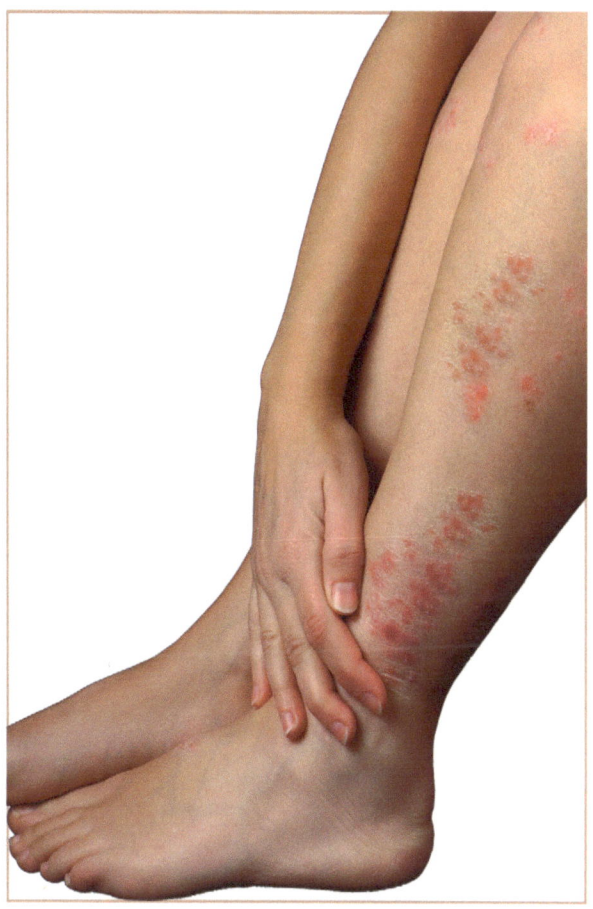

Fig 8-2 Psoriasis

The disease is characterized by well-defined red plaques with silvery scales which are clearly demarcated. These are compared to flakes of mica. The onset of psoriasis is typically slow starting with only one or few lesions which are reddish in colour covered by scales. When they are scratched the underlying blood vessels starts bleeding. By the age of 20 years, about 30 percent of the psoriasis patients have developed their first lesion. Once they develop, and if left untreated, they tend to stay around for several months. The common sites involved are elbows, knees, buttock and scalp. The nails are damaged occasionally. The whole body may be involved and this requires intensive care and treatment.

- The amount of production of the pigment melanin determines the color of the human skin. Large amount of melanin results in darker skin while small amount of melanin results in lighter skin
- Every minute our skin looses about 30,000 to 40,000 dead skin cells from its surface

ECZEMA

Eczema can refer to virtually any skin infections. The various causes are dandruff, irritants, allergens like nickel, wool, alcohol, and repeated rubbing or scratching. It has also got a genetic predisposition. The presenting symptoms often include dryness, itching, cracking of the skin, and edema. There are two types of eczema: (i) Acute (ii) Chronic.

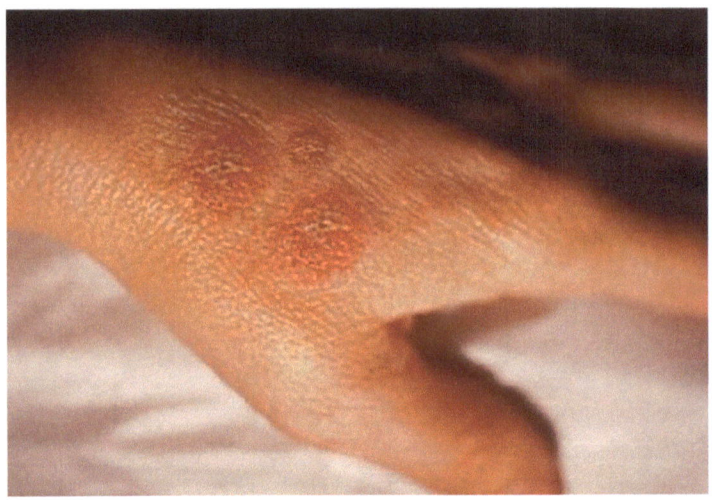

Fig 8-3 Eczema

Acute eczema is characterized by redness, swelling, papules, vesicles (an elevated lesion less than 0.5 centimeter in diameter filled with fluid and are often transparent), and blisters with fluid oozing out. In chronic eczema it is often dry leathery thickening with increased skin marking secondary to rubbing and scratching.

Hands and legs are the common sites involved. Individual causative factors should be identified and avoided.

IMPETIGO

Impetigo is skin infection caused by bacteria. The lesion of impetigo is a blister like pustule (a vesicle filled with pus). When this breaks open, another form of impetigo can manifest itself. When this ulcerates, it is called ecthyma.

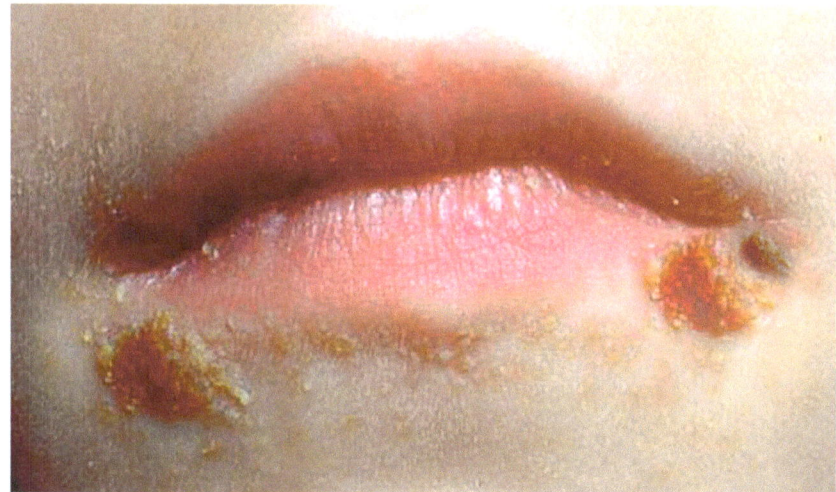

Fig 8-4 Impetigo

It occurs in arms and legs of children. The lesions are itchy and it spreads quickly due to the multiplication of bacteria to surrounding areas. If this disease is left untreated, it can cause permanent damage to the kidneys.

RING WORM

It is a fungal infection. This fungus tends to grow in the moist skin in between toes. It also causes ring shape rash that spreads all over the body. Sometimes it looks like dandruff when it involves the scalp. The other sites involved are the nails and genital area. This infection is contracted in places where people walk barefoot, have contact with pet animals, or if they wear tight inner garments. It has a characteristic ring like lesion. The lesion is red or brown in colour and has peripheral thickening.

Antifungal therapy is used and the patient is advised to wear loose inner garments.

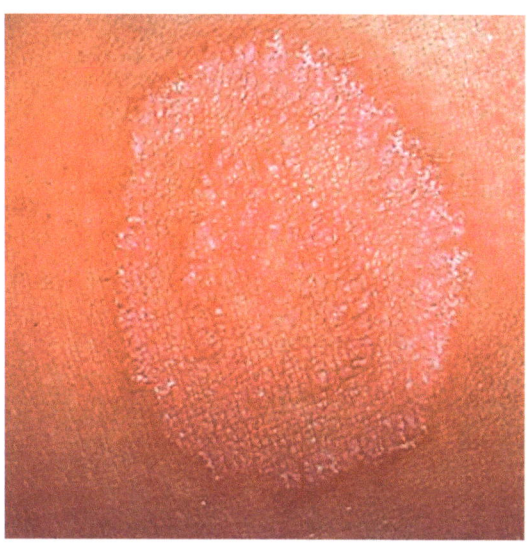

Fig 8-5 Ring worm

WARTS

It is a superficial skin infection caused by virus which multiplies in a single spot, enlarges and then produces a small protruding lump called wart. These are demarcated lesions which look like a cauliflower. It may bleed on injury and tend to grow slowly if not hurt.

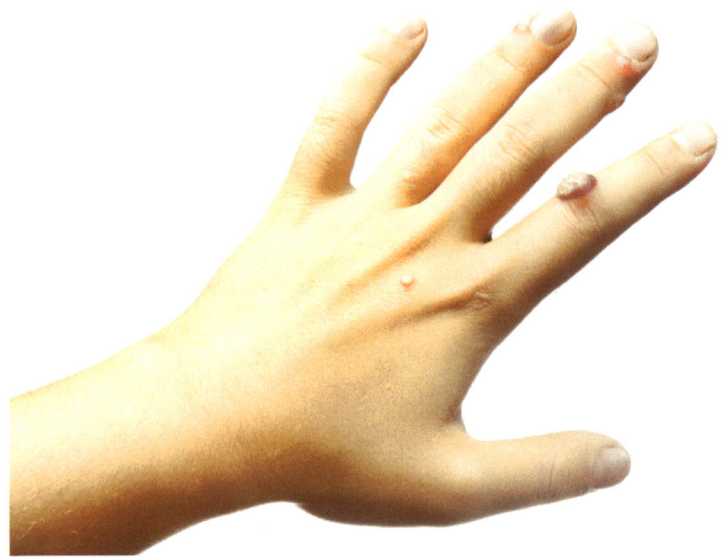

Fig 8-6 Warts

ALOPECIA

Alopecia means hair loss. There are various causes for loss of hair. The commonest is baldness; the pattern is common in whole families and is inherited. The other causes include infections, hormonal imbalance, vitamin deficiencies, stress etc.

- On an average we loose 100 hairs per day from the scalp

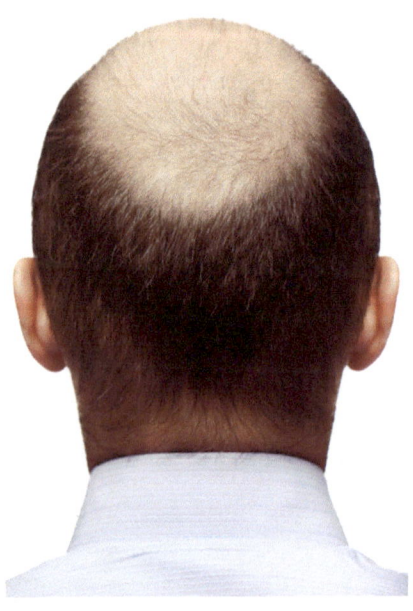

Fig 8-7 Alopecia

LEPROSY

Leprosy (hansen's disease) is a skin deforming disease which is a serious threat in many developing countries because of poverty, though it has lost its impact due to proper medications. It is caused by a bacteria. It mainly affects the skin, nerves, mucous membrane and is transmitted through nasal secretions that contain leprosy bacteria.

There are two types of leprosy. One is tuberculoid leprosy and the other is lepromatous leprosy. In tuberculoid leprosy, the patient will have few white lesions. The symptoms include loss of heat, cold and touch sensation, there is no itching. The bacteria multiply and invade the skin, nerves and lymph tissue. Since there is loss of pain perception, ulcers are common due to trauma. In case of lepromatous leprosy, the lesions are enormous with abundant multiplication of bacteria. The whole thickness of the skin is involved which produces disfigurement to the patient.

Multidrug therapy is recommended by WHO for leprosy since it cannot be treated by a single drug.

SHINGLES (or) HERPES ZOSTER

The virus that causes chicken pox causes shingles. This occurs in adults who had a prior exposure to the chicken pox virus in childhood. The virus is latent in the nerves of the spinal cord.

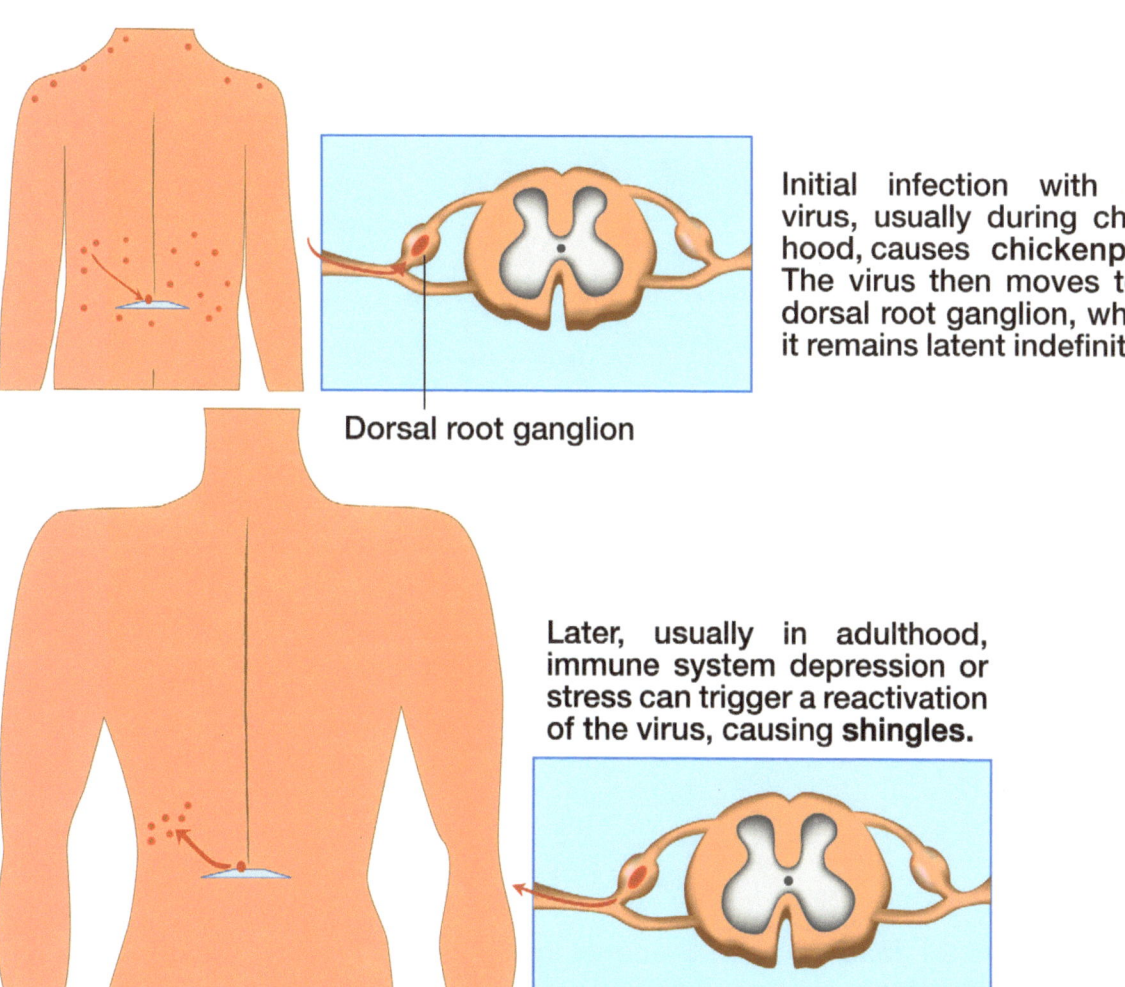

Fig 8-8 Shingles or Herpes zoster

Skin 159

In an adult when the person's immune status comes down due to stress or infection this virus starts migrating along the nerve fibers to the particular skin segment. It is confined to a single segment of the skin and hence called as shingles. It produces shooting-type of pain which lasts for 2 to 3 days. It produces a rash which lasts for 4 days and then produces blisters. The treatment is symptomatic with antiviral therapy.

ACNE VULGARIS (or) PIMPLES

Adolescents are usually affected when they attain puberty. It is a skin disease that affects the oil glands. It may be hereditary in origin or due to hormonal imbalance. The oily secretions from the skin glands are accumulated with the multiplication of bacteria and often aggravates the lesion and results in white heads and black heads.

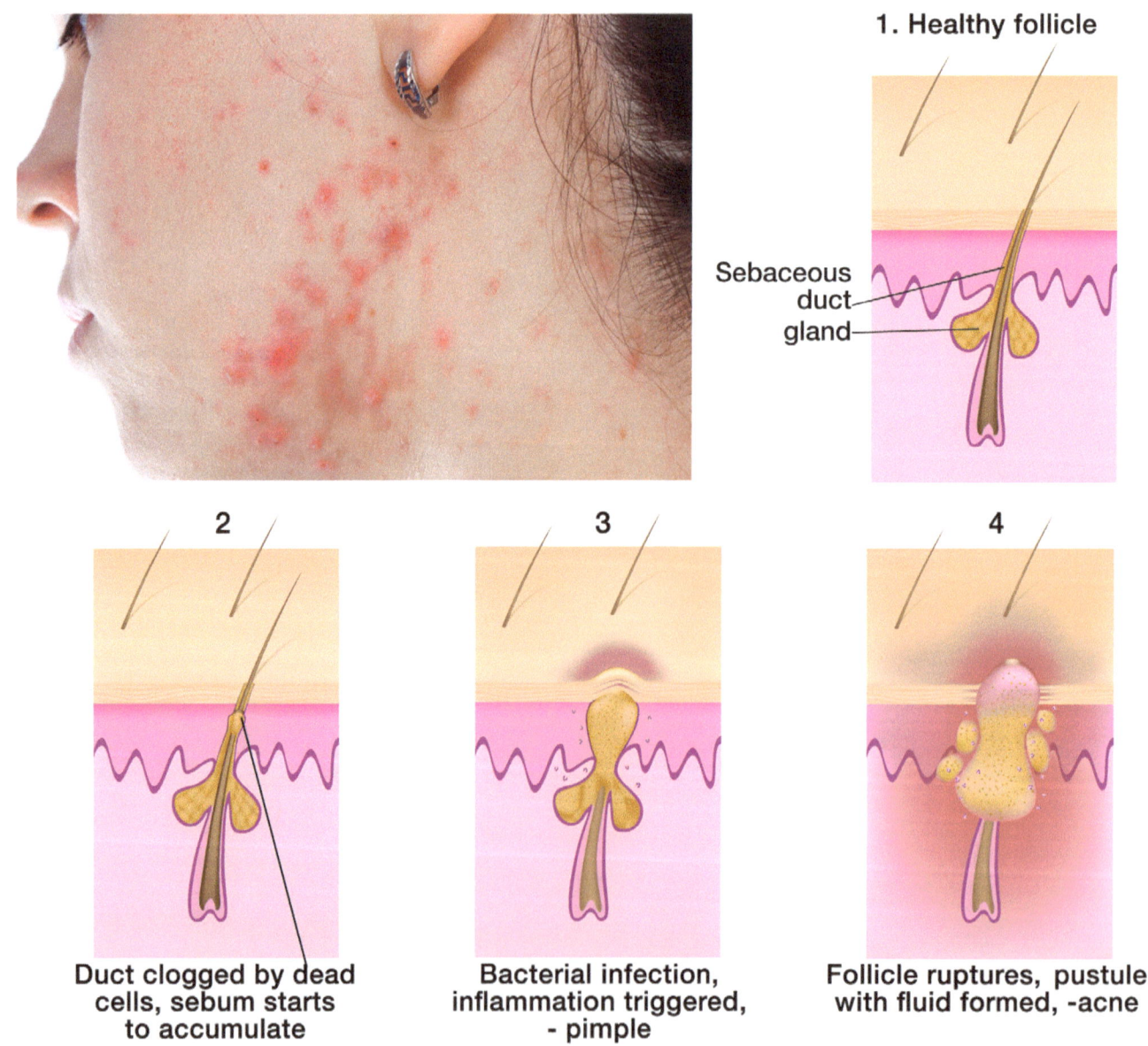

Fig 8-9 Formation of pimples and acne

WOUND HEALING

Wound healing is a complex process that begins at the moment of injury and can continue for a few days to a few months or even years.

It involves 1) Inflammatory phase, 2) Proliferative phase, 3) Remodeling phase.

Inflammatory phase- In this stage the blood vessels contract at the site of injury and blood clot is formed. After this stage the blood vessels dilate to allow the white blood cells, nutrients, antibodies, enzymes to reach the area of injury. This phase lasts from 2 to 5 days.

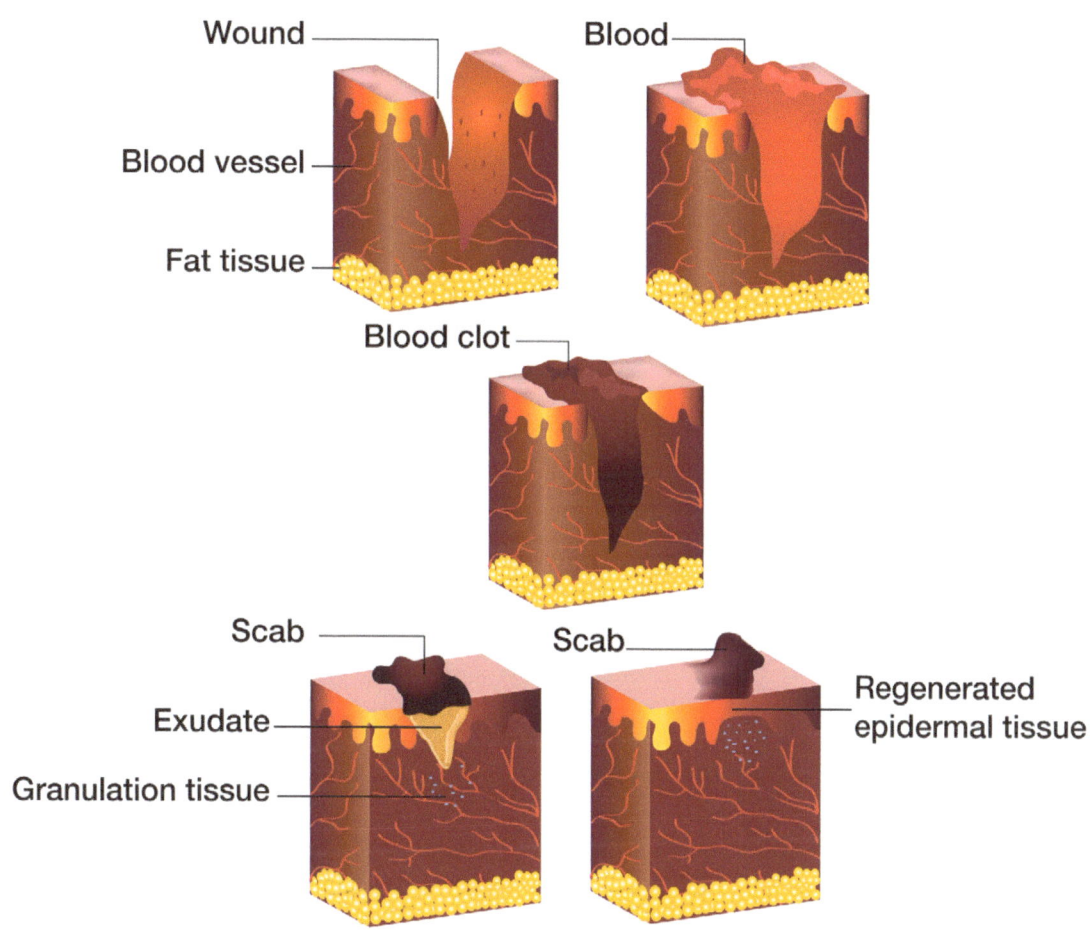

Fig 8-10 Wound healing

Proliferative phase last from 2 days to 3 weeks. In this phase new granulation tissue forms and the color of the tissue indicates how healthy the tissue is. The granulation tissue consists of collagens and a network of new capillaries. If the granulation tissue is red or pink it indicates that it is healthy and there is sufficient levels of oxygen and nutrient supply. If the granulation tissue is dark it indicates lack of oxygen and nutrient supply. This may be due to infection and ischemia.

In the remodeling phase the wound is closed and new collagen forms. This phase may last from 3 weeks to 2 years.

Chapter 9

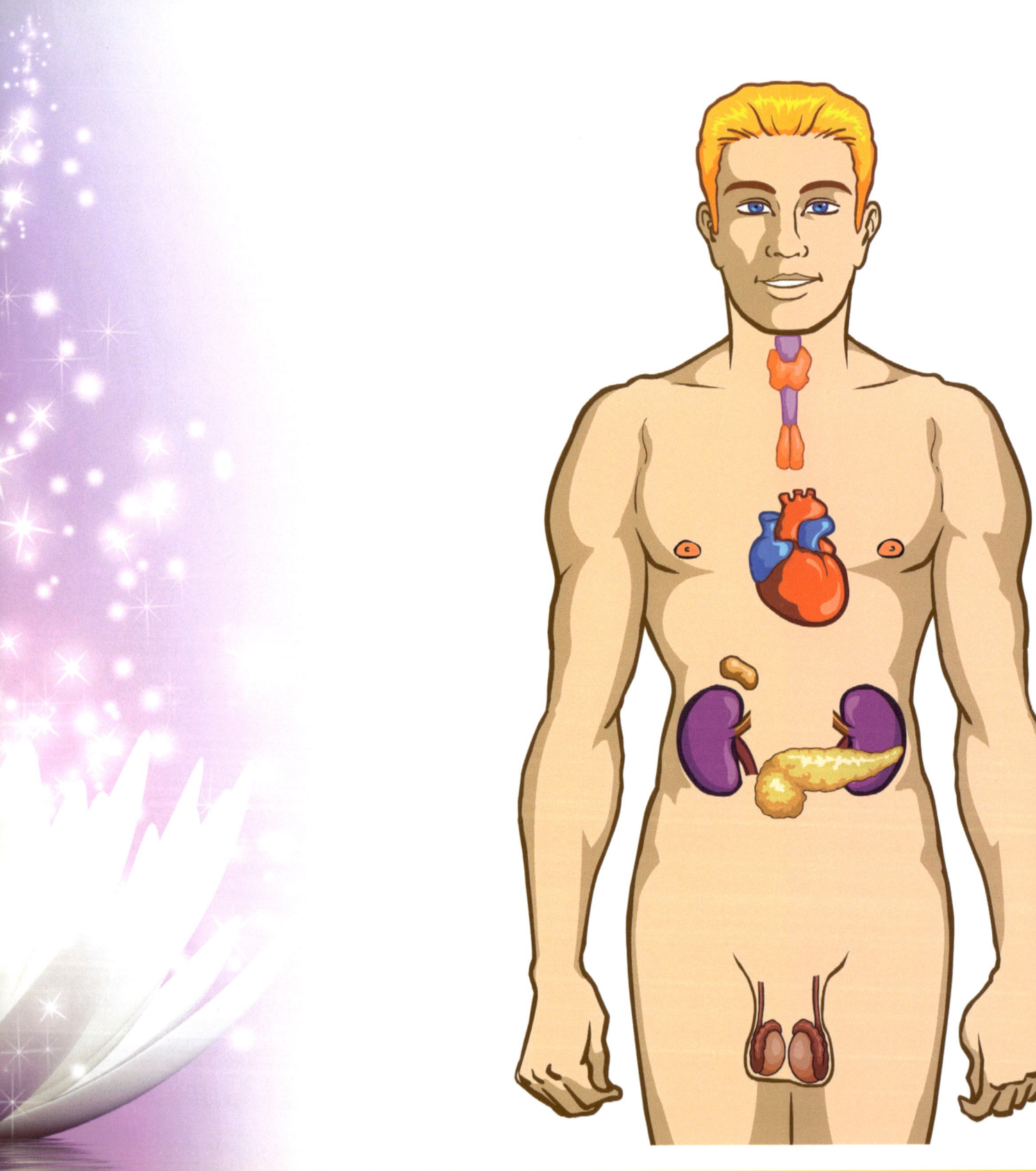

Endocrine system

TABLE OF CONTENTS

- **INTRODUCTION** 165
- **PITUITARY GLAND** 166
- **DISORDERS OF PITUITARY GLAND** 167
- **DISORDERS RELATED TO ANTERIOR LOBE** 167
  - Hyper-secretion 167
    - Acromegaly 167
    - Gigantism 168
  - Hypo-secretion 168
    - Dwarfism 168
    - Panhypopituitarism 168
- **DISORDERS RELATED TO POSTERIOR LOBE** 168
  - Hyper-secretion 168
    - Syndrome of inappropriate ADH (SIADH) 168
  - Hypo-secretion 168
    - Diabetes insipidus 168
- **THYROID GLAND** 168
- **DISORDERS OF THYROID GLAND** 169
  - Hyper-secretion 169
    - Hyperthyroidism 169
  - Hypo-secretion 170
    - Hypothyroidism 170
    - Myxedema 170
    - Cretinism 170
    - Goiter 170
- **PARATHYROID GLAND** 170
- **DISORDERS OF PARATHYROID GLAND** 171
  - Hyper-secretion 171
    - Hyperparathyroidism 171
  - Hypo-secretion 171
    - Hypoparathyroidism 171
- **ADRENAL GLANDS** 172
  - Glucocorticoids 172
  - Mineralocorticoids 172
  - Sex hormones 173
  - Epinephrine (Adrenaline) 173
  - Norepinephrine (Noradrenaline) 173

DISORDERS OF ADRENAL CORTEX 173
Hyper-secretion 173
Adrenal virilism 173
Cushing syndrome 173
Hypo-secretion 173
Addison's disease 174

DISORDERS OF ADRENAL MEDULLA 174
Hyper-secretion 174
Pheochromocytoma 174

PANCREAS 174
Hyper-secretion 175
Hypoglycemia 175
Hypo-secretion 175
Diabetes mellitus 175

OVARIES 177
TESTES 177

ENDOCRINE SYSTEM

INTRODUCTION

The collection of tissues that secrete hormones is referred to as the endocrine system. Endocrine literally means to secrete inside. The hormones are chemical messengers that are secreted by endocrine or ductless glands and are essential for vital functioning of the human body. Various endocrine glands that are present in the body are listed below:

1. Pituitary gland
2. Thyroid gland
3. Parathyroid gland
4. Islets of langerhans
5. Adrenal gland
6. Gonads (testes and ovaries)
7. Thymus.

- 'Hormone' comes from ancient Greek word hormon meaning "urging on"-they cause things to happen.
- There are about 30 distinct hormones produced by the endocrine glands.
- The endocrine gland influences the characteristic of a person to a great extent.

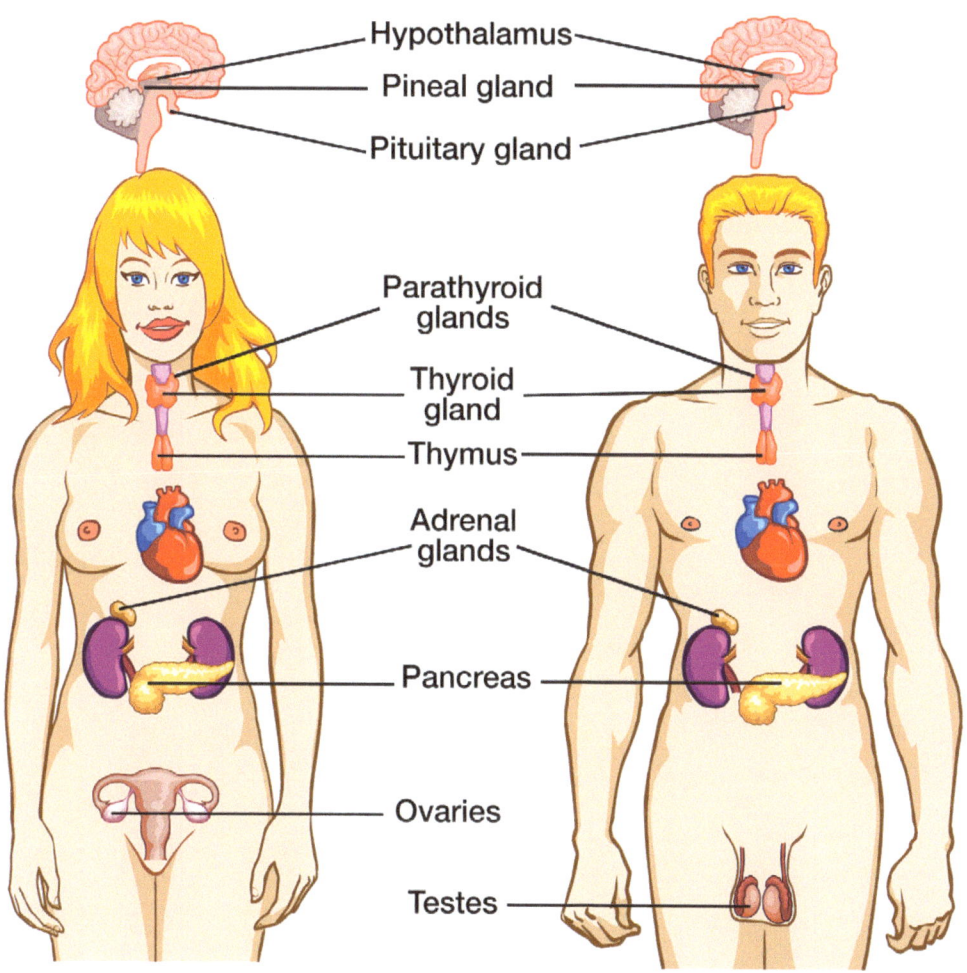

Fig 9-1 Endocrine system

Endocrine System 165

PITUITARY GLAND

The pituitary gland (otherwise called the master gland or hypophysis) is situated at the base of the brain, below the hypothalamus. Pituitary is the central endocrine gland that controls the other endocrine glands and consists of the two following parts:

1. Anterior pituitary or adenohypophysis
2. Posterior pituitary or neurohypophysis

The anterior pituitary secretes the growth hormone or somatotrophic hormone (GH), thyroid stimulating hormone (TSH), adrenocorticotropic hormone (ACTH), gonadotrophic hormone (GnH), follicle stimulating hormone (FSH) and luteinizing hormone (LH), prolactin and melanocyte stimulating hormone (MSH).

- The pituitary gland is the size of a pea and stimulates all other glands of the body. It is also called as the master gland

The hormones secreted by the posterior pituitary are oxytocin and anti-diuretic hormone or vasopressin.

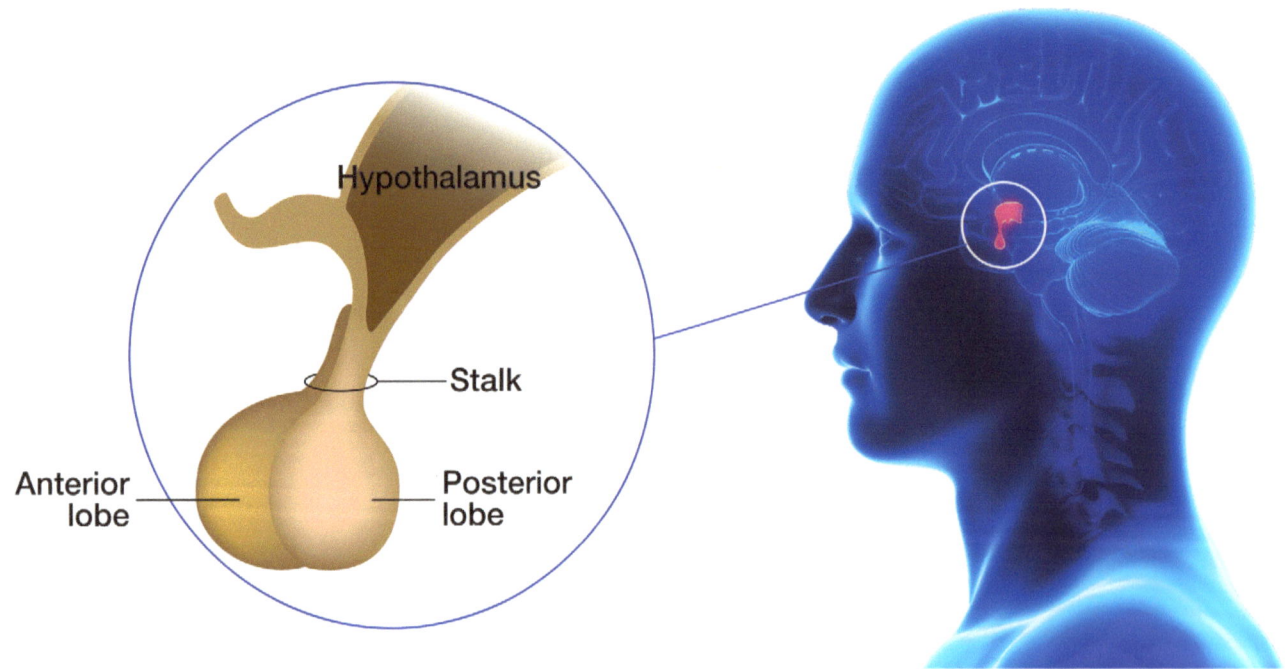

Fig 9-2 Anatomy of pituitary gland

Function of pituitary hormones

The anterior pituitary gland secretes following important hormones:

- The endocrine glands do not have ducts and therefore release the hormones directly into the blood stream

1. Growth hormone (somatotropin)

This hormone results in the growth of the bones and other tissues by promoting protein synthesis. Growth hormone also stimulates the liver to make insulin-like growth factor which enhances the growth of bones.

2. Thyroid-stimulating hormone or thyrotropin

This hormone stimulates the growth and normal secretion of thyroxine of the thyroid gland.

3. Adrenocorticotropic hormone

This hormone stimulates the growth of the adrenal cortex and increases its secretion of steroid hormones.

4. Gonadotropic hormone

The gonadotropic hormones stimulate the hormone secretion of the ovaries in females and the testes in males.

In the female, follicle-stimulating (FSH) hormone and luteinizing hormone (LH) stimulate the growth of ovum in the ovaries, the production of hormones, and ovulation. In the male, FSH influences the production of sperm while LH stimulates the testes to produce testosterone.

5. Prolactin

This hormone enhances and sustains milk production after birth.

6. Melanocyte-stimulating hormone

This hormone influences the formation of melanin and causes pigmentation of the skin. The melanin content in the body determines the color of the skin, hair, and eyes.

The posterior pituitary gland secretes two important hormones presented below which are formed in the hypothalamus and secreted through the posterior pituitary gland:

1. Antidiuretic hormone (ADH)

This hormone, also known as vasopressin, stimulates the reabsorption of water by the kidney tubules. ADH can also increase the blood pressure by constricting arterioles.

2. Oxytocin

During childbirth, oxytocin stimulates the uterus to contract and maintains the labor. Oxytocin is also secreted during suckling and causes the production of milk from the mammary glands.

DISORDERS OF PITUITARY GLAND

Appropriate secretion of glands provides a normal body functioning condition. Increased or decreased secretion may lead to disorders in the body.

DISORDERS RELATED TO ANTERIOR LOBE

HYPER-SECRETION

Acromegaly

It is an excess of growth hormone produced by tumors of the pituitary gland during adulthood causing acromegaly. It results in enlargement of the extremities and bones in the hands, feet, face, and jaw grow abnormally large.

Gigantism

Gigantism is the hyper-functioning of the pituitary gland before puberty, leading to abnormal overgrowth of the body. Gigantism can be corrected by early diagnosis in childhood, followed by removal of the tumor or appropriate treatment to the pituitary.

> - The nervous system controls the endocrine gland

HYPO-SECRETION

Dwarfism

Congenital hypo-secretion of growth hormone results in dwarfism. The children affected are normal mentally, but their bones remain small and underdeveloped.

Panhypopituitarism

Panhypopituiatarism is a condition where all the pituitary hormones are deficient. Functions of target glands such as adrenals, thyroid, ovaries, and testes are also adversely affected.

DISORDERS RELATED TO POSTERIOR LOBE

HYPER-SECRETION

Syndrome of inappropriate ADH (SIADH)

Excessive secretion of antidiuretic hormone produces excess water retention in the body. Treatment consists of dietary water restriction. Tumor, drug reactions, and head injury are among the possible causes.

HYPO-SECRETION

Diabetes Insipidus

Insufficient secretion of antidiuretic hormone causes the kidney tubules to fail to reabsorb water and salts needed. Insipidus means tasteless, reflecting the condition of the dilute urine. Symptoms include polyuria (increased urination) and polydipsia (increased thirst).

THYROID GLAND

The thyroid gland consists of two lobes located on either side of the trachea below thyroid cartilage and produces the prominence on the neck known as the Adam's apple. The isthmus of the thyroid gland is a narrow strip tissue that connects the two lobes. The thyroid glands secretions are tetraiodothyronine (T4),

> - The thyroid hormones regulate the proper growth and development of the brain and nervous system in small children

triiodothyronine (T3) and thyrocalcitonin. The T3 and T4 are hormones synthesized in the thyroid gland from iodine, which is picked up from the blood circulating through the gland.

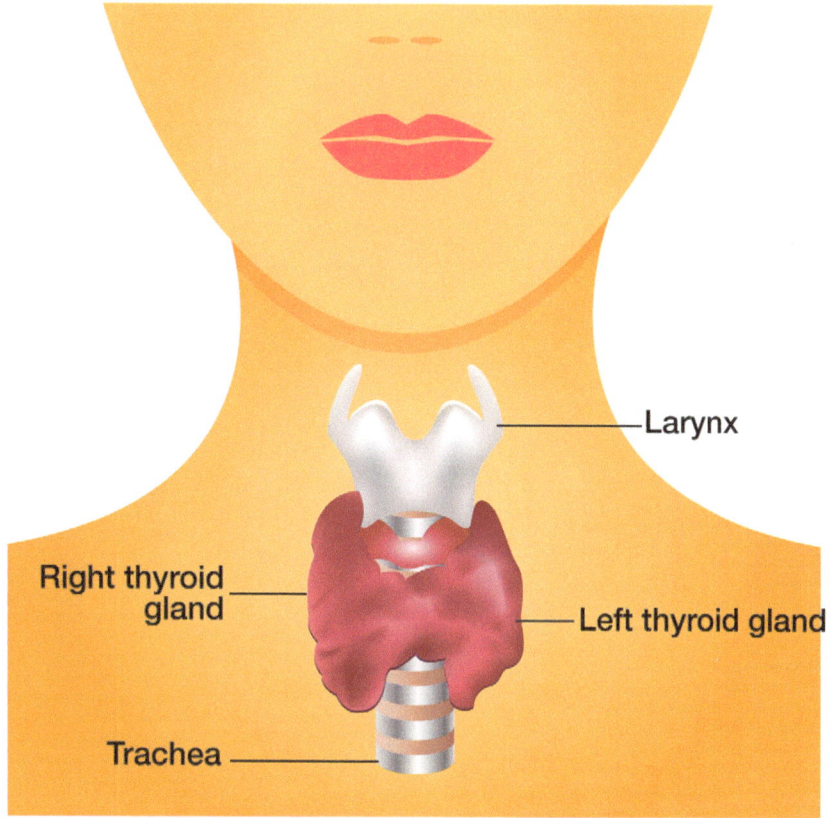

Fig 9-3 Thyroid gland

Function

T4 and T3 are necessary in the body to maintain a normal level of metabolism in all cells. Thyroid hormone aids cells in their uptake of oxygen and thus supports the metabolic rate in the body. Injections of thyroid hormone raise the metabolic rate, whereas removal of the thyroid gland, diminishes thyroid hormone content in the body and results in a lower metabolic rate, heat loss, and poor physical and mental development. Thyrocalcitonin, a more recently discovered hormone produced by the thyroid gland is secreted when calcium levels in the blood are high. It stimulates calcium to leave the blood and enter the bones, thus lowering blood calcium back to normal.

DISORDERS OF THYROID GLAND

HYPER-SECRETION

Hyperthyroidism

The overactivity of the thyroid gland is called hyperthyroidism, and the condition is referred to as thyrotoxicosis or graves disease. It can occur as a result of hyperplasia of the thyroid parenchyma and excessive hormone is released. The metabolic rate in cells is increased. The term 'thyroid storm' is used to indicate the abrupt onset of severe hyperthyroidism. In addition, exophthalmos (where the protrusion of the eyeballs occurs as a result of swelling of the tissue behind the eyeball) and tremors may be present. Treatment of this disease may include removal of thyroid gland, management with antithyroid drugs that reduce the amount of thyroid hormone produced by the gland.

HYPO-SECRETION

Hypothyroidism

This results because of underactivity of the thyroid gland. Several factors can produce hypothyroidism including thyroidectomy (removal of thyroid gland), endemic goiter, and destruction of the gland by irradiation. All these factors, however, have similar physiological effects such as fatigue, muscular and mental sluggishness and constipation. Two manifestations of hypothyroidism are myxedema and cretinism

Myxedema

Myxedema usually occurs in adults. It is a condition where the skin becomes dry and puffy because of the collection of mucus-like material under the skin. Rapid recovery may be noticed if thyroid hormone is provided soon after the symptoms appear.

Cretinism

Extreme hypothyroidism during infancy and childhood leads to lack of normal physical and mental growth known as cretinism. Skeletal growth is more inhibited than soft tissue growth, so the cretin has the appearance of an obese, short, and stocky child. Treatment consists of the administration of thyroid hormone, which may be able to reverse some of the hypothyroid effects.

Goiter

Enlargement of the thyroid gland is referred to as goiter. Goiter may be a symptom of many different conditions. It occurs in certain regions and persons as a result of deficiency of iodine in the diet. Treatment of this type of goitre is to increase the supply of iodine in the diet. Another type of goiter is nodular or adenomatous goiter, in which hyperplasia occurs as well as nodules and adenomas.

PARATHYROID GLAND

The parathyroid glands are four small oval bodies responsible for secretion of parathyroid hormone and located on the dorsal aspect of the thyroid gland. This hormone is also known as parathormone. It mobilizes calcium from bones into the bloodstream, where calcium is necessary for the proper functioning of body tissues and especially muscles. If there is a decrease in blood calcium as in pregnancy, rickets or a vitamin D deficiency disease, parathyroid hormone is secreted in larger amounts to cause calcium to leave the bones and enter the bloodstream. Thus, blood calcium levels are brought back to normal.

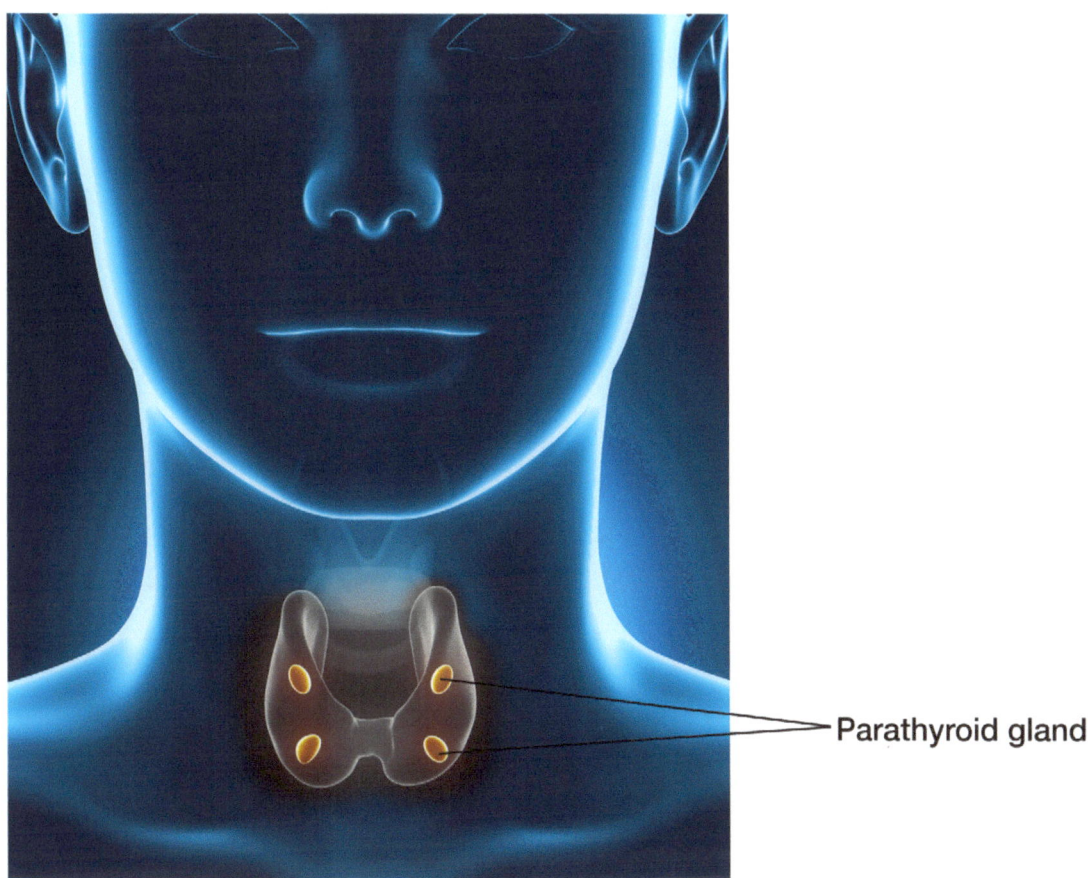

Fig 9-4 Parathyroid gland

DISORDERS OF PARATHYROID GLAND

HYPER-SECRETION

Hyperparathyroidism

Hyperparathyroidism is the excessive secretion of parathormone which results in calcium leaving the bones and entering the bloodstream (hypercalcemia). As a result of this bones become decalcified and susceptible to fractures and cysts. Kidney stones can also occur as a result of hypercalcemia. The cause is often a parathyroid tumor.

HYPO-SECRETION

Hypoparathyroidism

Hypoparathyroidism refers to deficient production of parathyroid hormone which leads to hypocalcemia where the calcium remains in bones and is unable to enter the bloodstream. This results in weakness in the muscles and the nerves accompanied with spasms of muscles and constant muscle contraction called tetany. Administration of calcium plus large quantities of vitamin D can control the calcium level in the bloodstream.

ADRENAL GLANDS

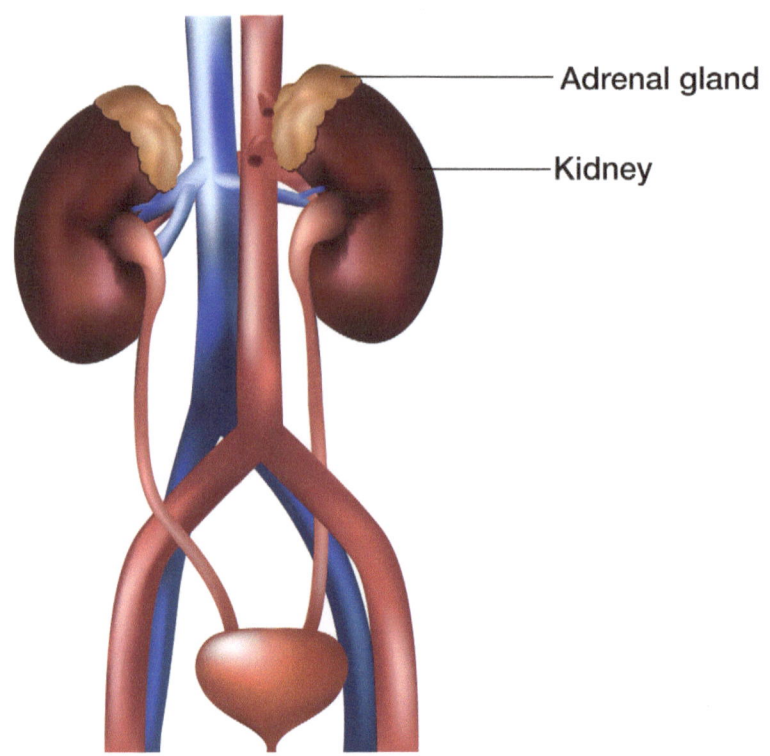

Fig 9-5 Adrenal gland

The adrenal glands also called the suprarenal glands are two small glands situated on top of each kidney. Each gland consists of two parts: an outer cortex and an inner medulla. The cortex secretes the hormones called corticosteroids, and the medulla secretes the hormones known as catecholamines. The adrenal cortex secretes three types of steroid hormones called corticosteroids.

They are as follows:

Glucocorticoids

These steroid hormones have an important influence on the metabolism of sugars, fats, and proteins within all body cells and have a powerful anti-inflammatory effect. Cortisol, a hormone increases the ability of cells to make new sugars out of fats and proteins and also regulates the quantity of sugars, fats, and proteins in the blood and cells. Cortisone is a hormone very similar to cortisol and is useful in treating inflammatory conditions such as rheumatoid arthritis.

Mineralocorticoids

These hormones regulate the amount of electrolytes that are retained in the body. A proper balance of water and salts in the blood and tissues is essential to normal functioning of the body. Aldosterone is a mineralocorticoid hormone that helps in reabsorption of sodium by the kidney tubules. At the same time, aldosterone stimulates the excretion of another electrolyte known as potassium.

Sex hormones

Androgens, estrogens, and progesterone are male and female hormones that maintain the secondary sex characteristics, such as beard and breast development, and are necessary for reproduction.

The adrenal medulla secretes two types of catecholamine hormones, epinephrine and norepinephrine.

Epinephrine (Adrenaline)

This hormone increases cardiac rate, dilates bronchial tubes, and stimulates the production of glucose from a storage substance called glycogen when the body needs glucose.

Norepinephrine (Noradrenaline)

This hormone constricts vessels and raises blood pressure. During times of stress, these hormones are secreted by the adrenal medulla in response to nervous stimulation. They help the body respond to crisis situations by raising blood pressure, increasing heartbeat and respiration, and bringing sugar out of storage in the cells.

DISORDERS OF ADRENAL CORTEX

HYPER-SECRETION

Adrenal virilism

Excessive secretion of adrenal androgens in adult women results in a condition known as adrenal virilism, the symptoms of which include amenorrhea, hirsutism (excessive hair on the face and body), acne, and deepening of the voice.

Cushing's syndrome

Cushing's syndrome includes a group of symptoms produced by the excess of cortisol from the adrenal cortex. Obesity, moon-like fullness of the face, excess deposition of fat in the back, hyperglycemia (increased sugar level), hypernatremia (increase sodium level), hypokalemia (decreased potassium level), osteoporosis, and hypertension occur with hypercortisolism. The cause of this condition may lie within the excess adrenocorticotrophic hormone secretion or tumor of the adrenal cortex.

HYPO-SECRETION

Addison's disease

The mineralocorticoids and glucocorticoids are produced in deficient amounts in addison's disease. The symptoms include hypoglycemia from deficient glucocorticoids, hyponatremia, excretion of large amounts of water and salts from deficient mineralocorticoids, fatigue, weakness, weight loss, low blood pressure, syncope and darker pigmentation of the skin.

DISORDERS OF ADRENAL MEDULLA

HYPER-SECRETION

Pheochromocytoma

Pheochromocytoma is a benign tumor of the adrenal medulla producing excess secretion of epinephrine and norepinephrine. Symptoms are hypertension, palpitations, severe headaches, sweating, flushing of the face, and muscle spasms. Surgery to remove the tumor and administration of antihypertensive drugs are among the possible treatments.

PANCREAS

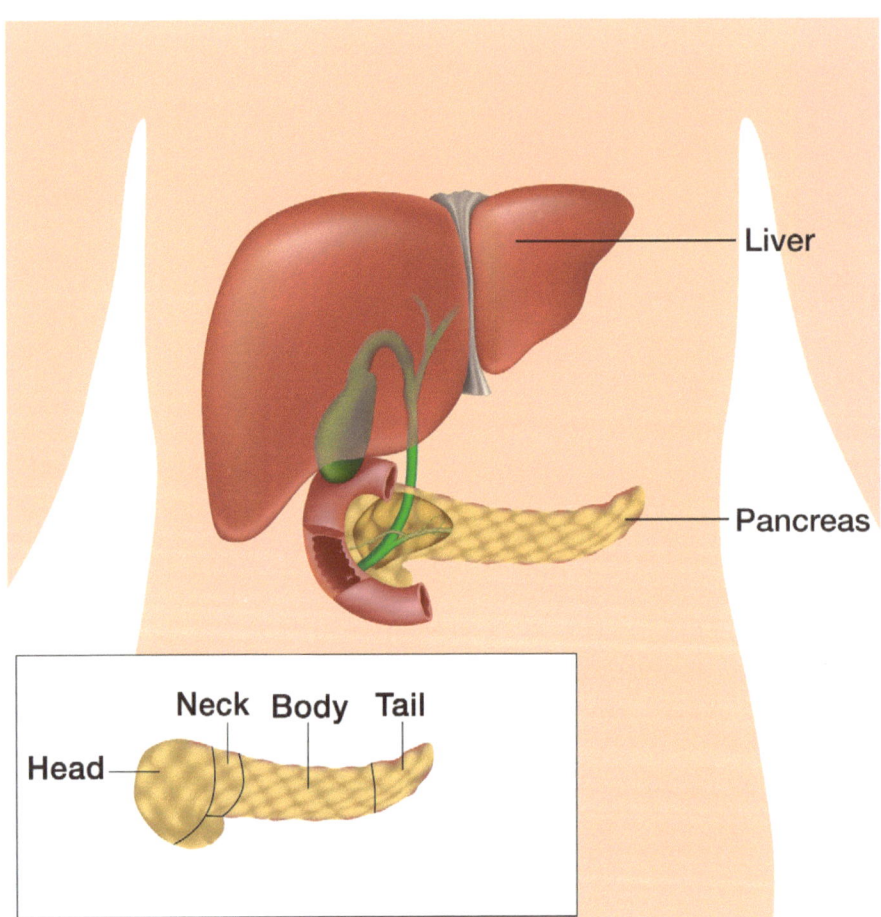

Fig 9-6 Pancreas

The pancreas is located near and partially behind the stomach in the region of the first and second lumbar vertebrae. The endocrine tissue of the pancreas consists of specialized hormone-producing cells called the islets of langerhans. The islets of langerhans produce two hormones: insulin produced by beta cells and glucagon produced by alpha cells. Insulin is necessary in the bloodstream so that sugars can pass from the blood into the cells of the body where they are burned to release energy or converted to glycogen and stored in the liver and the muscles. Glucagon is released into the blood when sugar levels are below normal. It causes the breakdown of stored liver glycogen which releases glucose in the blood and makes it available for cells.

HYPER-SECRETION

Hypoglycemia

Hypoglycemia is a condition of excess secretion of insulin. The cause may be a tumor of the pancreas or an overdose of insulin. It results in fainting spells, convulsions, and loss of consciousness, as a certain level of blood sugar is necessary for proper mental functioning.

HYPO-SECRETION

Diabetes mellitus

Diabetes mellitus is the lack of insulin secretion or resistance of insulin in promoting sugar, starch, and fat metabolism in cells. Insulin insufficiency or ineffectiveness prevents sugar from leaving the blood and entering the body cells, where it is normally used to produce energy. There are two major types of diabetes mellitus; Type 1 diabetes or Insulin dependent diabetes mellitus is a condition which involves destruction of the beta islet cells of the pancreas and complete deficiency of insulin in the body. Patients are usually thin and require frequent injections of insulin to maintain a normal level of glucose in the blood.

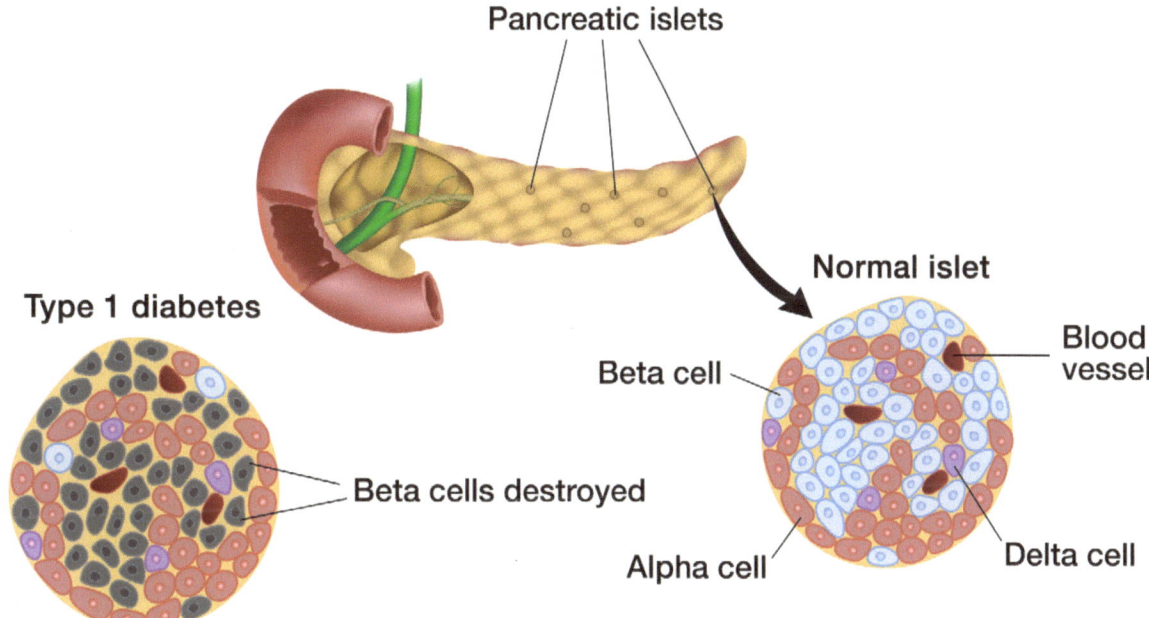

Fig 9-7 Type 1 diabetes

Type 2 diabetes or non-insulin dependent diabetes mellitus is a disease where the islet cells are not destroyed, and there is a relative deficiency of insulin secretion with a resistance by target tissues to the action of insulin. Treatment is with diet, weight reduction, exercise and, if necessary, insulin or oral hypoglycemic agents. The oral hypoglycemic agents can stimulate the release of insulin from the pancreas and improve the body's sensitivity to insulin. The symptoms of diabetes are listed and explained below.

Polyuria

Polyuria is the excessive excretion of urine as kidneys fail to reabsorb water.

Polydipsia

Polydipsia is the excessive thirst that is relatively prolonged because of dehydration.

Polyphagia

Polyphagia is the excessive eating as tissue breakdown causes hunger.

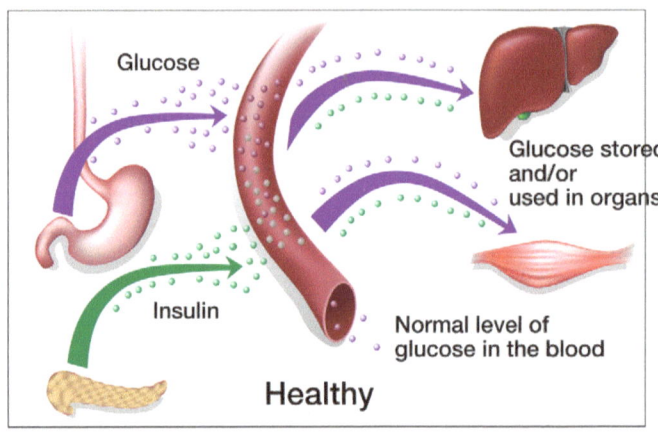

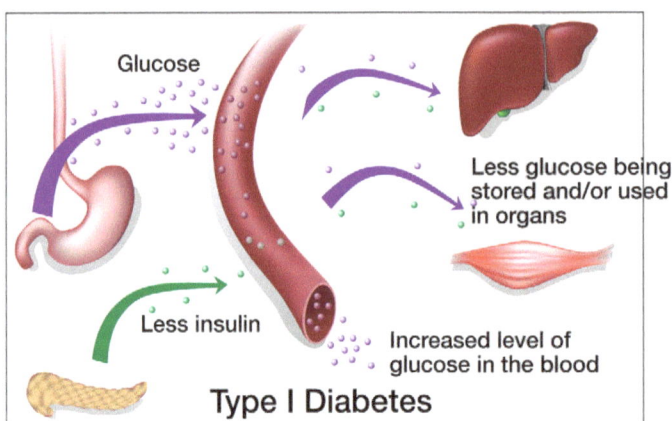

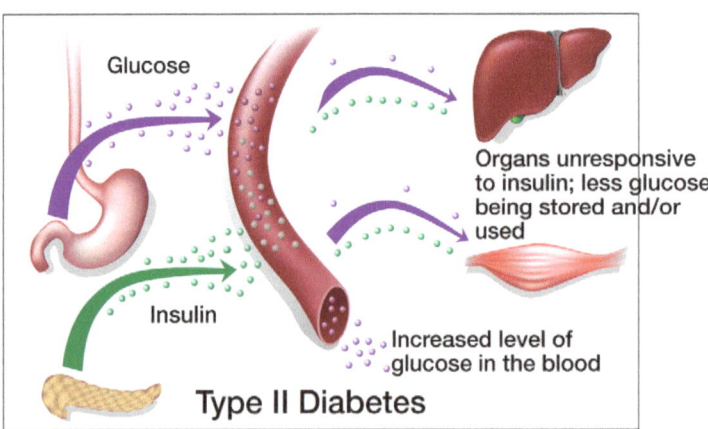

Fig 9-8 Type 1 & 2 diabetes mellitus

Complications:

Primary complications include ketoacidosis and coma when blood sugar concentration gets too high or the patient receives an insufficient amount of insulin. Hypoglycemia occurs when the patient takes excess amounts of insulin. Secondary or long-term complications include eye disorders such as glaucoma, cataract and destruction of the blood vessels of the retina known as diabetic retinopathy causing visual loss and blindness; destruction of the kidneys causing renal insufficiency and often requiring hemodialysis or renal transplantation; and destruction of blood vessels, with atherosclerosis leading to stroke or myocardial infarction.

OVARIES

The ovaries are two small glands located in the lower abdominal region of the female body. The ovaries produce the female gamete, the ovum, as well as hormones that are responsible for female sexual characteristics and regulation of the menstrual cycle. The ovaries secrete two hormones namely estrogen and progesterone. Estrogen is responsible for the development and maintenance of secondary sexual characteristics, such as pubic hair and breast development and deposition of subcutaneous fat. Progesterone is responsible for the preparation and maintenance of the uterus and support of pregnancy. (refer fig 6-2, page 106)

TESTES

Testes are male sex organs that produce the male gametes and the male sex hormone called testosterone. The testes are two small ovoid glands suspended from the inguinal region of the male by the spermatic cord and surrounded by the scrotal sac. Testosterone is an androgen, a male steroid hormone that stimulates and promotes the growth of secondary sexual characteristics in the male like development of beard and pubic hair, deepening of voice, and distribution of fat. (refer fig 6-16, page 119)

Chapter 10

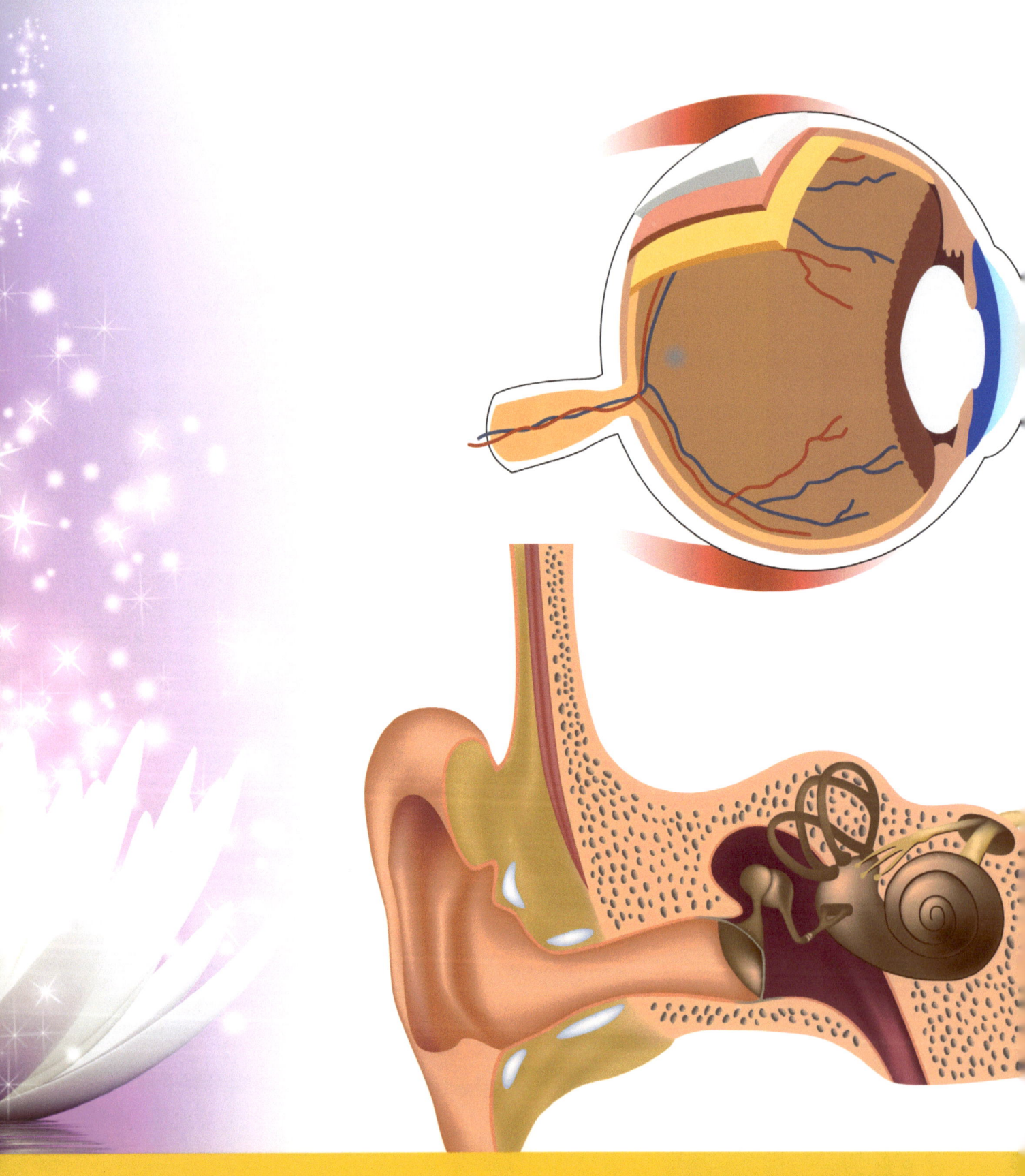

Eye and Ear

TABLE OF CONTENTS

EYE 180
DISORDERS OF THE EYE 182
    Astigmatism 182
    Cataract 183
    Conjunctivitis 183
    Detached retina 184
    Floaters 184
    Glaucoma 185
    Myopia or shortsightedness 186
    Squint 186
    Diabetic retinopathy 186
    Macular degeneration 188
EAR 190
DISORDERS OF EAR 191
    Deafness 191
    Tympanic membrane perforations 191
    Otitis media 192
    Tinnitus 193
    Vertigo 193

EYE

Eye is the organ of vision. The human eye works like a camera and it is a very complex organ. The eye is made up of three layers of tissue. The outermost fibrous tissue layer is called sclera. The middle tissue layer which has a good blood supply is referred to as choroid. The innermost light sensitive layer of the eye is called retina. Light rays enter the dark center of the eye called the pupil. The cornea is a fibrous, transparent tissue that extends over the pupil and colored portion of the eye. In bright sun it is nearly closed, on a dark night it is wide open. The amount of light entering the eye is controlled by the pupil. The conjunctiva is a mucous membrane that lines the eyelids and coats the anterior portion of the eyeball over the white of the eye.

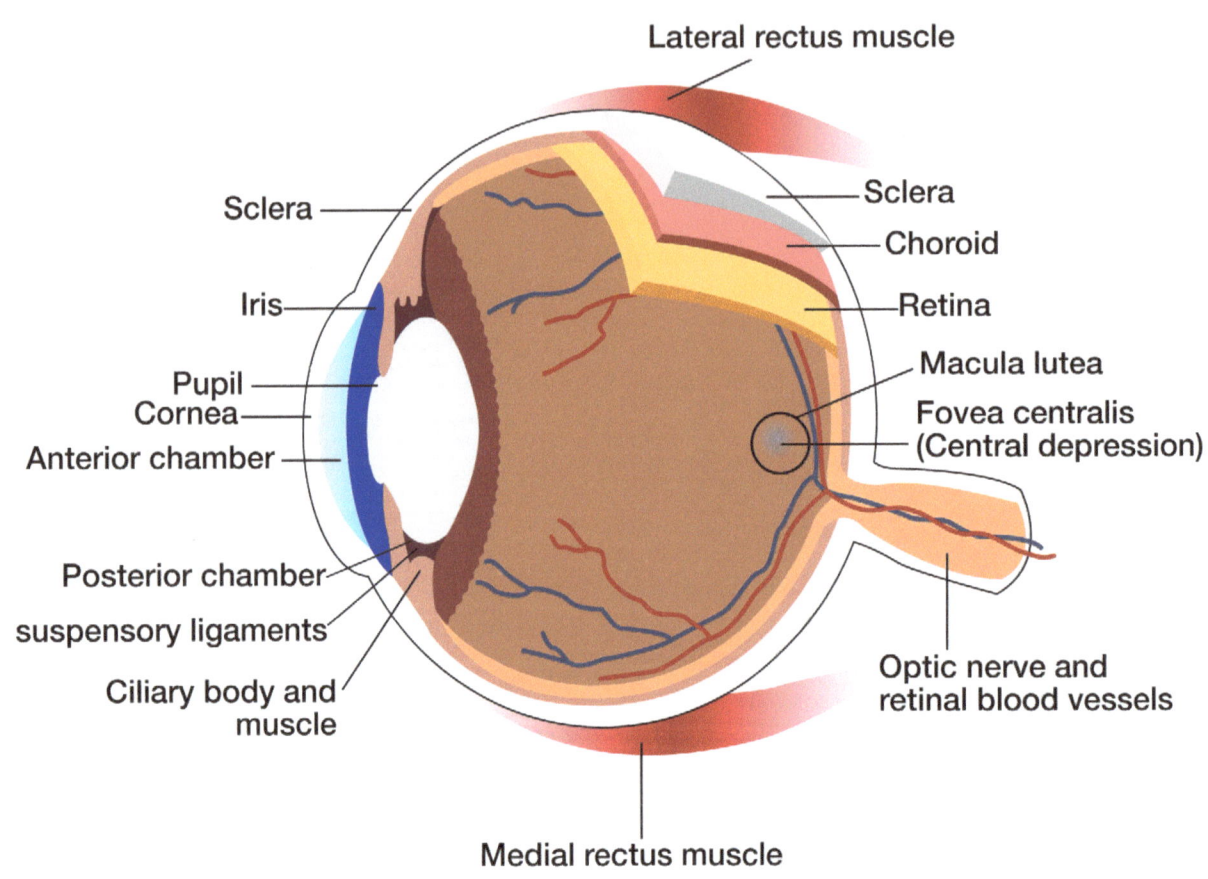

Fig 10-1 Eye anatomy

The eye is a hollow organ, it has two cavities namely anterior chamber and vitreous chamber. The anterior chamber contains fluid called aqueous humor. The posterior chamber consists of fluid called vitreous humor.

The choroid is continuous anteriorly with the pigment-containing iris and the ciliary body on the anterior surface of the eye. The iris can appear blue, green, hazel, gray, or brown in color. Muscles of the iris are responsible for constriction of pupil

- An average person blinks about 10,000 times a day
- The area between the eyebrows is called glabella
- The colored part of the eye is called iris and it appear blue, green, brown, gray or other colors
- The sclera is the 'white' of the eye

in response to light. The ciliary bodies are tiny muscles that hold the lens which is responsible for focussing of the light rays on the retina.

The lens is transparent biconvex cellular refractive structure consisting of a soft outer part and a dense inner part. The shape of the lens can be altered by contraction and relaxation of the ciliary bodies. When ciliary muscles contract the lens become rounded focusing on nearby objects and when they relax the lens flattens to focus on objects at a longer distance. This process of change in shape of the lens to view objects at different distances is referred to as accommodation.

- When we blink the eye lids move tears over our eyes washing specks of dust into the corner of the eyes. It also keeps the eye moist which makes it easy for the eyelids to glide across

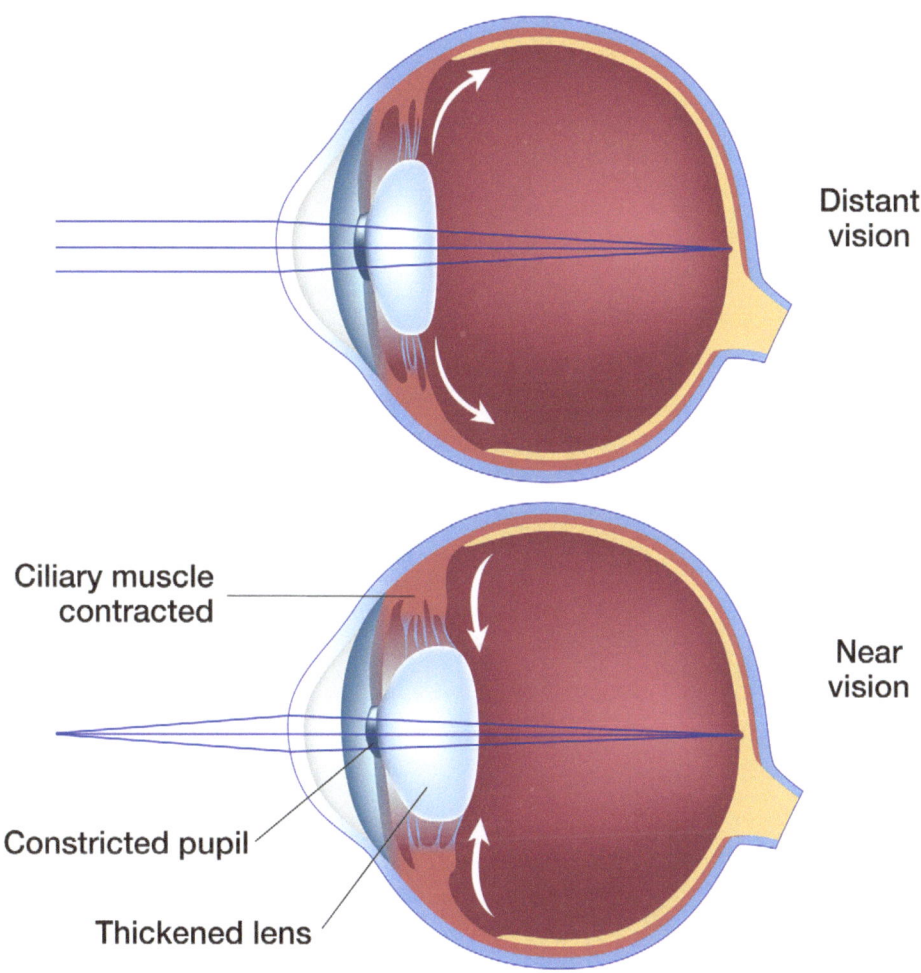

Fig 10-2 Accommodation of the lens

When an object is seen, the light passes through the lens which brings it into correct focus of the retina. The retina consists of light sensitive cones and rod cells. There are 130 million cones, shaped like cones for colour vision and rods which respond to shades of gray and important for night vision. These impulses are fed into optic nerve and transmitted to the brain. The image is inverted and reversed with respect to the object. However, the mind perceives objects in the upright position despite the upside-down orientation on the retina because the brain is trained to consider an inverted image as normal.

DISORDERS OF THE EYE

ASTIGMATISM

Astigmatism is an ailment where the cornea curves in one direction than the other distorting vision. Both cornea and the lens (normally totally transparent tissues) can cloud and lead to blindness.

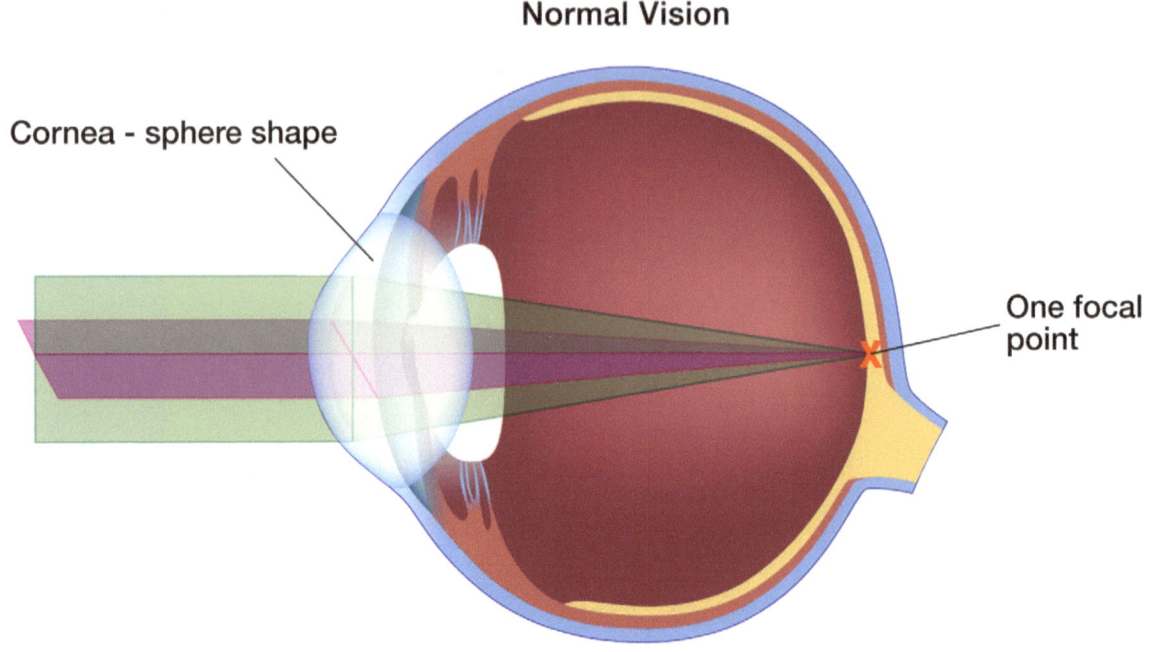

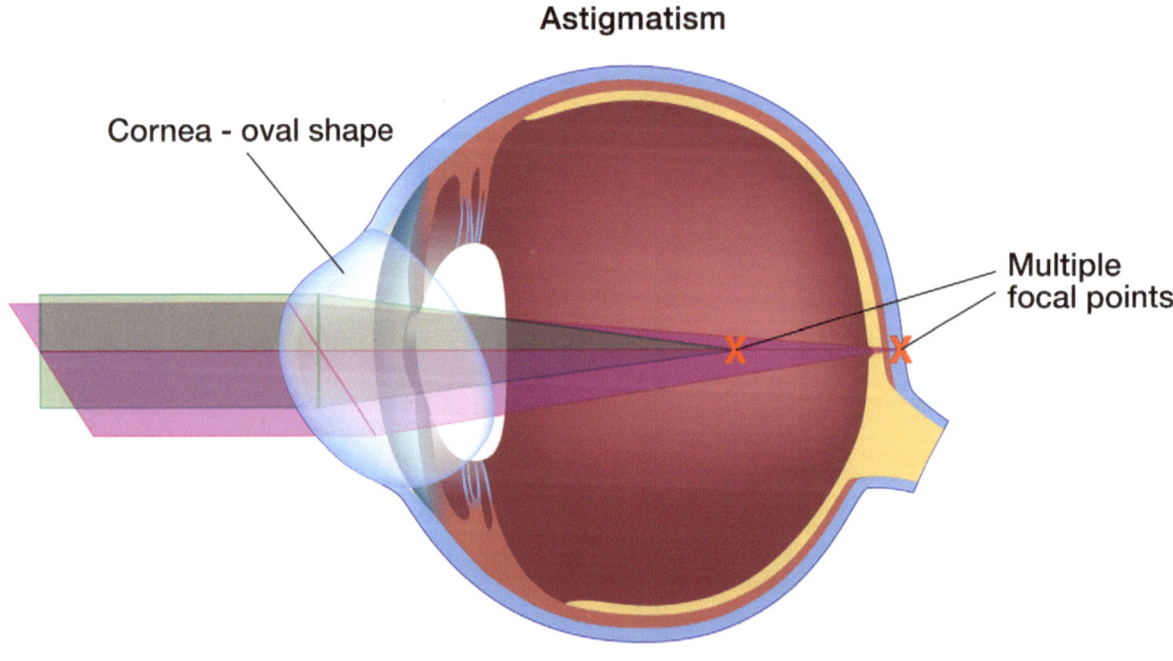

Fig 10-3 Astigmatism

CATARACT

A painless misting of the lens which in majority of cases does not cause inconvenience. This usually occurs in aged people. In early stage of cataract formation, the proteins in some of the lens fibers become denatured. Later, these same proteins coagulate to form opaque areas in place of the normal transparent protein fibers.

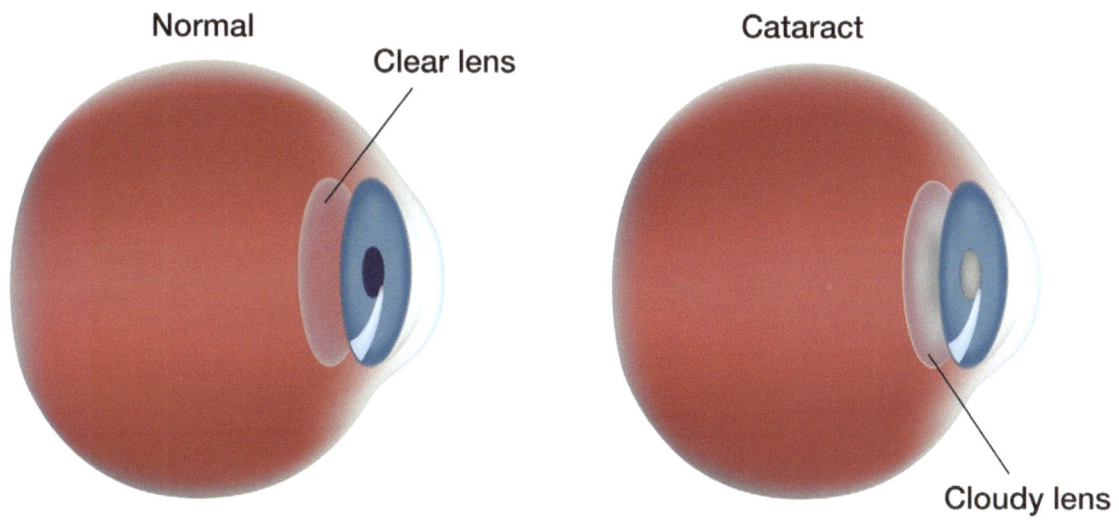

Fig 10-4 Cataract

The condition can be corrected by surgical removal of the lens. When this is done, the eye loses a large portion of refractive power, which must be replaced by a powerful convex lens in front of the eyes or an artificial lens may be implanted inside the eye in place of the removed lens. The vision may be cloudy and the individual's distant vision becomes foggy. Some of the causes for cataract are decreased nourishment and blood supply to the lens, diabetes, etc.

CONJUNCTIVITIS

It is inflammation of the conjunctiva, which covers the white of the eye and inner surface of the lids. The eye becomes red, sticky and feels irritated. The most common cause is bacterial or virus infection.

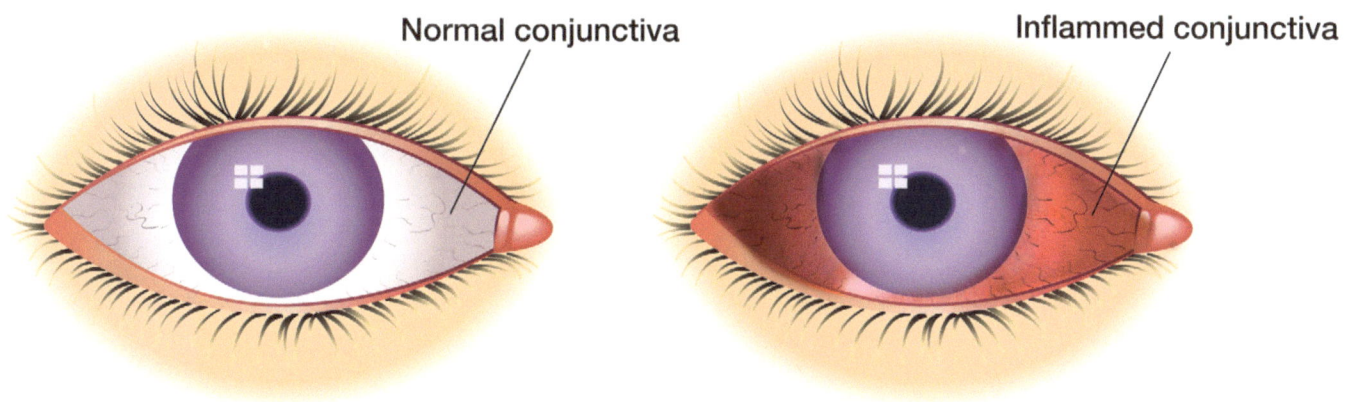

Fig 10-5 Conjunctivitis

DETACHED RETINA

Retina is formed from two layers. This is the light sensitive lining of the eye where objects are focused. If there is an injury or tear to the inner layer, fluid enters and separates the two layers and causes the detachment due to which there may be a sudden painless loss or change of vision. Sensation of flashing lights may precede this.

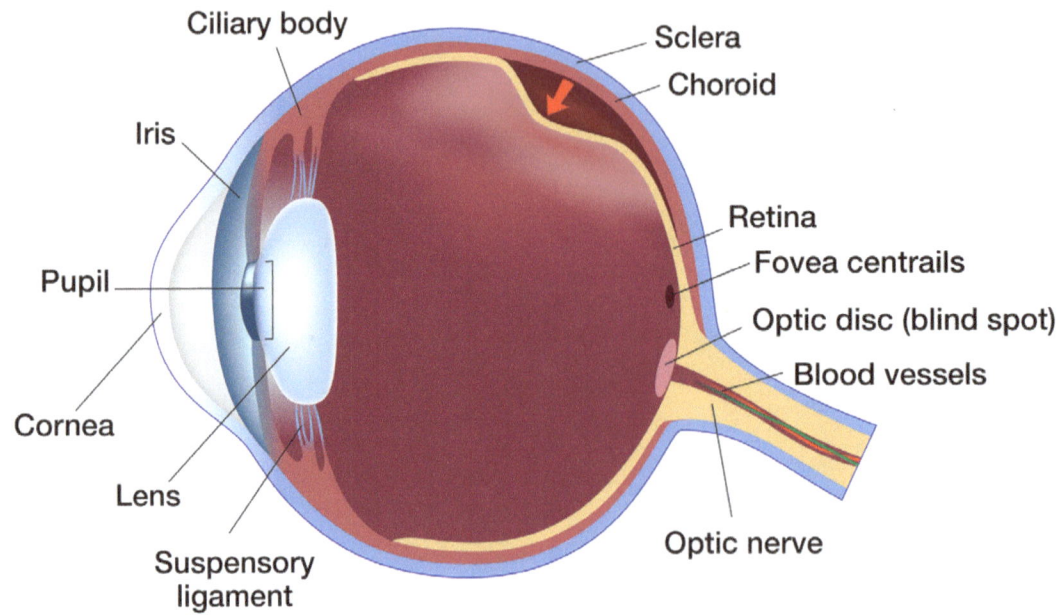

Fig 10-6 Retinal detachment

FLOATERS

The individual experiences black dots or threads floating in the field of vision. This may be caused by tiny leakages of blood into the fluid of the eyeball. Retinal hemorrhages and clots are responsible for floaters. Diabetes is one of the chief cause for this condition.

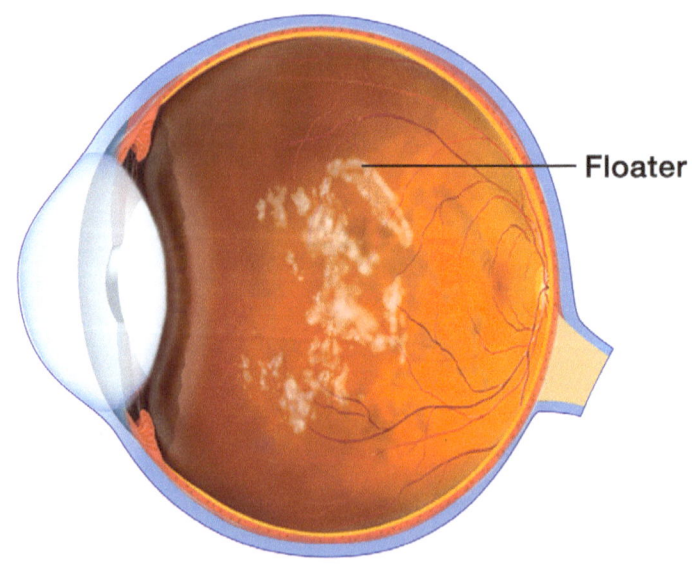

Fig 10-7 Floaters

GLAUCOMA

Glaucoma is caused by increased pressure in the eyes. People with diabetes and high blood pressure can develop this. The symptoms are coloured halos around bright lights, loss of side vision, difficulty in adjusting to dark, blurring of vision.

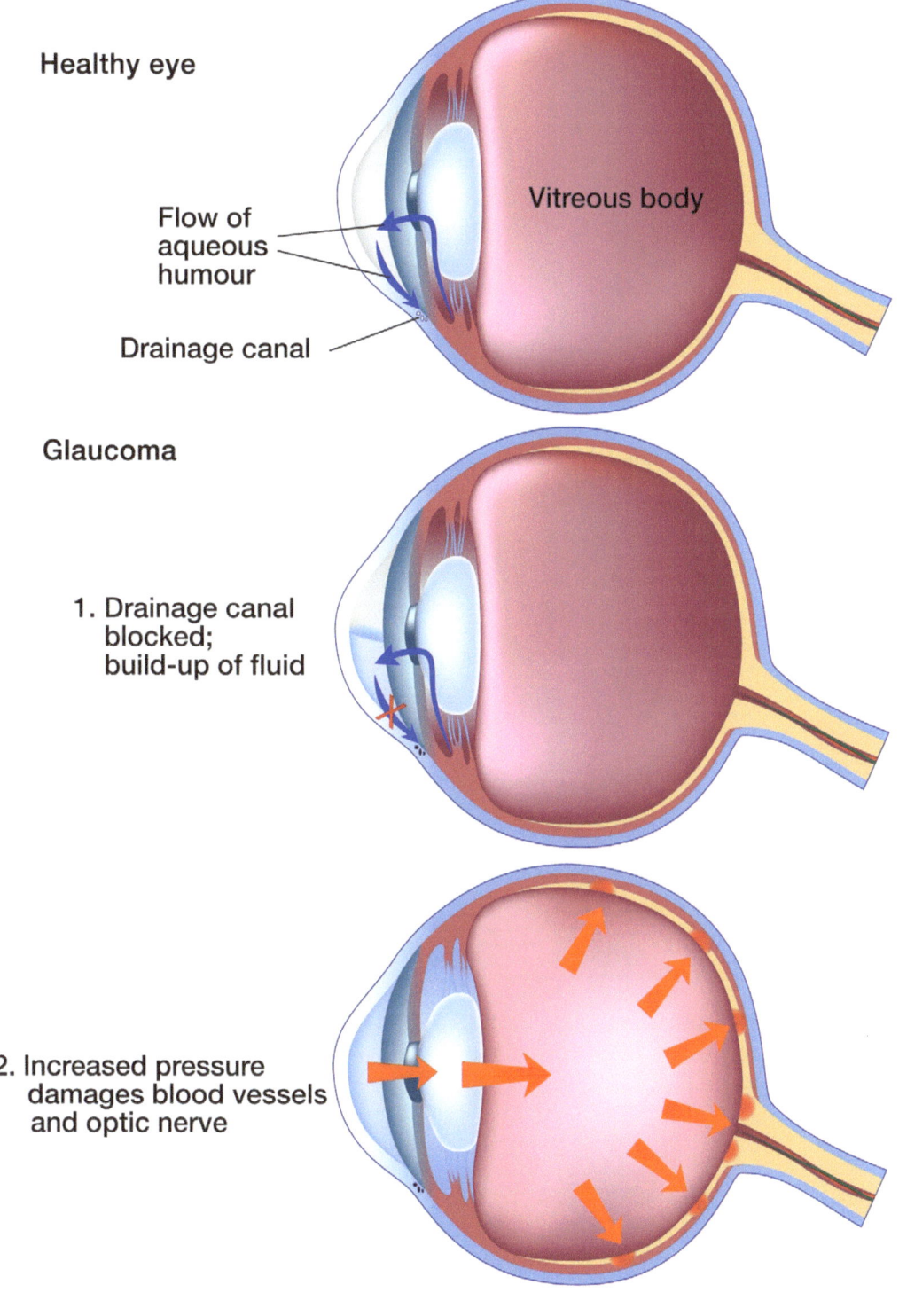

Fig 10-8 Glaucoma

MYOPIA OR SHORTSIGHTEDNESS

Myopia or shortsightedness is the inability to focus on distant objects. This happens when the light rays coming from distant objects are focused in front of retina.

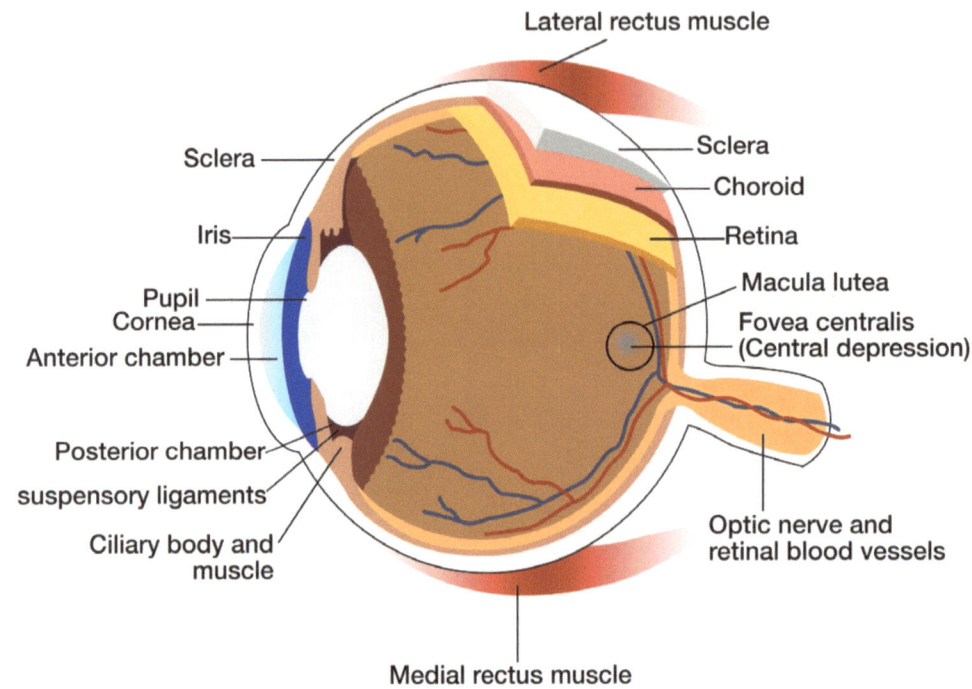

Fig 10-9 Myopia

SQUINT

A squint (which is usually congenital) is caused by incoordination of one or more muscles of the eyeball. A squint which appears in adult life is usually due to paralysis of one of the nerves of the eye muscles, due to damage or irritation or compression of the nerve. This type of squint results in double vision or diplopia.

DIABETIC RETINOPATHY

Diabetic retinopathy is a condition that results from changes and damage in the blood vessels of the retina, which is a light sensitive tissue at the back of the eye. It is a retinopathy (damage to the retina) resulting as a complication of diabetes and one of the leading causes of blindness in adults.

The are two types of diabetic retinopathy:

Nonproliferative diabetic retinopathy: This is the initial stage and it may not cause any symptoms or only mild vision problem. Here there are changes in the small blood vessels due to the over accumulation of glucose and/or fructose in the small blood vessels of the retina which are sensitive to the changes in the sugar levels. It is characterized by small bulges in the blood vessels of the retina that often leak fluid (micro aneurysm), closure of blood vessels (vascular closure), and small amount of bleeding in the retina (retinal hemorrhage).It shows up as cotton wool spots.

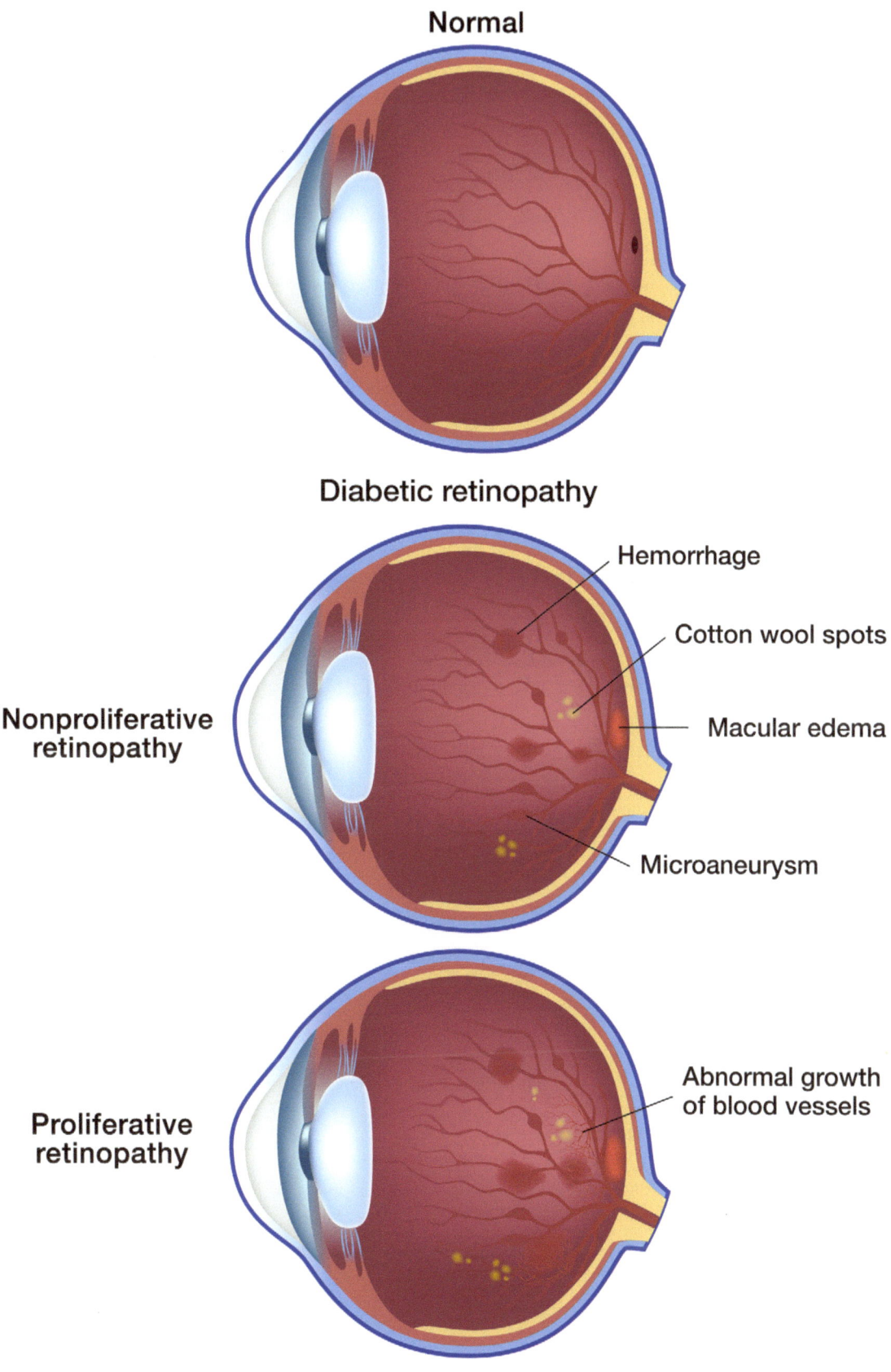

Fig 10-10 Diabetic retinopathy

Proliferative diabetic retinopathy: In this later stages the blood flow to the retina is blocked and also there is lack of oxygen to the retina. When this occurs the retina responds by growing new blood vessels on the surface of the retina and in the vitreous humour, the gel-like fluid that fills the eye. These new blood vessels are not as efficient and they do not supply enough blood to the retina. Due to this the retina wrinkles and detaches. During this stage the blood vessels bleed in the vitreous humour and a person may see dark floaters.

The symptoms of diabetic retinopathy are blurred vision, difficulty seeing at night, floaters and eventually loss of vision.

Control of blood sugar levels, blood pressure, cholesterol and quitting smoking are some of the preventative measures.

MACULAR DEGENERATION

This is a disease which affects the macula, the central area of the retina responsible for the finest details, sharp, central vision needed to read or to drive. The macula lines the inside of the back of the eye.

- Smoking increases the risk of macular degeneration

Age related macular degeneration often called AMD or ARMD affects the older adults usually 60 yrs or older. It is a major cause of blindness and visual impairment in elderly adults.

There are two forms of macular degeneration. They are the "dry and "wet" forms. In the "dry" form which accounts to about 90% of the cases the central part of the retina becomes distorted or thinned and cellular debris gets accumulated inside it. This causes the central part of the retina to become distorted. This is less severe compared to the "wet" form.

In the more severe "wet" form which occurs in 10% of the cases abnormal blood vessels develop beneath the retina and leaks fluid and blood under the macula. This causes permanent damage to the retinal cells affecting the field of vision. Treatment here is aimed to stop or reverse the growth of these abnormal new blood vessels.

A combination of vitamin C & E, beta-carotene and zinc are helpful to delay the visual loss with moderately advanced dry age-related macular degeneration.

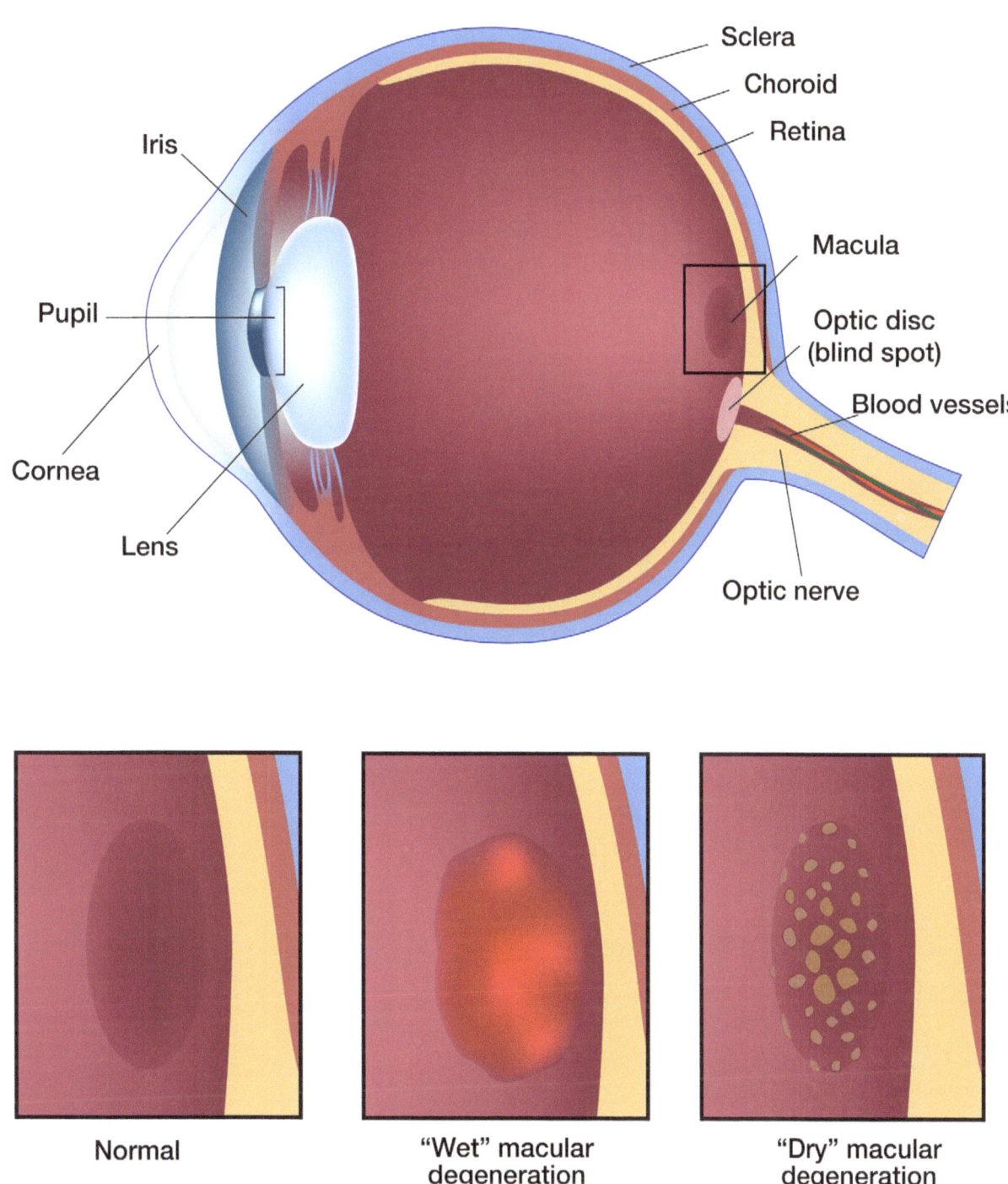

Fig 10-11 Macular degeneration

Eye 189

EAR

Ear is the principal organ of hearing. It also consists of components important to maintain balance and equilibrium. The ear can be divided into outer ear, middle ear and inner ear.

The outer ear consists of funnel-shaped structure called pinna that gathers sound and transmits it to the eardrum through a canal running obliquely to the eardrum. The canal is called external auditory canal or auditory meatus. It is oblique and twisted to protect the delicate inner components. This canal has numerous hair follicles and wax glands that prevent foreign agents like insects and dust from getting into the ear. The wax glands secrete a waxy substance called cerumen. This guards the inner ear from infecting organisms.

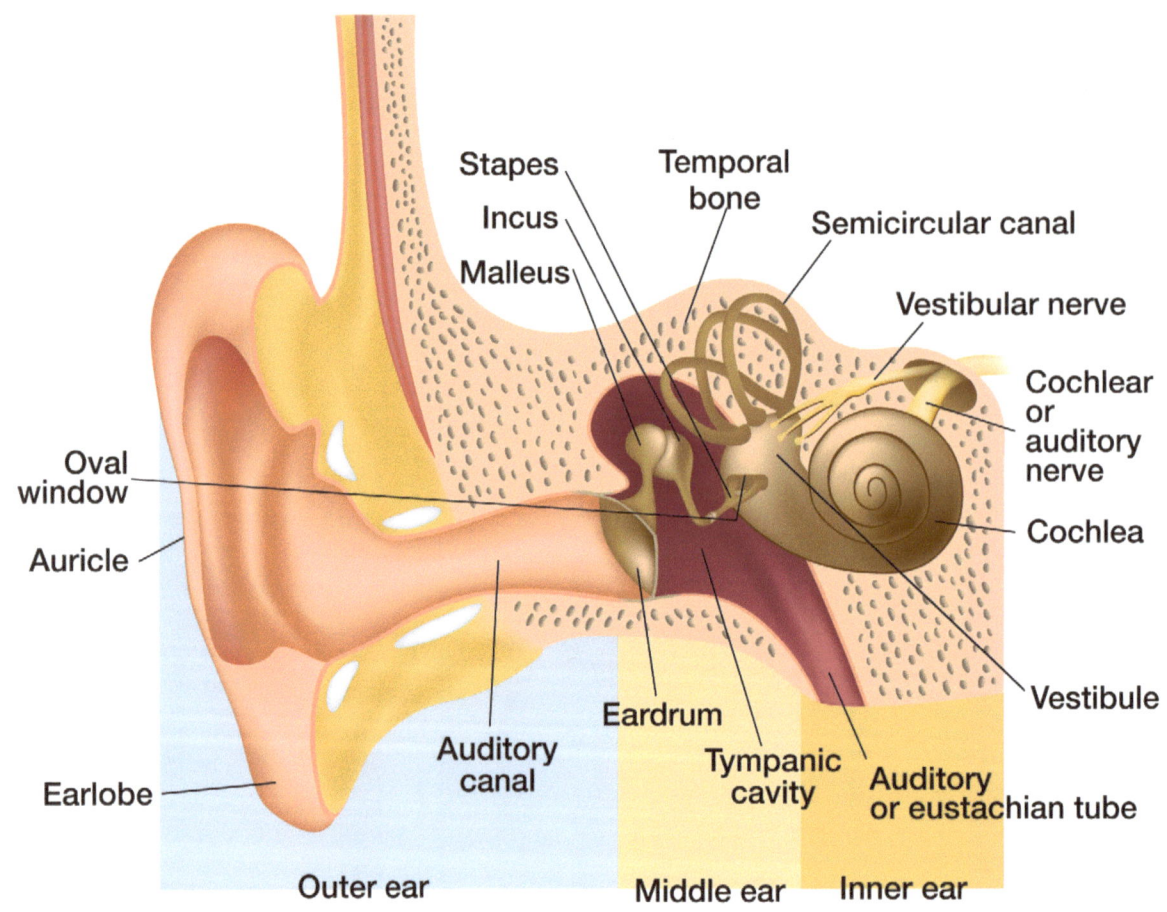

Fig 10-12 Ear anatomy

The eardrum otherwise called the tympanic membrane is an oval-shaped, stretched membrane less than 2 cm across present at the end of the auditory meatus. The sound waves from the outer ear strikes the tympanic membrane and starts the process that result in one hearing the sound. The tympanic membrane is connected to tiny bones called ear ossicles. They are three in number namely malleus, incus and stapes. The vibrations from the tympanic membrane created by the sound waves are transmitted to the ossicles, which

- The speed of sound is 770 miles per hour
- Ears not only helps in hearing but also keeping our balance. That is the reason why we feel dizzy sometimes when we have an ear infection

are passed on to the inner ear. The middle ear is connected to the throat (pharynx) by a slender tube called eustachian tube. This tube maintains the pressure in the middle ear and the respiratory passageways.

> • Our ear continues to hear sound while we sleep but the brain simply shuts them out

Inner ear is the region where the sound vibrations are converted into electrical impulses and transmitted to the brain through the auditory nerve. The inner ear consists of snail shell shaped coiled tube called cochlea. The last of the ossicle, the stapes is connected to a membrane called oval window in the cochlea through which the vibrations are transmitted from the middle ear to the inner ear. The cochlea consists of about 20,000 microscopic hair-like nerve cells, each one tuned to a particular vibration. The vibrations in the cochlea resulting in waving of the hair cells, this waving produces impulses that feed into the auditory nerve, then to the brainstem and then to the cortex of the brain where they are interpreted.

The inner ear also consists of vestibular apparatus which has three bony tubes in the inner ear within which the membranous semicircular ducts are located and the membranous sacs. They are three in number which lie in planes at right angles to each other and are known as anterior, posterior and lateral semicircular canals. The semicircular canals connect to two membranous sacs called vestibules. The smaller sac is called sacculus and the larger one is called utriculus. The semicircular canals and membranous sacs contain a fluid called endolymph. The movement of this fluid within the canals and the membranous sacs helps maintain the balance and equilibrium of an individual.

The auditory nerve has two components one from the cochlea which carries the sound signals and is important for the function of hearing. The other component is called a vestibular part which arises from the vestibular apparatus and is responsible for carrying impulses pertaining to balance and equilibrium.

DISORDERS OF EAR

DEAFNESS

Loss of ability to hear is referred to as deafness. It can be mild, partial or complete depending on the severity of the loss. It is divided into two types based on the region of lesion.

> • Irreversible hearing damage can be caused in less than 8 minutes by sitting in front of the speakers at a rock concert

Nerve deafness is caused by impairment of the cochlea or auditory nerve lesion. The lesion can be at its origin in the inner ear or can be anywhere in its course to the brain.

Conduction deafness is caused by impairment of the middle ear ossicles and membranes that transmit sound waves into the cochlea. This can be corrected in mild impairment with the use of hearing aids and in severe cases by surgical implantation of the ossicular prosthesis.

TYMPANIC MEMBRANE PERFORATIONS

The tympanic membrane or the eardrum gets punctured easily by external objects used to clean the auditory canal or by high sounds. Fortunately most of such punctures heal themselves; however, recurrent punctures or perforations can be repaired by surgical procedures such as tympanostomy tube placement.

OTITIS MEDIA

Inflammation of the middle ear is referred to as otitis media. There are two types of otitis media classified based on the cause.

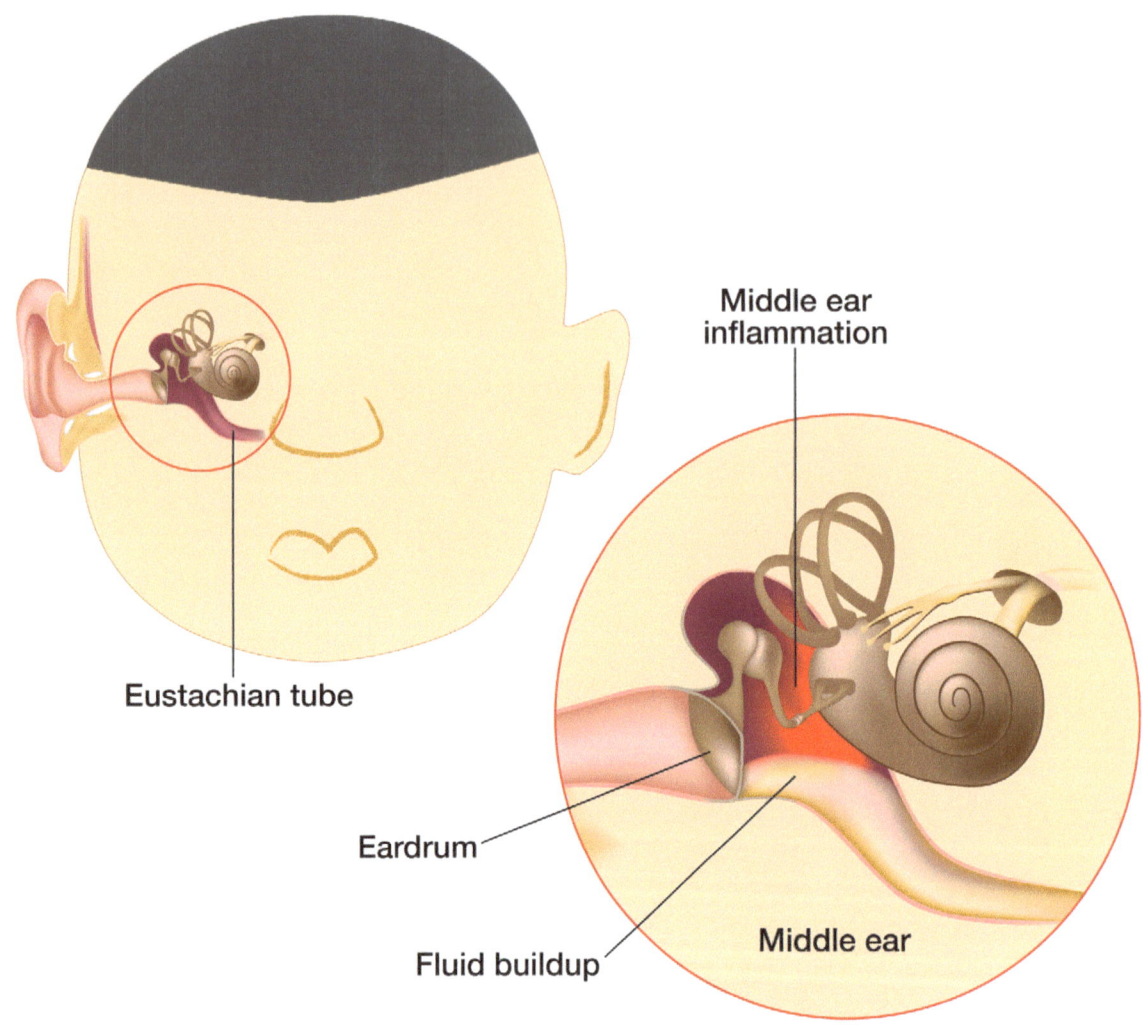

Fig 10-13 Otitis media

Acute otitis media is the inflammation of the middle ear due infection of the middle ear following an upper respiratory infection. Pain and fever with redness and loss of mobility of the eardrum are symptoms. As bacteria invade the middle ear, pus formation occurs resulting in a condition called suppurative otitis media. It can be treated with antibiotics, but if the condition becomes persistent a surgical procedure called myringotomy may be required to ventilate the middle ear.

In serous otitis media there is an accumulation of serous fluid. It often results from a dysfunction or obstruction of eustachian tube. Treatment includes aspiration fluid and tympanostomy tubes placement in the eardrum to allow ventilation of the middle ear.

TINNITUS

Tinnitus is a sensation of noises characterized by ringing, buzzing, whistling, booming in the ears. Tinnitus is caused by irritation of the delicate hair cells in the inner ear. Chronic otitis media, labyrinthitis, drugs, fever, tumors, disorders of auditory nerves can lead to tinnitus. The treatment includes techniques of relaxation and help the individual to reduce stress and anxiety if these are contributing factors.

Fig 10-14 Woman having tinnitus

VERTIGO

Vertigo is a condition where an individual has a sensation of irregular or whirling motion either of oneself or of external objects. It results from disease in the labyrinth of the inner ear or in the vestibular nerve that carries messages from the semicircular canals to the brain. Equilibrium and balance are affected, and nausea may occur as well.

Fig 10-15 Vertigo

Chapter 11

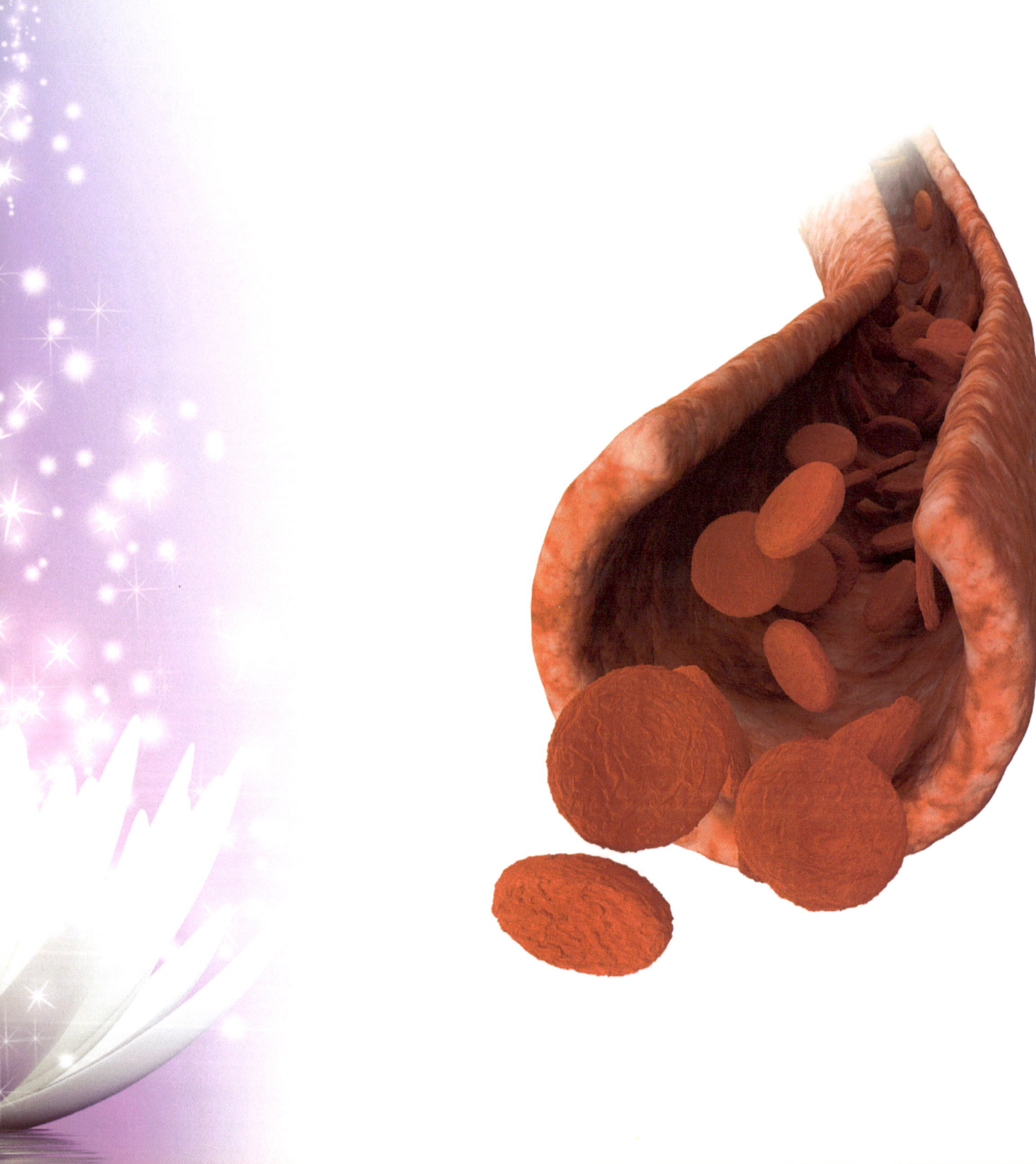

Blood

TABLE OF CONTENTS

RED BLOOD CELLS (RBC) OR ERYTHROCYTES 197
WHITE BLOOD CELLS (WBC) OR LEUCOCYTES 197
PLATELETS OR THROMBOCYTES 197
FUNCTIONS OF BLOOD 198
DISORDERS OF RED BLOOD CELLS 198
    Anemia 198
        Hemorrhagic anemia 198
        Hemolytic anemia 198
        Nutritional deficiency anemia 198
        Aplastic anemia 201
    Polycythemia 201
DISORDERS OF WHITE BLOOD CELLS 201
    Leukemia 201
DISORDERS OF PLATELETS 202
    Hemophilia 202
    Purpura 203

BLOOD

Blood is an opaque fluid, which is red in color, salty in taste and is present throughout the body. A normal adult has 5 litres of blood in their body. Blood contains the solid part called blood cells and the liquid portion called plasma. The plasma forms 55% and blood cells forms 45% of total blood.

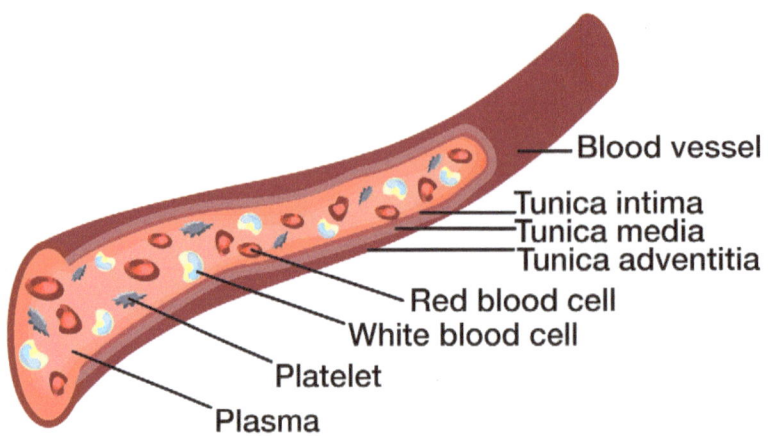

Fig 11-1 Composition of blood

The blood cells are as follows:
1. Red blood cells (RBC) or erythrocytes
2. White blood cells (WBC) or leucocytes
3. Platelets or thrombocytes.

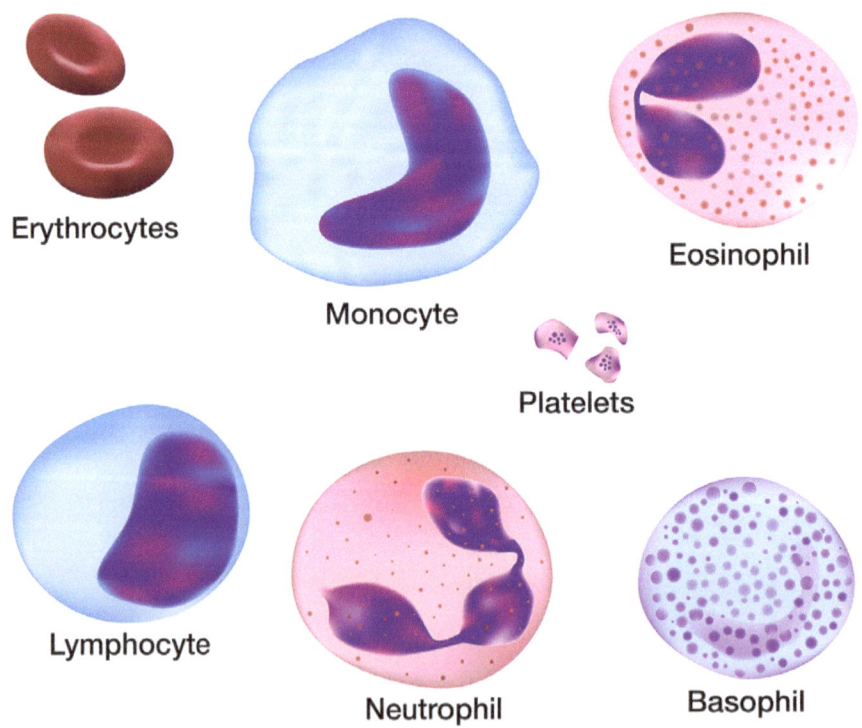

Fig 11-2 Elements of blood

RED BLOOD CELLS (RBC) OR ERYTHROCYTES

The red blood cells are formed elements in the blood. The red colour is due to the presence of hemoglobin which is present in the RBC. In an adult male it ranges from 5 to 5.5 million/cubic mm of blood and in adult female it ranges from 4 to 4.5 million/cubic mm of blood.

It is dumbbell shaped which helps in diffusion of oxygen and other substances to the interior of the cells. The dumbbell shape also helps the RBC's to be squeezed in the capillaries very easily. Average hemoglobin content is 14.16 gm/dl. In adult male it is 15gm/dl and adult female it is 14.5 gm/dl. The hemoglobin contains a protein part with a iron containing pigment. The protein part in globin and the iron containing pigment is heme.

WHITE BLOOD CELLS (WBC) OR LEUCOCYTES

They are colorless elements of the blood, which play an important role in the defense mechanism of the body. They are classified into 2 types. Granulocytes and agranulocytes. The granulocytes contain granules which are neutrophils, eosinophils and basophils. The agranulocytes are monocytes and lymphocytes. The total WBC count is 4,000 to 11,000 cells / cubic mm of blood.

NORMAL VALUES OF DIFFERENT WBC ARE AS FOLLOWS :

- Neutrophils   —   50% - 70%.
- Eosinophils   —   1% - 4 %
- Basophils   —   0% - 1 %
- Monocytes   —   2% - 8%
- Lymphocytes   —   20% - 30%

Neutrophils play an important role in the defense mechanism of the body. The granules of the neutrophils contain enzymes and antibodies. These help in protecting the body against foreign microorganisms.

The eosinophils play an important role in defense mechanism of the body. It is increased during parasitic infection and allergic condition.

The basophils play an important role in healing process after inflammation.

The monocytes also play an important role in defense mechanism of the body.

The lymphocytes helps in immunity by producing antibodies.

PLATELETS OR THROMBOCYTES

Platelets are small colorless elements of blood. Normally they are spherical or rod shaped and become oval or disc shaped when inactivated. The normal platelet count is 250,000 to 400,000 /mm of blood. Platelets have the property of sticking together or coming in contact with the wet surface. This is the property of adhesiveness. It also has the property of grouping together. The clumping of platelets is agglutination. All these properties help the formation of clots and prevent blood loss.

The liquid component of blood is plasma. It is formed by 91% – 92% of water and 8% – 9% of solid. The solid contains organic and inorganic substances. The organic substances of plasma contain proteins, carbohydrates, fats, enzymes and antibodies. The inorganic substances of plasma contain sodium, calcium, potassium, magnesium, iron etc.,

FUNCTIONS OF BLOOD

a. Acts as a transport medium which carries nutritive substances like glucose, lipids, amino acids derived from digested food to different parts of the body for the growth and production of energy.
b. It helps in transportation of oxygen from the lungs to different tissues and transportation of carbon-dioxide from the tissue to the lungs.
c. The hormones and enzymes are carried by the blood to different parts of the body.
d. The waste products of metabolism are carried by the blood to the excretory organs like kidney and liver.
e. It helps in the regulation of water.
f. It helps in maintaining the acid-base balance.
g. It helps in regulation of the body temperature.
h. It helps in the storage of protein and glucose which are taken from the blood during conditions like starvation, fluid loss, electrolyte loss.
i. It helps in maintaining the defense mechanism of the body.

DISORDERS OF RED BLOOD CELLS

ANEMIA

It is classified into

a. Hemorrhagic anemia
b. Hemolytic anemia
c. Nutritional deficiency anemia
d. Aplastic anemia

Hemorrhagic anemia

It occurs due to excessive blood loss in conditions like accident, ulcers, purpura, and hemophilia. There are 2 types, acute and chronic.

In acute there is sudden loss of blood due to injury and bleeding. There is a decrease in the RBC count but the size of RBC and hemoglobin is normal. However in this condition plasma is replaced within 24 hours but the replacement of RBC takes some time.

In chronic there is continuous loss of blood from the body wherein there is a great loss of iron.

Hemolytic anemia

As the word itself mean there is an excessive dysfunction of RBC. It occurs in various conditions like malaria, antigen antibody reaction. It may be congenital or acquired. There are different types of hemolytic anemia.

a. Sickle cell anemia.
b. Thalassemia

c. Autoimmune hemolytic anemia
d. Hereditary spherocytosis.

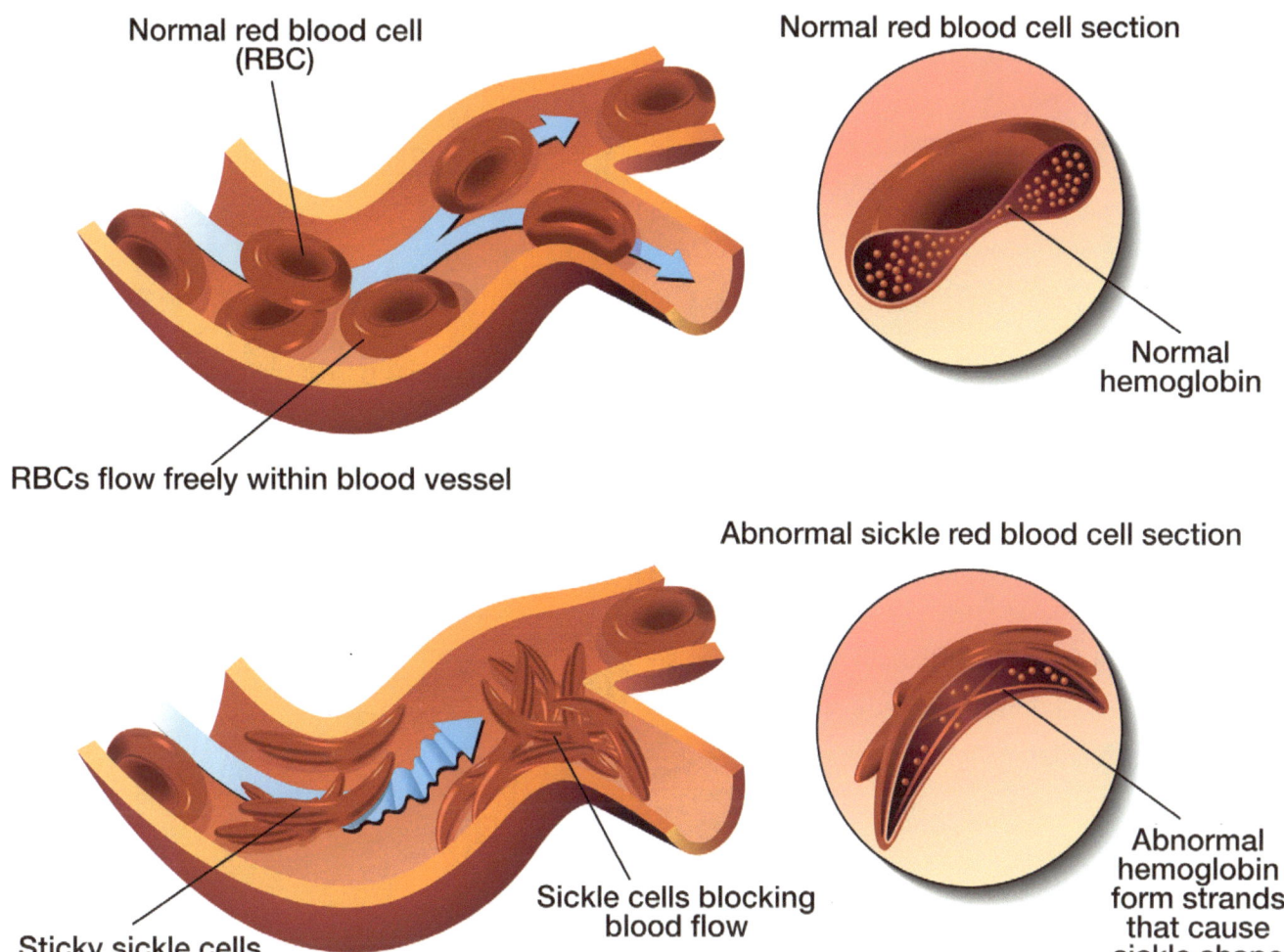

Fig 11-3 Sickle cell anemia

Sickle cell anemia

It is a congenital anomaly. Here the shape of the RBC's are changed into sickle shaped due to the abnormality in the hemoglobin. The abnormal hemoglobin tends to form a long chain and aggregates giving a sickle shape to RBC. The sickle cells are plugged in the small vessels resulting in anemia.

Thalassemia

It is a congenital condition in which there is an impairment of hemoglobin production. It is common in the mediterranean countries. There is decrease in the synthesis of hemoglobin. The lifespan of RBC is reduced resulting in anemia.

Autoimmune hemolytic anemia

This results from increased RBC destruction due to autoimmunity (where the body cells are destroyed by body's own defense mechanism). This is characterized by shortening of the lifespan of blood cells and premature destruction of RBC. There are two types, warm and cold.

Warm auto immune hemolytic anemia is common in middle age and in females. This occurs when the temperature is high.

In cold auto immune hemolytic anemia the antibodies tend to be produced and destruct the RBC at a temperature of 4 degree celcius or less.

Hereditary spherocytosis

It is a congenital condition in which there is impairment in the membrane formation of RBC resulting in the spherical shape of RBC. These spherical RBC's have a difficulty in leaving the capillaries. This sluggish circulation causes stagnation of RBC resulting in the injury to RBC resulting in anemia.

Nutritional deficiency anemia

Nutritive substances such as iron, protein and vitamin B12 and folic acid are necessary for synthesis of RBC. The deficiency to these substances result in nutritional deficiency anemia.

The anemia of these categories are as follows:
a. Iron deficiency anemia
b. Protein deficiency anemia
c. Pernicious anemia
d. Megaloblastic anemia
e. Aplastic anemia

Iron deficiency anemia

This is due to excessive loss of iron from the body or decrease intake or decrease absorption of iron from the body or due to excessive bleeding. Excessive blood loss occurs in conditions like gastric ulcers, stomach cancers, worm infection, excessive menstrual blood loss, pregnancy and drug intake. Iron deficiency anemia also occurs during breast feeding and during menstruating.

Protein deficiency anemia

This occurs due to deficiency in protein intake.

Pernicious anemia

This results in deficiency of vitamin B12 due to antibodies produced against the intrinsic factor which is present in the stomach responsible for the absorption of vitamin B12.

Megaloblastic anemia

This is due to deficiency of vitamin B12 or folic acid which plays an important role in the maturation of RBC. These immature RBC larger in size, width with deficient hemoglobin results in anemia.

Aplastic anemia

In this condition there is a disorder of the bone marrow. The bone marrow is reduced and replaced by fibrous tissue due to conditions like repeated exposure of x-rays or gamma radiation and hence the RBCs are not produced.

Symptoms are as follows:

- The colour of the skin becomes pale.
- The paleness is more visible in the palms, nail beds, lips and eyes.
- The skin becomes very thin and bright.
- The nail becomes brittle and is very easily breakable.
- The hair becomes thin and the roots become weak and there is excessive hair loss.
- The rate and force of respiration is increased to compensate for the deficient supply of oxygen. The heart has to pump more blood resulting in increasing in heart rate and increase in the size of the heart.

The other symptoms are nausea, vomiting, abdominal pain, constipation, headache, irritating cold & fainting sensation.

POLYCYTHEMIA

This a condition in which RBC count is increased above 7 million / cubic mm of blood.

There are 2 types.

a. Primary polycythemia
b. Secondary polycythemia

Primary polycythemia is a disease in which there is persistent increase in RBC above 14 million / cubic mm of blood. It occurs in condition like tumors of the bone marrow.

Secondary polycythemia is a condition in which there is increase in RBC secondary to other causes such as hypoxia, congenital heart diseases, carbon monoxide poisoning and repeated mild hemorrhage.

DISORDERS OF WHITE BLOOD CELLS

LEUKEMIA

Leukemia is a group of malignant disorders of the blood cells associated with the increase in the number of WBC. The WBC may be increased either in bone marrow or in the blood. Males are more affected than females. The cause is unknown but however there are various factors responsible such as radiation, exposure to benzene in the industries, drugs, viral infection and genetic causes.

Leukemia is classified into acute and chronic.

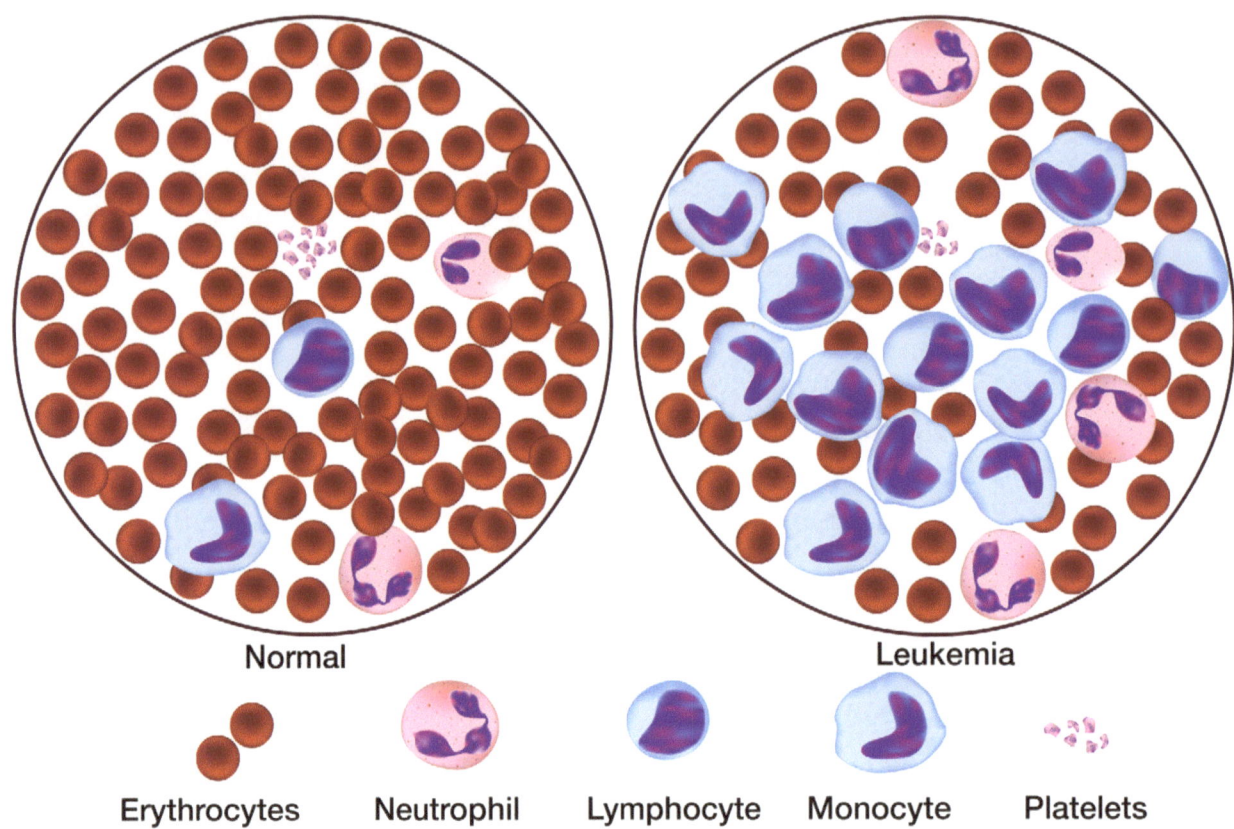

Fig 11-4 Leukemia

In acute leukemia the life expectancy is very short and in chronic leukemia the patient is not well for months together and the life span is reduced. The patient may complain with anemia, painless lymph node enlargement, enlargement of the spleen, enlargement of the liver in some cases, fever, loss of weight, loss of appetite, bleeding and infection. Infections are more common due to the defense mechanism of the body being affected. Sometimes the patient may have delusions and hallucinations.

DISORDERS OF PLATELETS

The diseases of the platelets result in prolonged bleeding or clotting time resulting in bleeding disorders. The bleeding disorders are hemophilia and purpura.

HEMOPHILIA

Hemophilia is a congenital disorder affecting the males. The disorder is characterized by prolonged clotting time due to deficiency of production of a factor which is responsible for the coagulation of blood. Even a mild trauma may lead to excessive bleeding or death.

Note : Bleeding time is the time taken from the puncture of blood vessel to the stoppage of bleeding. The normal time is 2-6 minutes. Clotting time is the time taken from the puncture of blood vessel to the formation of clot. The normal time taken is 4-8 minutes.

PURPURA

It is a disorder in which there is a prolonged bleeding time but the clotting time is normal. There is a deficiency in the number of platelets which results in spontaneous bleeding and produces hemorrhagic spots in the body. These appear as purple colour patches in the skin. That is why this disease is called purpura. The most common form of purpura is idiopathic thrombocytic purpura where there are multiple pinpoint hemorrhages under the skin giving purplish appearance to the skin.

Chapter 12

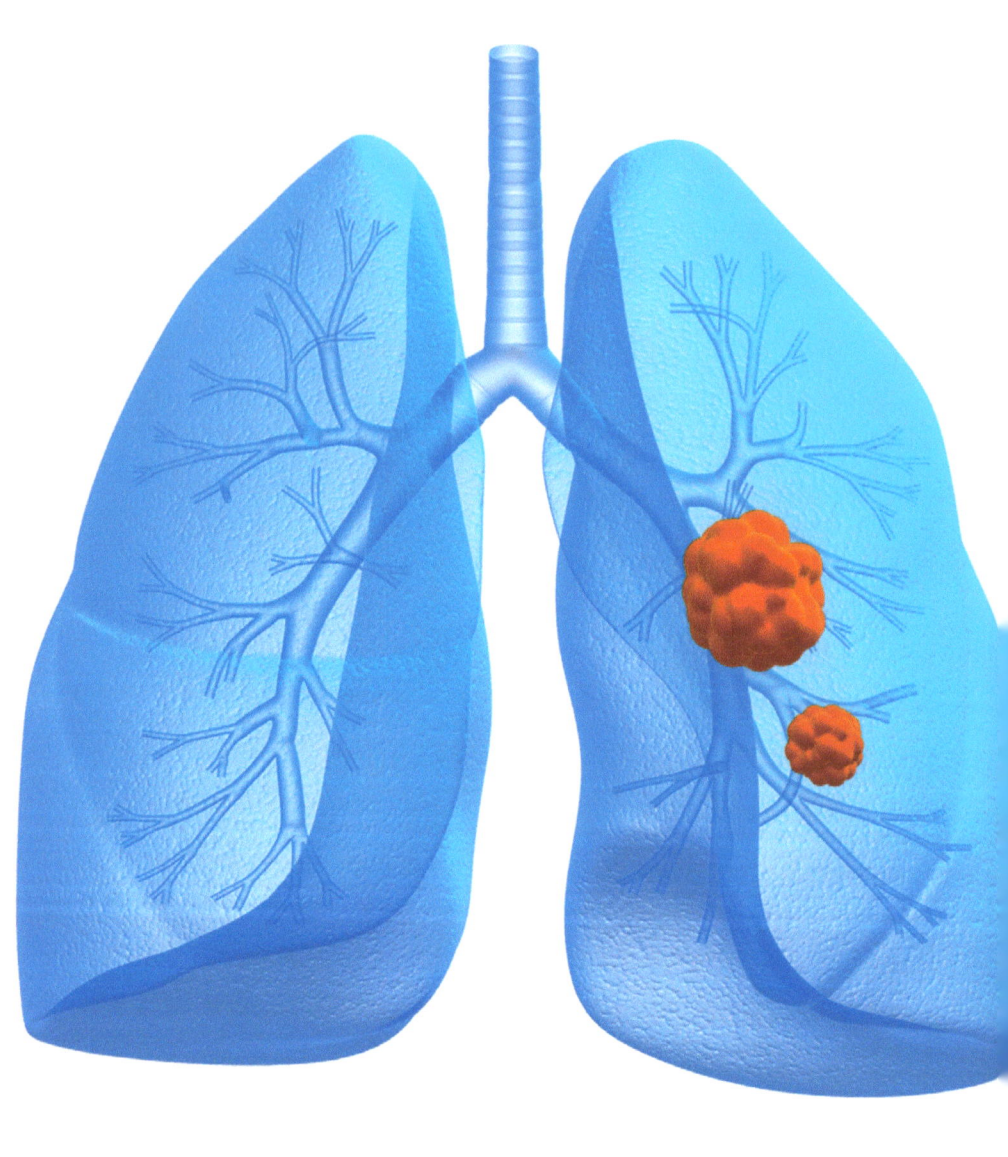

Cancer and Tumors

TABLE OF CONTENTS

CANCER AND TUMORS 206
    Carcinoma 206
    Sarcoma 206
    Leukemia 206
    Lymphoma and myeloma 207
    Central nervous system cancers 207

ORIGINS OF CANCER 207
    Benign tumors 207
    Malignant tumors 207

HOW CANCER SPREADS 207
    Local invasion 209
    Intravasation 210
    Circulation 210
    Arrest and extravasation 210
    Proliferation 210
    Angiogenesis 210

COMMON TYPES OF CANCER 211
    Breast cancer 211
    Carcinoma of cervix (cervical cancer) 212
    Colon and rectal cancer 213
    Kidney cancer 214
    Leukemia 215
    Liver cancer 215
    Lung cancer 216
    Thyroid cancer 217
    Vaginal cancer 218
    Prostate cancer 219
    Uterine (endometrial) cancer 220

CANCER AND TUMORS

Cancer is a term used for diseases in which abnormal cells divide without control and are able to invade other tissues. Cancer cells can spread to other parts of the body through the blood and lymph systems.

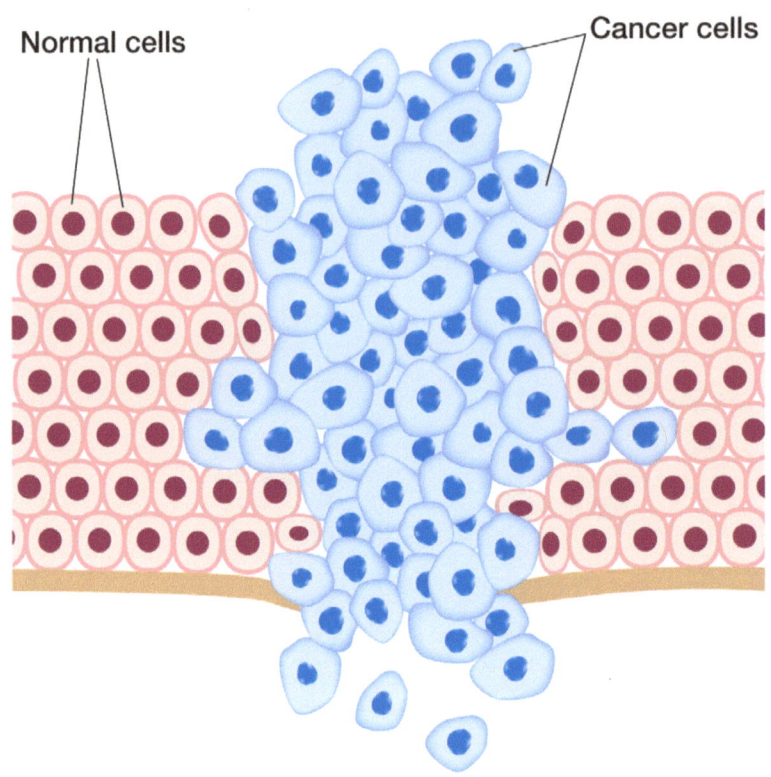

Fig 12-1 Cancer cells

Cancer is not just one disease but many diseases. There are more than 100 different types of cancer. Most cancers are named for the organ or type of cell in which they start - for example, cancer that begins in the colon is called colon cancer; cancer that begins in basal cells of the skin is called basal cell carcinoma.

Cancer types can be grouped into broader categories. The main categories of cancer include:

Carcinoma
Cancer that begins in the skin or in tissues that line or cover internal organs.

Sarcoma
Cancer that begins in bone, cartilage, fat, muscle, blood vessels, or other connective or supportive tissue.

Leukemia
Cancer that starts in blood-forming tissue such as the bone marrow and causes large numbers of abnormal blood cells to be produced and enter the blood.

Lymphoma and Myeloma

Cancers that begin in the cells of the immune system.

Central nervous system cancers

Cancers that begin in the tissues of the brain and spinal cord.

ORIGINS OF CANCER

- All cancers begin in cells, the body's basic unit of life. To understand cancer, it's helpful to know what happens when normal cells become cancer cells.
- The body is made up of many types of cells. These cells grow and divide in a controlled way to produce more cells as they are needed to keep the body healthy. When cells become old or damaged, they die and are replaced with new cells.
- However, sometimes this orderly process goes wrong. The genetic material (DNA) of a cell can become damaged or changed, producing mutations that affect normal cell growth and division. When this happens, cells do not die when they should and new cells form when the body does not need them. The extra cells may form a mass of tissue called a tumor.

Not all tumors are cancerous; tumors can be benign or malignant.

Benign tumors

Benign tumors aren't cancerous. They can often be removed, and, in most cases, they do not come back. Cells in benign tumors do not spread to other parts of the body.

Malignant tumors

Malignant tumors are cancerous. Cells in these tumors can invade nearby tissues and spread to other parts of the body. The spread of cancer from one part of the body to another is called metastasis.

- Preservatives such as nitrites which are chemical additives used to add flavouring in various food products such as hot dogs, lunch meats etc, turn into cancer causing carcinogens when they react with body chemicals.

Some cancers do not form tumors. For example, leukemia is a cancer of the bone marrow and blood.

HOW CANCER SPREADS

Cancer cells enters into the blood stream or lymph vessels and move through the circulatory system until they reach a suitable site and start growing and giving rise to new cancer cells. The process by which cancer cells spread to other parts of the body is also called metastasis.

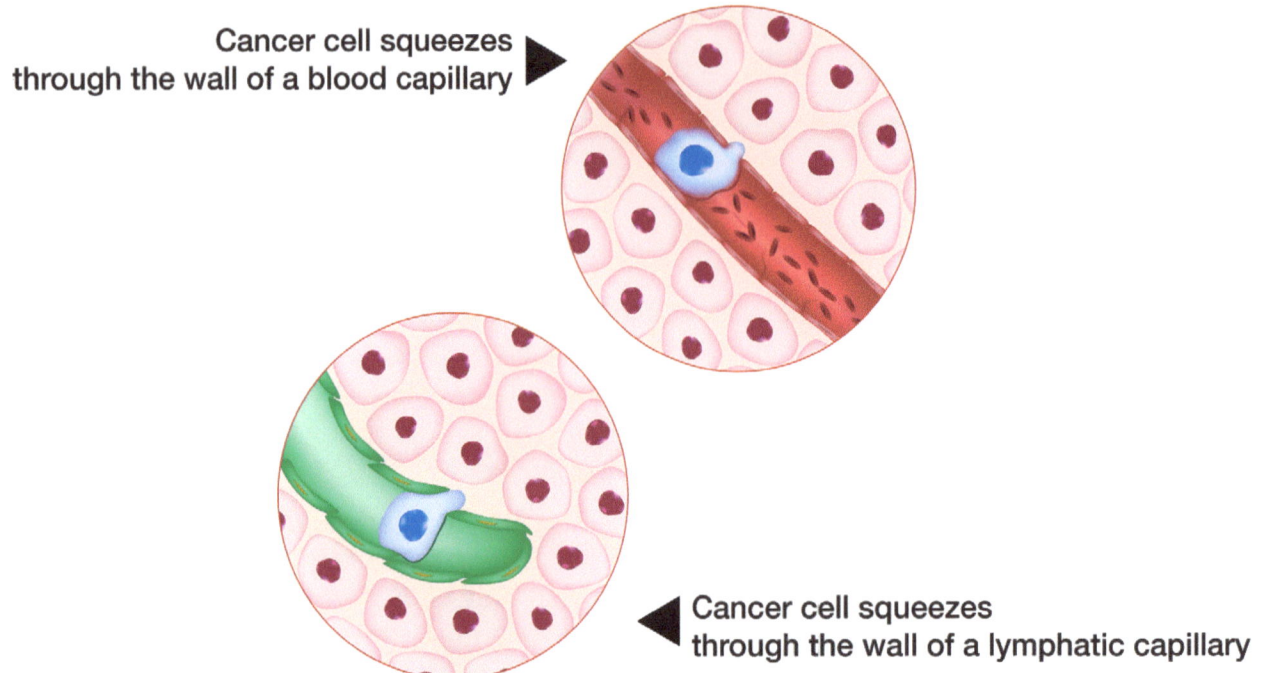

Fig 12-2 How cancer spreads

Metastatic cancer is cancer that has spread from the place where it first started to another place in the body. A tumor formed by metastatic cancer cells is called a metastatic tumor or a metastasis.

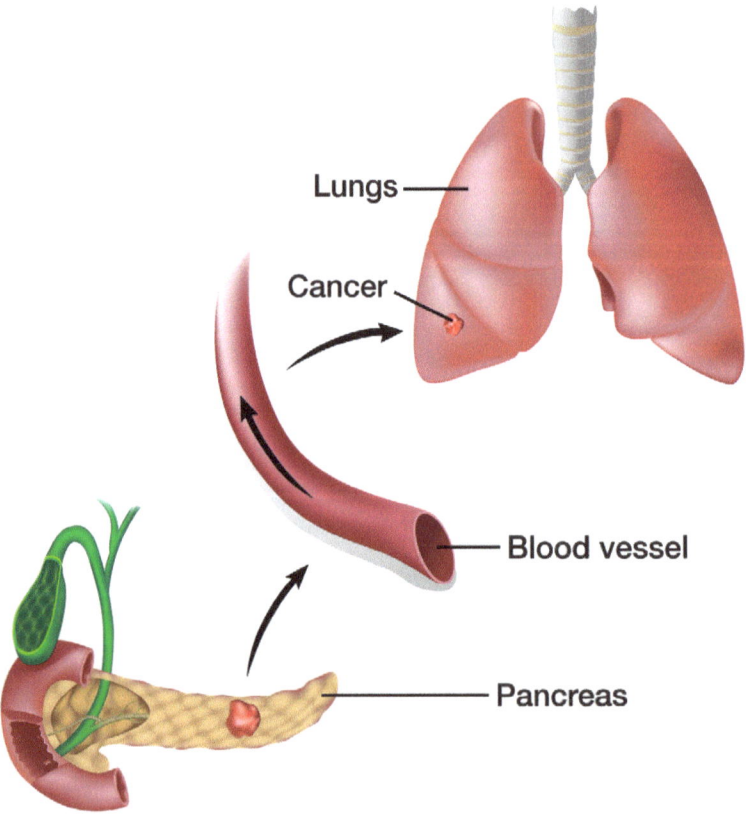

Fig 12-3 Metastatic cancer

Metastatic cancer has the same name and the same type of cancer cells as the original, or primary, cancer. For example, breast cancer that spreads to the lungs and forms a metastatic tumor is metastatic breast cancer, not lung cancer.

The most common sites of cancer metastasis are the lungs, bones, and liver. Although most cancers have the ability to spread to many different parts of the body, they usually spread to one site more often than others.

Cancer cell metastasis usually involves the following steps:

- An oxygenated environment makes it difficult for cancer cells to thrive. Regular deep breathing and physical exercises increases the oxygen at the cellular level and thereby helps against cancerous growth

Local invasion

Cancer cells invade nearby normal tissue.

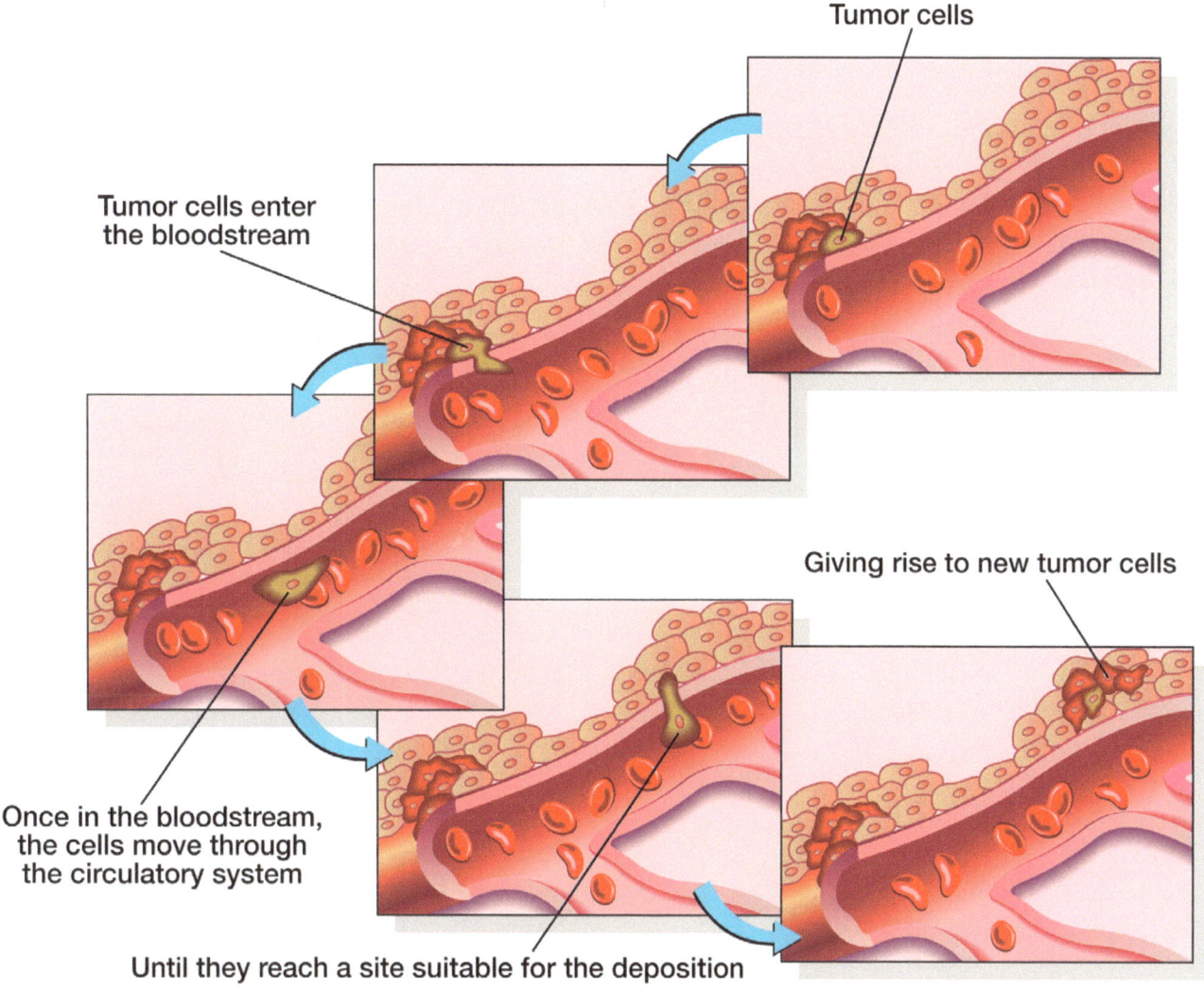

Fig 12-4 Stages of metastasis

Cancer and Tumors

Intravasation

Cancer cells invade and move through the walls of nearby lymph vessels or blood vessels.

Circulation

Cancer cells move through the lymphatic system and the bloodstream to other parts of the body.

Arrest and extravasation

Cancer cells arrest, or stop moving, in small blood vessels called capillaries at a distant location. They then invade the walls of the capillaries and migrate into the surrounding tissue.

Proliferation

Cancer cells multiply at the distant location to form small tumors known as micrometastases.

Angiogenesis

Micrometastases stimulate the growth of new blood vessels to obtain a blood supply. A blood supply is needed to obtain the oxygen and nutrients necessary for continued tumor growth.

- Negative lower emotions such as unforgiveness and bitterness causes the body to become an acidic cancer encouraging environment. Forgiveness and loving-kindness are very important for cancer warriors

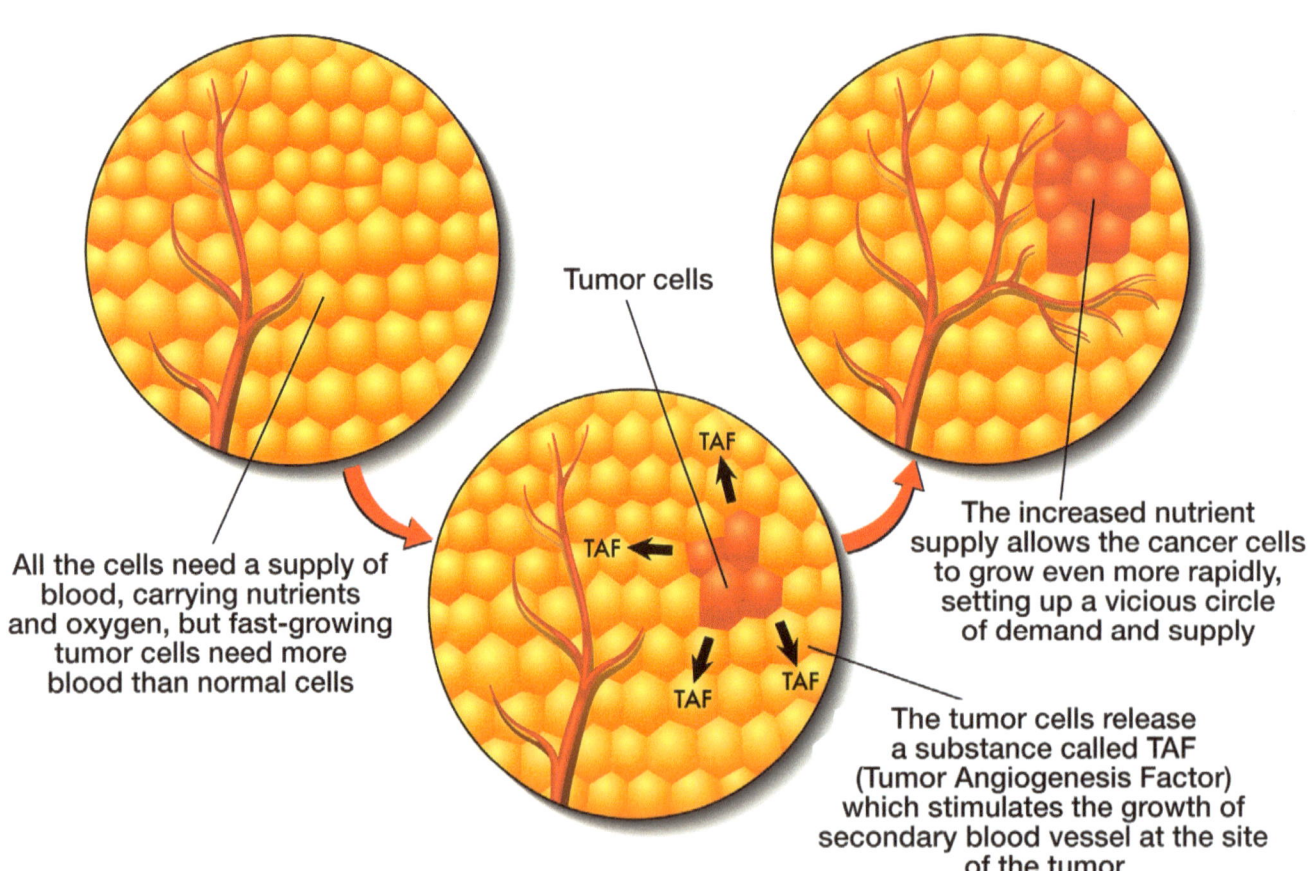

Fig 12-5 Angiogenesis

COMMON TYPES OF CANCER

BREAST CANCER

The malignant tumor of the breast arising from milk glands and ducts is referred to as carcinoma of breast. The mass is ususaly painful but there are times when the mass can be painless also. This tumor first spreads to the lymph nodes located in the axilla (armpit) adjacent to the affected breast and then to the skin and chest wall. From the lymph nodes it may spread to any of the other body organs, including bone, liver, lung, or brain.

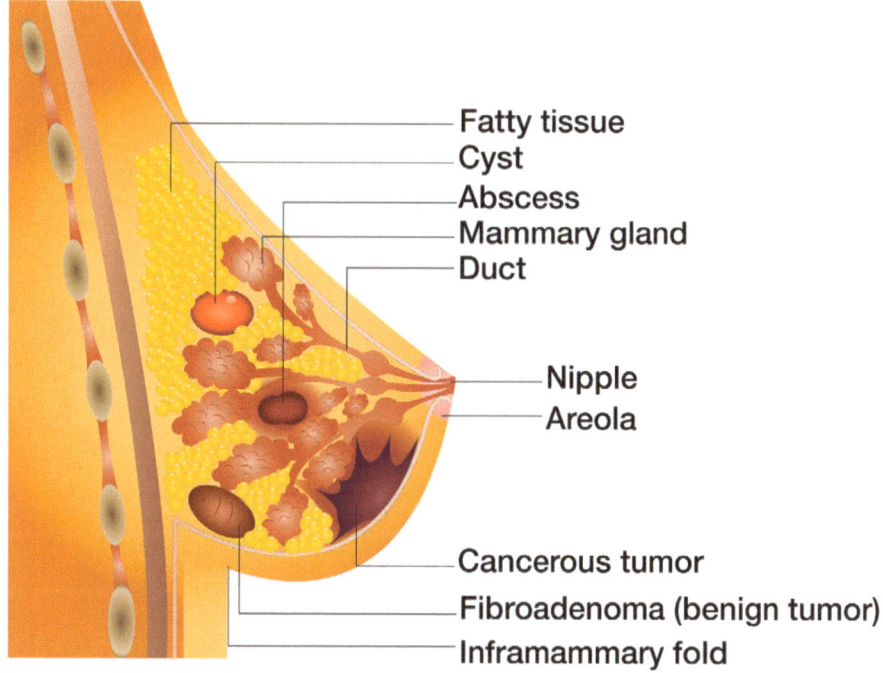

Fig 12-6 Breast cancer

Common signs and symptoms of breast cancer are:

- Inverted nipple (nipple turning inward).
- Change in the size or shape of the breast.
- A lump or thickening in the breast area that feels different.
- A swelling or lump in the armpit.
- Discharge from the nipple which is blood stained.
- Crusting, scaling or peeling of the nipple.

Conservative treatment includes chemotherapy where the cancer cells are destroyed by drugs; in advanced cases surgical options are considered. For small primary tumors the lump may be removed by surgery called lumpectomy, with the remainder of the breast left intact. This operation is usually followed by radiotherapy to the breast

- The most commonly diagnosed cancer in women are breast, cervical and colorectal cancer. The most commonly diagnosed cancer in men are prostate, lung and stomach cancer.

to kill remaining tumor cells. Alternatively, the surgeon may remove the entire breast by surgery called mastectomy. With either of these operations a separate incision is made to remove axillary lymph nodes to determine whether there is a spread.

Estimated new cases and deaths from breast cancer in the United States in 2012:

New cases: 226,870 (female); 2,190 (male)

Deaths: 39,510 (female); 410 (male)

CARCINOMA OF CERVIX (CERVICAL CANCER)

The condition of malignant cells present within the cervix is referred to as cervical cancer or cervical carcinoma. This is more common in women who have sexual intercourse at an early age, multiple sexual partners, a history of sexually transmitted diseases, and evidence of an HPV (human papilloma virus) infection.

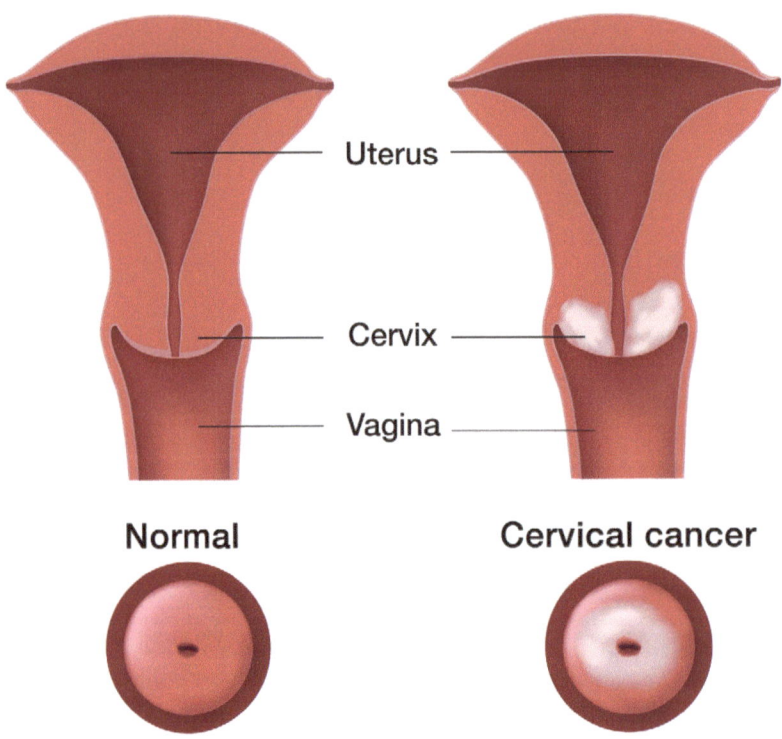

Fig 12-7 Cervical cancer

Early neoplastic changes in the cervix vary from dysplasia (abnormal cell growth) to carcinoma in situ (CIS), which is localized cancer growth. The diagnosis is done based on pap smear, which is pathologic examination of fluid with cell taken from the cervical opening. Further, biopsy and resection may be necessary to diagnose and treat CIS. Surgery or radiation therapy or both are used to treat more extensive and metastatic disease

Estimated new cases and deaths from cervical (uterine cervix) cancer in the United States in 2012:

New cases: 12,170

Deaths: 4,220

COLON AND RECTAL CANCER

Cancer in the colon ranges from very small ones to larger ones and mostly occurs low down in the bowel, i.e. in the rectum and the colon. In some cases it can occur in the transverse colon, the descending colon or the ascending colon. Most colon cancers are believed to start as polyps, which are growths or protrusions on the lining of the colon, although most polyps never change into a cancer. Uncontrolled negative lower emotions, low fiber diet and improper eating habits are the major causes of the colon cancer with the greatest risk for those who are 40 years of age or older.

Common signs and symptoms of colon cancer are:

- Passing dark bloods and red stools.
- Ulceration of this cancer site may lead to bleeding and bright red blood in the stools.
- Constipation with a frequent urge to empty the bowels or diarrhea, and change of bowel habits.
- Abdominal pain may be extended to or localized in the left lower abdomen.
- Loss of weight or appetite.
- Unexplained anemia.
- Fatigue.

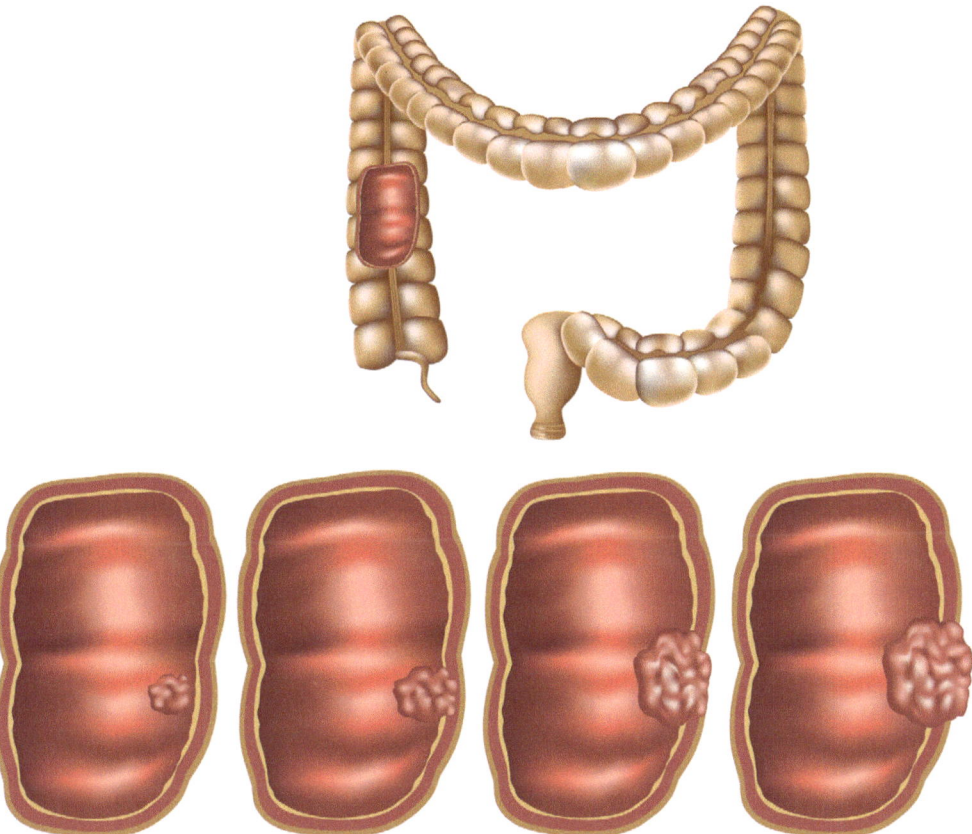

Fig 12-8 Stages of colon cancer

Complications include bowel obstruction where severe intermittent sharp pain is felt when growth is constricting the bowel. There is a spread of the cancerous growth to stomach, liver and urinary bladder. Cancer of the liver and ascites (buildup of fluid in the abdomen) are two of other possible complications

Estimated new cases and deaths from colon and rectal cancer in the United States in 2012:

New cases: 103,170 (colon); 40,290 (rectal)

Deaths: 51,690 (colon and rectal combined)

KIDNEY CANCER

Cancerous tumor of the kidney in adulthood is referred to as the renal cell carcinoma and hematuria (blood in the urine) is its main symptom. The tumor often spreads to the bones and lungs. Removal of the kidney and replacement is the treatment of choice. Kidney cancer includes renal cell carcinoma (cancer that forms in the lining of very small tubes in the kidney that filter the blood and remove waste products) and renal pelvis carcinoma (cancer that forms in the center of the kidney where urine collects).Malignant tumor of the kidney occurring in childhood is called the wilms tumor. This tumor is treated with surgery, radiation, and chemotherapy.

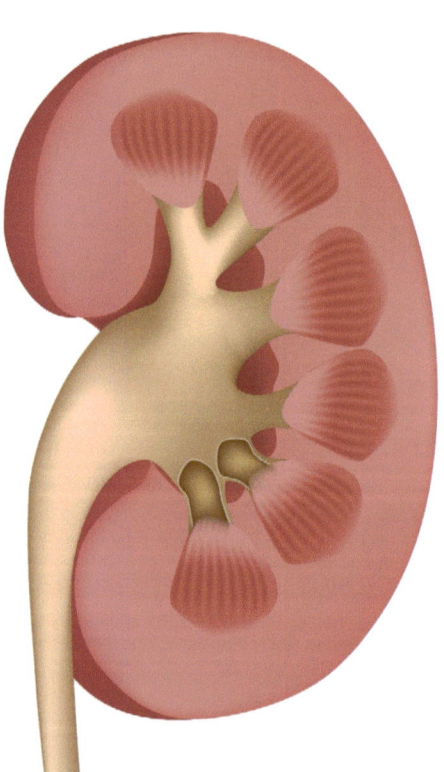
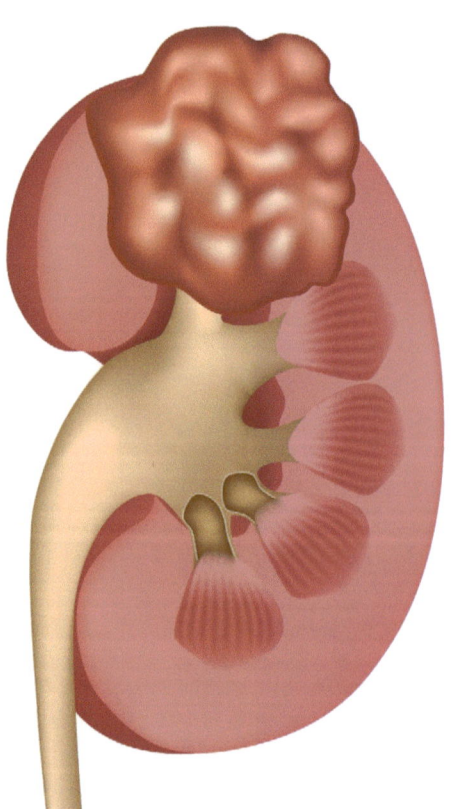

Healthy kidney   Kidney with tumor

Fig 12-9 Kidney cancer

Common signs and symptoms of kidney cancer are:
- Blood in the urine (hematuria).
- lump in the abdomen.
- Unexplained weight loss.

- Fever that lasts for weeks which is not caused by an infection.
- Swellings (edema) in the legs and ankles.
- Pain in the lower back just below the ribs.
- Extreme fatigue and lethargy.
- Night sweats.

Estimated new cases and deaths from kidney (renal cell and renal pelvis) cancer in the United States in 2012:

New cases: 64,770

Deaths: 13,570

LEUKEMIA

Leukemia is a group of malignant disorders of the blood cells associated with the increase in the number of WBC. The WBC may be increased either in bone marrow or in the blood. Males are more affected than females. The cause is unknown but however there are various factors responsible such as radiation, exposure to benzene in the industries, drugs, viral infection and genetic causes. Leukemia is classified into acute and chronic (Fig no:11.4, page 202)

In acute leukemia the life expectancy is very short and in chronic leukemia the patient is not well for months and the life span is reduced.

Common signs and symptoms of leukemia are:

- The patient may complain with anemia.
- Painless lymph node enlargement.
- Enlargement of the spleen.
- Enlargement of the liver in some cases.
- Fever.
- Loss of weight, loss of appetite.
- Bleeding and infection. Infections are more common due to the defense mechanism of the body being affected.
- Sometimes the patient have delusions and hallucinations.

Estimated new cases and deaths from leukemia in the United States in 2012:

New cases: 47,150

Deaths: 23,540

LIVER CANCER

Primary liver cancer is cancer that forms in the tissues of the liver. Secondary liver cancer is cancer that spreads to the liver from another part of the body.

- Alcohol and tobacco use, low fruit and vegetable consumption, lack of exercise and high body mass index cause 30% of cancer deaths

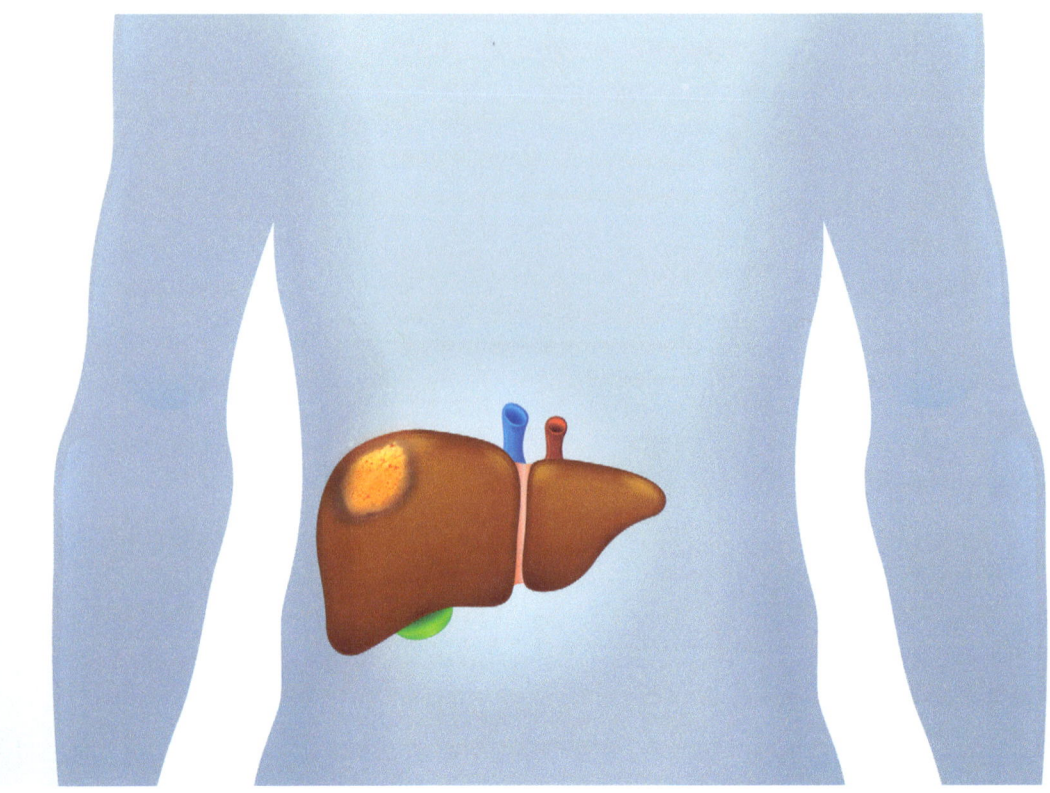

Fig 12-10 Liver cancer

Common signs and symptoms of liver cancer are:

- General fatigue which may not be relieved by rest.
- Pain and/or discomfort that occurs in the right shoulder blade area or in the right side of abdomen.
- Loss of appetite.
- Nausea or vomiting.
- Jaundice (causing yellowing of the skin and eyes).
- Enlarged liver and spleen which are felt as a mass under the right and left ribs respectively.

Estimated new cases and deaths from liver and intrahepatic bile duct cancer in the United States in 2012:

New cases: 28,720

Deaths: 20,550

LUNG CANCER

Cancerous tumor arising from bronchus or lung tissue is referred to as the lung cancer or the bronchiogenic carcinoma. This group of malignant tumors, associated with cigarette smoking, is responsible for 31% of cancer deaths in males. It usually starts on the bronchial tubes, then lung tissue, and spreads to other parts of the body. It is more prevalent among cigarette smokers.

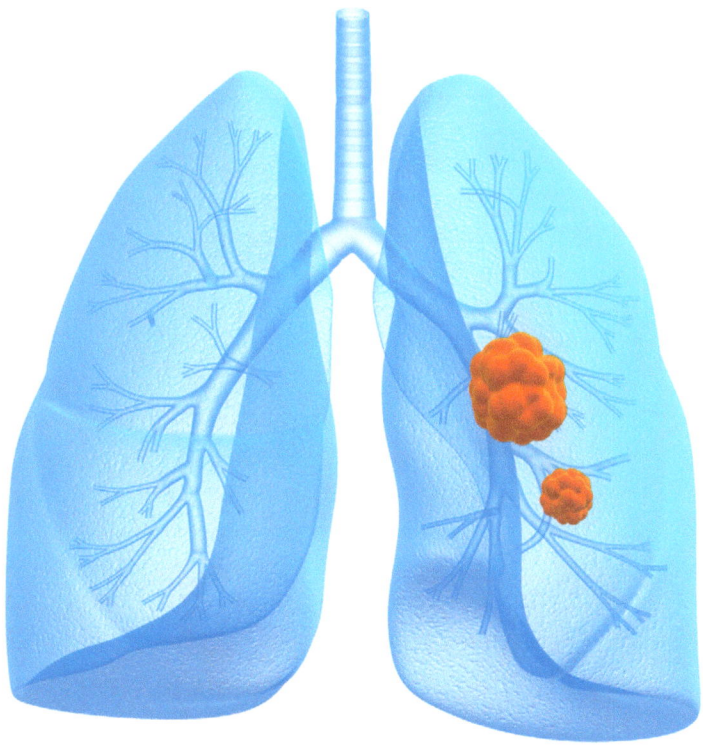

Fig 12-11 Lung cancer

Common signs and symptoms of lung cancer are:

- It starts with dry irritant cough and later the patient might cough up yellow phlegm.
- It can advance with expectoration of blood streaked sputum or frank blood (hemoptysis).
- There will be streaks of fresh red or altered brown blood mixed with phlegm during the course of this illness.
- Shortness of breathe.
- Loss of weight.
- Dull continuous pain in the chest or shoulders may also be experienced.

- Globally 22% of cancer deaths and 71% of lung cancer deaths are due to tobacco which is the most important risk factor for cancer

Estimated new cases and deaths from lung cancer in the United States in 2012:

New cases: 226,160

Deaths: 160,340

THYROID CANCER

Thyroid cancer forms in the thyroid gland (an organ at the base of the throat that makes hormones that help control heart rate, blood pressure, body temperature, and weight). Four main types of thyroid cancer are papillary, follicular, medullary, and anaplastic thyroid cancer. The four types are based on how the cancer cells look under a microscope.

Common signs and symptoms of thyroid cancer are:

- Lump or nodule in the neck which is usually painless.
- Persistent cough that is not due to cold or illness.
- Difficulty in breathing.
- Unexplained hoarseness of voice.
- Difficulty swallowing.
- Pain in throat and neck.

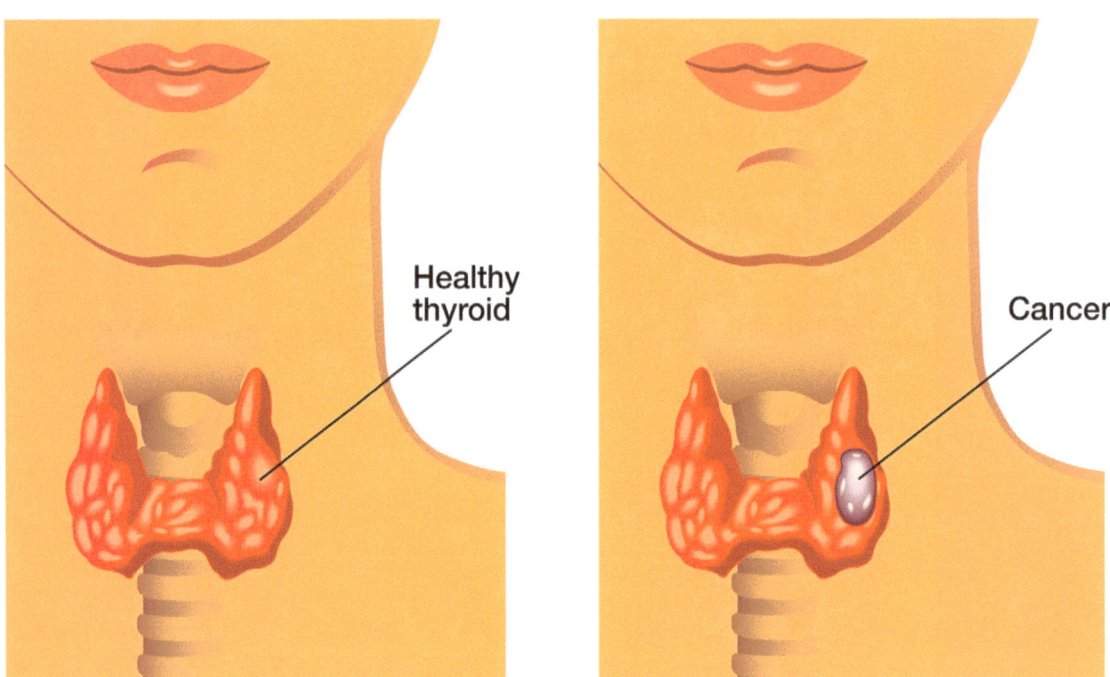

Fig 12-12 Thyroid cancer

Estimated new cases and deaths from thyroid cancer in the United States in 2012:

New cases: 56,460

Deaths: 1,780

VAGINAL CANCER

Vaginal cancer forms in the tissues of the vagina (birth canal). The vagina leads from the cervix (the opening of the uterus) to the outside of the body. The most common type of vaginal cancer is squamous cell carcinoma, which starts in the thin, flat cells lining the vagina. Another type of vaginal cancer is adenocarcinoma, cancer that begins in glandular cells in the lining of the vagina.

Common signs and symptoms of vaginal cancer are:

- Abnormal vaginal bleeding, common after intercourse or after menopause.
- Watery vaginal discharge.
- A lump or mass that can be felt in the vagina.
- Pain during urination.

- Constipation.
- Pain in the pelvis.

Estimated new cases and deaths from vaginal (and other female genital) cancer in the United States in 2012:

New cases: 2,680

Deaths: 840

PROSTATE CANCER

Prostate cancer forms in tissues of the prostate (a gland in the male reproductive system found below the bladder and in front of the rectum). Prostate cancer usually occurs in older men.

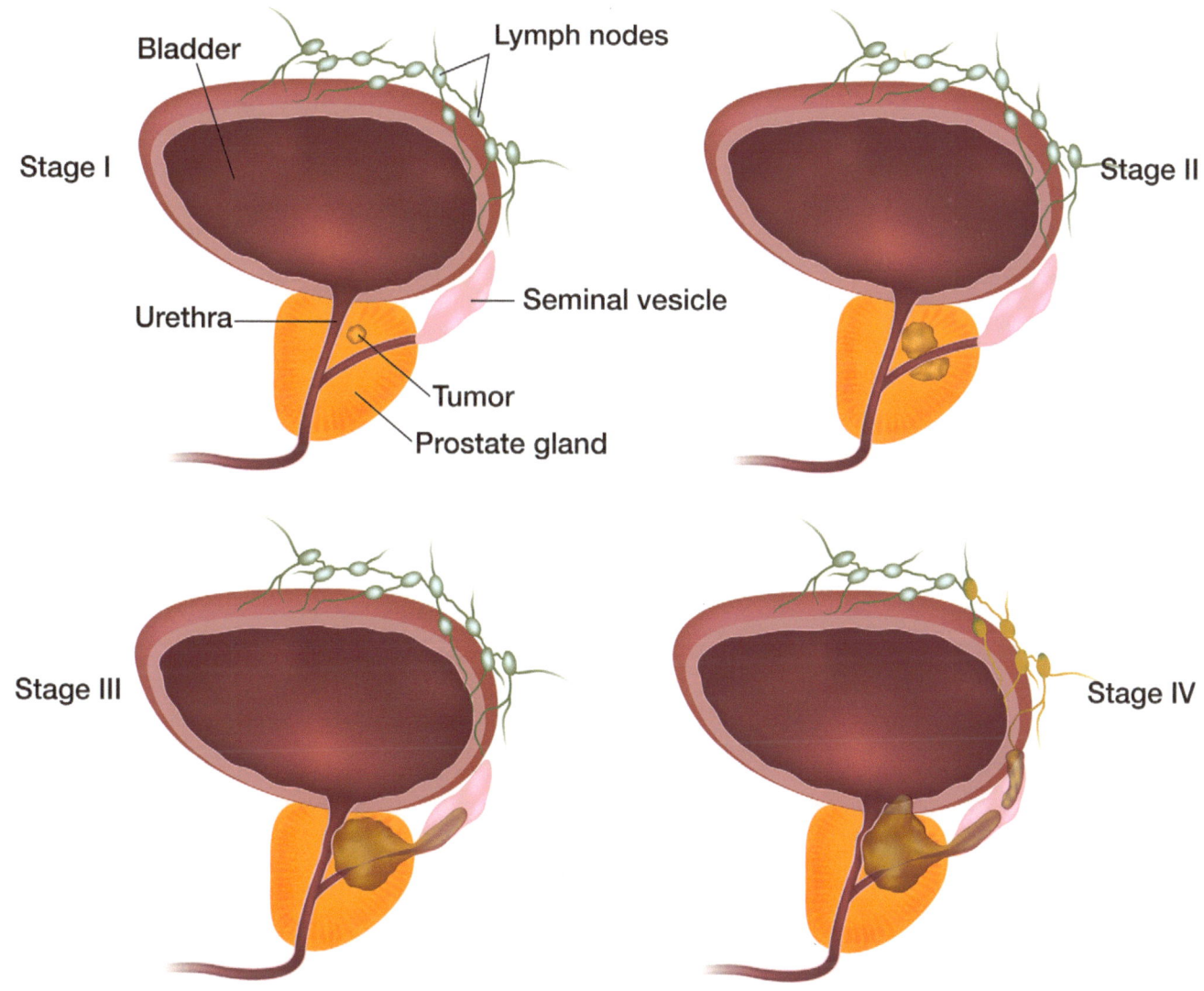

Fig 12-13 Prostate cancer

Common signs and symptoms of prostate cancer are:

- Frequent urination, especially at night.
- Burning sensation or pain while passing urine.

- Urgent need to pass urine.
- Blood in the urine (hematuria).
- Blood in the semen.
- Onset of erectile dysfunction (impotence).
- Pain in the bones (more common in lower back and hips).

Estimated new cases and deaths from prostate cancer in the United States in 2012:

New cases: 241,740

Deaths: 28,170

UTERINE (ENDOMETRIAL) CANCER

A cancerous growth in the uterus is more common after menopause unlike cancer of the cervix. The major symptom of adenocarcinoma of the uterus is postmenopausal bleeding. Endometrial cancer is more common in women who are exposed to high levels of estrogen from contraceptive pills, obesity, and in women who have not been pregnant. Dilation (opening the cervical canal) and curettage (scraping the inner lining of the uterus) is the best method of diagnosing the disease. If the tumor is confined to the uterus, it is treated by surgery, which involves removal of uterus, which is called hysterectomy. Radiation therapy is prescribed for patients with more advanced disease.

Common signs and symptoms of uterine cancer are:

- Heavy vaginal bleeding before or after menopause.
- Pain and bleeding during sex.
- Vaginal bleeding between normal menstrual periods.
- Foul smelling vaginal discharge.
- Pain in the lower abdomen, pelvic region, legs and back.

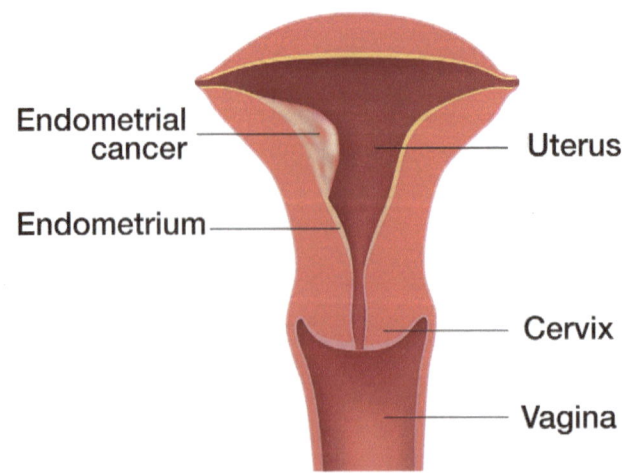

Fig 12-14 Uterine cancer

Estimated new cases and deaths from endometrial cancer in the United States in 2012:

New cases: 47,130

Deaths: 8,010

Source: National Cancer Institute; www.cancer.gov

Chapter 13

Lab investigations with interpretations

TABLE OF CONTENTS

VITAL SIGNS 224
    Blood pressure (BP) 224
    Temperature 224
    Pulse 224

COMMON LAB VALUES AND INTERPRETATIONS 225
    ESR (erythrocyte sedimentation rate) 225
    Hemoglobin 225
    Rbc's (red blood cell) 226
    Wbc's (white blood cell) 226
    Differential count 226
    Bleeding time and clotting time 227
    Packed cell volume 227
    Platelet count 227
    Blood urea 227
    Blood sugar 227
    Serum electrolytes 227
        Sodium 227
        Potassium 228
        Calcium 228
        Creatinine 228
        Cholesterol 228
    Liver function tests 228
        SAP (serum alkaline phosphatase) 228
        Serum bilirubin 228
        Serum proteins 229
    Urine 229
    Urine analysis 229

VITAL SIGNS, COMMON LAB VALUES AND INTERPRETATIONS

VITAL SIGNS

BLOOD PRESSURE (BP)

	Systolic (mm Hg)	Diastolic (mm Hg)	Average
Normal			
Adults	90 to 130	60 to 90	120/80
Children	80 to 100	50 to 70	100/60
Infants	70 to 95	40 to 80	90/60
Hypertension or high blood pressure for adults older than 18 years			
Stage 1	140 to 159	90 to 99	
Stage 2	160 or more	100 or more	

TEMPERATURE

The *Average oral temperature* is 37 degree C (98.6 degree F). This may slightly vary during the day time. It may be as low as 35.8 degree C (96.4 degree F) in the early morning and it may rise to 37.3 degree C (99.1 degree F) during the afternoon or evenings. If the temperature rises more than 37.2 degree C (98.9 degree F) in the early morning or higher than 37.7 degree C (99.9 degree F) in the afternoon or late afternoon it is considered a fever.

PULSE

The radial pulse is used to commonly assess the heart beat

The normal range for adults : 60 – 100 beats per minute

The normal range for children : 80 – 100 beats per minute

The normal range for infants (age 1 to 12 months) : 100 to 120 beats per minute

The normal range for neonates (age 1 to 28 days) : 120 to 160 beats per minute

COMMON LAB VALUES AND INTERPRETATIONS

Fig 13-1 Lab Investigations with Interpretation

ESR (ERYTHROCYTE SEDIMENTATION RATE)

- Normal value in Males – 0 – 9 mm/hr
- Normal value in Females – 0 – 20 mm/hr

This value has no use in diagnosing a disease. It only indicates the spread of disease and also worsening of the condition. An increase in ESR is seen in conditions like inflammation, anemia, infection, chronic illness like pulmonary tuberculosis and rheumatoid arthritis, malignancy and severe trauma.

However ESR value is low in newborns and higher in females and during pregnancy which should not be confused for any other disease.

HEMOGLOBIN

- Normal value in Males – 14 – 18 gm/dl
- Normal value in Females – 12 – 15.5 gm/dl

Investigations

When the hemoglobin level becomes low the condition is called anemia. Hemoglobin level of 8-12 gm/dl indicates the person is mildly anemic. Hemoglobin level 5-8 gm/dl indicates the person is moderately anemic. Hemoglobin level of less than 5 gm/dl indicates the person is severely anemic. Hemoglobin level is more in certain cardio respiratory disorders and polycythemia. In newborns, males and high altitude the hemoglobin count is higher which is normal.

RBC'S (RED BLOOD CELL)

Normal RBC count in males is 5 – 6 million / cu. mm and females is 4.5 – 5.5 million / cu. mm. In anemia the RBC count is less than 4 million / cu. mm. Polycythemia is a condition in which RBC count increases above 6 million / cu. mm. Polycythemia vera is cancerous condition of bone marrow which causes a marked increase in RBC count.

WBC'S (WHITE BLOOD CELL)

The total WBC count is 4000 – 11000 / cu. mm. Leucocytosis is the term used when the WBC count increases above 11000 / cu. mm. It increases during fever and pyogenic infections. Leukemia is a cancerous condition of blood in which WBC is more than 50000 / cu. mm. However, it is also increased in new born, stress, pregnancy, menstruation, lactation which is normal. When the WBC count goes below 4000 / cu. mm it is called leucopenia. The common causes of leucopenia are starvation, typhoid fever, viral infections etc.

DIFFERENTIAL COUNT

White blood cells consists of neutrophils, basophils, monocytes, eosinophils and lymphocytes

The normal value of:

- Neutrophils is 50 % – 70 %
- Basophils is < 1%
- Monocytes is 2 % – 8 %
- Eosinophils is 1 % – 4 %
- Lymphocytes is 20 % – 40 %

Neutrophil count increases after exercise, during pregnancy, menstruation, lactation, pus forming infection, burns and after surgery.

Neutrophil count decrease during typhoid fever, viral infection and bone marrow depression.

Eosinophil count increases in allergic conditions like bronchial asthma, worm infestations like skin disease.

Eosinophil count decreases after injection of steroids and cushing's syndrome.

Lymphocyte count increases in tuberculosis, leukemia and viral infection.

Lymphocyte count decreases in AIDS and decreased functioning of bone marrow.

Monocyte count increases in tuberculosis, syphilis and decreases in decreased functioning of bone marrow.

BLEEDING TIME AND CLOTTING TIME

Bleeding time is the time taken from the puncture of blood vessel to the stoppage of bleeding. The normal time is 2-6 minutes. Clotting time is the time taken from the puncture of blood vessel to the formation of the clot. The normal time taken is 4-8 minutes. Bleeding time is prolonged in thrombocytopenic purpura and high temperature. Clotting time is prolonged in hemophilia and vitamin k deficiency.

PACKED CELL VOLUME

Packed cell volume is a measure of the proportion of blood volume that is occupied by red blood cells .

- The normal value is 40 – 50% in males and 37 – 47 % in females.

It is increased in conditions like polycythemia, congestive cardiac failure, burns and dehydration. It is decreased in conditions like anemia, bone marrow leucopenia.

PLATELET COUNT

- The normal platelet count is 150,000- 350,000 / cu.mm

It is increased during trauma and after splenectomy (removal of spleen) It is decreased in bone marrow depression, viral infections, increased functioning of spleen.

BLOOD UREA

- The normal value is 20 – 40 mg / dl

It increases during dehydration, vomiting, diarrhea, diabetic coma, renal diseases, stones, enlarged prostate, tumour of bladder. It decreases during pregnancy, starvation, and diet deficient in protein.

BLOOD SUGAR

The patient is instructed to eat well 3 days before the test. Patient should avoid drugs like insulin. Patient has to be on 12 hours of fasting that is from previous night. In the morning fasting blood sample is taken for estimation of blood sugar level. Then 75gm of glucose is mixed in water and given to the patient and 2 hours later blood glucose level is estimated. Fasting level < 110 mg/dl is normal and > 126 mg/dl is diagnostic of diabetes. Post prandial level < 140 mg/dl is normal and > 200 mg/dl is diagnostic of diabetes.

SERUM ELECTROLYTES

SODIUM

- Normal serum sodium value is 130 mEq / L
- Sodium level < 130 mEq / L is hyponatremia

The causes are vomiting, diarrhea, sweating, renal failure, diuretics, cirrhosis, congestive cardiac failure, hypothyroidism.

- Sodium level > 150 mEq / L is hypernatremia.

The causes are increased saline infusion, vomiting, diarrhea, and diabetes insipidus.

POTASSIUM

- Normal serum value is 3.5 to 4.5 mEq / L

When the serum level falls below 3.5 mEq / L it is called hypokalemia. The causes are vomiting, diarrhea, cushing's syndrome. When the serum level increases above 5.5 mEq / L it is called hyperkalemia. The causes are renal failure, internal bleeding, blood transfusion.

CALCIUM

- The normal serum value is 9 – 11 mg /dl

Deficiency of calcium leads to tetany. Increased calcium level leads to the formation of renal stones

CREATININE

- The normal serum creatinine is 0.8 to 1.2 mg/dl

The value is raised in starvation, thyrotoxicosis, poorly controlled diabetes, muscle diseases

CHOLESTEROL

- The normal serum cholesterol level is 250 mg/dl. However less than 200 mg/dl is desirable.

Plasma cholesterol decreases by increased secretion of thyroid and oestrogen hormones. Plasma cholesterol level increases by intestinal obstruction and diabetes. Increased cholesterol level leads to atherosclerosis, obesity, CVA (cerebrovascular accidents), gallstones, CAD (Coronary artery disease).

LIVER FUNCTION TESTS

- SGOT & SGPT are normally present in the blood and is less than 40 units.
- SGOT – 10 – 35 U / L
- SGPT – 10 – 40 U / L
- They are indicators of liver cell damage.
- Value > 300 – 400 U / L indicates liver damage leading to jaundice.
- Value > 1000 U / L is seen in hepatitis and drugs damaging liver.
- Lesser degree of elevation is seen in chronic hepatitis, cirrhosis of liver.

SAP (SERUM ALKALINE PHOSPHATASE)

- Normal value is 30 – 120 U / L. The value is increased in biliary obstruction, diabetes and carcinoma of liver

SERUM BILIRUBIN

- Normal value 0.12 – 1.0 mg / dl. When it exceeds more than 2 mg / dl the condition is called jaundice.

SERUM PROTEINS
- Normal albumin level is 3.5 – 5 g / dl
- Normal globulin level is 2 – 3.5 g / dl

In progressive liver diseases serum albumin level is < 3 g / dl and serum globulin level is > 4 g/ dl. Serum albumin level is low in shock, protein deficiency, nephritic syndrome, edema.

URINE
- In urine we normally look for color and quantity.
- High coloured urine suggests jaundice.
- Normal individual excretes 1200 ml of urine per day.
- Less indicates renal failure.
- The routine investigations done in urine are urine albumin, sugar, ketone, pus cells, deposits, bile salts and bile pigments.
- Presence of glucose in the urine indicates diabetes.
- Presence of albumin in the urine indicates diabetes or nephrotic syndrome.
- Bile salts and bile pigments are present in urine in jaundice.
- Ketones are present in urine in diabetic coma.
- Pus cells are present in urine in urinary tract infection.

URINE ANALYSIS

Analysis of urine is a very important investigation in reaching upon diagnosis of major metabolic disorders. The parameters that are commonly looked for in a urine analysis are described below.

1. Color: Normal urine is yellow (amber) or straw-colored. A colorless, pale urine indicates a large amount of water in the urine, whereas a smoky-red or brown color of urine is due to the presence of large amounts of blood.
2. pH: The pH test indicates to what degree a solution is acidic or alkaline. Normal urine is slightly acidic (6.5). However, in infections of the bladder, the urine pH may be alkaline.
3. Glucose: Sugar is not normally found in the urine. In most cases, when it does appear (glycosuria), it indicates the diabetes mellitus. In diabetes mellitus, there is an excess of sugar in the bloodstream (hyperglycemia), which leads to the "spilling over" of sugar into the urine and the renal tubules are unable to reabsorb all the sugar that filters out through the glomerular membrane.
4. Protein: Small amounts of protein are normally found in the urine but not in significant quantities. Albumin is usually responsible for positive urinary tests for protein. Albumin is the major protein in blood plasma. Protein in urine is referred to as proteinuria, and in case of presence of albumin it is called albuminuria. It is a sign of renal involvement in diabetes mellitus and essential hypertension.
5. Ketone bodies: Ketones are the breakdown products resulting from fat decomposition in cells. Ketones accumulate in large quantities in blood and urine when, fat is used instead of sugar for energy formation. This condition occurs in diabetes mellitus or during starvation.

6. **Specific gravity:** The specific gravity of the urine is compared to that of water. The urine of patients with diabetes mellitus has a higher-than-normal specific gravity because of the presence of sugar.

7. **Bilirubin:** This is a pigment substance formed from hemoglobin breakdown. It may appear in the urine darkening it, as an indication of liver or gallbladder disease. The diseased liver has difficulty removing bilirubin from the blood (hyperbilirubinemia), which causes excessive bilirubin to appear in the urine (bilirubinuria) as in the case of jaundice.

8. **Sediment:** Presence of abnormal particles in the urine can be a sign of a pathological condition which may include cells, bacteria, crystals.

9. **Pus:** Pyuria gives a cloudy appearance to the urine and is observed in the case of infection or inflammation in the kidney or bladder.

Chapter 14

Psychiatric Disorders

TABLE OF CONTENTS

INTRODUCTION 234
DISORDERS OF CHILDREN 234
    Specific learning disability 234
        Pica 234
        Attention deficit hyperactivity disorder (ADHD) 235
    Functional enuresis 235
    Functional encopresis 235
TIC DISORDERS 236
    Gilles de la tourette syndrome 236
    Mental retardation 236
    Autism 237
ADULT PSYCHIATRIC DISORDERS 237
    Schizophrenia 237
        Paranoid type 237
        Disorganized type 237
        Catatonic type 238
        Residual type 238
        Undifferentiated type 238
    Schizophreniform disorder 238
    Schizoaffective disorder 238
    Delusional disorder 238
        Grandiose 238
        Erotomanic 238
        Jealous 238
        Persecutory 238
        Somatic 238
    Brief psychotic disorder 239
    Shared psychotic disorder 239
    Substance induced psychotic disorder 239
    Asperger's disorder 239
NEUROTIC DISORDERS 239
ANXIETY DISTORDERS 239
    Panic disorder 240
    Agoraphobia 240
    Specific and social phobia 240
    Obsessive compulsive disorder 240
    Post traumatic stress disorder 241
    Generalized anxiety disorder 241

SOMATOFORM DISORDERS ... 241
Somatization ... 241
Conversion ... 241
Hypochondriasis ... 241
Body dysmorphic disorder ... 242
Pain disorder ... 242

DISSOCIATIVE DISORDERS ... 242
Dissociative amnesia ... 242
Dissociate fugue ... 242
Dissociative identity disorder ... 243
Depersonalization disorder ... 243

EATING DISORDERS ... 243
Anorexia nervosa ... 243
Bulimia nervosa ... 243
Obesity ... 244

PERSONALITY DISORDERS ... 244
Cluster A ... 244
Paranoid personality disorder ... 244
Schizoid personality disorder ... 244
Schizotypal personality disorder ... 244
Cluster B ... 244
Antisocial personality disorder ... 244
Borderline personality disorder ... 244
Histrionic personality disorder ... 244
Narcissistic personality disorder ... 244
Cluster C ... 245
Dependent personality disorder ... 245
Obsessive compulsive personality disorder ... 245
Avoidant personality disorder ... 245

MOOD DISORDERS ... 245

LEARNING DISORDERS ... 245
Reading disorder ... 245
Mathematics disorders ... 245
Disorder of written expression ... 245

PSYCHIATRIC DISORDER

INTRODUCTION

Presented here is a brief account of mental ill health and the disorders that are prevalent today. The following information is just an overview of the vast categories of existing psychiatric disorders.

The two most important psychiatric classifications in use today are the diagnostic and statistical manual of mental disorders (DSM) and the international classification of diseases (ICD). The DSM-4-revised is the latest in use all over the world and it is published by American psychiatric association (APA). The ICD-10th edition is currently in use but mainly in European countries only. Both the classification systems include similar diagnostic criteria, which are a list of features that must be present for each disorder to arrive at a diagnosis.

DISORDERS OF CHILDREN

SPECIFIC LEARNING DISABILITY

A child with normal or above intelligence who is unable to perform well in reading, writing or arithmetic can have a specific learning disability. These children are usually able to function well but have severe problems with academic performance. Some of the common features are listed below:

1. They have reversal in writing (for example, they write 'b' as 'd' or "no" as "on" or '41' as '14').
2. They often forget the sequence of letters that make up a word.
3. They hear many noises but often cannot hear their mother or teacher talking to them. They find it difficult to discriminate the main sound from background noises.
4. They forget common and important things like the phone numbers or names of people, but remember television commercials or movie songs.
5. They can often be messy and often find it difficult to stand in a line.
6. They confuse "yesterday" with a "tomorrow", "breakfast" with "lunch" and have problems with tasks involving a sequence.
7. They miss steps in mathematics.
8. They do well orally but have poor spelling and find it difficult to write.
9. They do not complete their notes.
10. In addition to academic problems they may have general confusion with direction, sequences, and/or time. SLD can be specific reading disorder, specific arithmetic disorder and specific writing disorder. With proper diagnosis and good remedial education where specific individual needs are met, the child is able to manage an average performance in school.

Pica

Pica is eating of items that are generally regarded as inedible. (for example, mud, paint, eraser, pencils, etc.). The child may also have behavioral/emotional problems. Very often children with mental retardation and brain damage can also show symptoms of pica. Many times pica is reduced or resolved as the child grows older.

Attention deficit hyperactivity disorder (ADHD)

The child is often restless and is physically overactive. They cannot pay attention to simple tasks. They are often reckless, impulsive and prone to accidents. Since they have difficulty paying attention, they have problems in language communication and in learning. Many children with ADHD also are aggressive and prone to temper tantrums. They have extreme mood swings and have low self-esteem. They often find difficult to make friends and sustain relationships.

There can be three kinds of hyperkinesis or hyperactivity, which may occur separately or concurrently.

Physically hyperactive – The child keeps moving, running, climbing, and/or jumping, and does not seem to get tired.

Impulse control – The child is able to sit and do few simple tasks but suddenly engages in violent or aggressive behavior (for example, while playing, the child may suddenly run and bite or pinch someone, or deliberately spill water while eating, etc,.).

Inattentive – The child can sit still for long periods of time, but cannot pay attention. They are physically present in the same place but mentally they find it difficult to concentrate on the same thing for more than a few seconds or minutes.

These children generally do not complete tasks, miss out important information while learning and are prone to careless errors. Even in tasks they like, they find it difficult to pay attention. Though the root causes of ADHD are unknown, there is a correlation between the disorder and birth related injuries that involve brain damage, and genetics also play a role. Interventions include education for family and teachers, behavior modification for the child, and a consistent, predictable environment. Medication has been useful in abating symptoms, but long term impacts of these medications is still not conclusive.

FUNCTIONAL ENURESIS

A child with this disorder cannot control their bladder and urine after the appropriate age of toilet training. Nocturnal enuresis is night time urination or bed-wetting. Diurnal enuresis is daytime wetting. When the child wets at all times of the day and night, this is called primary enuresis. Treatment usually involves a combination of psychotherapy through play, art, and movement along with behavior modification.

FUNCTIONAL ENCOPRESIS

A child with this disorder has voluntary or involuntary passing of feces in inappropriate places, after the age when bowel control is expected. Enuresis and encopresis are now very common in children who have been sent to school very early or in homes when toilet habits have been very rigid.

TIC DISORDERS

Tics are purposeless, stereotyped, and repetitive jerking movements. Usually the tics are seen on the face and the neck though other parts of the body may also be involved. Usually the cause of tic disorder is emotional disturbance. This disorder is more common in boys and is made worse by anxiety (for example, it may take the form of the eyelids moving which may look like winking). Often tics cause a lot of embarrassment and this worsens the condition.

GILLES DE LA TOURETTE SYNDROME

This syndrome involves multiple tics, and the onset is before the age of 16 years. There can be vocal tics like grunting, snarling, or use of foul language. They may have movements like jumping, dancing etc. This affects the normal functioning of the individual. Many medications have been tried, and along with psychotherapy there has been improvement in some cases.

MENTAL RETARDATION

IQ range	Classification
Above 130	Gifted
120 – 129	Superior intelligence
110 – 139	High average
90 – 109	Average
80 – 89	Low average
70 – 79	Borderline intelligence (slow learners)
50 – 69	Mild mental retardation (educable)
40 – 49	Moderate mental retardation (trainable)
20 – 39	Severe mental retardation (home- based training)
Below 20	Profound mental retardation. – (home- based training)

Generally educational problems occur when IQ is 80 and below. Below an IQ of 60, there are generally significant problems in more areas of functioning. Genetic metabolic disorders, birth injuries, malnutrition, brain illnesses, diseases after birth, endocrine problems, and certain environmental factors are considered common causes of mental retardation.

Mental retardation is addressed through a combination of specialized training including special education, physiotherapy, occupational therapy, behavior modification, and vocational training. Medication can be used to control any specific endocrine or other concurrent conditions (such as epilepsy).

Mental retardation can often coexist with cerebral palsy, autism, personality disorders, schizophrenia, and behavior disorders. Early detection, diagnosis, and effective handling of the problem helps an individual function to the best of their capacity. Slow learners can be successful in school if the issues are detected early and handled effectively. With mild mental retardation, the individual can be taught to read and write, and even complete their education with special supports in place. In the case of moderate mental retardation more emphasis is made on teaching simple repetitive tasks, though depending on the degree of challenge, these learners may be able to read and/or write at basic levels. In the case of severe and profound mental retardation more emphasis is placed on helping the individual become self-sufficient in the areas of personal hygiene, self-care, and the activities of daily living.

AUTISM

Autism involves the impaired ability to reciprocate to social interaction including difficulties in communication and physical gestures. Restricted, stereotypical behavioral patterns may be present(for example, flapping arms, rocking back and forth etc.) IQ may be normal or even above normal. The onset of autism occurs around 2-3 years of age. The rate of this disorder is higher in boys than girls, though girls may be more severely affected. Evident language development problems are the main criteria for diagnosing autistic disorder. Aggressiveness, self-injurious behavior, and short attention are commonly observed in such children when they are in stressful situations.

The goal of treatment with autism is to increase socially acceptable behavior, improve and increase verbal and nonverbal communication, and to reduce socially unacceptable behaviors. Individual therapy, including physiotherapy, speech therapy, opportunities for creative expression and movement, and continuous individualized care helps children with autism function more easily within social expectations and teaches them strategies for self-soothing and emotional regulation during times of stress or in large groups.

ADULT PSYCHIATRIC DISORDERS

SCHIZOPHRENIA

It is a broad term to include a range of disordered thinking. Though the exact causes of schizophrenia are unclear, it is thought to be biologically based and is treated accordingly. The focus of treatment is on inhibiting and increasing the release of certain neurotransmitters in the brain. It usually has an earlier onset in men (15-25 years) than in women (25-35 years). Its treatment usually adopts a multimodal approach, including medications, therapy, diet, environment, and learning to cope with symptoms. For a diagnosis of schizophrenia to be made 2 or more of the following active phase symptoms have to be present for a minimum of 6 consecutive months: - delusions, hallucinations, disorganized speech (improper/inappropriate/illogical/senseless talking), major disorganized behavior (heightened physical activity or almost no movements) and negative symptoms (difficulty expressing appropriate emotion etc.)

Paranoid type includes delusions of persecution or grandeur. The person's mental faculties, emotional responses, and behavior tend to be relatively fair in functioning. Such people are typically suspicious, guarded, or sometimes hostile and aggressive by nature. Their intelligence is less impacted than those with other types of schizophrenia.

Disorganized type is characterized by primitive, uninhibited, and unorganized behavior. Such people spend a lot of time in non-constructive behavior. Their thoughts do not follow a logical progression and it seems they are not in touch with consensual reality (grinning/laughing without a reason, inappropriate emotional responses, odd personal appearance and social behavior).

Catatonic type includes disturbed physical functioning ranging from no movement at all to extreme physical activity. These people often need supervision to avoid unintentionally harming themselves.

Residual type are those who are diagnosed with schizophrenia but currently do not have active phase symptoms. Such patients usually exhibit emotional unresponsiveness, illogical thinking, social withdrawal, and talking for no reason without making "sense".

Undifferentiated type is a category for those people who do not fit into any of the above mentioned types of schizophrenia.

SCHIZOPHRENIFORM DISORDER

This condition is similar to schizophrenia except it has a much shorter active phase in its duration of the active phase symptoms. For this disorder, symptoms have to last for a minimum of one month but for less than six months. The person usually has a well-adjusted life before the abrupt onset of the symptoms. Usually, a psycho-social stressor triggers the onset of the symptoms. This is a rare disorder in adults, and more common in adolescents and young adults. Treatment for this disorder is short-term and tends to be effective.

SCHIZOAFFECTIVE DISORDER

In this condtion the patients exhibit symptoms of both active-phase schizophrenia as well as one or more mood disorders. It often occurs in adolescents who have no prior significant mental health issues until the sudden onset of symptoms. Often, a specific stressor may be linked to the onset of symptoms. Older people are also diagnosed with this disorder, and it is more prevalent in men than women. The specific cause of the disorder is unknown. Treatment involves hospitalization, appropriate medications, and psychosocial interventions.

DELUSIONAL DISORDER

This condition is different from a diagnosis of schizophrenia as hallucinations and some other symptoms are absent here. Prognosis of such patients depends upon how well the individual copes with daily affairs and interpersonal relationships, age of onset and type of delusion. Delusions fall in to the following categories:

Grandiose patients believe that they have a great but unacknowledged specialty (discovery, solution to a major problem that only they have, unique ability, insight into most difficult of matters, relationship with a famous public figure, etc.). Delusions may have religious content.

Erotomanic thoughts are centered around the belief that some famous public figure is infatuated with the patient, despite factual evidnce to the contrary.

Jealous delusion is about the infidelity of the patient's spouse despite evidence to the contrary. Though rare in occurrence, men are more affected by this delusion than women.

Persecutory usually involves a single theme or a series of connected themes about suspicion of being conspired against, spied on, being trapped into some harmful plot, or that someone or a team of people are trying to cause physical/mental/social harm to the patient. This is the most commonly occurring of all the types of delusions.

Somatic patient believes that they have a physical illness despite medical testing that proves contrary. Occurrence of this delusion is rare but is found the same degree in both sexes.

BRIEF PSYCHOTIC DISORDER

This disorder has a short duration (between 24 hours and one month). There may be symptoms of schizophrenia and it may have developed in response to a severe psychosocial stressor or group of stressors. The stressor is usually a major life event causing significant emotional upset to the patient. Patients that experience this disorder often have a pre-existing personality disorder and/or have experienced a major life change or transition. Symptoms include volatile emotions, unconventional dress, loud tone of voice, screaming and/or muteness, and impaired memory for recent events. Treatment includes hospitalization, antipsychotic medications and psychotherapy. This disorder is more common in younger adults.

SHARED PSYCHOTIC DISORDER

The key symptom in this disorder is the unchallenged acceptance of another person's delusions. It often involves two people who are very deeply connected to each other emotionally, and are likely to have schizophrenia in their family histories. Of the two people involved, the one who has a pre-existing psychotic disorder is usually older, more intelligent, better educated and dominant than the submissive person who shares the former's psychosis. The delusions are often persecutory or hypochondriacal in content. The treatment mainly involves separating the patient from the dominant person, providing antipsychotic medications and therapy. However, most of the patients fall back into the same cycle once out of the hospital as the dominant person is often a family member living in the same home. This disorder is more common in low socioeconomic groups and is more common in women than men.

SUBSTANCE INDUCED PSYCHOTIC DISORDER

The patient loses touch with reality either during intoxication or during the withdrawal period. Hallucination-like symptoms are present, ranging from auditory, visual, tactile, olfactory, and others.

ASPERGER'S DISORDER

Asperger's disorder is a type of autistic disorder where cognitive abilities and adaptive skills are mostly normal but the person has difficulty in social interactions and relationships. Making a diagnosis in favor of this disorder is difficult due to the instability in the diagnostic criteria. Treatment often depends upon the patient's level of adaptive functioning and somewhat similar techniques used for autistic children can be applied here for the severely disturbed social behavior.

NEUROTIC DISORDERS

'Neurosis' is a chronic or reappearing nonpsychotic disorder characterized mainly by anxiety. It often appears as a series of symptoms to which there are no provable organic factors/causes. The term 'neurosis' covers a wide range of disorders having different symptoms. The main difference between neurosis and psychosis is that in the former, a person is aware of what is real and what is not, and is able to function within consensual reality. The following is a list of disorders under the category of neurosis.

1) ANXIETY DISORDERS

Anxiety disorders are the most common of the neurotic disorders with symptoms varying from patient to patient. Anxiety disorder is more prevalent in women than men. There can be internal causes for this disorder (thoughts, beliefs, medical conditions) or external causes (environment, social settings etc.). There may also be a genetic basis for this disorder. A combination of medication and therapy are effective in managing and alleviating many anxiety disorders. The following is a list of anxiety disorders.

Panic disorder

This condition is characterized by the spontaneous and unexpected occurrence of a panic attack (discrete period of intense fear/discomfort) along with physical symptoms, thoughts, and/or emotions. The frequency of panic attacks may range from several attacks in one day to a few attacks in a year. They are often present in depressive mood disorders, substance intoxication and withdrawal. Panic disorder can develop at any age though onset is usually in young adulthood. Causes range from environmental stressors, life transitions, childhood trauma, etc. Research is exploring genetic causes and panic attacks as a learned response.

Agoraphobia

There is a fear of having a panic attack in a public place where there would be no help available. As such, people with this disorder often avoid crowds and/or open spaces. Many of these patients have been diagnosed with panic disorder. The treatment used for panic disorders and agoraphobia a combination of medication and therapy.

SPECIFIC AND SOCIAL PHOBIA

Specific phobia is defined as a strong persisting fear of an object or a situation. It is more commonly found than social phobia in women than men. The cause is an interaction of biological, genetic and environmental factors.

Social phobia is a strong persisting fear of situation in which embarrassment can occur. It is more common in women than men. The peak age of onset is in the teen years, though onset may be as early as 5 years or as late as 35 years age. Treatment includes insight oriented psychological therapies, family therapy, hypnosis, visualization techniques, relaxation techniques etc.

OBSESSIVE COMPULSIVE DISORDER

An obsession is a thought, feeling, idea, or sensation that occurs repetitively and is intrusive in nature. The obsession increases anxiety and the person is aware that it is a product of his/her mind. Compulsion is a conscious, standardized, recurring pattern of behavior (such as counting, checking, avoiding, etc.). The compulsive action helps to reduce the anxiety caused by the obsession.

Both the obsession and the compulsion can be very disabling and time consuming, and significantly interfere with one's normal routine. Men and women are equally affected but in adolescence more boys are affected than girls. The coexisting disorders in such patients are alcohol abuse, specific phobia, panic disorder, and eating disorders.

Causes include biological factors and psycho-social factors. Many patients exhibit depression symptoms and they do not necessarily have the diagnosis of obsessive compulsive personality disorder. More than half of these patients have a sudden onset of symptoms after experiencing a stressful event. Suicide risk is high for this disorder. Treatment involves a combination of medication and therapy.

POST TRAUMATIC STRESS DISORDER

There is a set of typical symptoms that develops after a person sees, is involved in, or hears of an extreme traumatic stressor (an event, experience, incident causing lot of stress). The person reacts to this event with fear and helplessness, constantly relives the event mentally and tries to avoid being reminded of it. Symptoms last for more than one month and significantly affect different areas of life. The symptoms can develop days, weeks, or months after the trauma. The onset can be at any age. Greater emphasis is placed on the person's subjective response to the event than on the severity of the event. Treatment includes a combination of medications, psychotherapy, hypnosis, and relaxation techniques.

GENERALIZED ANXIETY DISORDER

This condition is defined as excessive anxiety about several events/activities. The person may exhibit symptoms from social phobia, specific phobia, panic disorder, post-traumatic stress disorder, and depression. This disorder occurs more in women than men. It is generally diagnosed and treated by general practitioners rather than mental health professionals. The specific causes are not known at this time. Symptoms primarily include: physical tension (motor), cognitive alertness, shortness of breath, excessive sweating, heart palpitations, gastrointestinal symptoms, and anxiety. The course and prognosis of this disorder is difficult to predict due to coexistence of other mental disorders. Treatment includes a combination of anxiety-reducing medications and therapy

2) SOMATOFORM DISORDERS

These conditions are characterized by the presence of physical symptoms indicating a medical condition, but the symptoms are not supported by laboratory findings. However, the symptoms are severe enough to cause distress and they are not intentionally produced. Causes are generally a combination of biological, environmental, and psycho-social factors. The following disorders come under the category of somatoform disorders.

SOMATIZATION

This condtion is characterized by a combination of pain, gastrointestinal, sexual, and neurological symptoms. The focus is on physical symptoms for which there is no biological reason. Onset is usually before the age of 30 years. Individual and group therapy are effective treatment for this disorder.

CONVERSION

This condition is characterized by one or more neurological symptoms e.g. blindness, paralysis etc., which cannot be medically explained. For this diagnosis, certain psychological factors have to be linked with either the start or progression of the disorder. This disorder is more prevalent in women than men. Patients have a good prognosis when the onset of this disorder is sudden, has an easily identifiable stressor, and the person is generally well-adjusted before the onset of the disorder with no other pre-existing psychiatric or medical disorders. A combination of therapy and anxiety-reducing medication are effective treatment for conversion disorder.

HYPOCHONDRIASIS

This condition is a person's preoccupation with the fear of contracting or the belief that he already had a serious disease. The person misinterprets normal bodily sensations, understanding them as signs that something is medically wrong. Hypochondriasis occurs equally in men and women and the onset is usually between 20 -30 years of age. Causes are believed to be psycho-social in nature. Group therapy is effective for this condition, and medication can be given where a medically treatable condition is actually present.

BODY DYSMORPHIC DISORDER

This condition is characterized by a preoccupation with an imagined defect of the person's physical appearance, or an exaggerated distortion of a small defect in physical appearance and this preoccupation causes the patient significant distress or impairs his/her personal, social and/or occupational life. Patients will often avoid social settings and try to cover up their presumed defect with makeup or clothing. Women are more affected by this disorder than men, and common age of onset is between 15 - 20 years. The causes are not known. A combination of medication and therapy help to reduce symptoms.

PAIN DISORDER

This condition is characterized by the patient complaining of pain at one or more sites in the body with no medical explanation. The symptoms are often associated with emotional disturbance and of impaired functioning in different areas of life. The peak age of onset is between 40 - 50 years. The causes are biological and psycho-social in nature. The onset of this disorder is abrupt and can increase in severity for a few weeks to months. Antidepressant medication combined with therapy are useful in treatment.

3) DISSOCIATIVE DISORDERS

These conditions are characterized by a state of disrupted consciousness, memory, identity, or perception of the environment. Patients feel as though they don't have an identity, they are confused about who they are, or they experience multiple identities. Dissociative disorders often occur as a psychological defense against an extreme trauma. The following is a list of types of dissociative disorders.

DISSOCIATIVE AMNESIA

This condition is characterized by the inability to recall information about events in a person's life. The onset is usually an extreme trauma. After the trauma, the capacity to learn new information remains intact. This is the most common of all the dissociative disorders. Mostly the amnesia ends abruptly except in cases where the patient has a secondary gain (avoidance of responsibility, attention of people etc.,) Medication and hypnosis are used to help recover the lost memories followed by help to integrate those memories into present life.

DISSOCIATE FUGUE

This condition is characterized by the travelling to a certain distance and suddenly failing to remember important aspects of one's own identity. Old and new identities do not alternate, rather the person assumes or creates a new identity with no awareness of his/her previous life. It is rare in occurrence, but likely to increase during the war time, natural disaster, or as a result of personal crises. It lasts for hours or days, and at the most weeks. Patients generally recover from it fast and recurrences are rare. Treatment is similar to that of dissociative amnesia.

DISSOCIATIVE IDENTITY DISORDER

This condition is more commonly known as multiple personality disorder. It is chronic in nature and typically caused by traumatic abuse in childhood. This is the most serious of the dissociative disorders. It seems to be rare in occurance, but may be under-reported. Mostly women are affected. Although patients have had symptoms for 5 - 10 years, they are diagnosed around the age of 30 years. The cause is unknown, but almost all recorded cases includes a traumatic childhood event or environment. The transition from one personality to another is often sudden, and during each personality state, patients will not be able to recall anything about other personalities. Often there is one personality state known as the host, which has all the information of other states and knows that they alternate. These personality states have proper names, nature, behavior etc., and complete and discrete identities. Though full recovery is possible, it is rare. A combination of therapy and medication can be useful in keeping symptoms manageable.

DEPERSONALIZATION DISORDER

This condition is characterized by persistent and recurrent alteration in the perception of the self where the person feels estranged from their own body or personality. Anxiety and depression are often already present conditions. Onset is more sudden than gradual and often occurs between 15 - 30 years of age. There are limited results with a combination of medications and therapy.

4) EATING DISORDERS

The following types of disorders fall under this category.

ANOREXIA NERVOSA

This condition is where the patient is intensively fearful of gaining weight and highly misinterprets their own body and its shape. Its onset is during the adolescence and more women are affected than men. The patient's body weight is 15% or below the normal expected weight for their age and height. The two types of anorexia nervosa are (a) where the person restricts the amount of food intake and occasionally purges it out or (b) where patients engage in binge eating or frequent eating and remove the eaten food from their body through purging or laxatives. Causes include social influences, psychological makeup, and the extreme need to be in control. Past physical and/or sexual abuse has also been linked to this disorder. Suicide rate is higher in patients with the binge eating - purging type (b) than the restricting type (a). However the (b) type patients have a better prognosis than the (a) type. Treatment includes hospitalization when needed, and individual and family education and psychotherapy.

BULIMIA NERVOSA

This condition is defined by binge-eating combined with inappropriate ways of stopping weight gain. The binge is often followed by feelings of guilt, depression or self-disgust. Patients with this disorder may maintain their normal body weight. The two types are as follows: (a) purging type (vomiting/laxatives) or (b) non - purging type (fasting / excessive physical exercises). Onset is in late adolescence to early adulthood, and the disorder is more common in women than men. This disorder has a better prognosis than anorexia nervosa, though little is known about long term recovery of these patients. Treatment includes a combination of medication and therapy.

OBESITY

This is a condition where excessive fat is accumulated in the body and the person's weight is more than 20% of the expected standard. It occurs more frequently in women, especially those from lower socioeconomic backgrounds. Generally, this disorder affects people aged 20-50 years. The causes range from genetic predisposition to lifestyle. These patients may also develop mild anxiety and depression. Treatment may involve, weight reduction programs, adjustment to diet, increase in physical activity, surgery, and counselling.

5) PERSONALITY DISORDERS

Personality disorders are characterized by the presence of long- lasting subjective experiences and behavior that stray from cultural norms. Onset may begin in early childhood or adolescence, remains stable throughout adulthood, and symptoms cause distress and impairs functioning in significant areas of life. Often patients with a personality disorder do not think there in anything wrong with them, and so often refuse professional intervention. There may be a genetic predisposition to certain personality disorders though environment, life experiences and temperament also play a role. Treatment depends on the main symptoms present for each patient and specifically which type of a personality disorder one has. Hospitalization occurs whenever necessary and antipsychotic/antianxiety/antidepressant medicines are given according to the type of personality disorder combined with therapy.

Personality disorders are divided into three cluster groups as follows:

CLUSTER A

Paranoid personality disorder is characterized by chronic suspiciousness, distrust, irritability, and hostility towards others.

Schizoid personality disorder is characterized by a pattern of withdrawal from society, such patients feel uncomfortable with interacting with people, are introverted, prefer isolation to social gatherings, and can be eccentric and emotionally unresponsive.

Schizotypal personality disorder is characterized by outwardly strange behavior such as visual illusions, believing magical things to be real, and/or living in an unreal world.

CLUSTER B

Antisocial personality disorder is characterized by a person's constant inability to conform to the societal norms with disregard and/or hostility to social expectations.

Borderline personality disorder is characterized by social manipulation, mood swings, self destructive behaviours, emotional instability, low self-image and fear of being alone.

Histrionic personality disorder is where the person is very easily excited, very dramatic and loud in expressing themselves emotionally and behaviorally, and can be inappropriately seductive.

Narcissistic personality disorder is where the person has a unrealistic sense of self-importance and uniqueness, including feelings of grandiosity They except special treatment where they go and cannot take criticism.

CLUSTER C

Dependent personality disorder is where the person has low self-esteem, automatically puts others needs before their own, feels very uncomfortable when alone and makes others assume responsibility for their lives. People with this disorder tend to be very pessimistic, seek out people to depend on who will make decisions for them and find it difficult to express their anger and sexual feelings.

Obsessive compulsive personality disorder is where people exhibit indecisiveness, perseverance, controlled emotional responses and a 'perfectionist' approach in all area of life. People with this disorder are afraid of makings mistakes, are highly inflexible and have difficulty with interpersonal interaction.

Avoidant personality disorder is characterized by having a need for social company, but may be living a socially withdrawn life due to heightened sensitivity to rejection or criticism from others.

6) MOOD DISORDERS

Generally people experience a wide range of moods and emotions and to a large extent can keep them in control. With mood disorders this sense of control is absent/lost and this causes great distress to the patient. The mood disorder impairs the interpersonal, social, and occupational functioning of the patient. The causes for mood disorders are not known. Treatment often includes therapy, hospitalization (to avoid self destruction and harm to others, and for appropriate treatment) antipsychotic, antianxiety, antidepressants and other forms of psychotropic drugs as required.

7) LEARNING DISORDERS

Learning disorders are diagnosed when achievement on standardized tests in reading, mathematics or written expression are substantially below that expected for his/her age, education, and level of intelligence. These learning problems affect one's day-to-day activities as well. The causes could include a genetic link, prenatal injury, neurological factors and other medical conditions, as well as environmental factors. Treatment involves remedial teaching by professionals trained as special educators, psychotherapy aimed at improving the person's social skills, self esteem and assertiveness and education about the disorder for the child and family.

Reading disorder is characterized by impaired ability to recognize words, slow and inaccurate reading and poor understanding of words.

Mathematics disorders is characterized mainly by difficulty in understanding mathematical terms and in converting worded problems to symbols. These people also have difficulty with the basics of addition, subtraction, multiplication and division.

Disorder of written expression is characterized by poor spelling, writing, poor handwriting, difficulties with grammar

All the above learning disorders can occur in isolation or combination with each other.

Chapter 15

Aromatherapy and Colored Energy

TABLE OF CONTENTS

INTRODUCTION 248

    Basil (Holy basil, tulsi, tulasi) 248

    Black pepper 248

    Camphor 249

    Cedarwood 249

    Chamomile 250

    Cinnamon 250

    Clove bud 251

    Eucalyptus (Eucalyptus radiate) 251

    Frankincense (Olibanum) 252

    Geranium (Pelargonium graveolens) 252

    Grapefruit (Citrus paradise) -pink / white 253

    Hyssop (Hyssopus officinalis) 253

    Jasmine (Jasminum grandiflorum) 254

    Juniper berry (Juniperus indica) 254

    Lemongrass (Cymbopogon flexuosus) 255

    Lavender (Lavendula officinalis) 255

    Lemon (Citrus limonum) 256

    Lime (Citrus aurantifolia) 257

    Lotus (Nelumbo nucifera) - pink / white 257

    Myrrh (Commiphora myrrha) 258

    Neroli (Citrus aurantium) 258

    Orange sweet (citrus sinensis) 259

    Oregano (Origanum compactum) 259

    Palarosa (Cymbopogon martini) 260

    Patchouli dark (Pogostemon cablin) 260

    Peppermint redist (Mentha piperita) 261

    Rose (Rosa damascene) 261

    Rosemary (Rosmarinus officinalis) 262

    Sage (Salvia lavandulaefolia) 262

    Sandal wood (Santalum spicatum) 263

    Spearmint (Mentha spicata) 263

    Spikenard (Nardastachus jatamansi) 264

    Tangerine (Citrus reticulate) 264

    Tea tree (Melaleuca alternifolia) 265

    Ylang Ylang (Cananga odorata genuine) 265

AROMATHERAPY AND COLORED ENERGY

INTRODUCTION

In this chapter we will be discussing the healing properties of essential oils, their chakral application and their colored energy (*Please refer to 'Advanced Pranic Healing' book by Grandmaster Choa Kok Sui to know more about the function of Chakras and properties of Colored Energy or Prana*).

BASIL (HOLY BASIL, TULSI, TULASI)

Basil oil is a powerful antispasmodic, anti- infectious, antiviral, anti-inflammatory, decongestant (affecting veins, arteries of the lungs, prostate), and antibacterial. Helps with mental fatigue- inhale first, then apply to crown, forehead, heart and navel chakras. Basil is relaxing to striated and smooth muscles. It is soothing for insect bites. It can be applied on the tip of the nose, on temples and on specific locations. It can also be added to food or water as a dietary supplement.

Figure 15-1 Basil (Holy basil, tulsi, tulasi)

BLACK PEPPER

When taken internally it is used to stimulate the digestive system, and to stimulate the reproductive system as an aphrodisiac(increases sexual desire). It is considered useful to soothe stomach pains and as a preventive against food poisoning. For external use, it has always to be diluted. Can be added to lotions and creams and used in salt baths. Inhaling the scent is stimulating and comforting. It activates the basic chakra.

Figure 15-2 Black pepper

CAMPHOR

Camphor stimulates the function of the mucous membrane of the respiratory tract. It has an analgesic and sedative effect. Can be applied externally for muscular aches and pains or inhaled for rapidly opening of the respiratory channels. It can help cleanse the crown chakra.

Figure 15-3 Camphor

CEDARWOOD

Cedarwood oil is a fine addition to any massage oil, especially when the target is to improve respiratory system. It can be added to shampoos and facial washes. A drop of oil in ½ cup water is used as a gargle for sore throat. A few drops with eucalyptus in a steaming bowel of water is wonderful measure to reduce nasal and lung congestion.

Figure 15-4 Cedarwood

Aromatherapy and Colored Energy

CHAMOMILE

Chamomile oil promotes the regeneration of the skin. It has blue prana. Its calming properties help with insomnia, nervous tension, stress, soothe stomach aches, indigestion and relieve toothaches. Apply on the bottom of feet, ankles, wrists or on location. It is good to calm crying children.

Figure 15-5 Chamomile

CINNAMON

Cinnamon oil is very strong and should only be used highly diluted. Inhaling it works as a sudorific (increases sweating). The aroma of cinnamon is said to increase your ability to tap into your psychic mind and to increase financial prosperity. Can be sprayed (diluted in alcohol or water) or sprinkled on rolled cinnamon sticks and then placed in potpourri at stores and business places.

Figure 15-6 Cinnamon

CLOVE BUD

Clove bud oil is one of the first oils to be directly applied in therapy- in aching teeth to anesthetize them or on warts to remove them. It is antibacterial, antiseptic and analgesic and is good oil for the prevention of disease and infection. Clove is powerful oil that has been used for sterilization of surgical instruments. It should not be used undiluted on the skin. Being a spice it can be incorporated into your cooking. It is inhaled to stimulate memory, to stimulate the respiratory system and as an antiseptic for various infectious diseases. If too much is inhaled it acts as a soporific; it can cause a good sleep generally culminating in stimulating dreams. Clove oil is highest scoring essential oil in oxygen radical absorption capacity. The antioxidant score of carrots are 210, while the score of clove oil is 10,786,875. This means that one ounce of clove oil has the antioxidant capacity of 450 lbs of carrots.

Figure 15-7 Clove bud

EUCALYPTUS (EUCALYPTUS RADIATE)

Eucalyptus oil contains orange prana and works great in salt bath for deep cleansing of psychic and etheric bodies. It is anti inflammatory, antiseptic, antibiotic, diuretic, analgesic, deodorizing and antiviral properties. Eucalyptus oil is effective in killing bacteria and for clearing the system when used in vaporizer or a spray bottle.

Figure 15-8 Eucalyptus (Eucalyptus radiate)

Aromatherapy and Colored Energy

FRANKINCENSE (OLIBANUM)

Frankincense is one of the three gifts given to baby Jesus by the three Magi. It is one of the first oils used in rituals. During Roman times, when cremation was widely practiced, it was also customary to burn it in the funeral pyre. It contains orange prana, which has expelling effect, therefore helping the incarnated soul to detach from the body. It can be used in spray bottles or diffusers in funerals or in terminal patients' bedroom. It can also be used in salt- baths for a super cleansing effect.

Figure 15-9 Frankincense (Olibanum)

GERANIUM (PELARGONIUM GRAVEOLENS)

Geranium oil can be added to any beauty cosmetic like shampoos creams, etc,. It helps to balance the function of the oily glands, and can be used for dry or oil skin. When Inhaled, it acts as a stimulant to the thyroid and as an anti-inflammatory to the lungs. Can help people with adrenal function problems, or menopause.

Figure 15-10 Geranium (Pelargonium graveolens)

GRAPEFRUIT (PINK / WHITE) – CITRUS PARADISE

Grapefruit oil is good for detoxifying the body, also it helps to break up fat and cellulite. It can be used in the bath, rubbed on the body, taken internally or inhaled.

Figure 15-11 Grapefruit (Pink / White) – Citrus paradise

HYSSOP (HYSSOPUS OFFICINALIS)

The fragrance of Hyssop oil stimulates creativity and meditation. Hyssop raises low blood pressure, regulates menstrual flow, and increases perspiration. It is a decongestant, expectorant, cleansing, purifying and helps reduce fat in the tissues. Diffuse and apply topically. It can be added to food and also in baths.

Figure 15-12 Hyssop (Hyssopus officinalis)

Aromatherapy and Colored Energy

JASMINE (JASMINUM GRANDIFLORUM)

The jasmine flower is known as the "King of Flowers". The oil contains pink-green-violet- golden prana. It is used during child birth in India which is rubbed on the mother's belly, and is the first aroma the baby smells. It is also mentioned throughout Kama Sutra manual as a reputed aphrodisiac (increase sexual desire). Can be inhaled or applied on the heart or on any higher chakra. A drop rubbed on the temples will clear up a headache in moments. It is a powerful tool in prostate conditions or impotence.

Figure 15-13 Jasmine (Jasminum grandiflorum)

JUNIPER BERRY (JUNIPERUS INDICA)

Juniper berry is antiseptic, astringent, digestive, stimulant, purifying and detoxifying. It increases circulation through kidneys and promote excretion of uric acid and toxins. It may help acne, dermatitis, eczema, depression, fatigue, liver problems, sore muscles, rheumatism, ulcers, urinary infections, fluid retention and wounds. Diffuse or apply topically. It can be added to food.

Figure 15-14 Juniper berry (Juniperus indica)

LEMONGRASS (CYMBOPOGON FLEXUOSUS)

Lemongrass is a strong oil that should be used diluted. It is antiseptic, anti-bacterial and anti-fungal. It can be added in shampoos for oily hair, cellulite cream or blends for massage and to the bath. When inhaled it has a sedating action on the nervous system, can soothe headache and stimulate the thyroid gland.

Figure 15-15 Lemongrass (Cymbopogon flexuosus)

LAVENDER (LAVENDULA OFFICINALIS)

Grand Master Choa Kok Sui recommended the use of lavender oil on the hands during healing sessions to reduce contamination and to increase the size of the hand chakras.

Figure 15-16 Lavender (Lavendula officinalis)

It is natural antibiotic, antiseptic, antiviral and anti-fungal, also anti-depressive, sedative and detoxifying. It is excellent to be sprayed or used in a diffuser to clean the atmosphere physically and etherically.

Lavender oil stimulates the immune system and contributes to the healing process. It helps to deal with psychological shock or injury. It also has a multitude of other qualities which make it truly indispensible oil. It is great for bath, on chakras, and awesome on the bottom of the feet, especially before meditation or before sleep. It contains predominantly violet prana. It is used for stress relief and it has shown a significant cleansing effect on the front and back solar plexus and ajna chakras. Use 20 drops in your bath for relaxing purifying effect. You can mix it with alcohol or water to spray around the house and on your bed linens. Lavender oil is great for helping to relieve colds and coughs. It is safe for babies and children.

LEMON (CITRUS LIMONUM)

Lemon oil is a very powerful emotional and physical purifier. Lemon oil when absorbed into the blood stream actively stimulates and boosts the immune system. It helps in lymphatic drainage, thereby flushing out toxins from the body.

Figure 15-17 Lemon (Citrus limonum)

Lemon oil helps detoxify the liver, kidneys, blood and the cells of the body. It also helps in weight reduction. Lemon oil is a great way to help remove heavy metals from deep within the body. Use a few drops of lemon oil in your bath. Lemon oil along with orange oil helps excite people, and was proven to help boost sales when used in offices and show rooms. Spray lemon oil and water or alcohol into the air to help neutralize airborne pathogens, and make the place feel happy and cheerful. Is antibiotic, antiseptic and antifungal.

LIME (CITRUS AURANTIFOLIA)

Lime helps detoxify the cells of the body.

Figure 15-18 Lime (Citrus aurantifolia)

LOTUS (NELUMBO NUCIFERA) - PINK / WHITE

The lotus flower is a symbol of illumination for some cultures. The crown chakra, in a developed person looks like a flower blossom. It also symbolizes that mankind, with his "roots in the mud" can achieve illumination, like the lotus opens to the sun.

Figure 15-19 Lotus (Nelumbo nucifera) - pink / white

Aromatherapy and Colored Energy

MYRRH (COMMIPHORA MYRRHA)

The most mentioned oil in the bible, myrrh was gift given by the three Magi to baby Jesus. It vibrates in the color blue to indigo and is useful for problems of the throat regions.

Figure 15-20 Myrrh (Commiphora myrrha)

NEROLI (CITRUS AURANTIUM)

Neroli is made of the orange flower, and owes its name from a princess. It is indicated for cardiac spasm, chronic diarrhea and insomnia. It can be inhaled, used in diffuser or taken internally. It is soothing, calming and sedating.

Figure 15-21 Neroli (Citrus aurantium)

ORANGE SWEET (CITRUS SINENSIS)

Orange sweet is made from the peel of the fruit. It can be inhaled or taken internally, acting as an anti-depressive and nerve sedative. When sprayed in the air, it helps eliminate odors such as smoke.

Figure 15-22 Orange sweet (citrus sinensis)

OREGANO (ORIGANUM COMPACTUM)

This is one of the most potent antiviral and anti-bacterial oils on the planet, and a very potent antioxidant. It is a general tonic and immune stimulant. This oil may help in respiratory infections, digestive problems, balance metabolism, respiratory problems and strengthen the vital centers. Use on bottom of the feet or with food.

Figure 15-23 Oregano (Origanum compactum)

PALAROSA (CYMBOPOGON MARTINI)

Palarosa helps with skin problems. It is antimicrobial and supportive to the nerves and circulation. This oil may be beneficial for candida, cardiovascular system, circulation, digestion, infection, nervous system problems and rashes. Stimulates new growth, regulates oil production, and moisturizes the skin. Apply topically.

Figure 15-24 Palarosa (Cymbopogon martini)

PATCHOULI DARK (POGOSTEMON CABLIN)

Patchouli has been used for its beneficial properties in India for thousands of years. It activates the basic and sex chakras. Patchouli also contains many healing chemicals. It works great after meditation for helping to root to the earth.

Figure 15-25 Patchouli dark (Pogostemon cablin)

PEPPERMINT REDIST (MENTHA PIPERITA)

This is great for romance and love, try a few drops on the tongue before kissing, we call it peppermint kisses, very sweet. Peppermint is very cooling to the body, and also helps curb the appetite. Peppermint is very energizing. Contains blue prana.

Figure 15-26 Peppermint redist (Mentha piperita)

ROSE (ROSA DAMASCENE)

Master Choa Kok Sui states in the advanced pranic healing book on page 251-252: "Pink prana has a cleansing effect on the chakras and meridians. This is clairvoyantly seen as dirty red energy being dispersed and transmuted by the pink from the chakras and meridians. The cleansing of the chakras and the meridians allows the free flow of pranic energy and causes the chakras to normalize, therby enhancing the body's ability to normalize itself. Musk and rose oil contains a lot of pink prana. They can be taken internally. Since many ailments are emotional in origin, it is likely in the future that musk and rose oil will be widely used to normalize emotions, as well as for medication." The pink prana in rose is good to help transmute anger and unforgiveness. Rose oil also helps expand the heart chakra, and numb pain. When used on acupuncture meridians for front and back solar plexus, they instantly get smaller and cleaner and the heart chakra is increased in size. When rose oil is applied to heart chakra, its size increases significantly.

Figure 15-27 Rose (Rosa damascene)

Aromatherapy and Colored Energy

ROSEMARY (ROSMARINUS OFFICINALIS)

Rosemary oil is very emotionally and physically uplifting. It helps purify the respiratory tract and is also a powerful antiviral and immune system booster. It contains red prana.

Figure 15-28 Rosemary (Rosmarinus officinalis)

SAGE (SALVIA LAVANDULAEFOLIA)

Sage contains green, blue and violet pranas. It is very powerful for purification, both physically and emotionally. Use in bath with lavender, tea tree or eucalyptus oil.

Figure 15-29 Sage (Salvia lavandulaefolia)

SANDALWOOD (SANTALUM SPICATUM)

Sandalwood is a potent cleanser and purifier. It helps expand the heart chakra and is reputed love oil. It is referenced many times in the Kama Sutra, when applied directly on chakras, has a deep cleansing effect. It contains over 90% healing chemicals. These chemicals called sesquiterpenes can help people fight cancer. Sandalwood contains lots of green prana and some golden prana. It can be used in bath, at the bottom of the feet and on the chakras.It is very good as a natural deodorant.

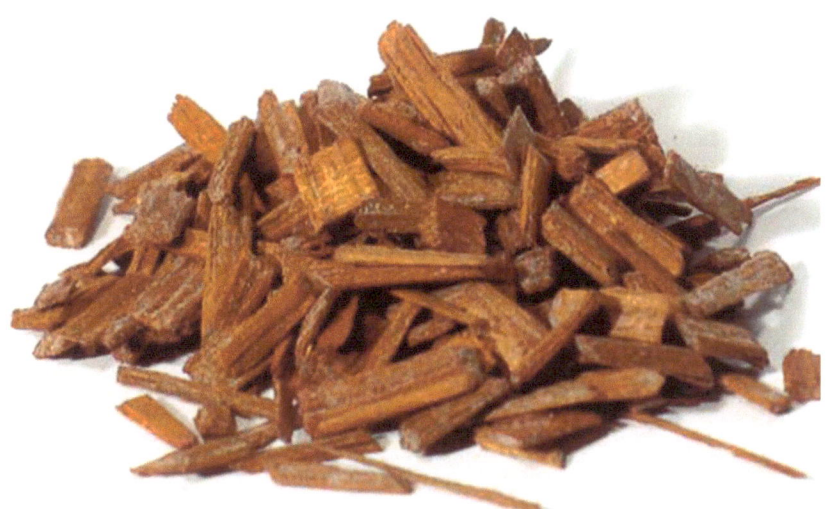

Figure 15-30 Sandalwood (Santalum spicatum)

SPEARMINT (MENTHA SPICATA)

It contains bluish violet prana, great for energizing and weight loss.

Figure 15-31 Spearmint (Mentha spicata)

Aromatherapy and Colored Energy

SPIKENARD (NARDASTACHUS JATAMANSI)

Spikenard is very potent for purification. It was the oil rubbed on Jesus's feet. Master Choa stated that when spikenard is used on the soles of the feet it enhances the ability to fly in the inner world.

Figure 15-32 Spikenard (Nardastachus jatamansi)

TANGERINE (CITRUS RETICULATE)

Tangerine helps energize and purify the body.

Figure 15-33 Tangerine (Citrus reticulate)

TEA TREE (MELALEUCA ALTERNIFOLIA)

Tea tree oil is antiviral and anti bacterial and has hundreds of uses. Tea tree oil is very good for the skin and for bug bites. It is predominantly green prana, with some pink and gold. It's great for breaking up energy congestion. Use in the bath with lavender oil or with eucalyptus oil. It is also very nice on the bottom of the feet, to pull out negative energy through the feet. It is not for internal use.

Figure 15-34 Tea Tree (Melaleuca alternifolia)

YLANG YLANG (CANANGA ODORATA GENUINE)

Ylang Ylang contains violet prana and is very powerful for purification and love. Used extensively during weddings and honeymoons in Indonesia. The bride wears a beautiful Ylang Ylang flower in her hair during wedding and later Ylang Ylang flowers are spread on the honeymoon bed. Use it on the chakras.

Figure 15-35 Ylang Ylang (Cananga odorata genuine)

Source: This chapter is based on the information provided by Rocky Patel, author of 'Golden Aromatherapy: A Symphony of Colored Energy and Aromatic scents'. He is also a senior student of Grandmaster Choa Kok Sui.

For more information please visit his website http://www.goldenaromatherapy.net

Chapter 16

General Health Forms

TABLE OF CONTENTS

CLIENT INTAKE FORM (SAMPLE 1 & 2) 268
PAIN ASSESSMENT SCALE FORM 273
FOLLOW-UP TREATMENT FORM 274
APPOINTMENT CARD 275

Client intake form

File No :

1. Name :
2. Age :
3. Sex : Male / Female
4. Address :

     Town / City :
     State :
     Zip / Pincode :

5. Home phone :
6. Work phone :
7. Cell phone :
8. E-mail :
9. Occupation :
10. Present medical condition :

11. Past medical history :

12. Purpose of visit :

13. What is your treatment goal? :

14. Do you have any infection? : Yes / No
    If yes, please specify

15. Are you pregnant? : Yes / No / Not applicable

16. Do you have menstrual periods? : Yes / No / Not applicable

17. Have you ever had organ transplant? : Yes / No
    If yes, please specify

18. Do you have any metal implants? : Yes / No
    If yes, please specify

19. Will you be able to continue the number of healing sessions as recommended? : Yes / No

20. Do you prefer distant healing or direct healing? :

21. How did you hear about us? :

Mark 'X' on the area of pain / discomfort

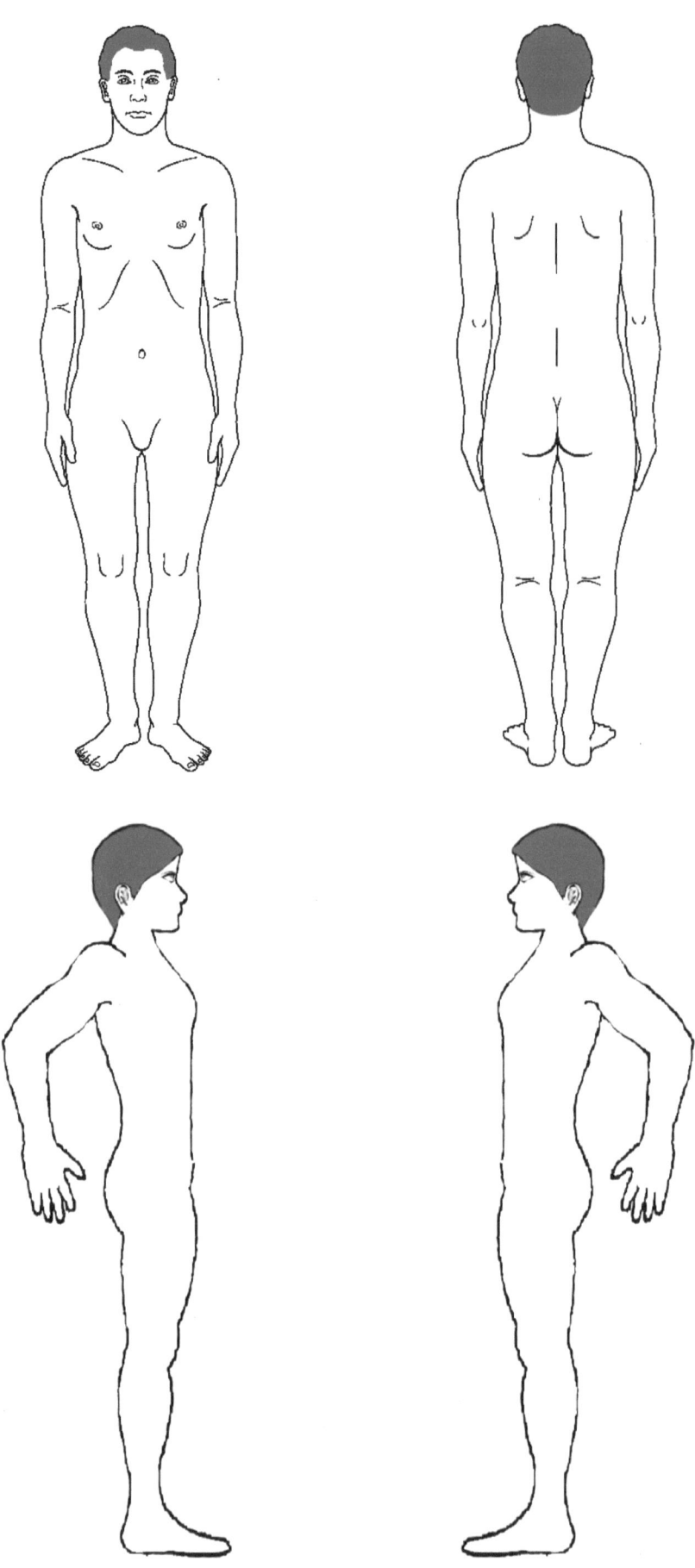

---FOR OFFICIAL USE ONLY---

22. Treatment goal

      Short term goal :

      Long term goal :

23. Treatment plan

      Duration of treatment :

      Number of treatment :
      sessions / week

Name of the client :   Signature :

                                                                            Date   :

Name of the healing practitioner :   Signature :

                                                                            Date   :

Energy treatment session form

Client name _____

Address _____

_____

Phone _____ Date _____

Email address _____

Date of birth _____ Sex _____

To better assist us, please answer the following questions:

Do you smoke? Yes _____ No _____

Do you drink Alcohol : Yes _____ Rarely _____ No _____

Are you pregnant? Yes _____ No _____

Do you have high blood pressure? Yes _____ No _____

Do you take any prescribed drugs or medications? Yes _____ No _____

If yes, please describe : _____

_____

Do you have of any history of disease ? Yes _____ No _____

If yes, please describe : _____

_____

Do you have any physical injuries? Yes _____ No _____

If yes, please describe : _____

_____

Do you have any psychological illness? Yes _____ No _____

If yes, please describe : _____

_____

Purpose of visit (Please state in detail symptoms, injuries, conditions, etc)

_____

_____

_____

Pain assessment scale

Patient Name :   File No:

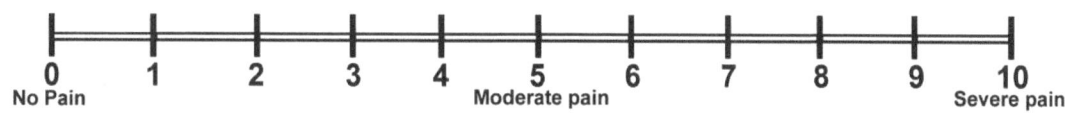

Days	Date	Level of pain										
Day 1		0	1	2	3	4	5	6	7	8	9	10
Day 2												
Day 3												
Day 4												
Day 5												
Day 6												
Day 7												
Day 8												
Day 9												
Day 10												
Day 11												
Day 12												
Day 13												
Day 14												
Day 15												
Day 16												
Day 17												
Day 18												
Day 19												
Day 20												
Day 21												
Day 22												
Day 23												
Day 24												
Day 25												
Day 26												
Day 27												
Day 28												
Day 29												
Day 30												

Follow-up treatment form

Name : File No:
Date :

1. How was the previous healing session? What positive changes did you notice in terms of symptoms, energy levels, improved sleep, etc.

2. Chief concerns today :

For official use only

3. Energetic diagnosis :

4. Changes in the treatment based on information documented, energetic diagnosis result:

- Appointment booked for :
- Healer's name :

Appointment card

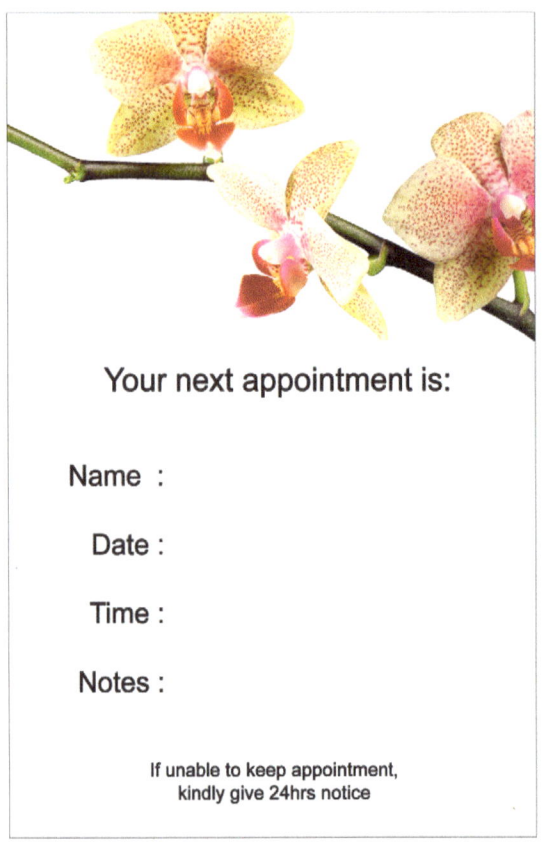

Your next appointment is:

Name :

Date :

Time :

Notes :

If unable to keep appointment,
kindly give 24hrs notice

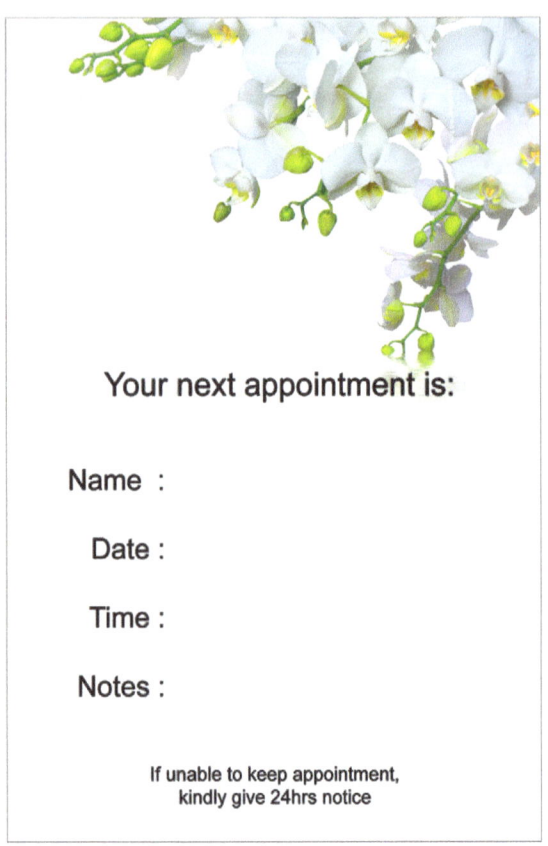

Your next appointment is:

Name :

Date :

Time :

Notes :

If unable to keep appointment,
kindly give 24hrs notice

WEEKLY APPOINTMENT

Name :

☐ Mon – Date:_____ Time:_____
☐ Tue – Date:_____ Time:_____
☐ Wed – Date:_____ Time:_____
☐ Thu – Date:_____ Time:_____
☐ Fri – Date:_____ Time:_____
☐ Sat – Date:_____ Time:_____
☐ Sun – Date:_____ Time:_____

Notes :

If unable to keep appointment, kindly give 24hrs notice

WEEKLY APPOINTMENT

Name :

☐ Mon – Date:_____ Time:_____
☐ Tue – Date:_____ Time:_____
☐ Wed – Date:_____ Time:_____
☐ Thu – Date:_____ Time:_____
☐ Fri – Date:_____ Time:_____
☐ Sat – Date:_____ Time:_____
☐ Sun – Date:_____ Time:_____

Notes :

If unable to keep appointment, kindly give 24hrs notice

COMMONLY USED MEDICAL TERMINOLOGY

Abscess	—	A collection of pus in the tissues of some part of the body resulting from an infection and often accompanied by inflammation.
Akinesia	—	Loss of movement.
Amnesia	—	Partial or entire loss of memory caused by injury to brain or by disease.
Amputation	—	Cutting off all or a part of a leg, arm, hand etc by surgery.
Anesthesia	—	Entire or partial loss of the feeling of pain, touch, cold etc,.
Analgesic agent	—	Drugs that relieves or lessens pain.
Antibodies	—	Protein substances produced in the blood or tissues that destroy bacteria.
Antigens	—	Any protein substance that causes the body to produce antibodies to counteract them.
Aphasia	—	Total a partial loss of the ability to use or understand words.
Arrhythmias	—	Irregular heart beats.
Arth	—	Refers to joints. eg, arthritis.
Atrophy	—	Weakening or shrinking away of the body or a part of it due to imperfect nourishment or disuse.
Auditory	—	Having to do with hearing (Auditory nerve transmits impulses from the ear to the brain).
Biopsy	—	Surgical removal of a sample of tissue from living body for examination and diagnosis.
Bradycardia	—	Decreased heart beat rate.
Bradypnea	—	Decreased breathing rate.
Bronchodilators	—	Substances which dilates the bronchial tubes in the lungs (used in case of asthma).
Bronchoscopy	—	Examination of bronchial tubes by passing a lighted, flexible fiberoptic tube through the nose, throat, laynx and trachea into the bronchi.
Benign	—	Not dangerous to health, (not malignant) a benign tumour.

Carcinoma	—	Any of various cancers of skin, gland, tissue, etc,.
Cardium	—	Having to do with muscles of the heart.
Cardiovascular	—	Having to do or affecting both heart and the blood vessels.
Casts	—	Made of plaster of paris to support a broken bone while it heals.
Catheter	—	A slender rigid or flexible tube to be inserted into a passage or cavity of the body. A catheter may be used to remove urine from the bladder.
Cephalo	—	Refers to head eg. encepholopathy.
Chorea	—	Uncontrolled jerky movements involving any part of the body.
Cirrhosis	—	A chronic disease of the liver marked by degeneration of the liver cells.
Coma	—	Prolonged unconsciousness caused by diseases, injury or poision.
Colonoscopy	—	An instrument to view the colon internally.
CT (CAT) Scan	—	Computed tomography (computed axial tomography). A series of X-ray pictures are taken and processed by a computer to show a cross-section (transverse) image of internal organs. Tomography means that a series of X-rays are taken to see an organ in depth.
Cyst	—	Small abnormal sac like growth usually containing liquid and diseased matter produced by inflammation.
Cysto	—	Refers to urinary bladder eg. cystoscopy.
Dementia	—	Partial or complete deterioration of mind.
Derm	—	Refers to skin eg. Dermatology.
Dysphagia	—	Difficulty in swallowing.
Dyspnea	—	Difficulty in breathing.
Dysentery	—	Disease of intestines producing diarrhea with blood and mucus caused by several micro organisms or by irritants.
Dysphasia	—	Difficulty in speaking
Effusion	—	The escape of fluid such as blood or lymph from its natural vessels into surrounding tissues or cavities.
Electrocardiograph (ECG)	—	Instrument that detects and records the electrical impulses produced by the action of the heart with each beat. It is used to diagnose diseases of the heart.

Embolus	—	A clot, air bubble, globule of fat etc, that is carried in the blood stream. It sometimes blocks a blood vessels.
Empyema	—	Pus in the body cavity..
Encephalo	—	Refers to brain
Edema	—	Swelling..
Fibrosis	—	A excessive growth of fibrous tissue in an organ or part of a body.
Fistula	—	A tube like abnormal passage connecting the surface of the body with some internal cavity or organ, caused by wound.
Flaccid	—	Lying loose eg. flaccid muscles can be seen in some stroke patients where the muscle tone is low or nil.
Gangrene	—	Death and decay of a tissue when the blood supply to the part is cut off by injury, infection or freezing.
Gastric	—	A part of or near the stomach
Gastritis	—	Inflammation of the stomach, especially of its lining.
Gastrointestinal	—	Of stomach and intestines.
Gastrointestinal Endoscopy	—	A flexible fiberoptic tube is placed through the mouth or anus to visualize parts of the gastrointestinal tract. eg. Colonoscopy, sigmoidoscopy.
Genital	—	Having to do with reproduction or sex organs
Geriatric	—	Old age
Gynec	—	Refers to female eg., gynecology
Haem	—	Refers to blood
Hemoptysis	—	Blood during vomiting.
Hematoma	—	Swelling or tumour composed of blood
Hematuria	—	Blood in the urine
Hemoglobin	—	Substance in the red blood cells made of iron and protein that carry oxygen from lung to the tissues and carries carbondioxide from tissues to the lungs.
Hemophilic	—	A condition of the blood in which clotting does not occur normally making it difficult to stop bleeding even after the slightest injury. It affect only males but is inherited from the mother.

Hemorrhoids	—	Painful swelling formed by dilation of blood vessels near the anus; piles.
Hepatic	—	Having to do with the liver, eg., hepatitis.
Hepatitis	—	Inflammation of the liver
Hepatomegaly	—	Enlargement of liver and spleen
Hernia	—	It is abnormal protrusion of an organ from one compartment of the body into another. Protrusion of some tissue or organ of the brain, especially a part of the intestine, through the wall of the cavity which should hold it in.
Hydrocephalus	—	Enlargement of the head usually in infants caused by accumulation of cerebrospinal fluid within the cranium.
Hydrocele	—	Enlargement of the testicles
Infarct	—	Portion of dying or dead tissue caused by the obstruction of blood supply.
Intravenous	—	Through the vein eg., Intravenous injection.
Insomnia	—	Loss of sleep
Ischemia	—	Loss of blood supply to a part caused by an obstruction of the supply of arterial blood.
Itis	—	Inflammation.
Laryngitis	—	Inflammation of the larynx.
Leukocyte	—	White blood cells.
Leucopenia	—	Lack of white blood cells in the blood.
Lithotripsy	—	Ultrasonic dissolution of kidney stones.
Malignant	—	Very dangerous, cancer is a malignant growth.
Metastasis	—	Which spreads eg., metastasis of cancer.
Megaly	—	Enlargement eg., splenomegaly.
MRI Scan	—	Magnetic resonance imaging. Magnetic waves are used to create detailed images. MRI scan brings abnormal lesion into sharper focus.
Muscular dystrophy	—	A disease characterized by muscle degeneration leading to progressive weakness.
Myasthenia	—	Extreme muscular weakness.

Myelitis	—	Inflammation of the spinal cord or of the bone marrow.
Narcotic	—	Any drug that produces drowsiness, sleep, dullness or an insensible condition and lessens pain by dulling the nerves.
Neurosis	—	Any of various mental or emotional disorder, less severe than a psychosis anxiety, abnormal fear, compulsive behavior.
Necrosis	—	Death of a part of the body from injury or disease.
Nephro	—	Refers to kidneys.
Nephritis	—	Inflammation of the kidneys.
Neuralgia	—	Sharp pain along the course of a nerve.
Neuro	—	Refers to nerve, eg., neurology.
Neuritis	—	Inflammation of a nerve.
Obstetrics	—	Branch of medicine concerned with caring for treating women before and after child birth.
Occlude	—	Block eg., occlusion of artery.
Optic	—	Having to do with eyes eg., optic nerve.
Orthopedics	—	Branch of surgery that deals with deformities and diseases of bones and joints.
Osteo	—	Having to do with bones.
Palsy	—	Paralysis.
Paresis	—	Partial paralysis eg., hemiparesis (Partial paralysis of one side of the body).
Pathology	—	Branch of medicine dealing with cause of a disease.
Pediatrics	—	Branch of medicine dealing with children's diseases and care of babies and children.
Physiology	—	Study of the function of various parts of the body.
Renal	—	Having to do with kidneys.
Regurgitation	—	Back ward flow eg., Aortic regurgitation backward flow of the blood through the aortic valve of the heart.
Sarcoma	—	Any of a number of malignant tumors that originate in bone or muscle.
Sensory	—	Having to do with the senses.

Shunt	—	Connection eg., Atrioventricular shunt.
Spasm	—	Sudden abnormal involuntary contraction of muscles.
Splenomegaly	—	Enlargement of spleen
Stenosis	—	Contraction, stricture or narrowing eg. Mitral or aortic stenosis.
Stethoscope	—	Instrument used by doctors to hear the sound produced in the lungs, heart, etc.
Tachypnea	—	Increased rate of breathing
Tachycardia	—	Increased rate of heart beat
Thrombus	—	A fibrous clot which forms in a blood vessel or within the heart and obstructs the circulation.
Tracheostomy	—	Creation of an opening into the trachea through the neck and insertion of a tube to create an airway where it may be permanent as well as emergency device.
Ultrasound	—	This technique employs high-frequency inaudible sound waves that bounce off body tissues and are then recorded to give information about the anatomy of an internal organ. Ultrasound is used as diagnostic tool to detect intracranial and ophthalmic lesions, heart valve and blood vessel disorders, locate abdominal masses outside the digestive organs and to locate tumors or cysts.
Umbilical cord	—	A cord like structure that connects the navel of the fetus to the placenta of the mother. It carries nourishment to the fetus and carries away.
Urinary incontinence	—	Loss of control of urinary bladder.
Urethritis	—	Inflammation of the urethra.

The language of surgery

Plasty	—	It is the refashioning of something to make it work (eg) Arthroplasty – Replacement of joints (usually performed in arthritis)
Ectomy	—	Cutting something out (eg) Appendectomy (Removal of vermiform appendix)
Otomy	—	Cutting something opens (eg) Laparotomy (cutting open the abdomen).
Scope	—	An instrument for looking into the body (eg) Cytoscope (a device for looking into the urinary bladder)

A

Abdomen 11, 13, 14, 16, 18, 20, 21, 22, 23, 24, 25, 40, 70, 97, 106, 116, 118, 213, 214, 216, 220, 281
Accommodate 96, 97
Accommodation 181
Ache 16, 114
Aches 249
Acid 3, 11, 14, 15, 16, 20, 22, 36, 95, 98, 99, 122, 136, 198, 200, 201, 254
Acne 153, 160, 173, 254
Acromegaly 163, 167
Addison's Disease 173
Adenocarcinoma 218, 220
Adenohypophysis 166
Adenoid 38
Adenoiditis 28, 38
Adenoids 31, 38
Adenomas 170
Adenomatous Goiter 170
Adh 163, 167, 168
Adhd 232, 235
Adnexitis 116
Adrenal 68, 78, 163, 164, 165, 167, 172, 173, 174, 252
Adrenalin 55
Adrenaline 163, 173
Adrenals 168
Adrenocorticotropic 166, 167
Agoraphobia 232, 240
Agranulocytes 197
Akinesia 276
Albumin 229
Albuminuria 99, 229
Alcohol 13, 14, 21, 23, 24, 95, 115, 156, 215, 240, 250, 256
Alkaline 223, 228, 229
Allergens 39, 156
Allergic 37, 39, 197, 226
Alopecia 153, 158
Alveolar 36, 41
Alveoli 6, 28, 30, 33, 34, 35, 41, 43
Alveolus 6, 43
Alzheimer 86
Amenorrhea 104, 114, 173
Amino 15, 198
Amnesia 233, 242, 276
Amniotic 112
Amputation 276
Amylase 15
Analgesic 249, 251, 276
Anatomy 5, 6, 32, 50, 51, 58, 75, 96, 126, 130, 147, 154, 166, 174, 180, 190, 281
Androgen 117, 177
Androgens 117, 173

Anemia 24, 116, 195, 198, 199, 200, 201, 202, 213, 215, 225, 226, 227
Aneurysm 47, 70, 186
Aneurysms 70
Anexitis 104
Angina 46, 58, 59, 65, 66, 69
Anginal 66
Angiogenesis 205, 210
Angioplasty 59
Ankylosing 124, 132
Anorexia 233, 243
Antacids 20
Anti-Depressive 259
Anti-Diuretic 166
Anti-Inflammatory 137, 149, 151, 172, 248
Antianxiety 244, 245
Antibacterial 248, 251
Antibiotic 121, 251, 255, 256
Antibiotics 101, 192
Antibodies 69, 90, 91, 161, 197, 198, 200, 276
Antibody 198
Antidepressant 242, 244
Antidepressants 245
Antidiuretic 102, 167, 168
Antifungal 157, 255, 256
Antigen 198
Antigens 276
Antihypertensive 174
Antiinflammatory 132, 136
Antimicrobial 260
Antioxidant 251, 259
Antipsychotic 239, 244, 245
Antirheumatic 132
Antiseptic 251, 254, 255, 256
Antisocial 233, 244
Antispasmodic 248
Antithyroid 170
Antiviral 160, 248, 251, 255
Anus 5, 13, 15, 22, 278, 279
Anxiety 21, 39, 193, 232, 236, 239, 240, 241, 243, 244, 280
Aorta 46, 48, 52, 55, 57, 60, 62, 63, 67, 70
Aortic 46, 47, 52, 60, 61, 67, 280, 281
Aphasia 276
Aphrodisiac 248, 254
Aplastic 195, 198, 200, 201
Apophyseal 148
Appendectomy 281
Appendicitis 3, 17
Appendix 13, 17, 18, 281
Arachnoid 81
Arches 7, 143
Areola 108
Aroma 1, 250, 254

Aromatherapy 248, 249, 250, 251, 252, 253, 254, 255, 256, 257, 258, 259, 260, 261, 262, 263, 264, 265
Aromatic 265
Arrhythmia 55, 64
Arrhythmias 46, 64, 276
Arterial 47, 56, 61, 62, 70, 279
Arteries 46, 48, 49, 50, 52, 57, 58, 65, 66, 67, 68, 69, 70, 71, 87, 98, 114, 248
Arteriole 98
Arterioles 48, 49, 98, 167
Arteriosclerosis 46, 65, 66, 67, 71
Artery 41, 46, 48, 52, 53, 55, 56, 57, 59, 60, 62, 63, 65, 66, 70, 71, 87, 98, 228, 280
Arthritis 99, 124, 132, 134, 135, 136, 148, 172, 225, 276, 281
Arthroplasty 281
Ascites 3, 24, 214
Aseptic 89
Asperger‚Äôs Disorder 232, 239
Aspirated 121
Aspiration 32, 39, 192
Assessment 267
Asthma 28, 39, 67, 226, 276
Asthmaticus 39
Astigmatism 179, 182
Astringent 254
Atheroma 70
Atherosclerosis 46, 59, 65, 68, 177, 228
Athetosis 73, 85
Atrioventricular 51, 52, 53, 54, 64, 67, 281
Atrium 49, 50, 52, 53, 55, 56, 57, 61, 67
Atrophied 86
Atrophy 24, 138, 139, 276
Attention 232, 235, 237, 242
Aura 90, 92
Autism 232, 236, 237
Autistic 237, 239
Autoimmune 90, 199, 200
Autoimmunity 200
Autonomic 73, 80
Axon 84, 90
Axons 85

B

Backache 116
Bacteria 8, 15, 21, 43, 44, 89, 90, 116, 156, 157, 159, 160, 192, 230, 251, 276
Bacterial 18, 88, 89, 101, 121, 183, 255, 259, 265
Basil 247, 248
Basophils 197, 226
Bed-Wetting 235
Bell's Palsy 73, 85
Benign 104, 122, 174, 205, 207, 276
Benzene 201, 215

Beta-Blockers 68
Beta-Carotene 188
Bicuspid 52
Bile 12, 14, 15, 23, 25, 26, 216, 229
Bilirubin 15, 23, 95, 223, 228, 230
Bilirubinuria 230
Biliverdin 15, 23
Binge-Eating 243
Biopsy 122, 212, 276
Bladder 3, 13, 14, 15, 23, 24, 25, 81, 85, 88, 91, 94, 96, 97, 99, 100, 102, 107, 119, 120, 122, 151, 214, 219, 227, 229, 230, 235, 277, 281
Blastocyst 111
Bleeding 17, 19, 21, 39, 156, 186, 198, 200, 202, 203, 213, 215, 218, 220, 223, 227, 228, 278
Blindness 87, 177, 182, 186, 188, 241
Blisters 121, 156, 160
Bone 30, 58, 66, 115, 116, 126, 127, 130, 131, 132, 134, 137, 141, 143, 146, 148, 201, 206, 207, 211, 215, 226, 227, 277, 280
Bowel 13, 18, 19, 20, 23, 85, 88, 91, 132, 151, 213, 235, 249
Bowman Capsule 97, 98
Bradycardia 276
Bradypnea 276
Brain 14, 44, 57, 65, 66, 68, 70, 73, 74, 75, 76, 77, 78, 79, 80, 81, 82, 85, 86, 87, 88, 91, 99, 121, 143, 166, 168, 181, 191, 193, 207, 211, 234, 235, 236, 237, 276, 278, 279
Brainstem 86, 191
Breast 58, 66, 79, 104, 108, 111, 173, 177, 200, 205, 209, 211, 212
Breastbone 15, 20, 49
Bronchi 28, 30, 32, 33, 34, 40, 276
Bronchial 33, 40, 41, 173, 216, 226, 276
Bronchiectasis 28, 40
Bronchiole 33, 41
Bronchioles 28, 30, 33, 34, 39, 40
Bronchiolitis 28, 40
Bronchitis 28, 40, 41, 66, 67
Bronchodilators 276
Bronchoscopy 276
Bronchus 33, 40, 216
Buccal Cavity 5
Buerger's Discease 71
Bulimia 233, 243
Bursa 124, 130
Bursae 130, 132
Bursitis 124, 132, 133
Bypass 59, 60

C

Calcium 8, 68, 99, 114, 115, 116, 126, 169, 170, 171, 198, 223, 228

Calculi 99
Calyces 97
Camphor 247, 249
Cancer 23, 122, 205, 206, 207, 208, 209, 210, 211, 212, 213, 214, 215, 216, 217, 218, 219, 220, 221, 263, 279
Cancerous 21, 207, 209, 213, 214, 216, 220, 226
Cancers 1, 200, 205, 206, 207, 209, 213, 277
Candida 260
Canine 7
Capillaries 33, 46, 48, 49, 60, 71, 97, 98, 161, 197, 200, 210
Capillary 71
Capsule 87, 97, 98, 130, 133, 137
Capsulitis 137
Carbohydrates 15, 198
Carcinoma 205, 206, 211, 212, 214, 216, 218, 228, 277
Cardiac 11, 15, 55, 56, 57, 58, 64, 71, 79, 137, 173, 227, 258
Cardio-Vascular 79
Cardiomyopathy 47, 69
Cardiorespiratory 86
Cardiovascular 1, 48, 49, 50, 51, 52, 53, 54, 55, 56, 57, 58, 59, 60, 61, 62, 63, 64, 65, 66, 67, 68, 69, 70, 71, 260, 277
Cardioverter 65
Carotid 57
Carpal 124, 136, 148
Cartilage 31, 33, 69, 126, 127, 130, 133, 136, 143, 168, 206
Cartilaginous 32, 147
Cataract 177, 179, 183
Catecholamine 173
Catheter 277
Cecum 5, 12, 13, 15
Cedarwood 247, 249
Cellulite 253, 255
Cementum 6
Cerebellum 73, 75, 79, 80
Cerebrospinal 74, 279
Cerebrovascular 228
Cerebrum 73, 75, 77, 78, 79, 80, 86
Cervical 17, 81, 82, 91, 107, 143, 144, 148, 205, 211, 212, 220
Cervicitis 104, 116
Cervix 107, 113, 121, 205, 212, 218, 220
Chakra 248, 249, 254, 257, 261, 263
Chamomile 247, 250
Chemotherapy 211, 214
Chest 15, 21, 22, 32, 41, 42, 43, 55, 59, 64, 65, 67, 69, 70, 108, 143, 211, 217
Cholesterol 25, 59, 188, 223, 228
Chorea 73, 85, 277
Chromosomes 105
Chyme 14, 15
Cilia 33

Ciliary 180, 181
Cinnamon 247, 250
Circumflex 53
Cirrhosis 3, 24, 25, 227, 228, 277
Citrus 247, 253, 256, 257, 258, 259, 264
Clairvoyantly 261
Claudication 47
Clitoris 108
Coarctation 46, 62
Coccygeal 82
Coccyx 146
Cochlea 191
Colic 114
Collagen 126, 161
Collagens 154, 161
Colon 5, 12, 13, 15, 18, 19, 23, 205, 206, 213, 214, 277
Colonoscopy 277, 278
Coma 76, 79, 86, 177, 227, 229, 277
Cone-Shaped 49
Cones 181
Congenital 40, 62, 63, 64, 66, 67, 70, 151, 168, 186, 198, 199, 200, 201, 202
Conjunctiva 180, 183
Conjunctivitis 179, 183
Constipation 3, 18, 19, 23, 170, 201, 213, 219
Contraceptive 114, 220
Convex 183
Convulsions 85, 175
Cornea 180, 182
Coronary 46, 50, 52, 53, 56, 57, 58, 59, 60, 65, 66, 69, 228
Corticosteroids 137, 172
Cortisone 172
Cough 38, 39, 40, 41, 43, 69, 217, 218
Coughing 32, 42, 43, 79, 116
Cramp 21
Cramps 23
Cranial Nerves 81
Cranium 143, 279
Creatinine 95, 98, 223, 228
Cretinism 163, 170
Cushing 164, 173
Cushing's Syndrome 226, 228
Cyanosis 62, 63
Cyst 277
Cystitis 94, 102
Cystoscopy 277
Cysts 100, 117, 171, 281
Cytoscope 281

D

Dandruff 156, 157
Deafness 179, 191
Defibrillator 65

Degenerative 70, 71, 86, 148
Delusions 202, 215, 237, 238, 239
Dementia 73, 86, 87, 277
Dendrites 84, 85
Depolarization 46, 55
Depression 90, 111, 114, 226, 227, 240, 241, 243, 244, 254
Dermatitis 254
Dermatology 277
Dermis 154
Diabetes 17, 66, 71, 94, 99, 102, 137, 163, 164, 168, 175, 176, 183, 184, 185, 186, 227, 228, 229, 230
Dialysis 99, 101
Diaphragm 11, 14, 22, 23, 34, 35, 114
Diaphysis 126
Diarrhea 3, 18, 20, 22, 23, 26, 213, 227, 228, 258, 277
Diastole 56, 61
Diastolic 56, 61, 62, 224
Digestion 4, 5, 11, 12, 13, 14, 15, 23, 24, 25, 26, 260
Diplopia 91, 186
Disc 124, 149, 150, 151, 197
Discs 147, 148
Dissociative 233, 242, 243
Diuretic 251
Diuretics 67, 68, 227
Diverticulitis 18
Diverticulosis 3, 18
Dizziness 37, 66, 67
Drug 86, 132, 159, 168, 200, 280
Ductless 165
Ducts 14, 105, 108, 166, 191, 211
Duodenal 3, 20, 21
Duodenum 5, 11, 12, 14, 15, 20, 21, 23
Dwarfism 163, 168
Dysentery 3, 20, 277
Dysfunction 77, 86, 148, 192, 198, 220
Dysmenorrhea 104, 114, 115
Dysphagia 277
Dysphasia 277
Dysplasia 212
Dyspnea 39, 277
Dystrophy 279
Dysuria 121

E

Eardrum 190, 191, 192
Ecg 46, 54, 55, 277
Eczema 153, 156, 254
Edema 47, 61, 67, 71, 99, 121, 156, 215, 229, 278
Effusion 277
Electrical 46, 54, 55, 65, 86, 191, 277
Electrocardiogram 55
Electrocardiograph 277
Electrolyte 86, 94, 172, 198

Electrolytes 99, 172, 223
Embolus 278
Embryo 53, 106, 112
Emphysema 28, 41
Emphysematous 42
Empyema 278
Enamel 6, 8
Encephalitis 73, 86, 91
Encepholopathy 277
Encopresis 232, 235
Endocrine 1, 78, 102, 111, 113, 117, 165, 166, 167, 168, 169, 170, 171, 172, 173, 174, 175, 176, 177, 236
Endometrium 107, 110, 111, 112
Endoscopy 278
Enuresis 232, 235
Enzymes 5, 12, 14, 15, 161, 197, 198
Eosinophils 197, 226
Epicondylitis 141
Epidermis 154
Epididymis 104, 119
Epiglottis 10, 14, 31
Epilepsy 73, 86, 87, 89, 236
Epiphysis 126
Epistaxis 28, 39
Epithelial 33, 49, 107
Erythrocyte 223
Erythrocytes 195, 196
Esophagus 3, 5, 10, 11, 14, 15, 19, 22
Esr 223, 225
Estrogen 106, 110, 111, 112, 113, 114, 115, 116, 177, 220
Etheric 251
Etherically 255
Eucalyptus 41, 247, 249, 251, 262, 265
Eustachian Tube 191, 192
Exophthalmos 169
Expectorant 253
Expectoration 41, 217
Extrapyramidal 85
Eye 1, 15, 23, 69, 177, 179, 180, 181, 182, 183, 184, 185, 186, 187, 188, 189

F

Fallopian Tube 104, 106, 107, 110, 116
Fascia 142, 143
Fasciitis 124, 142, 143
Fats 14, 15, 172, 198
Fecal 4, 17, 18
Feces 13, 15, 18, 235
Femur 126, 148
Fertilization 111
Fertilized 111
Fetus 85, 112, 113, 151, 281
Fever 19, 22, 23, 25, 37, 40, 43, 64, 67, 69, 192, 193, 202, 215, 224, 226

Fibrillation 46, 64, 65
Fibroids 104, 116
Fibrosis 67, 147, 278
Fibrous 24, 108, 126, 127, 130, 136, 137, 147, 180, 278, 281
Fibula 126, 148
Filariasis 71
Fistula 278
Flaccid 91, 278
Flaccidity 88
Floaters 179, 184, 188
Follicle 106, 109, 110, 111, 166
Forebrain 75, 78, 79
Forgiveness 210
Fracture 44, 115, 124, 131, 132, 149
Frankincense 247, 252
Fungus 157

G

Gallbladder 3, 13, 14, 15, 25, 230
Gallstones 3, 25, 26, 228
Gamete 105, 118, 177
Ganglia 73, 80, 91
Gangrene 47, 71, 278
Gastritis 3, 22, 278
Gastrointestinal 1, 3, 4, 5, 6, 7, 8, 9, 10, 11, 12, 13, 14, 15, 16, 17, 18, 19, 20, 21, 22, 23, 24, 25, 26, 241, 278
Genetic 91, 155, 156, 201, 207, 215, 236, 240, 244, 245
Genital 17, 119, 121, 155, 157, 219, 278
Genitalia 105, 106, 108, 121
Gigantism 163, 168
Glands 3, 5, 9, 13, 14, 23, 38, 68, 78, 80, 81, 101, 108, 118, 119, 154, 160, 163, 165, 166, 167, 168, 170, 172, 177, 190, 211, 252
Glaucoma 177, 179, 185
Glomerulonephritis 68, 94, 99
Glomerulus 97, 98, 99
Glucagon 174
Glucocorticoids 163, 172, 173
Glucose 14, 102, 173, 175, 186, 198, 227, 229
Gluteus 139
Glycerol 15
Glycogen 173, 174, 175
Gonadotrophic Hormones 166
Gonadotropin 113
Gonads 105, 118, 165
Gonococci 121
Gonorrhea 104, 121
Gout 124, 136
Graafian 106, 110, 111
Granulocytes 197
Grapefruit 247, 253
Greenstick 131
Gynecology 278

H

Hallucination 202, 215
Hallucinations 78, 237, 238
Hamstring 149
Hansen's Disease 159
Haversian Canals 127
Headache 26, 37, 38, 89, 90, 201, 254, 255
Heart 3, 15, 23, 24, 38, 41, 46, 47, 48, 49, 50, 51, 52, 53, 54, 55, 56, 57, 58, 59, 60, 61, 62, 63, 64, 65, 66, 67, 69, 70, 71, 76, 79, 80, 81, 91, 114, 121, 201, 217, 224, 241, 248, 254, 261, 263, 271, 276, 277, 280, 281
Heartbeat 53, 55, 64, 66, 173
Heartburn 15, 16, 22
Hematoma 278
Hematuria 102, 214, 220, 278
Hemiparesis 87, 280, 73, 87
Hemiplegia 66, 73, 87
Hemodialysis 177
Hemoglobin 35, 197, 198, 199, 201, 223, 225, 226, 230, 278
Hemolytic Anemia 195, 198, 199, 200
Hemophilia 39, 195, 198, 202, 227
Hemophilic 278
Hemoptysis 217, 278
Hemorrhage 23, 39, 87, 186, 201
Hemorrhagic 195, 198, 203
Hemorrhoids 279
Hemothorax 42
Hepatic 23, 24, 279
Hepatitis 3, 24, 26, 228, 279
Hepatocytes 14, 23
Hepatomegaly 279
Hernia 3, 21, 22, 150, 279
Herniated 22, 124, 150, 151
Herpes 89, 104, 121, 153, 159
Hiatal Hernia 3, 21
Hiatus 21, 22
Hilum 97
Homeostasis 99
Hormone 79, 97, 102, 110, 113, 114, 116, 117, 118, 165, 166, 167, 168, 169, 170, 171, 172, 173, 177
Hormones 25, 106, 108, 111, 113, 114, 117, 118, 163, 165, 166, 167, 168, 169, 172, 173, 174, 177, 198, 217, 228
Humerus 126, 148
Hydrocele 104, 121, 279
Hydrocelectomy 121
Hydrocephalus 279
Hyperbilirubinemia 230
Hypercalcemia 171
Hyperglycemia 102, 173, 229
Hyperkalemia 228
Hyperkinesis 235
Hypernatremia 173, 227

Hyperparathyroidism 163, 171
Hyperplasia 169, 170
Hypersecretion 41
Hypertension 47, 68, 94, 101, 173, 174, 224, 229
Hyperthyroidism 163, 169
Hypertrophy 41, 46, 60, 61, 63, 104, 122, 138
Hypocalcemia 171
Hypochondria 241
Hypochondriasis 233, 241
Hypoglycemia 164, 173, 175, 177
Hypokalemia 173, 228
Hyponatremia 173, 227
Hypoparathyroidism 163, 171
Hypophysis 166
Hypothalamus 73, 78, 79, 166, 167
Hypothyroid 170
Hypothyroidism 163, 170, 227
Hypotonia 85
Hypoxia 35, 201
Hysterectomy 220

I

Idiopathic 91, 99, 203
Ileum 5, 12
Immune 160, 200, 207, 256, 259, 262
Immunity 197
Impetigo 153, 156, 157
Implantation 64, 111, 112, 191
Impotence 220, 254
Impulsive 235
Incisors 7
Infection 17, 19, 20, 22, 24, 26, 38, 40, 41, 42, 43, 44, 67, 69, 85, 86, 89, 90, 91, 99, 101, 102, 104, 115, 116, 121, 134, 155, 156, 157, 158, 160, 161, 183, 190, 192, 197, 200, 201, 202, 212, 215, 225, 226, 229, 230, 251, 260, 269, 276, 278
Infertility 115, 116
Inflammation 15, 16, 17, 18, 19, 23, 24, 25, 26, 37, 38, 39, 40, 42, 71, 85, 88, 90, 99, 101, 102, 114, 116, 121, 132, 134, 137, 142, 149, 183, 192, 197, 225, 230, 276, 277, 278, 279, 280, 281
Inguinal 177
Insomnia 250, 258, 279
Inspiration 31, 34
Insulin 102, 174, 175, 177, 227
Intercostal 35
Intercourse 120, 212, 218
Interstitial 118
Interventricular 63
Intervertebral 124, 147
Intestine 3, 5, 11, 12, 13, 14, 15, 18, 19, 26, 81, 279
Intestines 12, 18, 26, 277, 278
Intracranial 39, 86, 281
Intrauterine 114

Intravenous 279
Ischemia 161, 279
Ischemic 46, 64, 65
Islets Of Langerhans 165, 174

J

Jasmine 247, 254
Jaundice 3, 23, 24, 26, 216, 228, 229, 230
Jaw 5, 7, 9, 65, 66, 92, 126, 134, 167, 271
Jejunum 5, 12
Jesus 252, 258
Juniper 247, 254

K

Keratin 154
Ketone 229
Kidney 17, 24, 65, 69, 71, 94, 96, 97, 98, 99, 100, 101, 102, 136, 167, 168, 171, 172, 198, 205, 214, 215, 230, 279
Kidneys 17, 94, 96, 97, 98, 99, 100, 101, 122, 157, 176, 177, 254, 256, 280
Knee 129, 130, 132, 134, 148, 271

L

Labor 112, 113, 167
Laboratory 241
Labyrinth 193
Lacrimal 80, 81
Lactation 226
Laparotomy 281
Laryngitis 28, 39, 279
Larynx 28, 30, 31, 32, 34, 39, 91, 279
Lavender 41, 247, 255, 256, 262, 265
Laxatives 243
Legs 67, 70, 71, 87, 126, 134, 149, 150, 156, 157, 215, 220
Lemon 247, 256
Lemongrass 247, 255
Lens 181, 182, 183
Leprosy 153, 159
Lesion 16, 68, 85, 155, 156, 157, 160, 191, 279
Lesions 61, 85, 87, 155, 157, 158, 159, 281
Leucocytes 195, 196
Leucocytosis 226
Leucopenia 226, 227, 279
Leukemia 39, 195, 201, 202, 205, 206, 207, 215, 226
Leukocyte 279
Leukorrhea 104, 115
Ligaments 97, 116, 124, 125, 130, 133, 137, 140, 148
Lithotripsy 100, 279

Liver 3, 5, 13, 14, 15, 23, 24, 25, 26, 67, 96, 97, 166, 174, 175, 198, 202, 205, 209, 211, 213, 214, 215, 216, 223, 228, 229, 230, 254, 256, 277, 279
Lobe 14, 23, 77, 78, 163, 167, 168
Lobes 77, 78, 168
Lotus 247, 257
Loving-Kindness 210
Lumbar 81, 82, 91, 115, 146, 148, 149, 174
Lump 158, 211, 214, 218
Lumpectomy 211
Lung 32, 33, 40, 41, 42, 43, 46, 61, 66, 67, 205, 209, 211, 216, 217, 249, 278
Lungs 10, 14, 26, 28, 29, 30, 33, 34, 35, 36, 39, 40, 42, 43, 44, 49, 57, 61, 63, 67, 80, 90, 132, 198, 209, 214, 248, 252, 276, 278, 281
Lymph 121, 159, 202, 206, 207, 210, 211, 212, 215, 277
Lymphatic 31, 71, 210, 256
Lymphocytes 197, 226
Lymphoid 38
Lymphoma 205

M

Macula 188
Magnesium 126, 198
Malaria 198
Malignancy 225
Malignant 201, 205, 207, 211, 212, 214, 215, 216, 276, 279, 280
Malnutrition 24, 236
Mammary 108, 167
Mandible 5, 9
Mastectomy 137, 212
Maxillary Sinuses 30, 92
Medulla 75, 79, 81, 101, 164, 172, 173, 174
Medullary 217
Melanocyte 166
Menarche 109
Meninges 44, 75, 76, 81, 88, 89, 90
Meningitis 73, 88, 89, 90
Menopause 106, 114, 115, 218, 220, 252
Menstrual 17, 104, 109, 110, 111, 113, 114, 177, 200, 220, 253, 269
Menstruation 109, 111, 114, 226
Metabolic 23, 29, 48, 115, 169, 229, 236
Metabolism 95, 97, 98, 101, 136, 169, 172, 175, 198, 259
Metacarpal 148
Metastasis 207, 208, 209, 279
Metatarsal 148
Microorganisms 37, 38, 197
Microscope 217
Midbrain 75, 79
Migraine 73, 90
Mineralocorticoids 163, 172, 173

Miscarriage 117
Mitral 47, 52, 67, 281
Molar 7
Molecules 4, 35
Monocytes 197, 226
Motor 79, 80, 82, 83, 85, 86, 241
Mouth 3, 5, 9, 10, 14, 31, 38, 85, 134, 278
Mucosa 5, 9, 18, 21, 32, 63
Mucous 15, 30, 33, 107, 108, 121, 159, 180, 249
Mucus 14, 18, 20, 40, 41, 113, 277
Muscle 14, 15, 18, 53, 55, 56, 57, 59, 66, 79, 80, 83, 87, 91, 116, 130, 137, 138, 139, 140, 149, 151, 171, 174, 206, 228, 278, 279, 280
Musculoskeletal 125, 126, 127, 128, 129, 130, 131, 132, 133, 134, 135, 136, 137, 138, 139, 140, 141, 142, 143, 144, 145, 146, 147, 148, 149, 150, 151
Musk 261
Myasthenia 73, 91, 279
Mycobacterium 44
Myelin 85, 90
Myelitis 73, 91, 280
Myeloma 205, 207
Myocardial Infarction 46, 57, 64, 66, 177
Myocardium 46, 49, 53, 54, 63
Myopia 179, 186
Myrrh 247, 258
Myxedema 163, 170

N

Nasal 28, 30, 31, 37, 38, 39, 85, 159, 168, 249
Nasopharynx 30, 31, 34, 38
Nausea 19, 20, 22, 23, 25, 26, 90, 193, 201, 216
Navel 18, 20, 248, 271, 281
Neck 6, 15, 32, 38, 58, 66, 81, 107, 116, 143, 146, 148, 150, 151, 168, 218, 236, 281
Necrosis 280
Neoplastic 212
Nephritis 71, 280
Nephrolithiasis 99
Nephromegaly 100
Nephrons 71, 97, 99
Nephrosis 99
Nephrotic 94, 99, 229
Nerve 53, 79, 80, 81, 84, 85, 87, 92, 139, 149, 160, 181, 186, 191, 193, 259, 276, 280
Nerves 6, 8, 14, 53, 66, 77, 81, 82, 84, 86, 148, 149, 150, 159, 171, 186, 193, 260, 280
Neuritis 91, 280
Neurohypophysis 166
Neurology 280
Neuron 84
Neurosis 239, 280
Neurotic 232, 239
Neurotransmitters 85, 237

289

Neutrophils 197, 226
Nipple 108, 211
Nipples 79
Node 53, 55, 64, 202, 215
Nodes 31, 121, 211, 212
Nodule 218
Nodules 24, 170
Noradrenaline 163, 173
Norepinephrine 163, 173, 174
Nose 28, 30, 31, 34, 37, 38, 39, 248, 276
Nostrils 30
Nucleus 147, 150
Nutrients 4, 12, 48, 95, 113, 127, 161, 210

O

Obese 170
Obesity 66, 143, 173, 220, 228, 233, 244
Obsession 240
Obsessive 232, 233, 240, 245
Obstetrics 280
Occipital 77, 78
Occlude 280
Occlusion 57, 59, 280
Oestrogen 228
Olfactory 239
Olibanum 247, 252
Ophthalmic 92, 281
Oral 5, 9, 31, 63, 137, 175, 224
Oropharynx 30, 31, 34, 38
Orthopedics 280
Osteoarthritis 124, 133, 134
Osteoarthrosis 133
Osteomyelitis 124, 134
Osteoporosis 104, 114, 115, 116, 173
Ova 106
Ovaries 104, 105, 106, 107, 108, 109, 110, 114, 117, 164, 165, 167, 168, 177
Ovary 104, 106, 107, 110, 111, 112, 117
Ovulation 110, 114, 115, 167
Ovum 105, 106, 107, 109, 110, 114, 167, 177
Oxyhemoglobin 35
Oxytocin 79, 166, 167

P

Pacemaker 53, 54, 55, 64
Palpitation 64, 114
Palpitations 55, 174, 241
Pancreas 5, 13, 14, 15, 174, 175
Pancreatic 12, 14, 15
Panhypopituitarism 163, 168
Papules 155, 156
Paralysis 66, 76, 79, 83, 85, 87, 91, 186, 241, 280

Paralyzed 87, 91
Paranoid 232, 233, 237, 244
Paraplegia 73, 91
Parasitic 71, 155, 197
Parasympathetic 80, 81
Parathormone 170, 171
Parathyroid 99, 165, 170, 171
Paresis 91, 280
Parietal 33, 77
Parkinson's 73, 86, 91
Parotid 9
Patchouli 247, 260
Patella 148
Pathogens 256
Pathologist 122
Pathology 39, 280
Pediatrics 280
Pelvic 12, 97, 113, 114, 115, 119, 220
Pelvis 97, 99, 100, 101, 113, 116, 214, 215, 219
Penis 118, 120, 121, 154
Peppermint 247, 261
Peptic 3, 20
Periarthritis 137
Pericardium 49
Periosteum 126, 127
Peristalsis 5, 14
Peritoneum 16
Peritonitis 16, 21
Phalanges 148
Pharyngeal 38
Pharyngitis 28, 38
Pharynx 3, 5, 10, 14, 28, 30, 31, 91, 191
Phimosis 104, 121
Phlegm 40, 43, 217
Phobia 232, 240, 241
Photophobia 89, 90
Pigments 15, 23, 229
Piles 22, 279
Pimples 153, 160
Pituitary 78, 114, 165, 166, 167, 168
Placenta 112, 113, 281
Pneumonia 28, 40, 42, 43, 89, 259
Pneumothorax 28, 42
Polycystic 94, 100, 104, 117
Polycythemia 195, 201, 226, 227
Polydipsia 102, 168, 176
Polyphagia 176
Polyps 213
Polyuria 102, 168, 176
Pons 75, 79
Post-Menopausal 115
Post-Traumatic 241
Prana 250, 251, 252, 254, 256, 261, 262, 263, 265
Pregnancy 66, 79, 104, 111, 112, 113, 114, 115, 143, 170, 177, 200, 225, 226, 227

Pregnant 66, 113, 114, 220, 269
Premenstrual 111
Premolars 7
Progesterone 106, 111, 112, 113, 114, 177
Prolapse 3, 22, 104
Prolapsed 22, 117
Prostate 97, 104, 118, 120, 122, 205, 211, 219, 220, 227, 248, 254
Protein 71, 84, 99, 166, 183, 197, 198, 200, 227, 229, 276, 278
Proteins 14, 15, 71, 98, 172, 183, 198, 223
Psychiatric 86, 234, 235, 236, 237, 238, 239, 240, 241, 242, 243, 244, 245
Psycho-Social 238, 240, 241, 242
Psychological 90, 240, 241, 242, 243, 256
Psychosis 239, 280
Psychosocial 238, 239
Psychotherapy 235, 236, 239, 241, 243, 245
Psychotic 232, 239
Psychotropic 245
Puberty 106, 108, 109, 160, 168
Pulmonary 28, 34, 41, 48, 49, 52, 55, 57, 61, 62, 63, 67, 225
Pyelonephritis 68, 94, 101
Pyloric 11, 14

Q

Quadriplegia 73, 91

R

Radial 56, 224
Radiotherapy 211
Radius 126, 148
Rash 157, 160
Rashes 260
Rbc 195, 196, 197, 198, 199, 200, 201, 226
Rbc's 197, 199, 200, 223, 226
Receptors 91
Rectum 5, 12, 13, 15, 22, 107, 108, 213, 219
Reflex 14, 18, 91
Reflexes 18
Reflux 16, 22
Regenerate 24
Regurgitation 3, 11, 15, 22, 46, 47, 60, 61, 67, 280
Rehabilitation 85
Repolarization 46, 55
Reproduction 105, 108, 173, 278
Reproductive 1, 78, 97, 104, 105, 106, 107, 108, 109, 110, 111, 112, 113, 114, 115, 116, 117, 118, 119, 120, 121, 122, 219, 248
Respiration 29, 34, 83, 91, 173, 201
Retardation 85, 232, 236, 237

Retina 69, 177, 179, 181, 184, 186, 188
Rheumatic 38, 47, 64, 67, 69
Rheumatism 254
Rheumatoid 124, 134, 135, 172, 225
Rods 132, 181
Rose 247, 261
Rosemary 41, 247, 262

S

Sacral 81, 82, 146, 149
Sacrum 146
Sacs 18, 30, 33, 41, 100, 130, 191
Saliva 5, 9, 14
Salivary 3, 5, 9, 14, 80, 81
Salpingitis 104, 116, 121
Sandalwood 263
Sarcoma 205, 206, 280
Scabies 153, 155
Scalp 156, 157, 158
Schizoaffective 232, 238
Schizoid 233, 244
Schizophrenia 232, 236, 237, 238, 239
Schizophreniform 232, 238
Schizotypal 233, 244
Sciatica 124, 149, 150
Sclera 180
Scrotum 118, 121
Sebaceous 154
Seizures 86, 89, 90
Semen 97, 119, 120, 220
Semicircular 191, 193
Semilunar 52
Seminal 120
Seminiferous Tubules 118, 119
Sensory 14, 80, 82, 83, 85, 86, 92, 280
Septal 46, 62, 63
Septum 30, 50, 53, 62, 63
Sex 25, 105, 106, 111, 114, 163, 173, 177, 220, 260, 268, 269, 271, 278
Sgot 228
Sgpt 228
Shingles 153, 159, 160
Shortsightedness 179, 186
Sigmoid 5, 13
Sigmoidoscopy 278
Sino-Atrial 55
Sinus 37
Sinuses 28, 30, 37, 108
Sinusitis 28, 37
Skeletal 5, 85, 125, 127, 137, 138, 140, 145, 170
Skeleton 115, 126, 143
Skin 1, 5, 15, 23, 26, 33, 63, 77, 114, 120, 121, 130, 131, 134, 136, 153, 154, 155, 156, 157, 158, 159, 160, 161, 167, 170, 173, 193, 201, 203, 206, 211, 216, 226, 250,

251, 252, 260, 265, 277
Skull 30, 39, 74, 77, 124, 127, 143, 148
Somatotrophic 166
Somatotropin 166
Spasm 86, 114, 258, 281
Spasmodic 85, 114
Spasms 149, 171, 174
Spasticity 88, 91
Sperm 105, 106, 118, 119, 120, 121, 167
Spermatic Cord 177
Spermatozoa 118, 119
Spermatozoon 105, 111
Spikenard 247, 264
Spinal 44, 73, 74, 75, 79, 80, 81, 82, 83, 84, 86, 91, 121, 143, 146, 148, 150, 151, 159, 207, 280
Spine 44, 67, 81, 91, 124, 132, 143, 144, 146, 147, 148, 149, 151
Spleen 24, 26, 67, 202, 215, 216, 227, 279, 281
Splenectomy 227
Splenomegaly 279, 281
Spondylitis 124, 132
Spondylolisthesis 124, 149
Spondylolysis 124, 149
Spondylosis 124, 148, 149
Spur 149
Sputum 41, 217
Squamous Cell Carcinoma 218
Squint 179, 186
Stenosed 60
Stenosis 46, 47, 60, 61, 63, 67, 281
Stereotyped 236
Stereotypical 237
Sterilization 251
Sternum 49, 58, 66, 143
Steroid 167, 172, 177
Steroids 136, 226
Stethoscope 281
Stomach 3, 5, 10, 11, 12, 13, 14, 15, 16, 17, 19, 20, 21, 22, 81, 174, 200, 211, 213, 248, 278
Stomachaches 250
Stones 17, 25, 94, 99, 100, 171, 227, 228, 279
Strengthen 259
Stroke 56, 66, 69, 73, 86, 87, 88, 139, 177, 278
Sub-Lingual 9
Sub-Mandibular 9
Subacromial 130
Subcutaneous 67, 154, 177
Sugar 98, 102, 173, 175, 177, 186, 188, 223, 227, 229, 230
Sugars 14, 15, 172, 174
Surgery 18, 46, 59, 60, 62, 149, 174, 211, 212, 214, 220, 226, 244, 276, 280, 281
Surgical 63, 67, 101, 120, 122, 132, 136, 149, 151, 183, 191, 192, 211, 251, 276
Swelling 17, 24, 37, 67, 70, 71, 116, 121, 131, 136, 140, 156, 169, 211, 278, 279
Syncope 173
Synovial 127, 130, 133
Systole 54, 56, 61
Systolic 61, 62, 224

T

Tangerine 264
Tantrums 235
Temporal 77, 78
Tendinitis 137
Tendon 141
Tendons 130, 137, 141
Testes 105, 118, 164, 165, 167, 168, 177
Testicles 24, 118, 121, 279
Testosterone 118, 167, 177
Tetany 171, 228
Tetralogy 62, 63
Thalamus 73, 75, 79, 86
Thalassemia 199
Thigh 127, 148, 149
Thighbone 148
Thoracic 33, 34, 35, 49, 81, 82, 91, 132, 143
Thorax 21, 22, 124, 146
Throat 15, 31, 38, 39, 69, 134, 191, 217, 218, 249, 258, 271, 276
Thrombocytes 195, 196
Thrombosis 46, 47, 66, 70, 71
Thrombus 65, 66, 281
Thyroid 78, 163, 165, 166, 167, 168, 169, 170, 205, 217, 218, 228, 252, 255
Thyroid-Stimulating 167
Thyroidectomy 170
Thyrotoxicosis 169, 228
Thyrotropin 167
Thyroxine 167
Tibia 126, 148
Tinnitus 179, 193
Tongue 9, 38, 86, 261
Tonsillitis 38
Tonsils 9, 31, 38
Tooth 3, 6, 8
Toothaches 250
Toxic 15, 23, 98
Toxins 23, 86, 95, 99, 254, 256
Trachea 28, 30, 31, 32, 33, 34, 168, 276, 281
Transplant 99, 269
Trauma 39, 85, 86, 115, 141, 159, 202, 225, 227, 240, 241, 242
Tremor 79, 91
Tricuspid Valve 52
Trigeminal Neuralgia 91, 92
Tuberculosis 40, 44, 86, 88, 90, 225, 226
Tumor 85, 86, 87, 131, 149, 168, 171, 173, 174, 175, 207,

208, 209, 210, 211, 212, 214, 216, 220
Tumors 1, 18, 86, 99, 116, 121, 167, 193, 201, 205, 206, 207, 208, 209, 210, 211, 212, 213, 214, 215, 216, 217, 218, 219, 220, 221, 280, 281
Tympanic 190, 191

U

Ulcer 3, 15, 16, 20, 21, 121
Ulcers 21, 121, 159, 198, 200, 254
Ulna 126, 148
Ultrasound 281
Umbilical 12, 113, 281
Urea 95, 98, 101, 223, 227
Uremia 17, 99
Ureter 97, 99, 100
Ureters 94, 96, 97, 122
Urethra 94, 96, 97, 99, 118, 119, 120, 121, 281
Urination 86, 88, 99, 102, 121, 122, 168, 218, 219, 235
Urine 26, 71, 79, 94, 97, 98, 99, 100, 101, 102, 113, 116, 136, 168, 176, 214, 219, 220, 223, 229, 230, 235, 277, 278
Uterine 104, 107, 111, 112, 116, 205, 212, 220, 221
Uterus 79, 104, 106, 107, 108, 109, 111, 113, 114, 116, 117, 167, 177, 218, 220

V

Vagina 17, 106, 107, 108, 109, 113, 115, 116, 121, 218
Vaginal 108, 116, 121, 205, 218, 219, 220
Vaginitis 104, 116
Valve 11, 46, 47, 52, 60, 61, 67, 280, 281
Valves 51, 52, 67, 69
Vasectomy 120
Vasomotor 79
Vasopressin 166, 167
Vein 57, 279
Veins 24, 46, 48, 49, 56, 57, 59, 71, 248
Vertebra 44, 81, 149
Vertebrae 82, 127, 131, 143, 146, 147, 149, 174
Vertigo 179, 193
Vesicles 156
Virus 43, 89, 121, 158, 159, 160, 183, 212
Vitreous 180, 188
Vomiting 20, 21, 22, 25, 26, 79, 86, 89, 90, 201, 216, 227, 228, 243, 278
Vulva 97, 108

W

Walnut 9
Wbc 195, 196, 197, 201, 215, 226
Wbc's 223, 226
Wheeze 40
Wheezing 39

Windpipe 10, 14, 31, 32

X

X-Ray 277

Y

Ylang Ylang 247, 265

Z

Zygote 111

ABOUT THE AUTHOR

Dr. Syed A. Afzal has a degree in Physiotherapy and a Doctorate in Acupuncture. He has been a Pranic Healer since 1996. He has personally trained with Grandmaster Choa Kok Sui.

Syed has treated world class sportsmen and athletes using Pranic Healing, Acupuncture and Physiotherapy at Fitness Foundation Academy of YMCA college in India for more than four years. He has worked with many Cancer Patients using Pranic healing at Apollo Cancer Hospital, India. He has practiced as a Pranic Healer at Ashwini Soundarya Hospital. He currently lives in Canada and continues to practice Pranic Healing.

POEM ABOUT SICKNESS
by Jigme Lingpa

Sicknesses are the brooms sweeping your evil deeds.

Seeing the sicknesses as the teachers, pray to them.

Sicknesses are coming to you by the kindness of the masters and the Three Jewels.

Sicknesses are your accomplishments, so worship them as the deities.

Sicknesses are the signs that your bad karmas are being exhausted.

Do not look at the face of your sickness, but at the one (the mind) who is sick.

Do not place the sicknesses on your mind, but place your naked intrinsic awareness upon your sickness.

This is the instruction on sickness arising as the Dharmakaya.

The body is inanimate and mind is emptiness.

What can cause pain to an inanimate thing or harm to the emptiness?

Search for where the sicknesses are coming from, where they go, and where they dwell.

Sicknesses are mere sudden projections of your thoughts.

When those thoughts disappear, the sicknesses dissolve too.

There is not better fuel (than sicknesses) to burn off the bad karmas.

Don't get into entertaining a sad mind or negative views (over the sicknesses),

But see them as the signs of the waning of your bad karmas, and rejoice over them.

This poem comes from Masters of Meditation and Miracles, p. 126, translated by Tulku Thondup

WE APPRECIATE YOUR FEEDBACK

The information in this book is constantly evolving and we appreciate your help!
If any information needs to be added, deleted, changed or updated in any way, please email us.
We are eager to hear from you about this 2nd edition.

Please give us feedback and let us know what you would like to see in the future versions of this book by contacting us at
westernmedicalguide4ehp@gmail.com